SAFETY MANAGEMENT

SAFETY MANAGEMENT

R.K. MISHRA

Sr. Faculty and Safety Advisor
O&M Solutions P. Ltd., Bhubaneswar, Odisha
and
Formerly 'Chief of Safety' and
Chief Manager (Operation Technologies)
Tata Refractories Ltd., Belpahar, Odisha

A.I.T.B.S.

AITBS PUBLISHERS, INDIA

J-5/6, Krishan Nagar, Delhi-110051 (INDIA)
Phone: 011-40167052, 49067602; Fax: 011-22009074
E-mail: aitbsindia@gmail.com & aitbsindia@hotmail.com

First Edition : 2013
Second Edition : 2023

ISBN: 978-93-7473-498-8

Published by:
Virender Kumar Arya for
AITBS Publishers, India
J-5/6, Krishan Nagar, Delhi-110051 (INDIA)
Phone: 011-40167052, 49067602; Fax: 011-22009074
E-mail: aitbsindia@gmail.com & aitbsindia@hotmail.com

Printed by AITBS, Delhi

This Book is Dedicated to

Students, the Workers, the Supervisors,
the Officers, the Managers and
the Sr. Managers to whom
I have taught these subjects

Preface

Safety of human beings poses utmost importance due to rapid industrialization, globalization and competitive environmental conditions. Due to inbuilt hazards, safety of men and machines has a great concern for any industry. With the increased awareness coupled with rapid automation, the safety performance ought to increase over the years.

Safety in work place is paramount to boost the productivity. Safe working conditions are as important as the production and the productivity. The commitment for adherence to safety practices will not only create a safe environment but also boost up the morale and confidence of employees.

Safety is an integral part of industrial excellence and organizational culture. There are growing concerns and consciousness of safety issues in every gamut of our life. Therefore it is essential for the organizations to give utmost importance to safety for further excellence in the business. It is said 'safety pays'. In other words plants following safety in true spirit are most productive ones.

The first and foremost step in the field of safety is awareness in the subject. The human factor plays a key role in any enterprise in achieving the goal of safety. Therefore, it is necessary to constantly educate, train and motivate them in adopting a transformational work culture besides close monitoring of the safety management system in all sphere of life.

With this in mind we have tried our best to collect and present the materials in this book for the benefit of all. If this effort will help in this direction we feel our motive has been fulfilled.

We are also thankful to Virender Kumar Arya and his team at AITBS Publishers, India, Delhi, for their meticulous efforts in the direction of bringing out this book on time.

Any suggestion for further improvement will be gladly accepted.

–R.K. Mishra

Contents

1

CHAPTER

Accident Causation and Prevention

INTRODUCTION

Accident prevention is nothing but a problem solving, and this kind of problem solving involves two basic principles:

1. Establish the causes of accident.
2. Eliminate the causes of accident.

All organized accident prevention flows from these two principles. They do not require lengthy explanations. It is obvious that all accidents are caused and that we must know what the causes are before we can do anything about them. It is also obvious that merely knowing the causes is not enough. Something has to be done about them, and that something is to eliminate them.

Although these two principles are logical and obvious, and we usually apply them without thinking, we often overlook these principles at the time we need them most. Have you ever seen an inexperienced person run into trouble on a job? Did he patiently try to establish the causes of his problem before he acted? Or did he act on a hit or miss, trial and error basis? It was probably the later. We all make the same mistakes at times. We try to solve problems without understanding the causes. That is why a lot of our remedies do not work. Always go back to them, first establish the causes, then act to eliminate them. That is how accident problems are solved.

ARE THERE DIFFERENT TYPES OF CAUSES?

People generally are concerned with causes only after something has happened or after there is a problem. In accident prevention, there must be a concern with causes both before and after accidents have occurred. It is just as important for supervisors to be concerned with what can cause an accident as with what has caused an accident.

There are two kinds of causes:

1. Potential causes and
2. Actual causes.

Potential Causes are those that at any moment could cause an accident. Unsafe Acts and Unsafe Conditions are potential causes because they may cause an accident. Similarly, personal factor causes like lack of skill, poor vision, being 'under the influence', etc. are potential causes of accidents.

Actual Causes are those that can be specifically related to an accident that has already occurred. They are the cause that can be identified after an accident occurred.

An unsafe condition (or an unsafe practice) may be a potential cause at one time and an actual cause at another time. For example, say a puddle of oil has accumulated on a shop floor, before any one steps into it. The oil puddle is a potential cause of a fall. It could be said that there is a cause waiting to produce an accident. Now say somebody steps into the oil and slipped and fell down. The oil puddle is now the actual cause of accident (fall down). However, if the oil is not cleaned up after the same accident, it will again a potential cause waiting to produce another accident.

The distinction just made between potential and actual causes changes, in an important way, now they are:

- Establish both potential and actual accident causes.
- Eliminate both potential and actual causes of accident.

The first principle now tells us that we must not wait for accident to happen before we spot causes. To prevent accidents, we must always be alert for potential causes. When accidents do occur, we must identify the actual causes so we can take corrective action to keep them from being potential causes again.

The second principle now emphasizes that we must be just as vigorous in the elimination of potential causes before accident occur as we are in eliminating actual causes after accidents have occurred.

ESTABLISHING POTENTIAL CAUSES

Identifying potential causes of accidents is related to the four major categories of direct and indirect causes. These are:

- Detect unsafe conditions promptly
- Identify their source causes
- Detect unsafe practices promptly
- Identify their personal factor causes.

HOW TO DETECT UNSAFE CONDITIONS PROMPTLY?

This means that supervisors should make regular inspections and must be alert all the time for unsafe conditions. Unsafe conditions are always created by the actions of worker on the shop floor, normal wear and tear, and errors in equipment and facility design. Unless the newly developed unsafe conditions are promptly detected and eliminated, they will increase the number of accidents. That is why the early detection of unsafe conditions must be regarded as a basic principle of accident prevention. The basic tools for putting this principle to work are:

- Safety inspections by immediate supervisors.
- Safety inspection by employees.
- Safety inspection by department head.
- Safety inspection by plant manager.
- Safety inspection by safety department.
- Safety inspection by safety specialist.
- Safety inspection by interdepartmental groups.

HOW TO IDENTIFY SOURCE CAUSES?

The principle of identifying source causes has two meanings:

The First is preventing the initial occurrence of an unsafe condition. Supervisors should always be alert for both the actions of employees and the conditions of equipment that will develop into unsafe conditions. The idea is to nip the unsafe condition in the bud.

The Second meaning of the principle is preventing repeated recurrence of an unsafe condition. Many unsafe conditions that are corrected occur again in a short time because correction was not applied to the source of the unsafe condition. Supervisors should always identify the source causes of any unsafe condition they see. The idea is to prevent repetition of the unsafe condition by evaluating and correcting the source causes. The wise supervisor will always ask 'Why?', 'How come?', 'What's the reason?', when he spots an unsafe condition.

WHAT ARE THE TOOLS TO DETECT PROMPTLY UNSAFE PRACTICES?

Unsafe practices must be detected promptly, if accidents are to be prevented. Supervisors must always be alert for unsafe practices. Moreover, they tend to spread from one employee to another. That is especially true if those who work unsafely are the kind of informal leaders who influence younger and less experienced men. These are one of the reasons why the early detection of unsafe practices is another basic principle of accident prevention. The basic tools that put this principle to work in safety program are:

- Job safety analysis.
- Supervisory safety observations.
- Higher supervision safety observation.
- Safety department observation.

WHY IS IT IMPORTANT TO SPOT 'PERSONAL FACTOR CAUSES?'

There are two meaning to this principle:

The First is preventing the occurrence of an unsafe practice. Supervisor should always be alert for personal factors that may cause a man to work unsafely. It is important to look for signs of inadequate job knowledge or skill, conditions of physical or mental unfitness to work safely, or attitudes that conflict with safety, by acting promptly on personal factor causes, prevention of unsafe practices that could cause a man's disability or death.

The Second meaning is preventing repetition of unsafe practices. How to correct a man seen working unsafely. A supervisor should always try to find out why a man acted unsafely before he decides how to correct him. The most effective correction depends upon knowing what caused or influenced a man to work unsafely. It would be a mistake to discipline a man for working unsafely when he really did not know that he was working unsafely. Honest ignorance calls for patient instruction, not discipline. Similarly, it would not be effective to lecture a man on the importance of paying attention to signals when he missed a signal because of poor eye sight. An effective correction can be done when it is understood why a man acted unsafely.

There is no basic procedure for identifying personal factor causes. It takes a lot of knowledge and skill to establish such causes with any accuracy. It is difficult to establish personal factor causes in all the cases.

Establishing Actual Causes

The four principles of establishing actual causes are:

- Establish all contributing conditions.
- Determine the causes of any contributing conditions.

- Establish all contributing actions.
- Determine the causes of any contributing actions.

HOW TO ESTABLISH ALL CONTRIBUTING CONDITIONS?

All environmental conditions that have contributed to an accident must be clearly established. When the environmental causes of an accident go unrecognized, they invariably go un-corrected. There may be more than one contributing condition. Therefore, while investigating an accident the pertinent question that should be asked – What are the environmental condition that caused, made possible, or contributed in any way to the accident?

IS IT POSSIBLE TO DETERMINE THE CAUSES OF THE CONTRIBUTING CONDITIONS?

Unsafe conditions or contributing conditions, like accidents, are caused. These causes are likely to repeat again and bring about the same unsafe condition. For example, a man slipped and fell when he stepped into an oil puddle. The oil puddle was caused by a slow leak in an oil line on a nearby machine. The leak was caused by excessive vibration of machine. The excessive vibration was caused by the fact that the machine was not bolted securely to the floor. Some bolts have been replaced. Would it be sufficient to merely clean up the oil puddle after this accident?

Accident investigators must always ask themselves this question when environmental conditions contributed to an accident – What caused, made possible, or contributed to the environmental conditions. The question gets at the root of the environmental problems.

HOW TO ESTABLISH ALL CONTRIBUTING ACTIONS?

The great majority of accidents involve some action or lack of action on the part of the person to whom accident happened. Such contributing actions must be established and steps taken to prevent their recurrence not only by the man who had the accident but by others as well. Otherwise, the accident is certain to occur again. All contributing actions must be identified in specific and concrete details.

IS IT POSSIBLE TO DETERMINE THE CAUSES OF CONTRIBUTING ACTIONS?

Accident investigators must always try to determine the personal factor causes of any contributing actions associated with an accident. It must be known why the man did what he did. Exactly what went wrong? Such information will help to decide what kind of corrective actions is best to make sure that, the man does not repeat his unsafe practices.

There is another important reason for wanting to know the causes behind the contributing actions. Such causes often point out weaknesses on the part of the management. For example, if many men are having accidents because of lack of job knowledge or job skill, there may be a training weakness in the organization. Similarly, if many accidents are traced to defective physical and mental conditions, it suggests a review of the measures taken to ensure employee fitness.

To help decide corrective actions intelligently and to learn about possible weaknesses in management activities, accident investigators should always ask this question – Are there and what are the personal factor causes of the actions that contributed to the man's accident?

PRINCIPLES FOR ELIMINATING ACCIDENT CAUSES

The only sure way to prevent unsafe practices is to eliminate their causes. The following short coming have to be overcome:

- Lack of knowledge of hazards and safe procedures.
- Inadequate job skills.
- Lack of incentives to work safely.
- Motivations that conflicts with working safely.
- Physical and mental unfitness to work safely.
- Other personal factors which causes unsafe practices.

The way to eliminate unsafe conditions is to correct the conditions plus the causes of the condition.

Eliminating Unsafe Practices Caused by Insufficient Awareness, Knowledge, or Job Skill

The following principles point out what should be done:

- Provide position safety orientation for employees assigned to work in new positions (occupations).
- Conduct thorough initial job safety training, including use of JSA's.
- Follow up training with planned safety observations.
- Use of your safety contacts to re-emphasize major hazards and precautions.
- Provide pre job instructions on especially hazardous jobs that are infrequently done.
- Always correct men you see working unsafely, unless another kind of correction in order.

Discuss with the employee who is new to a position.

- Major area hazards.
- Required personal protective equipment.
- Specific house keeping and clean up responsibilities.
- Important safety rules that need special emphasis on his first day in the new position.

Eliminating Unsafe Practices Caused by Conflicting Motivations and Attitudes

Workers sometimes deliberately risk unsafe practices to save time or effort, to avoid discomfort, to attract attention – and for many other reasons. When they do, supervision must recognize the problems as one of the conflicting motivations and attitudes rather than one of not knowing better. The motivation problem is a combination of too little incentive to work safely and too much incentive to work unsafely.

THE MOTIVATION PROBLEM

It represents the employee who has to make the choice between doing a job the safe way or of doing it an unsafe way.

Example:

If the worker's ladder is too short to reach his work, he can get a long ladder (the safe way) or can try to make the ladder do by standing on the top rung of the ladder (one of several unsafe alternatives).

The worker in this case must make a choice between the safe and unsafe way. Some things about the safe way may attract him, others repel him.

The same holds true about the unsafe way. The choice he makes will depend on which alternative attract him the most.

The Safe Way

- Go back and get the longer ladder!
- Turn that tool now!
- Do not rush the work!
- Wear it! It will protect you!

The Unsafe Way

- Now! Step on the top rung instead.
- It's good for a few more days.
- Throw it! It's easier.
- Let's hurry so we can take a break!
- It's too uncomfortable, take it off!

THE FOUR BASIC MOTIVATION PRINCIPLES

1. Emphasize and increase the advantages and satisfactions of working safely.
2. Eliminate, where possible, any disadvantages or dissatisfactions of working unsafely.
3. Emphasize and increase the disadvantages and dissatisfactions of working unsafely.
4. Eliminate, where possible, any advantages or satisfactions associated with working unsafely.

The Motivation Problem Resolved

The best way to make the worker chose the safe way is to be sure he realizes fully the advantages of the safe way and the disadvantages of the unsafe way. The worker must be able to weigh the alternatives himself and chooses to do his job the safe way.

The Safe Way

- Safety awards.
- Sense of personal pride.
- Greater personal security.
- Clear personal record.
- Less time and effort.
- Respects for safety know how.
- Good safety reputation.
- Better promotion potential.
- Greater peace of mind.
- Harmony with supervision.
- Recognition and compliments.
- Greater work efficiency.
- Special commendation.

The Unsafe Way

- More things go wrong.
- Loss of hobbies.
- Family life disruption.
- More time and effort.
- Injury, illness or death.
- Poor safety reputation.
- Disciplininary action.

- Lost ambition, hope etc.
- Friction with supervision.
- Loss of earning power.
- Co-worker resentment.
- Feeling of insecurity.
- Poor personal record.

Eliminating Unsafe Practices Caused by Physical or Mental Unfitness

To prevent or eliminate the underlying conditions of unfitness:

- Determine fitness before hiring.
- Establish special fitness for certain jobs.
- Detect unfitness to work safely.
- Correct unfitness to work safely.
- Move the unfit man to a job which he can perform safely.

Eliminating Unsafe Conditions

- When you have authority, order prompt corrections of unsafe conditions.
- When such authority is lacking, report the unsafe condition to higher supervision together with recommendations for corrective action.
- When you have authority, correct the unsafe conditions as the source.
- When such authority is lacking, report the source causes to higher supervision, together with recommendations for corrective action.
- When correction of an unsafe condition is delayed, take whatever temporary precautions are necessary to reduce the hazard.
- Always follow up to be sure that correction has been applied.

APPROACH TO ACCIDENT PREVENTION POLICY AND RESPOSIBILITIES

Policy on accident prevention can be best described by the objective; to achieve, year by year, a continuing reduction in the number of accidents. No potential causes of accidents should be permitted to interfere with this basic objective.

All accidents regardless of their consequences are symptoms of production inefficiency. Really efficient production is accident free production. Good safety and good production go together hand in hand. Safety and productivity are the two faces of the same coin.

Top officials must have a concern for employee safety. It should not be a lip concern only. Top persons concern and their qualified support for the safety program should be demonstrated in their behaviors, speeches, letters, and directives etc.

Organized accident prevention requires a team work-approach. No single level management can do the job alone. It requires the efforts of all level, from top most level to first line supervisors and to lower most worker level.

The team work approach means a proper division of responsibilities. Each level of management must do what it can best do to promote accident prevention. There are four requirements for an organized accident prevention program based upon the team work concept:

- Establishment of management responsibilities.
- Communication of management responsibilities.
- Development of required knowledge and skill.
- Development of favorable motivation.

Safety starts at the top. The truth of this statement has long been recognized by professional safety people, who know that the driving force behind and effective accident prevention program is Management's Board directions and their support to safety. They establish basic accident prevention objective; to achieve a continuing year by year reduction in all accidents. It is the source that sets the wheel in motion.

Management's Responsibilities in the Safety Programs

Operation Head's Responsibilities:

- Establishment of a basic accident prevention program.
- Communication of safety objectives.
- Provision of the necessary means.
- Stimulation of earnest effort.
- Evaluation of progress made.
- Adherence to safety rules and codes.

Departmental Safety Head's Responsibilities:

- Management of the program.
- Basic supervisory safety training.
- Safety meetings with supervisors.
- Accident investigation.
- Safety inspections.
- Job safety analysis.
- Planned safety observations.

- Planned safety contacts.
- Initial safety orientation and job instructions.
- Maintenance of safety disciplines.
- Analysis of accident data.
- Adherence to statutory safety rules and regulations.
- Interdepartmental co-operation on safety matters.
- Development of proper safety attitudes.
- Personal protective equipment (PPE) program.
- Emergency readiness training.
- Mobile equipment operator selection and training.
- Miscellaneous responsibilities.

General Supervisor's Safety Responsibilities:

- Management of safety program.
- Supervisory safety training.
- Supervisory safety meeting.
- Accident investigation.
- Planned safety inspection.
- Job safety analysis.
- Planned safety observations.
- Planned safety contacts.
- Initial safety orientation and job instruction.
- Maintenance of safety disciplines.
- Personal protective equipment.
- Other safety responsibilities.

THE FIRST LINE SUPERVISOR'S SAFETY RESPONSIBILITIES

The first line supervisor, more than other members of management, has day in, day out contact with employees and their work areas. He has the best opportunity to train, guide and influence employees to work safely. That is why he plays the key role in accident prevention.

- Responsibility for assigned personnel.
- Responsibility for personnel not normally under his supervision.
- Initial safety orientation and job instructions.
- Employee safety attitudes.

- Maintenance of safety disciplines.
- Job safety analysis.
- Planned safety observations.
- Planned safety contacts.
- Planned safety inspections.
- Area house keeping.
- Employee medical care.
- Accident investigations.
- Employee fitness to work.
- Personal protective equipment.
- Mobile equipment operation.
- Emergency readiness.

RESPONSIBILITIES OF SAFETY DEPARTMENT

- Advisory and consultative services.
- Special safety studies.
- New equipment installations.
- Participation in accident investigation.

The above responsibilities of managers, assistants, department heads, assistant departmental heads, general supervisors, first line supervisors, and safety department personnel constitute basic accident prevention program. Their effectiveness lies in their collective application. Only if all levels of management accept their responsibility with conviction and willingness will the operation achieve its accident prevention objective; to achieve a continuing year by year reduction in accidents.

ACCIDENT PREVENTION MEASURES

The following steps are involved in an accident prevention program:

- 5 E's for accident prevention.
- Preventing unsafe acts.
- Preventing unsafe conditions.
- Safety tag system.
- Safety in house keeping.
- Employee's training in safety.
- Hazard check list.

- Color coding system.
- Motivating employees for safety.
- Safety auditing.

5 E'S FOR ACCIDENT PREVENTION

***1st E* – Engineering:**

Higher level of safety could be achieved through engineering controls only. Safety should be integrated with engineering from the design stage only. Project stage is the appropriate time for planning future safety. While the management has the obligation to make the work environment safer by using all available latest techniques, government agencies should exercise more control in the project stage itself. Engineering control is the best control; therefore, updated technology should be given preference over outdated ones even if these are costlier. It is the responsibility of government authorities that in granting industrial license, special emphasis should be given to safety measures and anti pollution measures.

***2nd E* – Education:**

It has been proved that over 98% accidents are due to human failure only. If adequate steps are taken to overcome human failure by proper education, then accident prevention will be a reality. The most important steps of education for safety consist of job training, knowledge of hazard and its control, procedure for the repair/maintenance etc., permit system, tag system, fire and its prevention, control and fighting equipment, use of personal protective equipment and first aid measures. As safety is gaining importance, the study of safety should be induced in school and university curriculum. Safety education and training is the most powerful tool which needs maximum publicity so that message of accident prevention reaches every individual and its importance is understood and appreciated by them.

***3rd E* – Enforcement:**

When employee fail to observe safe practices which they have been taught through the educational part of their training program, it become necessary to enforce them. In some instances drastic measures or penalties may become necessary to prevent the spread of unsafe practices. Enforcing safety disciplines to one and all is vital for the healthy growth of the nation. Safety enforcement can be better done in industry by including safety codes in standing orders. Anything enforced is resisted at the outset. Let the workers frame the rules and the managers follow. Finally the Government has to enforce the standard.

***4th E* – Enthusiasm:**

According to the different studies it has been proved that product from industrial workers was 8% higher when they are happy and satisfied. Maintaining the morale of workers is the prime duty of the management. All kinds of motivational techniques like individual safety awards, departmental safety contests, safety slogan, safety essay, spot the hazard contest etc. goes a long way to motivate the workers. For this purpose a safety suggestion scheme and giving suitable award for implemented suggestions is worth complementing. Most important of all is the participation of workers in all the deliberations of safety. Government can appreciate good safety record by issuing medals, trophies and certificates.

***5th E* – Evaluation:**

Continuous evaluation of programs, procedure and performance is a must for improvement in safety. Safety committee is an important medium to enhance this activity. Job safety analysis and statistics also help in this direction. The quality of personal protective equipment (PPE) is also to be evaluated.

PREVENTING UNSAFE ACTS

- Immediate supervisors should take corrective action. A well trained shop floor supervisor can easily detect unsafe acts while supervising and can take steps to eradicate such unsafe acts. Some unsafe acts are being done by the workers without knowledge and wrong training, which are very old habits. Supervisor may felt difficulty to prevent/overcome such long outstanding bad habits.
- Supervisors must see that all persons working under his guidance are using personal protective equipments while working. Use of proper protective equipments such as steel toed shoes, helmets, goggles and hand gloves etc. by the employees must be made compulsory. It is the duty of the supervisors to ensure the use of personal protective equipments by all and if required counsel, educate, caution, warn and take disciplinary measures.
- Action must be taken to create general awareness of bad habits. A general awareness of bad habits can be developed through safety literatures, safety training, proper skill training, and conducting regular works committee meetings etc. Above all help from union is very much essential to sustain these things.

PREVENTING UNSAFE CONDITIONS

Removing unsafe conditions is also an effective method of preventing accidents. The factors of eliminating unsafe conditions are:

- Safe guarding of all machines/equipments and moving parts. Machines should be adequately guarded or fenced against accidental contacts with dangerous parts and properly maintained to prevent accident.
- Suitable and safe design and construction. Unsafe design or installations are unergonomical design of machine (control of machine not matching with the physical capabilities of human beings) or improper foundation, grounding or lay

outs. Every machine should therefore be safely designed and installed to control accidents.

- Safe arrangement of materials, process and methods of work.
- Suitable safety devices of a machine, wearing tight fitting clothes to work on a machine, using brush or proper tool to remove swarf from a machine, not leaning over a running machine, cleaning machines after the work, not over speeding a machine, not leaving a machine in running condition, using safety goggles when chances of flying particles or splashes of oil/cutting fluid exist. So safety rules for operation in machine should be adhered to prevent accidents.
- Adequate and suitable ventilation.
- Adequate and suitable illumination.
- Maintenance of good house keeping.
- Proper maintenance of machines, e.g., oiling, greasing, adjusting, cleaning, replacing worn out or damaged machine parts in time.

SAFETY TAG SYSTEM

The tags are temporary means of warning all concerned of a hazardous condition, defective equipment, radiation hazards etc. These tags are not to be considered as a complete warning method, but used until positive means can be employed to eliminate the hazard. Accident prevention tags are used as a temporary means of warning employees of an existing hazard. It should not be used in place of or as a substitute for accident prevention signs.

Tags can be defined as a surface made of card board, paper board, plastic board or some temporary/non-permanent material on which letters or markings or both appear. They are for warning or cautioning or for giving safety instructions to employees who will be exposed to hazards. Tags are fixed to the equipment/device/system, by string or wire or adhesive tapes. Tags should be made preferably in two languages, i.e., English and local or regional languages so that the person can understand.

There is no fixed size for a tag. It should be suitable size. Material of the tag depends on the use on which they are to be put. The diameter of the hole of the tag may be varying. It is generally kept as 5 mm. As an additional reinforcement metal eye lets may be inserted into the hole. Tags may be attached to the re-enforcing substance with water proof and adhesive when it is subjected to abnormal humid conditions. Tags shall be attached either by a twine of minimum 9 numbers or steel wire of less than 0.6 mm diameters. The general tag colors are red indicates danger, green indicates O.K. and yellow indicates work in progress.

SAFETY IN HOUSE KEEPING

The term house keeping is defined as "A place for every thing and every thing in its place." House keeping means not only cleanliness but also orderly arrangement of tools, equipments, storage facilities and supplies. It is a practical method of increasing production, reducing accident and improving employee morale and public relations.

Aids to Good House Keeping

The following aids and equipments are to be provided and policies must be established by the management to achieve good house keeping standards.

- Proper lay out of work area.
- The marking of aisles and storage area.
- Provision of cabinets and holders for tools and portable equipment.
- Proper storage arrangement for materials.
- Provision of containers for materials in process.
- Efficient sequence of operations to avoid bottlenecks.
- Anticipation of wastes, scrap, dust, spillage, liquid splashes etc. and inclusion of means of control such as:
  - Providing overflow pans.
  - Receptacles for waste and scrap with orderly means of disposal.
  - Provision of scrap guards, chip screens, chutes, exhaust and collector systems, drains for liquid splash and vacuum cleaners etc.
- Efficient transportation of raw materials, the finished products and refuse etc.
- Efficient cleaning methods and scientific scheduling of cleaning without interference with production schedules.
- Training of employees for good house keeping.

This is not a complete list. Many more items can be added to the above list. However, the list is depending upon the requirements of a particular shop to suit the type of activities undertaken there.

Measures to Improve House Keeping

- Layout of machinery, equipments, storage space, aisles, and material movement facilities should be preplanned.
- All work places, aisles, and work surrounding areas should be kept clean and free from all obstructions.
- All materials should be stacked tidily up to a safe height in proper place. No material should lie in passenger aisles and walk ways.
- Do not pile wide or long material on top of narrow short material.
- Keep material a minimum distance of 3 ft. from power panels or light panels and 6 ft. from the nearest rail track or road.

- Do not allow keeping temporarily unwanted things on windows, edges or work tables etc., which may lead to hazards.
- Grease or oil if spilled on floor should be cleaned immediately.
- Nails, planks with protruding nails and other sharp cutting etc. should not be left on the floor.
- On completion of job all tools, ladders, chain pulley blocks and other equipment should be removed to proper place for storage.
- Eliminate the practice of keeping excess materials at work spot.
- Scrap bins should be provided at strategic locations. Scrap should be regularly cleaned from work places and should not allow to be accumulated in work area. Separate bins should used for rags and oily materials.
- Uniform color coding should be applied for pipe lines carrying gases, water, air, steam etc.
- Good ventilation and hygienic conditions should be maintained in buildings, sheds, canteens, rest rooms, lavatories etc.
- Illumination level should be adequate in buildings/yards through natural or artificial lighting.
- All defective tools should be removed from the tool box. No tool should be put to use for which they are not meant.
- All moving machine parts and live electric lines should be properly guarded.
- All man holes must be closed with suitable covers. If opened for some work, these should be guarded immediately. A red flag in day and a red light in the night should be placed by the side of the man hole.
- A first aid box shall be provided in a suitable place in each department. It's contents should be checked by the shift supervisor periodically.
- Oil, grease, lubricants and other combustible materials and explosives should be stored away from the work area.
- Fire extinguisher should be provided at all fire hazardous places. These should be checked periodically.
- A definite schedule should be carried out. Departmental house keeping inspections should be developed.

EMPLOYEES TRAINING IN SAFETY

For any successful accident prevention program safety training at all levels of management and employee's skill development is a must. Safety training develops skill, aptitude and insights among the employees which ultimately reflect in their work efficiency and adaptation of correct method of doing a job. It has been found that the root cause of most of the accidents whether they arise out of unsafe act or unsafe condition are attributed to lack of safety training. On the other hand success stories of industrial units with good safety performance give evidence of planned safety efforts.

Training should cover all levels of the organization. While safety training of workers usually covers safety at work, training of supervisors and managers should also cover other aspects such as legal aspects of safety, rules and regulations, company's safety policy, safety engineering and safety auditing etc.

As a general rule, safety training must form an integral part of the employee's job training. Right after joining employees must be taught a safe way of doing their jobs. Each employee must assume full responsibility for his own personal safety and well being. Each employee must be made to realize that it is his duty to perform the job safely so as to there should not be any risk to him, to his fellow workers and not to damage the company property while doing a job.

Advantages of Training in Safety

- Training imparts knowledge and skill which improve precautions and leads to safe work performance on the part of the employee.
- Training helps to develop safety consciousness among the employees and build up favorable attitudes on their part to wards safety measures and safety precautions.
- Training activity directly demonstrate company's interest in employees which leads to good human relations at work.
- Training saves the supervisors' time to instruct and correct employees.
- Training improves employees' understanding of:
  - Hazards associated with their work in a particular department or a particular job.
  - Causes of the accidents and how they are prevented.
  - The need for a prompt report on any personal injury.
- Training impresses upon an employee that he has a duty to his fellow workers and the company so that he may not endanger the lives of others or cause damage to the company's property.

Differences Between Education and Training

Education	Training
• Increases person's general knowledge.	• Develops person's skill in doing specific job.
• It is a life long phenomenon. It is a continuous process.	• It is of short duration say a few days, weeks, months or years.
• Education is imparted in schools, collages, and universities.	• Training is arranged in the industry or any other work place.
• Education is primarily the responsibility of the society and family is the primary unit of society.	• Training is the responsibility of the employer.
• The cost of the education is to be borne by the society.	• The cost of the training has to be borne by the employer.

ASSESSMENT OF TRAINING NEEDS

Safety training can give valuable results only if it is designed as per the need of the trainees and the organization. Need assessment generally deals with some of the safety related problems currently being faced by the organization. It is therefore, essential to assess training needs of the organization.

5 W'S to Assess Training Needs

- What are the current safety problems of the organization? (i.e., accidents/ occupational diseases or fires etc.)
- What are areas of safety training?
- When training should be imparted?
- Who should be given training?
- When and how to evaluate effectiveness of training?

Examples of Assessment of Training Needs

Level	Training Needs
Helpers (I day)	• Need for safety at work. • Hazards connected with their tasks and ways to safeguard. • Safety in handling and storage. • Steps to be taken in emergency.
Operators (3 days)	• Introduction to safety and company's policy. • Common causes of accidents.

	• Accident prevention. • Safety requirement in the job. • Role of worker in safety. • Safety in handling and storage. • Industrial hygiene and occupational health. • Personal protective equipment. • Steps to be taken in emergency and first aid.
Supervisors (5 days)	• Safety and company's policy. • Safety and the law. • Plant house keeping. • Common causes of accident in the plant. • Accident investigation and analysis. • Plant safety inspection. • Fire prevention and control. • Personal protective equipment. • Employee's education and motivation. • Role of supervisor in safety.
Managers (2 days)	• Introduction to safety and health and company's policy. • Legal responsibility of the employer. • Identification and control of hazards. • Elements of industrial hygiene and environmental monitoring. • Occupational health. • Accidents and associated costs. • Managing safety. • Human side of safety. • Role of management in safety. • Preventive and control measures.

SAFETY TRAINING DURING CONSTRUCTION

Safety training is given every person in the project. All site staff including site manager, erection – commissioning groups, control room engineers, operating staff and maintenance staff, testing engineers, quality control engineers, stores supervisors, safety engineers etc. are trained to ensure they are competent to carry out their work and they have understanding and knowledge of their functions and safety.

The activities in the training include:

- Study of documentation and procedures.
- Technical study.
- Attending lectures and workshops.
- Practical demonstration.
- Training in manufacturer's works and laboratories.
- Training at other connected stations in operation.
- On the spot training under guidance of experienced staff.
- Departmental examinations.

A good practice is to associate young personnel in various erection, commissioning, operation, and maintenance activities during the execution of project.

RECORD OF TRAINING

Training manager identifies the training needs of every person in the organization/ construction with long range and short range planning. Training card is made for every person. The training is reviewed on six monthly basis by the plant manager.

METHODS OF TRAINING

Training is the method of transfer of knowledge, skill or information which can be achieved through the following:

- On the job instructions by the supervisor or a senior worker at the time of allocation of job to the worker.
- Lecture on safety by external/internal faculty utilizing suitable blend of oral instructions and audio visual aids.
- Discussion led by expert faculty members covering relevant safety issues.
- Case study followed by a short lecture by the expert faculty involving participants to analyze an accident/dangerous occurrence. Discuss the issues involved and draw their own conclusions which may be moderated and corrected to impart instructions.
- Learning by doing is a method wherein the participants are expected after the lecture on safety to make "plant safety inspection" using a check list, brain storm their findings among themselves, and present a report to the trainer to demonstrate their understanding of the subject.
- Demonstration/visit are excellent method of training in topics like machinery guarding, measurement of noise/light intensity/dust and/or study good safety practices.

- Modern techniques (audio visual methods) using programmed instruction packages, computer assisted teaching aids and electronic aids like closed circuit camera/television etc.

HAZARD CHECK LIST

In a machine shop the following hazard check list will help the observer to make the safety appraisal.

- **House keeping:** State whether or not aisles are clear, stock properly piled, floor free from slipping and tipping hazards, and work area orderly.
- **Machine hazards:** State what guards are found not in use and where guards should be provided. This should include gears, sprockets, chains, bolts shafting etc.
- **Fire hazards:** Are all fire fighting appliances and fire exits are ready for immediate use? Are inflammable materials properly handled and stored?
- **Protective equipment:** Are goggles, respirators, safety caps, and other equipment being worn as required? Jewellery rings and wrist watch are a potential source of danger around moving machinery.
- **Electrical equipment:** Note conditions of switches, out lets, light cords and ground wires etc.
- **Tools:**
  - Are proper tools being used for each job?
  - Are handles missing from files, chisels mushroomed, hammers, wrenches and screw drivers defective?
  - Are feeds and speeds properly set?
- **General conditions:**
  - Are boards with nails left on floor?
  - Are ladders, stairs, guards and other equipments in need of repair?
  - Is cutting fluid likely to spill on the floor?

COLOR CODING SYSTEM

Color codes are used for:

- Stimulate a constant awareness of the presence of hazards.
- Expedite fire fighting and other emergency procedures.
- Marking physical hazards.

The color code is given below:

Red: Used exclusively in connection with fire prevention and fire fighting equipment.

Orange: Indicates dangerous points of machinery that cut, crush, shock or otherwise injure.

Yellow: The universal signal for caution. It is used most often to mark areas when there are tripping, falling, storing against or being cut in between hazards.

Green: The basic safety color. It should be used to indicate the location of first aid equipment, gas masks, safety deluge showers, and safety bulletin boards.

Blue: A cautionary color. It is a specific warning against starting that equipment as elevators, boilers, scaffolding ladders etc.

Purple: Indicates the presence of radiation hazards. Tags, labels, signs, and floor markings are made with a purple and yellow color combination.

Black, White or Black and White Combinations: Indicate traffic and house keeping locations, such as stair ways, dead ends of aisles and the location of refuge cans etc.

Black and Yellow Combinations: Used on overhead cranes, load carrying moving machineries etc.

MOTIVATING EMPLOYEES FOR SAFETY

'Motivation' is the act of stimulating someone or oneself to get desired course of action, to push the right button to get the desired action. Motivation in the context of safety, is the act of stimulating employees to perform their tasks the way it should be performed so that their own safety as well as those of others is not endangered.

Every employee has the responsibility to his own safety as well as that of the others whom their actions may affect. Management on the other hand has the responsibility of safe working conditions, i.e., safe design, proper machine guarding and proper maintenance of inherently dangerous machines/systems. Management is also responsible for persuading employees to undertake acts that ensure safe operation, i.e., management must secure safe behavior. A worker can be motivated in so many ways, i.e., by arranging good work place, good tools, good machines, good PPE's, promotions, good training, recognizing the work, and small fringe benefits. The management in order to motivate the worker may consider all the above points for improvements. Management will not be in a position to satisfy the worker by monetary benefits all the time; but other benefits like good work place, good personal protective equipment, good tools/machines etc. can be considered.

Characteristics of Motivation

- **Motivation is phychological act:** It relates to those forces within the individual employee which impel him to act or not act in certain ways.
- **Motivation is created from aims:** To motivate employees some targets must be set.
- **Motivation is an unending process:** Man is a social animal whose needs are unending. Fulfillment of first need gives rise to second need; second need leads to

third and so on. Need instigate to motivation. Man, therefore, can be kept motivated on continuous basis.

- **Motivation is the strength of work:** Motivation instigates a man to do or not a work in the specific direction.

Importance of Motivation

The sole objective of motivation is to instigate the employees to work effectively so that desired results are achieved through less effort. Motivation is the oxygen that keeps the fire in the man burning, i.e., desire to work even if the organization have the best equipment, best and sufficient quantity of material, men and money but their proper use will not be possible till the employee use them properly.

Advantages of Motivation

- Motivation enables effectiveness of resources.
- Motivation kindles in an employee the desire to work. Once the desire to work in the employee is actuated, then he works to his full capacity. Desire to work and capacity to work, therefore, are two different things. Even a highly effective person will not achieve much (not do appropriate work) in the absence of desire to work.
- Motivation increases productivity and safety both. The increase in productivity results because motivated workers work to their full capacity which leads to increase in production and therefore increase in productivity per worker per hour.
- Motivation develops in workers a sense of co-operation. Motivation improves job satisfaction and improved job satisfaction raises employees interest in the organization, which ultimately develops a sense of co-operation among them which is also essential for safe working.
- Motivation reduces accidents, labor turn over and absenteeism. Reduction in labor turn over enables management to have a pool of efficient workers. It also reduces the need to make substitute arrangement in the place of absent employees. Reduced labor turnover and absenteeism helps to reduce accidents.

Kinds of Motivation

Motivation is of two kinds:

1. Positive motivation
2. Negative motivation.

Positive motivation is based on the concept of "rewards for better performance". Employees may be motivated with some prize or facilities to do good or more work than was done previously.

Negative motivation is based on the concept of punishment. Employees may be fined if work is done poorly or not done in the manner it is supposed to be done.

Both positive and negative motivations may be applied according to the needs at different times. Good work should be rewarded but wrong work or no work should be punished. Similarly, employees should be encouraged (prized) for safe working and punished for unsafe acts.

Different Methods to Motivate Employees for Safety

- **Posters:** Posters are one of the simplest and excellent techniques to communicate with employees on safe practices. Posters with humorous or instructive text generally make good impact on the reader. However, to be effective, posters should be appropriate to the situation and changed frequently.
- House journal, a weekly or monthly news letter distributed to the company employees by the personnel department, is another good technique to publicize safety. The news letter may carry news of injury, severe occurrence of hazardous situations that have been corrected, details of proposed safety contest or result of safety contest, photographs of employees giving details of their contribution to safety/prevention of accident/innovative suggestions on safety etc. house journal to be an effective media for motivating towards safety must be interesting enough to read.
- Supervisors contacts are undoubtedly an excellent means of motivating employees for safety. A supervisor/foreman can contribute in the following ways to make a safety program work or wreck it:
  - Setting an example by wearing safety appliances and following safety practices.
  - Demonstrating positive attitude towards safety. He should never ask the worker to speed up at the cost of safety or express annoyance when worker requests time to go to dispensary for first aid treatment.
  - Holding short meetings popularly known as tool box meetings or pep talk to workers about safe work practices. Such meetings should be organized daily at the shift beginning or when there is something to be shown or some discussion is wanted. These meetings provide excellent opportunity to the supervisor to emphasis the importance of safety in work or pass on a reminder on certain safe practices.
  - Talking nice about safety specialist or safety regulations. A casual derogatory remark about safety engineer or safety regulation by a supervisor can easily kill company's safety program.
- Safety contest among different companies or among departments within a firm can provide good motivation. Such contests if conducted periodically can help in maintaining employees' interest in safety.

- Certain awards have proved very effective in certain industries in keeping employees' interest in safety. Safety awards (individual contests) where in awards are given to employees for working a long period with no injury. Many transport companies offer substantial rewards to their drivers who have worked without accident over extended periods. Safety awards may also be given to a department or a division for achieving zero lost time injury recorded over a long period. Such records when kept in prominent place and updated each day, e.g., accident free operation for X days (say 200 days) can prove very effective in kindling and maintaining employee interest in safety.
- Congratulatory messages from senior management are excellent motivation for most employees. Commendation letters for superior safety performance signed by chief executive/chairman/M.D. gives the recipients the feeling that the "big boss" is interested in the safety and welfare of the employees. Personal letters addressed to new employees at the time of joining and or on confirmation, emphasizing importance of safety, usually help in starting the new worker with the positive attitude.
- Employees' participation through the medium of safety committees, suggestion scheme or work simplification program is an excellent method for improving methods and morale. When one or more such concepts are in use, suggestion from employees to correct hazardous conditions or practices can be invited and employees can be suitably rewarded.

SAFETY AUDITING

Safety auditing is a very effective tool with safety management for identifying weak spot and planning corrective actions. The safety audit is the process that identifies unsafe condition and unsafe acts in the plant and recommends safety improvements. There are three types of safety audits:

- Walk through safety audit.
- Intermediate safety audit.
- Comprehensive safety audit.

These audits are different but they do not have rigid boundaries. They may have some overlap.

Walk Through Safety Audit

It evaluates the unsafe conditions noticeable to naked eye during walk through the plant with keen observation from safety view point. It is the least expensive safety audit during the walk through, many unsafe conditions may be noticed. These are listed, discussed and commitments for their dissolving are taken from line managers/supervisors.

During construction phase walk through safety audits may be carried out for stores, civil works, erection works, documentation and commissioning work etc. Security requirements are also audited.

During operation and maintenance, safety auditors observe the process, unsafe acts, and unsafe conditions.

The safety auditors discuss their observation with safety managers, line managers and line supervisors. Audit reports and recommendations are submitted to the plant manager and safety manager for taking corrective actions to eliminate unsafe conditions and prevent unsafe acts.

The teams for walk through safety audits include:

- Safety manager
- Safety consultant
- Insurance inspector
- Electrical inspector
- Manager civil/erection/commissioning/operation and maintenance.

The entire plant and its stores, documents, procedures are reviewed, interviews are conducted, observations are noted, and report is submitted. The report gives recommendations.

Intermediate Safety Audit

The intermediate safety audit involves more detailed study and review of plant design and plant operation than a walk through audit. Detailed measurements of high risk zones are conducted. These measurements are related with factor of safety. Tests may be conducted on unsafe conditions/equipment. Intermediate audit identifies weakness in plant design, equipment and substances and operation/maintenance procedures and improvements are also suggested.

Comprehensive Safety Audit

The comprehensive safety audit is a full scale audit that evaluates the safety factors in the plant on the basis of engineering, analysis testing, measurement, module analysis etc. full scale improvements in the plant design, renovation, operating procedures, staffing etc. are recommended. The comprehensive audit consists of the following:

Envelop Audit

This covers civil works, switch yard, electrical plant auxiliaries, stores, offices, canteen, ventilation systems, security arrangements and lightings etc.

Functional Audit

This covers organizational weakness, training requirements, clarity of responsibilities and delegation, documentation etc.

Safety Facility Audit

This audit reviews unsafe conditions of high risk and the existing safety facilities vis a vis recommended safety facility of high risk, medium risk and low risk zones.

Recommendations

The unsafe condition and unsafe acts are listed. The corrective actions and improvements are recommended. The unsafe conditions and unsafe acts observed are subjected to A, B, C analysis. A stands for high risk, B for moderate risk and C for low risk. Attention is focused on A and B categories.

MANAGEMENT RESPONSE

The safety audit is a powerful tool available to the management to take actions in right directions without hesitation/confusion. As mentioned earlier the management must be concerned about achieving hundred percent safety of personnel and plant. The recommendations of A and B category must be considered first. The action planned is mentioned for C category suggestions are implemented side by side.

Some commonly used accident prevention procedures

- Regular safety coaching class for workers. They should be explained for hazards, safety precautions and methods, safety duties and procedure in their own language.
- Periodical safety class for supervisors, managers and top executives for co-ordinate efforts from all.
- Safety meeting, conference, seminar, exhibition etc.
- Publicity safety posters, slogans, maxims, notices, bulletins, pay pocket inserts, stickers, slides, film, house magazines etc.
- Safety books, pamphlets, periodicals etc.
- Safety contests, essays etc.
- Safety plays and similar programs.
- Preparation of safety codes, standards etc.
- Use of safe employees in setting a good example.
- Safety message on work orders, correspondence etc.
- Featuring specific safe practice rules.

- Investigation of accidents and explaining their analysis of unsafe actions, unsafe conditions and their remedial measures.
- Hiring and training programs.
- Sending persons to outside safety courses.
- Specific programs as per own need and nature of work.
- Conducting short term safety courses for all employees in rotation.

2 CHAPTER

Be A Successful Safety Manager

INTRODUCTION

How you communicate affects your abilities as a safety manager. To be a more effective communicator, follow these guidelines:

Listen: To know what the employee thinks about the issues that affects employee safety, you must listen carefully to what is said, what others try to tell you or try not to tell you.

Do not be too quick ... or too slow: Do not wait to discuss bad news. Bring it up promptly. Delaying may hurt others. But do not jump the gun until you are sure you have the facts regarding hazardous situations.

Watch: Communications also happens with non verbal expressions. Be aware of body language. What message do you give to employees? For example, do you ignore an unsafe situation?

Be a problem solver: Keep discussions problem oriented rather than personality oriented. Define the safety problem and ask for help to solve it.

Look for ares of agreement: Begin with similarities and build on them. Retain your flexibility – do not say "absolute no" unless you mean it.

Ask questions: One of the best ways to obtain information is to ask questions. If you do not understand an answer, ask for clarification. Encourage workers to ask questions.

Persuade and explain: Avoid arguments use persuasion. Tactfully explain your reasons for taking an action or rejecting a safety related request.

Be patient: If you are too important, you probably will not get the results you want. If you have doubts about a decision or action, do not delay because an employee's safety is involved.

Maintain your composure: If you lose control of your emotions, you lose control over the situation. When emotions run high, the offended party is often filled with righteous indignations at what he or she considers unfair treatment. This can be especially true when you investigate a serious incident.

Think, practice, talk safety. An idea can be a shield.

Keep your word: Successful safety managers need the respect and trust of employees. In the long run integrity and sincerity may be more important than skill or knowledge.

PERSONAL QUALITIES OF A SAFETY MAN

The following are essential qualities:

- **Sincerity and Honesty:** The safety man must be sincere and honest in his approach. He must try to gain the confidence and respect of the persons for whom he is working.
- **Enthusiasm:** He must be loyal to his job, believe in the importance of what he is doing and be able to transmit his enthusiasm to the people around him.
- **Interest in and Sympathy with People:** He must be able to get along with people at all levels to get along with people it is necessary to be interested in them. Also he must able to see their view points and to understand the motives behind their behavior.
- **Tact:** Tact in dealing with people comes from understanding people and not wishing to hurt their feelings by unkind or thoughtless words, even when these may be justified. Without tact no safety man is going to get very far.
- **Good Appearance:** He must be neat and tidy and look efficient. This will inspire confidence in him among the people with whom he is to propagate the message of safety.
- **Self Confidence:** This can only come with good mental set up and experience of applying safety norms successfully. The safety man must be able to stand up to top management, shop floor managers, on line supervisors, trade union officials, or workers in defense of his opinions and findings and do so in such a way that he must gain respect.

Some Basics to Become a Good Safety Professional

Safety is a noble profession. The person engaged in this profession must be proud of it, because serving human life is next to creating it. If only for the sake of fulfilling the statutory obligation somebody engaged in this profession, then neither he can satisfy himself nor can anybody else be satisfied by him. Hence to become a good safety professional some of the basics are given below.

- Selling safety is the first job of safety professional. He must put forth such proposals to the company, which ultimately adds to the profit. Under such circumstances the top management is likely to hear his say.
- As a Safety Officer he should not be very much after "to whom he will be reporting?" Rather top man must consider him the right man to be reporting to him.
- A Safety Officer must not be a man of power crazy. In other words he should be reluctant to power and authority. These things automatically come as per the work effectiveness.
- A Safety Officer must develop the ability to solve safety problems through proper maintenance, good house keeping and reliable instrumentation. Fixing an annual target of accident reduction for each department is a practicable goal setting process.
- The Safety Officer has to be an expert system evaluator. He must work like a consultant to the shop level executives. Analyzing a safety problem and taking it up at appropriate level is a managerial skill. The Safety Officer must cultivate this habit.
- The Safety Officer should be competent to manage critical situations. He must be able to organize his safety schemes in line with company's annual business target. He must be thorough in his inspections and report making. These things ultimately bring his status.
- As a Safety Officer one must know how to talk and behave on the Shop floor, failing which he will not be acceptable to the workers. A Safety Officer's heart must bleed at the blood stain of an injured worker. If the Safety Officer encourages the workers, supervisors and shop executives, they will solve the problems themselves. People, especially industrial workers behave differently in a group than individually. Arguments on Shop floor must be avoided at all costs.
- Safety Officer must realize that house keeping is the single largest contributor to accident prevention endeavors.
- Safety Officer has to limit himself to the hazards present and expected to his factory only. He has to supplement his knowledge with the knowledge and experience of Shop floor Engineers. He has to go through the operation and maintenance manual of all the equipments in his charge. A thorough knowledge of pressure gauges, flow meters, relays, alarms systems, interlocking devices, signals, color codes, safety

factors, fire control systems, gas monitoring devices, effluent control measures, underground pipes, cables, drains, work places etc. is a must for every Safety Officer.

SALIENT FEATURES OF SAFETY MANAGEMENT SYSTEM

Proactive Measures

- Culture of safety-first. Safety should be discussed as the first agenda in all performance review meetings.
- Preparing and establishing the safety/project safety plan
- Forming of site safety committee
- Screening and safety induction of all new workmen/employees
- Pep talks/Toolbox meetings
- Job safety analysis of all critical activities
- Equipment Fitness certification for Plant and machinery equipment
- Work permit system
- Quality in procurement-PPE and safety devices.

HSE Monitoring Measures

- General safety inspections
- Electrical safety inspection
- Inspection of PPE and safety devices on receipt
- Inspection of plant and machinery and equipment including vehicles.

Performance Measurement and Review Systems

- Internal quality audits
- Control of non-conforming services
- Management review
- Evaluation of sub-contractors
- Safety performance monitoring and measurement
- Customer feedback.

Corrective and Preventive Measures

- Accident/dangerous occurrence reporting
- Accident/dangerous occurrence investigation and disseminating the lesson learnt to all sites
- Accident/dangerous occurrence analysis

Motivational Schemes

- Merit certificate for zero accident for the whole year.
- Merit certificates for achieving accident free millions of man hours.
- Annual safety bonus schemes.
- Annual safety campaign schemes.
- Motivational schemes for workers at site.
- Safety performance measurement and comparison with benchmark.

CHARACTERISTICS OF A SAFETY OFFICER

- An ideal safety officer is like the Father of a church.
- A safety officer with a missionary zeal and reluctance for power or authority is the ideal one.
- Selling safety is the first job of a safety officer. If the safety officer has a concrete proposal as to how he is going to help the company during coming year, the top management is likely to hear his say.
- Safety officer has a staff function and shall advise the lower, middle and top level management. He must report to the number one and never below the number two in the works organization.
- The safety officer must develop the ability to solve safety problems through proper maintenance, good house keeping and reliable instructions.
- Fixing an annual target of accident reduction for each department is the practicable goal setting process.
- The safety officer has to organize his safety schemes in line with company management techniques.
- The safety officer must know the techniques of shop floor inspection thoroughly and use them meticulously.
- The safety officer must know the report writing techniques. Each inspection must be properly worded and directed to concerned personnel. It is futile to discuss non use of face shield by a particular welder with the managing director and to discuss about shifting a railway track in front of a godown to its back side with the go-down supervisor. The safety officer makes himself ridiculous this way.
- The safety officer should be competent enough to manage critical situations.
- Analyzing a safety problem and taking it up at appropriate level is a managerial skill, the safety officer must cultivate.
- The safety officer has to be an expert system evaluator. He must work like a consultant to the shop level executives.

- The safety officer has to study the plant lay out thoroughly. He must look for repeated flow of intermediate materials in process and do needful to avoid them.
- The safety officer is concerned for the accident and the doctor is concerned for the injury. Doctor takes up the issue after the safety officer's failure.
- The safety officer has to develop a reliable accident record of the plant such record must contain all accidents with or without injury.
- The safety officer has the correct philosophy of accident investigation, i.e., to establish the system defect and not to find a scapegoat.
- Safety officer can advise for quality, periodicity, and suitability of PPE used by the employees. He must not interfere its procurement, distributions and use in particular; because these are line functions.

List of Institutions Offering Post/Advanced Diploma Courses in Industrial Safety:

- Central Labor Institute, N.S. Mankikar Marg, Sion, Mumbai – 400 022.
- Regional Labour Institute, Patipukur, Kolkata – 700 089.
- Regional Labour Institute, TTTI Post Office, Tharamani, Chennai – 600 113.•. Regional Labour Institute, Sarvoday Nagar, Kanpur – 208 005.
- Institute of Industrial Safety Professionals of India, C/o. Shri J.V. Mulik, RVM Cottage, G.P. Road, Dahisar (W) Mumbai – 400 068.
- Thane Belapur Industries Association, P – 14, MIDC, Rabale, P.O. Ghansole, New Mumbai – 400 701.
- National Safety Organization, 5, Sahakar Nagar No. 2, Parvati, Pune – 410 009.
- Gandhi Labour Institute, Ahmedabad – 380 052.
- Delhi Productivity Council, New Delhi.
- Supervisory Development Centre of the Directorate of Technical Education of Kerala.
- Asian Workers Development Institute, Sector – 6, Rourkela – 769 002, Orissa.
- Indian Institue of Social Welfare & Business Management, Kolkata-700 073.
- Indian School of Labour Education, Chennai.
- Regional Engineering College, Trichy, conducting Post Graduate Degree 'M.E.' in Safety Engineering.

HAZARDS IN SAFETY PROFESSION

A safety officer in any industrial undertaking spends maximum time of his job in recording, reporting, investigating and analyzing work accidents. To be more precise, there is hardly any free day when safety officer is not worried of minor/major accidents/incidents.

Everyday there may not be a fatal, serious or reportable accident in the industry but non-reportable minor cases or near miss cases without injury are not rare. Most of times these cases are ignored either for convenience or due to complacency since they do not create turmoil at the work place.

There is no denying of the fact that safety is synonymous with accident (prevention) in many organizations. The safety officer has to shallow the bitter remarks of superiors, workman and statutory authorities when a major or fatal accident occurs.

In an anxiety to set the things in order, he has to spend many busy days and sleepless nights running from pillar to post without much appreciation from any corner. This type of episode occurs a few times in a year depending on the time gap between two such accidents. As a result, minor incidents are lost sight off. This type of safety activity considered by others as more negative than positive. Therefore, when the functions of the safety officer is evaluated critically, it becomes mostly accident oriented and negative. The efforts put in for developing a safety culture and safety promotion are pushed to the back door. With a defensive behavior, the safety officer also tries to bring out less and less of accident facts unconsciously in the form of a camouflaged statistics to please the statutory authorities and top bosses as a result, true picture of the safety performance of the company is not reflected and even the laudable efforts for safety promotion are undermined for years together.

Through Others Eye

Then, what next? Can it not be possible to look 'safety' as an important function of the business strategy of the company like quality, productivity, profitability, customer satisfaction and cost reduction ? This will be possible if the true safety picture is placed before the board of directors without any inhibition or apprehension. The facts have to be accepted and gray areas have to be identified to adopt remedial measures. The words like negligent behavior, carelessness, overconfidence, human failure, ignorance and indifference to safety are considered to be 'words of yore' in modern safety process and the management has to take the legal and moral responsibility of ensuring safety of employees engaged in various production processes. Safety is a balanced function of management leadership and employee involvement. It can not be left to the employees and supervisors alone. Safe behavior of the employees have to be promoted through skill development, safety training, behavioral modification, constant interaction and participate solution to the problem.

The role of the shop managers, supervisors and union representatives are also important to bring about cultural changes at the workplace by shading the old axioms and giving place to new concepts. Initially there may be some resistances; but it can be overcome by regular review discussions. Identification of hazards, elimination of unsafe conditions, educating the workers and supervisors on hazard monitoring and safe practices on the job and providing appropriate personal protective equipment to employees are some of the responsibilities of the management. Following the operating procedures, use of safety appliances, participating in identification and elimination of hazards, influencing the colleagues and subordinates to adopt the safe behavior, ensuring safety to follow workmen at the work place, implementation of the recommendations of the safety committee are some of the responsibilities of the workers and trade unions.

To make the safety process effective, both the partners should fulfill their responsibilities. The basic responsibility of safety should lie with the plant manager where as the safety officer should be an advisor, trainer and facilitator. This should be the approach of safety management.

Total involvement of all the employees in the safety movement of the company can bring about success in safety management. How it should be achieved is the key question. Appreciating good work, awarding safe action, encouraging to bring out safety suggestions and developing leadership in safety for long term benefit are some of the positive actions for ensuring employee involvement. Consistent effort to develop a participative culture at all levels should be done with sincerity, trust and mutual co-operation. The achievements should be highlighted but the lapses should not be lost sight of. Today the thrust is on changing attitude of employees towards safety. Attitude can be changed through behavior changes only. Therefore thrust on safe behavior practices should be encouraged.

If a safety audit is conducted every year, it will reveal that the new safety process thus adopted would generate profit by reducing cost. Safety pays and it does not really cost much.

Is the Safety Officer/Safety Department Responsible for any Accident?

A very tricky question indeed! The answer could be yes or no depending on the circumstances of each accident case.

In a country where safety officers are considered to be an appendage or a necessary evil and their role perceived as merely that of preventing the devilish Inspector of factories from enjoying piggy back rides on the back of the managements the helpless safety officers are invariably made a scapegoat irrespective of whether an accident occurs due to a technical lapse, murder, suicide or plain lunacy. With no ammunition in his arsenal and no support from the top management, the safety officer's plight is really most pathetic. Let us examine this question from a rational view point.

The two main issues involved herein are:

- **Responsibility:** This must be commensurate with the delegated authority and accountability. Since the line managers are delegated full power/authority within their jurisdiction of activity, it follows that they are fully responsible for ensuring safety also.
- **Staff relationships:** A safety organization have staff relationships with the line and hence a safety officer's role is essentially to advise and guide the line managers as well as the top management and also to catalyze all activities related with safety.

Even the Factories Act 1948, read with the relevant section of the Factories Rules, has prescribed similar duties for the safety officers as given below:

- ***Sec. 40-B(2):*** The duties, qualifications and conditions of service of safety officers shall be such as may be prescribed by the State Government.
- ***Rule 61-AA(4):*** The duties of the Safety Officers shall be to advise and assist the factory management in the fulfillment of its obligations, statutory or otherwise, concerning prevention of personal injuries and maintaining a safe work environment.......

On the basis of the above logic one may be inclined to let the Safety Officer go Scot free every time. However, there is a catch here. Consider the case of a major out break of fire in a chemical factory which is gutted due to failure of the fire detectors to sense the fire in its incipient stage, and the fire hydrants failing to supply water due to inadequate line-pressure. Though the front line managers as well as the Head of Department are primarily responsible for the disaster, the safety officer can not be absolved of his responsibility to have at least given timely feedback to the management regarding the ill health of the fire-detectors and inadequate water pressure. After all, this is what he is paid for. Hence, has the safety officer conducted mock drills/safety audits and exonerated full responsibility for the accident may then be fixed on the line manager/HOD/top management. If not, then a major portion of the blame for the disaster must definitely be assigned to the lethargy and inaction of the safety officers. It was on this reasoning that The Chief Inspector of Factories, Madhya Pradesh was sacked after the tragic MIC disaster in Bhopal on 3rd December, 1984. Of course, it would require a very objective enquiry into the circumstances leading to the accidents so as to assess if any lapses was there on the part of the safety officer.

At any rate, the wrath and fury always directed against the safety officer, particularly by belligerent unions, is retrograde step signifying the general mental and intellectual backwardness of our society. High emotional outbursts, especially during fatal accidents, are understandable, but rationality demands a more humane and scientific approach to accident prevention.

SAFEST WAY TO KILL SAFETY

When somebody wants to kill mosquitoes or mad dogs then he needs to plan carefully. But if somebody wants to kill SAFETY, which have been promoted many years of sincere efforts; he need not plan anything, just be indifferent, just ignore safety, it will die.

Safety is like a flower plant. To grow a flower plant, you need watering, manuring, weeding, love and care. Just ignore the plant for a few days, it will die. Likewise, ignore to attend a safety committee meeting, be indifferent to celebration of a safety week, if there is an invitation to address a safety rally say "I am too busy", and within a year or so, SAFETY will have its natural death.

Nobody will blame you; even none will know that you have harmed safety, what a safe and sure way to murder SAFETY!

Of course, Accidents will not appear all of a sudden. Out of inertia, the system will work safely for another year or so. Around the third year or so, the terrible teeth of Mr. Accident will be clearly visible.

Safety needs every one's gentle touch, love and care to flourish.

Indifference and negligence are the worst enemies of safety.

3 CHAPTER

Behavioural Based Safety

HISTORY OF BEHAVIOURAL BASED SAFETY

Dr. E. Scott Geller of safety performance Solutions in 1979 used the phrase 'Behavioural Based Safety' for the first time. It then became the catch phrase of the safety systems industry.

Behavioural safety grew out of the early work done by early pioneers who were applying behavioural principles in organizations. Behavioural Based Safety originated with the early work of Herbert William Heinrich. H.W. Heinrich who was basically an Insurance Agent working for Traveler's Insurance Company in 1930's. Due to his own interest he has reviewed thousands of accident reports completed by the Supervisors and from those drew the conclusion that most accidents, illness and injuries in the workplace are directly attributable to 'Human Failures', or the unsafe acts of the persons. In 1930's, not unlike today, supervisors' accident reports blame workers for the accidents. H.W. Heinrich came to the conclusion that roughly 90% of all accidents are caused by human error. Heinrich's data does not tell why the person did what they did to cause the accident; he could not justify rather termed 'Human Failure' only.

Later this conclusion became the foundation of Behavioural Based Safety (BBS). BBS addresses the fact that there are additional reasons for injuries in the work place; those are environmental factors, equipment, procedures and attitudes. Traditionally BBS has been used in industrial settings, but the new generation has found success of using BBS in office/laboratory settings as well.

BEHAVIOUR BASED SAFETY (BBS)

Objective

A behaviour based operation to safety and health will edge closer to achieving of **"Zero Accidents".**

A key factor for success is that employees learn to identify and correct at risk behaviour.

1. Consequence the Root of Change

- The conditions in a given environment, we can predict and change behaviour. To change a behaviour, we must specifically identify the factors in the environment that contribute to it and at before and after.

  Example: The seat belt is installed as a safety device. Although wearing a seat belt is known to save lives, many people do not wear them, either out of habit, comfort or a feeling of mortality.

2. An Employee Driven Process

- More than 95% of accidents are due to at risk behaviour.
- BBS training are taking place at two levels both management and employees are also be trained in the BBS process.
- Health and safety performance requires constant attention to both safe working conditions and safe working behaviours.

BBS Must be an Employee Driven

The implementation and acceptance of BBS will be a greater challenge.

3. BBS at the Industries

Industries have to develop and implement on occupational health and safety management system. The structured empowerment and involvement of employees is a key element of the system and clearly sets the stage to more deeply into behaviour based safety.

- BBS is not a quick fix program.
- BBS based safety alone can not guarantee success.
- It is to everyone's success.

Steps to BBS

1. Identify the critical behaviour.
2. Conduct observation on the behaviour.
3. Provide feedback and positive reinforcement on the execution of safe behaviours. Remove the barriers impeding safe behaviour.

WHAT IS BEHAVIOURAL BASED SAFETY

Behavioural based safety is the use of behavioural psychology to promote safety at home and at work places. BBS typically involves creating a systematic and on-going process that clearly defines a set of behaviours which ultimately reduces the injury, collects data on the frequency of those behaviours, then ensures feedback and reinforcement to ensure support of those behaviours.

Total safety culture encompasses that when safety mechanisms are in place then implementing BBS gives wonderful results. BBS believes that psychological change can be achieved with repeated and active care of each other. BBS underlines that when 80 to 90 percent of accidents and injuries are due to unsafe behaviours; one must focus on unsafe as well as safe behaviours. Behaviour is objective, definable, observable, correctable and measurable. One can accomplish this objective by training employees on the concept and process of behavioural safety.

A chief objective of each plant is to achieve Zero accident. Since safety in the organization can not be less than 100%; therefore the participation of employees in safety also has to be 100%. That is what BBS is all about.

Research and experience indicate that:

- 90% or more of the accidents are due to unsafe human act or behaviours.
- 50% of unsafe behaviours are identified or noticeable.
- 25-30% of safety awareness is lacking among employees which gets reflected in their unsafe behaviours.
- Unsafe behaviours are the core of any near misses, injury and accidents. If we control unsafe behaviours, we may not even have near misses.

So, in safety it is needed to focus on unsafe and safe behaviours. The secret of success of BBS is that the safety control is in the hands of employees and it depends on, when they feel empowered and responsible.

BEHAVIOURAL BASED SAFETY APPROACH

BBS is one of the best and latest safety approaches. BBS process is repeatedly going to an employee and making random observations till he reaches safe behaviours and learns the concept of self observation and observing others for safe performance. The aspects that BBS takes care in order to prevent unsafe behaviour and promote safe behaviour are:

- Maintenance of good house keeping.
- Proper using of tools and equipments.
- Proper body positioning.
- Taking proper protective measures while working.

- Correct material handling.
- Means of communication.
- Following correct procedure.
- Visual focusing.

With the help of a checklist BBS trained observers create data on the above eight critical behaviours to guide their observations. Each observer observes at least one of his co-workers daily. If there are 500 workmen, 500 checklists are created per day on unsafe and safe behaviours in the organization. By this way safety becomes a daily reminder which in essence builds safety culture. Besides the data created gives an idea of daily increase or decrease of unsafe and safe behaviours.

BEHAVIOUR BASED SAFETY PROCESS

BBS is based on the following four key components:

1. A behavioural observation and feed back process.
2. A formal review of observation data.
3. Improvement goals.
4. Reinforcement for improvement and goal attainment.

1. Behavioural Observations and Feedback Process

Employees are observed performing their routine task. The observer documents both safe and unsafe behaviours. The employee is then provided positive feedback on the safe behaviours and non threatening feedback on the unsafe behaviours. They are also provided with suggestions on correcting on the unsafe behaviours.

Observation/Feedback Works because:

- Motivates and involves people in safety.
- Generates two way communications.
- Empowers employees to improve their own safety and the safety of others.
- Creates volunteers who want to work safely.
- Impacts on people's behaviour.
- Focuses peoples mind on safety.
- Turn safety into a positive experience.

2. Formal Review of Observation Data

The data is then analyzed to determine the employee's improvement in safe behaviours. It can be looked into as an overall percentage. If there are 20 items in the checklist and the worker performed 17 of them safely, then he would get a score of 85% safe. The improvement between observations could be graphed and displayed for workers to view.

When the graph shows improvement, it provides positive reinforcing feedback to employees.

3. Improvement Goals

Setting improvement goals increases the effectiveness of feedback and the success of the behaviour based safety process. These goals can take different forms. Such as:

- Percent safe goals
- Process goals
- Implementation goals.

4. Reinforcement for Improvement and Goal Attainment

Management must provide immediate, positive feedback to reinforce safe behaviour. Rewards can be an effective means of reinforcing goal attainment.

Many approaches are used to make employees more safety conscious. However, the following elements are present in most successful safety programs:

- All employees are trained in safety procedures and understand relevant company rules.
- Management is willing to spend money and budget for safety.
- Safety programs have the support of top and middle management.
- Management and supervisors follow safety rules and confirm to regulations.
- Responsibility for safety is an integral part of manager's job.
- Positive attitude towards safety is maintained throughout the organization.
- Safety efforts are monitored and regularly evaluated.

Results of BBS

- Increased efficiency
- Increased morale
- Positive safety culture
- Job satisfaction
- Bonding
- Teamwork
- Fearlessness
- Feeling to help
- Openness
- Increased productivity
- Increase profitability
- Increase in production
- Love and affection
- Ownership
- Confidence
- Active care
- Feeling of joy
- Decrease in unsafe acts.

Problems in Observing and Giving Feedback

- Handing over checklist to observe and asking him to do the job.

- Only observing, not giving feedback.
- Two observers may not agree with each other.
- Observer may not allow an observe to speak.
- Comments column kept blank.
- Only criticism and not appreciation.
- Inadequate time for giving proper feedback.
- The person observed behaves smart, does not accept the observer.

Reasons of Failure of BBS Observer

- An aggressive way of responding.
- Giving feedback in front of others.
- Observer may not following standard operating practices himself.
- Improper communication.
- Incorrect way to pass feedback.
- Lack of correct relations.
- Lack of knowledge about the job of an observer.
- Lack of patience to correct an observe.
- Lack of responding skills.
- Mentioning person instead of behaviour.
- No proper follow up.
- Personal grudge.
- Superiority complex.
- Unable to convey that we are concerned about injury free culture.

WHY – WHY ANALYSIS

It is not always the workers fault because of which accidents take place. To know the actual reason of mishap the why – why analysis helps to reach the root cause of faulty behaviour. If a job is being done 'unsafely', a good rule of thumb is to ask **'why five times'.**

Example: A worker was not wearing safety glasses and something fell in his eyes causes' injury. The five why method can be applied to find the root cause of the injury.

The worker got something in his eye while at work. But why? Because he was not wearing his safety glasses. But why?

> Because they were all scratched up and not wearable.
>
> But why?
>
> Because the employer brought the cheap glasses.
>
> But why?
>
> Because his employer wanted to save money.
>
> But why?
>
> Because the profits are more important to the employer than worker safety.

Asking why questions allows an inquiry to got to root causes – the source of problem that will need to change in order to bring about a safer work place. Union can then strategize about what it would take to get an employer to purchase adequate personal protective equipment, or use engineering control to eliminate the need for workers to wear personal protective equipment, or in some other way make the work place safer. An approach that blames worker for their 'bad behaviour' not only prevents root cause analysis but also real prevention action.

BBS Basics

- Actively caring of unsafe and safe behaviours leads to improved safety behaviour.
- Listening, praising, group problem solving, and celebrating safety achievements can increase actively caring behaviours.
- Attitude and behaviour link is weak. What we teach does not necessarily get converted into behaviour.
- Attitude is internal, refers to thinking and realization; where as behaviour is external, observable, and an active experience.
- BBS addresses individual and social dynamics for safety.
- BBS does not substitute or replace process hazard evaluation, incident analysis, environmental or cultural solutions. When at-risk behaviours are identified, the comments are made on the organizational cultural factors that reduce or prevent such behaviours.
- BBS effects can be seen by measuring safety climate on awareness before and after its implementation for understanding change in safety performance.
- BBS finally needs customized approach as per needs of the organization.
- BBS follows DO-IT: define, observe, intervene and test.
- BBS has shown positive results in terms of safe behaviour and reduction in accident rates across industries and countries.
- BBS increases safe behaviours and therefore reduces injuries, illness and related financial costs.

- BBS involves a process of observation and feedback, a system of collecting, analyzing and dissemination of data, and a proactive support of management.
- BBS is 'actively caring': its beyond the call of duty for safety for self and others.
- BBS is 'safety for each other'.
- BBS is a continuous process till you intend to prevent unsafe behaviours at work place.
- BBS is a peer to peer learning about safe behaviours.
- BBS is a process of determining progress in the reduction of unsafe behaviours.
- BBS is more than safety regulations.
- BBS is not magic. It's a gradual process.
- BBS is not punishment or disciplinary action or focusing on incident rate, or personal prejudice, or top-down implementation. It's a praise, encouragement and reinforcement of safe behaviours.
- BBS is though a top driven but bottom-up approach.
- BBS is one of the best and latest safety approaches that will help improving safe behaviours and discourage unsafe behaviours in your organization if applied with full commitment of everyday.
- BBS is to ultimately develop concern for each other's safety at the workplace and developing empathy for each other.
- BBS is based on the established principles of behaviour theory in psychology.
- Principles of BBS are based on research and an established theory.

Action Plan Desirable in Launching BBS

- Commitment from management.
- Training of employees across the plant.
- Select and train observers from BBS trained employees.
- Forming steering committee consisting of 8 to 10 BBS trained persons.
- Develop checklists.
- Selection of areas/departments for behaviour observation and feedback process.
- Develop time table.
- Documentation, analysis and display.
- Review to determine BBS progress in the organization.
- Allocate time for BBS observations and meetings etc.

Management Questionnaire before Launching BBS

- How to select observers?

- How to launch BBS?
- Are there any implementation problems?
- How to form and who should form a steering committee?
- Is separate training necessary for observers on interpersonal skills?
- Is separate training required for steering committee on their roles and responsibilities?
- Does an observer require a badge on his chest?
- What should be the title for BBS project?
- Who should be an observer?

Pre-requisites for BBS Launching

- An accident history of past 5 years of the organization.
- List of existing safety measures.
- The organizational profile.
- Existing injury/accident rate.
- Near misses reported in the past one year.
- Management's readiness to implement a BBS process/BBS readiness survey.

Components of BBS Training

- What is BBS?
- Myths of BBS?
- How does BBS work?
- Why all the interest in BBS?
- Out comes of a BBS project.
- Psychology and BBS.
- What BBS is not?
- Implementation problem in BBS.
- BBS observation and feedback process.
- Manager's role in developing BBS culture.

Ten Expectations of BBS Training Participants

- How can we be #1 in accident prevention?
- How can we correct human behaviour?
- How behaviour is important in safety?
- How can we change attitude and behaviour?

- How can we analyze safe behaviour?
- How to implement BBS?
- How to find unsafe behaviour?
- How to make workers understand safety?
- Can safe behaviour be measured?
- How to sustain 'safe behaviour' is a challenge?

HOW TO SUSTAIN BBS CULTURE IN ORGANIZATION

- Monitor BBS data daily as being received from trained observers on prescribed format.
- Review meeting every month to be held.
- Form core committee of BBS trained persons.
- Display BBS banners of eight behaviours on a board across plant.
- Train all workers/employees phase wise.
- To report to management every month by core committee.
- Allow only trained workers to observe.
- Analyze and display weekly/monthly percentages and graphs of safe and unsafe behaviours of 'behaviour sampling checklist'.
- Quarterly BBS progress audit.
- Include BBS under EHS policy/framework.
- Action plan for rectifying unsafe conditions.
- Analysis of BBS data should be done per week/month of each observer, each behaviours and total of unsafe and safe behaviours. Data need to be entered daily in computer. In the morning, blank form of behaviour sampling to be distributed and filled in form to be collected in the evening from each observer by the core committee member.
- The major objective of BBS is to achieve progress in reduction of unsafe behaviours and increase of safe behaviours.
- Ensure positive attitude and whole hearted approach of everyone involved.
- Introduce train the trainer program. This way BBS trained members of each department take responsibility to train all members in their respective departments.
- Ceremonial lunch of BBS in the organization.

MAJOR HIGHLIGHTS OF BBS

- BBS is an employee movement with support and commitment of management.

- BBS is a continuous process till you intend to prevent unsafe behaviours at workplace.
- It requires a steering committee comprising of a senior manager, a front line manager and about ten of BBS trained observers.
- BBS should have pre and post measures of safety awareness levels of employees in all departments by safety awareness survey.
- 'Behavioural change' brings 'attitudinal change', not vice versa, so focus on behaviour and feedback process.
- BBS needs to be integrated as an organizational system. It is a new initiative, new direction and new emphasis on safety.
- It is by the people, of the people and for the people. It is based on the established principles of behaviour theory in psychology.
- The role of middle, senior, and top management in BBS is to motivate the observers, monitor progress, and to mentor them.
- BBS approach needs a 'visible presence, and a clear management adoption and open communication down the line for its launch with full breath, failing which it is difficult to succeed.
- BBS audit is needed after three months of launching BBS in an organization which includes:
  - Critically looking at the progress graphs across plants,
  - Meet/discuss with observers for understanding their issues,
  - Understanding execution of responsibilities of BBS core team,
  - Analysis of unsafe/safe behaviours, and
  - Setting further goals/challenges for BBS core team/observation etc.

BBS IN ORGANIZATIONS

- The key words of BBS are: unsafe and safe behaviour, observation, feedback, and steering committee.
- Engineering solutions have been achieved to a great extent in organizations but behavioural engineering in managing safety is a challenge to the organization.
- BBS concept of safety is not only useful for safety professionals but also everyone who is concerned in correcting unsafe behaviours for reduction of accidents.
- BBS emphasizes that if the employees behave unsafe, they are not punished, instead they are repeatedly told to correct; and when they behave safe, they are encouraged.
- Both unsafe and safe behaviours are counted and displayed. BBS also discusses the unsafe conditions that influence unsafe behaviours.

- BBS is a data driven decision making process. BBS believes that what gets measured gets done and each employee can make a difference in organizational safety.
- BBS begins by briefing sessions for all work areas and departments. BBS is a team work; it is company wide, and people driven.
- BBS purpose is not to enforce safety rules, but to identify safe and at-risk behaviours for safer solutions.
- BBS is not a management driven tool for safety, it's an employee driven approach with management support.

BBS CONCLUSIONS

The managements have taken many safety initiatives to reduce accidents in organizations such as:

- Risk assessment
- Suggestion schemes
- Auditing
- Standard operating practices
- Works permit systems etc.
- Safety training
- Safety committee
- Motivational programs
- Plant inspections

Most of these systems are able to control unsafe conditions successfully, because unsafe conditions are visible; whereas it is found that 80 to 90 percent of accidents are happened due to unsafe acts which are not visible and is the outcome of the unsafe behaviour of the person himself.

People behave unsafe because it saves their time and effort by taking short cut or not using personal protective equipments. Punishment may lead to positive or negative effects. Attitude change does not help much because it does not change into behaviour until the person wants to change his behaviour. Here lies the importance of BBS, which can be tried for better safety results. BBS is based on Stimulus Response Theory, which assumes that unsafe behaviour is to be changed and safe behaviour to be reinforced require repeated external stimuli which is prevented through Behaviour Observation and Feedback Process (BOFP).

BBS underlines that take active responsibility for safety of each other. Target observable behaviour, focus on positive consequences. We expect to receive, i.e., change unsafe to safe behaviour; monitor behavioural trend of each individual or group everyday/ week/ month in order to understand percentage of safe and at-risk behaviours across departments during the years.

Non use of appropriate personal protective equipment by the worker is an unsafe act and considered an unsafe behaviour but simultaneously it is considered a system failure also. Total safety culture encompasses that when the safety mechanisms are in place and active then implementing BBS gives wonderful results. To set right the system punishment should be the last resort as 'punishment never works for sustainable results for safety in the organizations. BBS is going to be one of the best components of safety in the years to come. BBS believes that psychological change can be achieved with repeated and active care of each other. In spite of best operational controls at the work place, workers still meet with accidents due to unsafe behaviours. BBS emphasizes that when 80-90 percent of accidents and injuries are due to unsafe behaviours; let us focus on unsafe as well as on safe behaviours more than the unsafe conditions. Behaviour is objective, desirable, observable, correctable and measurable.

BBS approach needs a visible presence and a clear management adoption and open communication down the line for its launch with full breath, failing which it is difficult to succeed. BBS is ABC of safety means 'Always Be Careful'.

4

CHAPTER

Electrical Safety

CAUSES OF ELECTRICAL ACCIDENTS

The main causes of electrical accidents are exposed wires, bare conductors, open switches, temporary/loose/hanging wires, no ear thing/inadequate ear thing, use of wrong fuses, inadequate knowledge and unsafe work methods.

Do's

- Only qualified persons should undertake electric repairs.
- Treat all circuits as live unless ensured dead by testing.
- Ensure extension cords are free from cuts, damaged insulations, kinks or joints.
- Ensure that pins of the socket/plug are not loose.
- Ensure easy access to put off the power supply.
- While using any portable electrical equipment ensure that it is properly earthed, there is no leakage of current through the body of the equipment.
- Report all electrical hazards to the competent person.
- In case of short-circuit or fire put off main switches immediately.

- Place rubber mats in front of the distribution boards.
- Use protection such as rubber gloves, shoes and insulated tools while working with electricity.
- Remove the fuse cutouts and keep them in self-custody while undertaking repairs.

Don'ts

- Don't tamper settings of Earth Leakage Circuit Breakers/Relays.
- Don't have any unsafe temporary connections, naked joints/wirings.
- Don't work wet, on electrical equipment.
- Don't just operate any switch unless you know the consequences.
- Don't overload an electrical point.
- Don't use water for extinguishing electrical fire.
- Don't take short cuts in tapping electric current.
- Don't store any material near the electrical Mains/ switch boards.
- Don't work on live circuits, even when the job is very small.

Electricity can not be seen, can not be tasted, use electricity carefully to avoid accidents.

ELECTRICAL SHOCK

It is sudden and accidental stimulation of the body's nervous system by an electric current. Current will flow through the body when it becomes part of an electrical circuit, which has a potential difference adequate to overcome the body's resistance to current flow.

Note: Although potential difference determines whether the resistance can be overcome, the damaging factor in electric shock is current flow.

Effect of Electric Current (50-60 Hz AC) on Personnel

Magnitude of Current	Effect on Personnel
• 1.0 mA (0.001 amp)	Shock perceptible, involuntary reflex action causing inadvertent motion, loss of balance causing fall or violent jerk.
• 5-25 mA (0.005-0.025 A)	Loss of control of muscles, freezing to the conductor.
• 25-75 mA (0.025-0.075 A)	Shock painful and injurious, prolonged contact may produce collapse, unconsciousness and death. (Death occurs if respiratory paralysis lasts more than 3 days.)

• 75-300 mA (0.075-0.3 A)	Fatal if it lasts a quarter of a second or more ventricular fibrillation (muscle fiber of heart twitch or fibrillation in self perpetrating waves instead of contracting in a coordinated beat)
• 2.5A mp and above	Clamping of heart as long as current flows. Fall of BP, unconsciousness, and burn to both skin and internal organs.

Human Resistance to Electrical Current

Body Area	Resistance in Ohms
Dry, clean and unburn skin	100,000-600,000
Wet or broken skin	Less than 500
Internal body resistance	300
Ear to ear	100
Head to foot	400-600

Note: Current through the heart, respiratory muscle or brain are most critical.

ELECTRICAL PROTECTION DEVICES

Electrical protection devices offer protection only if they are selected and installed properly. Temporary measures such as replacing the fuse wire with copper of any size may result in accidents, leading to fires. Here are a few tips for proper selection and utilization of electrical protection devices :

- Use only standard fuse wires with appropriate fuse rating for replacement. Non-standard wires may not clear faults in time and lead to fires.
- Investigate, identify and rectify the reason/defect for supply failure before re-energizing the circuit.
- Use ISI marked MCBs (miniature circuit breakers) or HRC (High Rupturing Capacity) fuses instead of re-wearable fuses.

Operation of protection devices for earth faults depends on earth resistance. Maintain low earth resistance values as per standards.

Electricity is Useful But it Can be Dangerous too

- Check all wires regularly to ensure that they are in perfect condition. If unsure about an electrical wire, assume it is energized. Do not touch it and report to a supervisor.
- Never insert a bare wire into a socket, always use a plug.

- Use three-pin plugs to protect yourself from shock. Keep electrical equipment properly grounded.
- Never remove a ground pin to fit a plug into a two-pin ungrounded outlet.
- While inserting or removing a plug from a socket, take care that your fingers do not touch the pin of the plug.
- Do not pull out the plug by the cord. Remove it with a firm grip on the plug.
- Wear approved rubber gloves when working near live-wires/terminals.
- Do not try to repair electrical equipment if you are not an electrician.
- Only qualified electricians should work on electrical equipment.
- Never use electrical equipment if your hands are wet or if you are standing on a wet surface. Water and electricity can be a fatal combination.
- Immediately switch off electrical equipment that sparks and report the condition to the supervisor.

Be alert use electricity safely.

Electricity at Home

Electricity is a wonderful servant in the house and the numbers of electrical accidents are very small considering its widespread use. Unfortunately however, an electric shock can very easily be fatal. There is a lot you can do to help prevent electrical accidents.

Modern electrical installations and appliances are controlled by regulations and the safety standards applied by electricity authorities. But old or badly maintained flexible cords and appliances can be dangerous, as can any "do-it-yourself" wiring or repairs.

Electrical repairs are for the electrician, not for the home handyperson. Each year wrongly wired extension cords; house wiring and appliances kill several "do-it-yourself" and their family members.

You need to inspect plugs, cords and appliances to see if they are in good condition and make arrangement for all necessary repairs immediately. If you feel a tingle or electric shock from an appliance, immediately switch off the power and remove the plug. Have it checked out by an electrician before using it again.

An earth leakage circuit breaker can be installed at a moderate cost to protect against electrocution.

Means of Protecting Personal Against Shock

Insulation: Insulating parts of electrical equipments, which a person will contact routinely or accidentally during operation of the system, is advisable. Insulated knobs, dials, buttons on controls, switches, meters are such items.

Personnel can be insulated: Mats of rubber or other non-conductive material can be provided on which to stand when electrical equipment is being operated on, repaired or maintained. Use of rubber gloves and non-conductive shoes help protect the persons from accidental contacts.

Interlocks: Interlocks are one of the most commonly used safety devices, especially with electrically operated equipment. Examples are: limit switches, proximity switches, key interlocks, timers and time delays, sequential controls, photoelectric devices, and magnetic sensing etc.

Isolation: Electrical equipment, HT type should be isolated to keep unauthorized personnel from approaching too close. Large transformers should be located in vaults or fenced enclosures. Panel boards, generators, large motors, bus bars should be enclosed to prevent accidental contacts.

Marking: Points of access to hazardous electrical equipment should be marked with suitable warnings.

Warning devices: A suitable warning device may be connected to electrical equipment to indicate when it is energized. This may be a light, steady or flashing, a suitable color indicator, an on-off sign or an audible signal.

GROUND FAULT CIRCUIT INTERRUPTER (GFCI) OR ELCB

It is a devise whose function is to interrupt the electrical circuit to the load when a fault current to ground exceeds some predetermined value that is less than that required to operate the over-current protective device of the supply circuit. It is intended for protection of personnel against shock. It is sensitive to very small currents is short enough to open the circuit before a person can be electrocuted.

If current greater than the level for which the GFCI is set passes to ground by any route other than the one designated into the system, an imbalance in current flow is created and sensed, and a circuit breaker opens. GFCI provides protection only in a ground fault situation. It does not provide protection when a person forms the path between two phases.

Use of ELCB

Home supply system, Industrial canteen, Bathroom, Individual supply system for portable tools and lighting etc.

YOUR FIRE PROTECTION CHECKLIST

Electrical Fire Hazards

- Do your electrical installations comply with regulations?
- Have they been checked?
- Do electrical faults receive prompt attention by a qualified electrician?

- Do you have any temporary extension wiring, which has been in position more than six months?
- Are you satisfied that all electrical installations in hazardous locations are the correct type for the risk?
- Are all electric heaters located in safe positions and fixed so that they can not be moved?
- Are all electrical installations rendered safe in idle periods?
- It is possible for combustible materials to be stacked close to electric lights, heaters, air conditioning units, fuse boxes or switch boards?
- Is all electrical process heating fitted with adequate controls and thermal cutouts?
- Do you have oil filled transformers or switchgear installed in unsuitable locations? If so, can any improvements be effected?

Avoid Fires – Check Wires

Faulty wiring is the cause for most of the electrical fires. Buildings where the wiring is old and the insulation has become brittle, fall pray to these fires. Many a times the fire starts from sparking and short circuits in frayed and worn-out wiring. Broken plugs, switches and frayed wires increase the chances of electrical shocks. These leads to an inflated electricity bill. Get them replaced immediately by a certified electrician.

Temporary or naked points or wiring may prove fatal. See that wires never trail over hot or wet surfaces. Never keep wires under mats, carpets or door-ways where they can get crushed and loose their insulation without your knowledge.

Don't Touch That Wire

Most office environments appear safe and sound. However, today's high-tech equipment can pose potential electrical and fire hazards.

Here are some guidelines to follow when your office machines go on the blink:

- Call for professional service if copier or fax machine paper jams are not easily fixed. Never take off covers and touch the machine; you could get an electrical shock.
- Tinkering inside your computer or monitor poses considerable risk because of high-voltage CRT tubes and other internal electronics. Again, call a qualified service representative. If there is a short circuit and you see smoke, pull the plug. And although modems run on low voltage, it's best not to open them, either.
- New laser printers have invisible lasers that can damage your eyes if exposure lasts for any length of time. Although the laser is deep inside the machine, an employee who takes apart the printer could accidentally suffer eye damage and

get an electrical shock. Likewise, electric/electronic typewriters can also give off an electrical shock.

- Office space heaters pose a serious fire hazard because they generate a lot of heat in small area. Do not drape coats over a space heater or place it near cushions or wastebaskets. Position the heater so it does not tip over or force heat down into the floor or carpet. And never leave your space heater on when the office is closed.
- If a circuit breaker trips, it's overloaded. Use a dedicated outlet for a copy machine, and keep each computer and its peripheral on one designated outlet. Check with your computer technician about power strips and surge protectors.
- Use extension cords only for a temporary fix. Instead, have an electrician install more outlet circuits or move the outlet to a more convenient location.
- When you must use an extension cord, use the proper-sized extension cord for the situation and make sure it does not get pinched, stepped on, run over placed under carpets or draped over doorways.

Misuse of Elctricity Can Shock You

Electricity makes life easier for every one. But if it is misused, it becomes dangerous. Commonwealth simple suggestions can ensure that electricity continues to help you not hurt you:

- Never overload outlets. An extension cord should never be used for more than one appliances through a single socket can cause the wire to overheat and can lead to a fire. It's safer to have a qualified electrician install additional outlets.
- Do not use frayed or punctured cords. If you touch an exposed wire, you may receive a shock. Worse yet, improperly maintained cords can cause fires. Inspect cords regularly and replace them when they are damaged.
- Never run cords under carpets. Never staple or nail cords to the floor. They should be secured with tape and kept away from walk areas.
- Do not use electrical appliances near water, if possible. And when you must-in the bathroom or kitchen, for example – dry your hands and keep them away from water, and do not touch the faucets at the same time that you touch the appliances. To guard against shock, install ground fault circuit interrupters in outlets near water sources and outside.
- Never go into a flooded basement until you are sure the power has been turned off. Submerged electrical appliances can electrify water. Call an electrician or the local fire department to disconnect the power.
- Never clean or repair appliances while they are plugged in.
- Do not go near fallen power lines or objects that touch them.

The shock you receive could be deadly. If you see a downed power line, call your local electrician.

Recommended Inter Distances for Electrical Installations

The basic objectives for observing safe distances are:

- Carry out operation and maintenance work safely.
- Allowing for easy movements/access or restrict for access.
- Reduce or minimize the damages to adjoining equipments.
- Reduce the thermal electrical load and congestion within restricted areas.

Some of the important provisions for observing the distances under the Indian Electricity (IE) Rules, 1956 are as follows:

Switch Board (IE Rule 51)

Sl. No.	Pre-requisite	Position	Distance Specified
1.	Switchboard	Clear space in front of switch board.	Not less than 1 metre.
2.	Any attachments or bare connections at the back of the switchboard.	Space if any behind the switchboard.	Either less than 20 cm or more than 75 cm in width measured from farthest outstanding point of any attachment or conductor.
3.	Space behind the switch-board exceeding 75 cm in width.	There shall be a passage way from either end of the switchboard.	Clear up to a height of 1.8 metres.

Minimum Clearance Between Lines Crossing Each Other (IE Rule 87)

(Recommended inter distances for electrical installations)

Sl. No.	Normal system voltage	Minimum clearance in metres between lines crossing each other				
		11-6 kV	110-132 kV	220 kV	400 kV	800 kV
1.	Low and medium	2.44	3.05	4.58	5.49	7.94
2.	11-66 kV	2.45	3.05	4.58	5.49	7.94
3.	110-132 kV	2.46	3.05	4.58	5.49	7.94
4.	220 kV	2.47	4.58	4.58	5.49	7.94
5.	400 kV	2.48	5.49	5.49	5.49	7.94
6.	800 kV	2.49	7.94	7.94	7.94	7.94

Cable Trenches

Sl. No.	Item	Distance (Recommended)
1.	Cable inside trench.	At least 75 mm above the trench bottom.
2.	Intervals between incombustible barriers for trenches above 1000 cm cross sectioned area.	Not less than 45 metres. Barriers to be at least 50 mm in thickness and at the same height of cable trench.

Clearances above Ground of The Lowest Conductor (IE Rule 77)

(Recommended inter distances for electrical installations)

Sl. No.	Pre-requisite	Position	Height not less than
1.	Conductor of overhead line including service lines across a street.	(a) Low and medium voltage lines (b) High voltage lines	5.8 metres 6.1 metres
2.	Conductor as above along any street as part there of.	(a) Low and medium voltage lines (b) High voltage lines	5.5 metres 5.8 metres
3.	Conductor as above erected elsewhere than along or across any street.	(a) Low, medium, high voltage lines up to and including 11000 volts. • If bare • If insulated (b) High voltage lines above 11 kV (c) Extra high voltage lines	4.6 metres 4.0 metres 5.2 metres not less than 5.2 metres plus 0.3 metre for every additional 33 kV or part thereof provided minimum clearance along and across street not less than 6.1 metres.

Clearances from Buildings (IE Rules 79 and 80)

(Recommended inter distances for electrical installations)

Sl. No.	Voltage lines	Passes above or adjacent	Minimum clearance in meters vertical	Horizontal
1.	Low and medium	• Flat roof, open balcony, varandas, roof and lean to roof • Pitched roof	2.5 metres from the highest point 2.5 metres immedia-tely under the lines	1.2 metres from the nearest point 1.2 metres line passes adjacent to building
2.	High and extra high • Up to 11 KV • Up to 33 kV • Extra-high	Any building or Part of building	3.7 m 3.7 m plus 0.3 m for every additional 33 kV or part thereof	1.2 m 2.0 m 2.0 m plus 0.3 m for every additional 33 kV or part thereof

Outdoor Transformers (Oil Filled)

(Recommended inter distances for electrical installations)

The oil capacity of the individual transformers is larger than 5000 litres, separating walls must be provided in all such cases unless all other equipment/building/plant are located at a clear distance of not less than the following from the transformer.

Sl. No.	Oil capacity of Individual transformer	Clear separating distances (recommended)
1.	5000 to 1000 litres	8 metres
2.	Above 10000 litres and upto 20000 litres	10 metres
3.	Above 20000 litres and upto 300000 litres	12.5 metres
4.	Over 30000 litres	12.5 metres

Ref.: The Indian Electricity Rules, 1956 and the Rules for Electrical Installations, 1998 published by the Tariff Advisory Committee.

IEC SAFETY HANDBOOK

(International Electrical Commission, Safety Handbook, Geneva)

The growing complexity and widespread use of a large variety of electrical equipment has resulted in greater awareness about the need for uniform safety standards in design, development, production, testing and maintenance of such equipment. Their existence and application is an important tool for the protection of user interests.

The standard included in this handbook – all 23 of them are published by IEC – concern the safety of people, surroundings livestock and domestic animals. They cover, for example, personal protection against electric shock; effects of excessive temperature, radiation, explosion, implosion, medical instability and moving parts; and protection against fire. Both safeties in the home and workplace are covered. The Handbook also provides guidance of drafting safety standards using a safety pilot function denotes the treatment of a specific safety aspect concerning the majority of Electro technical products.

The information given in the handbook is covered in the following seven sections:

(1) Drafting of safety standards and role of committees with safety pilot functions and safety group functions, including principal elements of the safety objectives for electrical equipment;

(2) Protection against electric shock;

(3) Insulation coordination for low voltage;

(4) Test methods for resistance to tracking;

(5) Test methods for assessing fire hazards;

(6) Identification system; and

(7) Degrees of protection by enclosures.

The IEC Safety Handbook will be found useful by technical departments in industry, testing laboratories and those responsible for public safety as well as others involved in the preparation of safety standards at the national and international level.

SAFETY IN ELECTRICAL INSTALLATIONS AND USAGE

(Hazard identification and preventive measures at project site)

Hazard	Consequences	Preventive Measures
Short circuiting	• Electrocution • Fire	• Ensure usage of only fully insulated wires or cables • Ensure earthing of equipment • Provide all connection through ELCB • Protect electrical cables or wires and equipment from water and naked flames

		• Avoid loose temporary connection • Do not use damaged cords • Do not allow open bare connection • Do not place bare wire ends in a socket • Use one socket for one appliance • Engage licensed electricians to carry out electrical installations • Do not lay wire under doorways • Use insulated hand tools and PPE • Check all connections before energizing
Overloading electrical system	• Bursting of system • Fire	• Ensure approved cable size, voltage grade and type • Display voltage and current rating prominently with "Danger" sign • Ensure proper grid wise distribution of power • Do not allow unauthorized connection • Switch off the electrical utilities when not in use
Improper laying of overhead and under-ground transmission lines/cables	• Electrocution • Fatal	• Do not lay unarmored cable directly on ground, wall, top of trees • Maintain 3 m distance from HT cables • All temporary cables should be laid at least 750 mm below ground on 100 mm fine sand overlaying by brick soling • Proper sleeves should be provided at road crossings • Provide cable route makers indicating the type and depth of cables at intervals not exceeding 30 m and at the diversion/termination.

DO'S OF AN ELECTRICIAN

- Obtain work permit before starting the work on an electrical equipment or installation.
- Ensure that all the control switches are opened and locked in off position and/or fuses withdrawn before commencing work on any electrical equipment or installation.
- When carrying out repairs of any equipment, follow scrupulously the maintenance instructions of the manufacturer as given in the manual.

- Know voltage and frequency of the circuit.
- Confirm color-coding used for the wiring in making connection is correct.
- Confirm the abbreviations and symbols used in the circuit diagram are as per the manual.
- Use appropriate personal protective equipments.
- Confirm from manual supplied by the manufacturer of equipment under fault conditions, that if provide for:
  - personal safety against electrical shock,
  - personal safety against effect of excessive temperature,
  - safety against fire, and
  - Appliances designed to contain liquid or provided with steam producing devices shall have adequate safeguards against the risk of explosion.
- Treat circuits as live until they are proved to be dead.
- Where a fuse or cut out is incorporated in any appliance its location should be clearly indicated by suitable visible marking.
- Ensure that the internal wiring and connection are adequately protected or enclosed so that they are not exposed to steam, vapor or spillage during normal operation.
- Internal wiring should be fixed in such a way that the functional insulation does not come into contact with external parts.
- Insulation shall be such that it is not damaged in normal use.
- Before energizing any equipment ensure that the permanent grounding are properly connected.

DON'TS OF AN ELECTRICIAN

- Do not touch electrical equipment with wet hand.
- Do not put off any switch unless you are familiar with the circuit, which it controls and know the reason for it being left on.
- Don't touch or tamper with any electrical switchgear or conductor, unless you have made sure it is dead and properly earthed.
- Don't test circuit with bare finger or hand.
- Don't use metal scales or tapes near electrical circuit.
- Don't use wires with poor and deteriorated insulation.
- Don't allow visitors or unauthorized persons to touch or handle electrical apparatus or come near the danger zone of high voltage apparatus.

- Don't use wood, cotton, silk, paper and similar hydroscopic material for insulation unless otherwise specified.

ELECTRICAL SAFETY MANAGEMENT

Dangers from electricity are due to:

- Electric flashovers resulting in deaths, fires and damages.
- Electric shocks resulting in burns, injury and deaths.
- Electrical faults resulting in arcing, explosions and fires.
- Explosion in electrical equipments resulting in damage to installations and deaths.
- Fire hazards resulting in destructions, loss of life and release of smoke, dust, gases which spread over large areas quickly.
- Pollution by thermal power plants.

Be Aware of Electrical Fires

Fires caused by electric loose connection, electric arcs, electric short circuits, electric flash-overs. Fires quickly spread and cause death due to burn injuries and release of poisonous gases. Fires cause loss to properly/installation.

Fires are caused by:

- Loose connection in power circuits.
- Loose connection in auxiliary circuit.
- Loose connection at terminals.
- Breaking of conductors.
- Overheating of conductor and burning of insulation.
- Welding of oil filled equipment.
- Electric fault in oil filled equipment.
- Electric arcs or faults in equipment having inflammable materials.
- Static electric charges, discharged through sparks.
- Lightning discharge.
- Flashovers.

5

CHAPTER

Energy Conservation

SOURCES OF ENERGY

Over the ages, humankind's energy problem consistently has been to develop the means to convert available sources of energy into the particular form needed to perform a specific task. The total energy available is almost limiting less. However as the more convenient sources become scarce; there can be legs in developing the know-how to convert alternative sources into usable forms.

What does it take for a form of energy to be useful as a source?

- It must be plentiful and easy to acquire;
- It must be easily converted into a form which our machines can use;
- It must be easy to transport and store.

Up to now, only a few energy sources have been developed that fit all these requirements: They are:

- Hydrocarbons or fossil fuels, which include natural gas, coal and petroleum;
- Nuclear energy;
- Hydroelectric power and
- Biomass.

Other sources are available which may not now meet all the requirements as well as those just listed. However, they could be developed to the point of meeting the requirements to a higher degree. This group includes:

- Solar energy;
- Forms of kinetic energy, including tidal wave, and wind energy;
- Thermal energy. This includes geothermal (heat from center of earth and the heat stored in the ocean waters);
- Biofuels.

Renewable sources	Forms of energy	Used for	Conversion devices
Solar	Thermal energy	Cooking Heating	Flat plate solar collector Concentrating collectors Solar hot water systems Solar pond Solar hot air systems
		Drying/ Timber seasoning	Solar drier Solar timber kiln
		Electricity/ Power generation	Solar photo voltaic systems Solar pond Concentrating collectors Power tower
		Cooling	Solar collectors Coupled to absorption Refrigeration systems
Biomass	Chemical energy	Cooking	Bioplant/ Gasifier/burner
		Mechanical Applications/ Dumping Power generation	Gasifier engine pump sets Stirling engine pump sets Producer gas/biogas based engine generator sets
Wind	Kinetic energy	Sailing ships Pumping water/ Irrigation Grinding grains Power generation	Sails Windmills Wind turbines

Water, waves and tides	Potential/ kinetic energy	Power generation	Turbine generators
Geothermal	Thermal energy	Heating/ Power generation	Heat exchanger Steam turbines
Nuclear	Automatic energy	Power generation	Nuclear reactor/ Turbine generator

ENERGY CONSERVATION

Fast depletion of precious resources of energy is quite alarming and hence their conservation is imperative. Following are some simple tips emphasizing upon use of efficient and energy saving equipment and practices, which would certainly benefit all of us.

Illumination

- Switch off tube lights, fans etc. when not required.
- Prefer task lighting instead of uniform all over.
- Follow recommended illumination levels.
- Use energy efficient lamps and luminaries.
- Keep clean all lighting equipments and reflectors.
- Optimize use of natural lighting.
- Prefer electronic ballast instead of conventional chokes.
- Prefer compact fluorescent lamps.
- Use current voltage reducer.

At Work Place

General:

- Use high efficiency and optimum size equipment.
- Optimize use of plant utilities such as steam, cooling water, compressed air etc.
- Monitor and control all plant parameters strictly. Install monitoring equipments like flow meter, pressure and temperature gauges, ammeter, etc. Wherever necessary.
- Carry out periodic maintenance. Remove the scaling sediments regularly.
- Stop all leakages. Avoid unnecessary long distribution pipelines.

Pumps and Compressors:

- Avoid throttling and if possible, trim the impellers.
- Use more small pumps/compressors instead of one large one.
- Use direct coupled and high efficiency flat belt driven system.

Cooling Towers and Refrigeration System:

- Use thermostatic controller for cooling tower fan.
- Use high efficiency drift eliminator and FRP blades.
- Use PVC fills instead of concrete or lumber.
- Optimize need of refrigeration and refrigeration temperature.
- Do not use weak or broken insulation.
- Store chilled water/ice during off peak hours and use it during peak hours.

Motive Load:

- Avoid idle/redundant running of motors.
- Use star delta changeover.
- Use soft starter for high torque.

Control of Maximum Demand:

- Improve load factor to maximum.
- Improve power factor by installing capacitor bank and automatic power factor correction system.
- Install automatic demand controller system.
- Select optimum sanctioned demand. Maximize peak demand.

In the Kitchen:

- Keep the entire cooking material ready before lighting the stove.
- Let cold materials attain room temperature before cooking.
- Soak the grains and cereals before you cook them.
- Avoid use of excessive water in cooking.
- Use utensils having broad base. Use lid on cooking utensils.
- Prefer small burner and light flame.
- Ensure stable, bright and blue flame. Reduce flame when boiling starts.
- Use pressure cooker. Cook different types of food simultaneously by using separators.
- Avoid often re-heating of food. Store food in insulated containers.

On the Road:

- Get the vehicles regularly serviced and engine tuned.

- Maintain correct tyre pressure.
- Clean air filter regularly.
- Drive in correct gears and at optimum and uniform speed.
- Keep your foot off the clutch and use it only while changing gears.
- Avoid idle running of engine.
- Make the vehicle lighter. Reduce unnecessary load.
- Plan your trips and route and avoid rush – hour traffic.
- Prefer cycle than fuel operated vehicles.

EFFICIENT ENERGY CONSERVATION

Energy Is Precious – Conserve It

When you look around you at all the machines that are running, the lights, fans, cars, etc., you simply can not imagine life without all these. But can you imagine the amount of energy that is being used to run all these? Fortunately, people all over the world are becoming aware of the problem of consuming too much energy and are making a conscious effort to conserve it and thereby put less pressure on the earth. By conserving energy we also lower the amount of pollutants we release into the air and thereby help to keep the air clean.

The interaction between the natural resources and the population has to be maintained at a balance in order to ensure the continuity of the human race. Energy is essential to life and its conservation has become an absolute necessity.

There are two types of energy, renewable and non-renewable sources of energy. The non-renewable resources of energy such as coal, natural gas, and mineral oil are gradually becoming exhausted as we are over tapping these resources. People are now looking towards alternative sources of energy such as wind, sun, the ocean, etc. for tapping energy. These are the renewable sources of energy and will not exhaust.

India's overall consumption of energy is very low, but compared to its gross domestic production its relative consumption is very high. The cost of commercial energy is also high compared to that in most other countries. The industrial sector consumes about 50% of the total commercial energy produced. There is a growing need to bring about improvement in the efficiency of energy use in the industrial sector.

Concerns over the negative environmental impacts of inefficient uses of energy are growing, both globally and regionally. Such concerns require greater national efforts and greater international cooperation to promote energy efficiency and energy conservation. Local air pollution, emissions of green house gases, and addiction of soil and water can all be reduced if energy and resource conservation concepts are more widely applied. Such concerns require greater national efforts and greater international cooperation to promote energy efficiency and energy conservation. More efficient energy use can increase productivity and economic competitiveness as well as lower green house gas emissions per unit of out put.

Loss of Water Due to Various Activities

Activity	Method being adopted	Quantity used	Method to be adopted	Quantity required	Quantity saved
Brushing	Running tap for 5 minutes	45 ltrs.	Tumbler or glass	0.5 ltr.	44.5 ltrs.
Shaving	Running tap for 2 minutes	18 ltrs.	Shaving mug	0.25 ltr.	17.75 ltrs.
Shower	Letting shower running while soaping staying under shower too long	90 ltrs.	Wet down tap off soap up, rinse off	20 ltrs.	70 ltrs.
Flushing toilet	Using old fashioned large capacity cistern	14 ltrs.	Dual system short flush liquid waste. Full flush solid waste	4.5 to 9 ltrs.	4.5 ltrs.
Washing floor	Running hose for 5 minutes	200 ltrs.	Bucket	18 ltrs.	182 ltrs.
Washing car	Running tap for 10 minutes	400 ltrs.	Two nos. of buckets	18 ltrs.	382 ltrs.

Methods to be Adopted for Water Conservation

In order to achieve the water conservation in a long-term basis for a sure future the following methods are to be adopted:

- Development of plenty numbers of watersheds to harvest and store of rainwater (primary source of fresh water) which will recharge the ground water.
- To conserve, every drop of rain water and roof top water as soil moisture and ground water.
- To prevent polluting the water through proper treatment.
- To prevent water losses due to leakage and illegal water hook-up operation from the domestic and industrial water supply.

- Loss of water due to evaporation (about 60%) during irrigation should minimize by deploying proper techniques in irrigation.
- Minimize ground water use.
- Hiking of water taxes and provision for meter reading in industrial sector to inculcate water use.
- Mass awareness.

Therefore it is proposed to create mass awareness among the people about judicious use of water, conserve for conservation of water resources to focus and solve the problems of water logging by involving the youth (age in between 15-25 years) with community, to prevent misuse and wastage of water, to inculcate in general masses a sense of importance for safe and clean drinking water to train a cadre of youth in development of huge numbers of water shades, roof-top and rain water harvesting structure to conserve fresh water for their followers is required. To overcome this fresh water problem United Nations government and many non-governmental and private sectors area are planning a wide range of events and activities for international year of fresh water which is being coordinated by the UN department of economic and social affair and UNESCO.

Energy Conservation in Domestic Sector

Did you know that to bring a megawatt of electricity to your homes, 30-40 million rupees is spent? Building a new power plant would cost millions. Isn't this reason enough for you to begin conserving energy in your house?

Distribution of Electricity End-Use in Domestic Sector in India

Fans	34%
Lighting	28%
Refrigerators	13%
Room AC	7%
Evaporative coolers	4%
Televisions	4%
Others	4%

Electricity saved is money saved; in fact, it is worth much more than the electricity generated. Every time your electricity bill reaches home, you realize there is no need for so many lights and fans around you. All you have to do is be slightly more alert and careful. And the best thing is, you can start right away. Involve the rest of your family in this effort, and see the difference.

Energy Conservation in Household

- Begin by switching off the lights and fans in the rooms that are not occupied. Make sure that every one in the family does the same.
- Use CFLs (compact fluorescent lamps) instead of ordinary incandescent lamps. These lamps may be more expensive but that last longer than the ordinary bulbs and are very energy efficient as they consume much less power.
- Use the washing machines at full loads, as the consumption of water will be the same whether you put in half a load of clothes or a full load.
- Mix hot water in the bucket for a bath rather than using a geyser shower. Showers consume more power and up to 90 ltrs. of water for a bath.
- Change the heat element in the geyser every 5-6 years; this will enable heating to be faster and also save valuable power.
- Try using the AC an hour or two less everyday. Switch on the air conditioner only when you go into the room and switch it off after a few hours as the room will remain cool for the next few hours. Keep the doors and windows shut even after it is switched off. Clean the filter at least once a fortnight. A choked filter means improper cooling and more power consumption.
- Plug on your iron only after you get all your clothes together.
- Replace traditional chokes of tube lights with electronic chokes. They save two-third energy lost in chokes.
- Use light colors on the walls of your rooms; this helps reducing lighting requirements up to 40%.
- Keep the lights and fixtures clean and dirt free. Dust and dirt reduce lighting levels by as much as 30%.
- Clean and lubricate your fans regularly and replace old regulators with electronic regulators. This helps reduce electricity consumption significantly at low speeds.
- Cool the food properly before storing in the fridge. Check on gasket lining or the seal of the fridge. Avoid opening the door frequently. Defrost the fridge regularly, this reduces the power consumption.
- Buy only those appliances that are essential and try to get the maximum benefit from them.

Energy Conservation in the Kitchen

- While cooking, use wide bottom vessels with lids.
- Allow food articles taken out of the fridge to attain room temperature before cooking them.
- Soak cereals and dals for sometime before cooking them to reduce the cooking time as well as the fuel consumption. Use just sufficient water for cooking.

- Pressure cookers used with separators lead to substantial fuel saving.
- Reduce flame by bringing the burner knob to the simmer position as soon as the water starts boiling.
- Try to eat together to avoid repeated warming of food. This not only saves the fuel but also preserves the nutritional value of food.
- Light the flame only after all preparations have been made and the vessel is ready to be put on the stove.
- Use hot water from solar water heaters for cooking if the facility is available. Try to use a solar cooker if facility and time permit.

Whenever you save energy – or use it more efficiently – you reduce the demand for gasoline, oil, coal, and natural gas. All these sources of energy are used to generate power. Less burning of these fossil fuels means lower emissions of carbon dioxide, the major contributor to global warming, and other harmful gases.

It has been estimated that good house keeping measures, use of more efficient equipment, and better control methods can save 35-40% electricity in the domestic sector.

Energy Conservation in Industrial Sector

The industrial sector uses about 50% of the total commercial energy available in India. Of the commercial source of energy, coal, lignite, and oil and natural gas are mainly used. The Indian energy sector is highly energy intensive and efficiency is well below that of other industrialized countries. Efforts are made on a regular basis to promote energy conservation in these countries as this will help reduce the cost of production.

There is considerable scope for improving energy efficiency in industries dealing with iron and steel, chemicals, cement, pulp and paper, fertilizers, textiles, etc. If such industries can promote energy conservation, it could lead to substantial reduction in their costs of production.

Energy management is very important as all well planned actions can help reduce an organization's energy bills and minimize the damage it does to the environment. The two main energy management strategies are conservation and efficiency. This requires the establishment of a system of collection, analysis, and reporting on the organization's energy consumption and costs.

In the industrial sector, the major consumers of energy are fertilizer, textile, sugar, cement, and steel. It has been estimated that the total conservation potential of this sector is around 25% of the total energy used by it.

Conservation Initiatives

Waste heat recovery systems, cogeneration, and the utilization of alternative sources of energy are also important for the conservation of energy.

Technology, up gradation, modernization, and the introduction of control instrumentation are necessary to realize the full potential of energy conservation in industry.

To motivate the industrial sector to take up energy conservation seriously, the government has from time to time introduced fiscal incentives such as cut on import duty for specific items. Effectively from 1983 certain tax benefits have been given to energy-saving devices and systems in the industrial sector such as cogeneration systems, power factor correcting devices, and specialized boiler and furnaces.

The coal industry is both a source of energy and a consumer of energy. Energy can be conserved in both these areas. Coal reserves can be conserved through proper methods of exploration, improved recovery, and introduction of new mining technologies.

Hydrocarbons continue to be the major source of energy. The conservation of this form of energy is essential as it will reduce environmental pollution.

Energy Conservation in Industrial Equipments

Boilers are used in various industrial units to convey heat for different process applications. Though boilers can be categorized into different types and have different efficiency levels, the motive of the industry should be to generate the required quantity and quality of steam at minimum cost. An optimum level of excess air level should be maintained. The method of return steam condensate to the boiler helps reduce fuel consumption; along with this method various other methods could be applied to minimize the loss of energy.

Steam plays an important part in chemical plants for process heating and turbine drives. The rising cost of fuel has made it necessary to adopt measures to reduce energy losses in the steam distribution network. The insulation should be kept in good condition, all valves and other parts of the system should be constantly checked. Condensation recovery in the steam system is very important. When steam condenses, it transfers about 75% of the heat content to the process and the remaining is with held in the condensed water. It is very important to install a good condensate recovery system to collect the condensate from the process.

Compressed air is used in almost all types of industries and accounts for a major share of the electricity used in some of the plants. It is utilized for a variety of end uses such as pneumatic tools and equipments, instrumentation, conveying, etc. and is preferred in industries because it is more convenient and safe. The compressor is the main component of this system and its selection must be done carefully. Leakage points have to be identified and sealed, and proper pressure has to be maintained.

Refrigeration is done by various methods such as the vapor compression system, absorption system, and the steam jet system. An air conditioning and a refrigeration plant are efficient when all the system components, i.e., the compressor, the condenser, the evaporator, the cooling tower, etc., are working in matching condition. Other than the servicing of the components and their maintenance, care should be taken to ensure that the outdoor air is kept at a minimum.

Most of the industrial processes in and out of plants involve transportation of fluids and the pump is the mechanical equipment that is used to facilitate this movement. It can be operated either through a diesel engine, an electrical motor, or a gas or steam turbine. All these consume energy either in the form of electric power or petroleum products like diesel, oil, or gas. The pumps have to be well maintained and under constant supervision.

Of the total electricity consumed in the industrial sector, electric motor account for approximately 70%. These motors are classified under DC (direct current) and AC (alternate current). Electricity consumption in these motors can be reduced if the cooling is improved along with the controls, if they are operated at the rated voltage, and are regularly maintained. The new energy efficient motors have better performance as they have incorporated design improvement to reduce energy loss.

Energy at High or Extra-high Voltage [IE Rule 64-2(a)]

(Recommended inter distances for electrical installations)

Safety work clearance for bare conductors or live parts of any apparatus in outdoor sub-stations excluding overhead lines of HV and EHV installations.

Highest system voltage	Safe working clearance in metres (m)
12 kV	2.6
36 kV	2.8
72.5 kV	3.1
145 kV	3.7
245 kV	4.3
20 kV	6.4
800 kV	10.4

- The above values are valid for altitude not exceeding 1000 m a correction factor of 1.25% per 100 m is to be applied for increase the clearance for altitude more than 1000 m and up to 3000 m.
- Safety working clearances are based on an insulation height of 2.4 m, which is the height of lowest point on the insulator (where it meets the earthed metal) from the ground.
- "Safety working clearances" is the minimum clearance to be maintained in air between the live part of the equipment or conductor on which it is necessary to carry out the work, on the other.

Energy Conservation in Transport Sector

Without proper means of transport, it is not possible for a person to get from one place to another. It is also not possible to move goods and other essential items.

Over the years, more and more people have moved from the traditional systems of transport to the mechanized ones, i.e., car, scooter, bus, truck etc. These methods of transport have till recently been running on fossil fuel sources of energy. these are not only burning out a non-renewable source of energy, but also causing a great deal of pollution.

Therefore, the need of the hour is conservation of energy in the transport sector. There are a number of rules to be followed for the conservation of energy, i.e., fuel, in transport sector.

- The first rule of fuel conservation would be to plan travel in such a manner that will curtail wasteful driving.
- Wherever possible and convenient, use public transport instead of using personal transport.
- If you have a option of personal car and a scooter, use the scooter when only two persons have to travel and the car if more persons have to travel or heavy luggage needs to be transported. This will go a long way in conserving fuel.
- Car-pulling to work is a very effective means of conserving fuel.
- Following traffic signals will help avoid traffic jams that lead to a great deal of wastage of fuel.
- As far as possible avoid idling the vehicle, be it a car, scooter, or any other mechanized transport.
- Regular servicing and tuning of the vehicle makes it more efficient and thereby helps in fuel conservation and emission control. This should include checking of injectors and spark plugs, correct tyre pressure, re-greasing, tapping up, or renewal of lubricants for engine and gearboxes.
- The use of quality lubricant is extremely important and should not be compromised.
- Correct driving habits are important for conservation. Try to avoid sudden speeding, breaking and stopping, clutch riding, idling, over-speeding.
- The use of public transport should be encouraged and priority should be given to improving public transport system. Improving and streamlining of mass transportation systems will lower energy consumption.

Have your vehicle checked for emission control regularly – not only because defaulters are fined, but because it leads to fuel conservation and pollution control. It is time we inculcate these habits to become a part of our daily routines. Only by practicing and preaching these conservation tips can we think of future progress. Good habits taught early will salvage the oil shortage to a great extent.

Alternative fuels such as CNG (compressed natural gas), propane, and electricity have been introduced; the others are being tested and will probably be introduced in the transport sector soon.

What the Industries Should do to Conserve Energy

Industries must try to improve the existing systems of their equipment and units and increase efficiency. This can be done through energy audits.

Attention should move from existing sources of energy to the new renewable sources. For instance, the sugar industry can start using the bagasse to generate power – a large number of sugar mills in the country are already using power generated from the residue.

House keeping methods should be improved by maintaining the systems as per the laid down norms.

New technologies with the state of the art machines, new processes, etc. which will help in saving energy have to be introduced. Good examples of this are the dry process as against the wet process in the cement industry. Another is the electric arc furnace versus the conventional method of steel production.

Lighting Options

A good supply of light does not necessarily mean the consumption of a great deal of energy. If the right lamp is selected for the right type of function, it is possible to save energy. There are four basic types of lighting; incandescent, fluorescent, high intensity discharge, and low pressure sodium.

Incandescent lamps are the least expensive to buy but are the most expensive to operate. They have the shortest lives and are inefficient compared with other lighting types.

Fluorescent lighting is used mainly indoors and is about three to four times as efficient as incandescent lighting. They last about ten times longer than the incandescent types.

Compact fluorescent lamps or **CFL** are the most significant lighting devices developed for homes in recent years. They combine the efficiency of fluorescent lighting with the convenience and popularity of the incandescent fixtures. They can replace incandescent ones that are roughly three to four times their wattage, saving up to 70% of the initial lighting energy. Although these bulbs cost ten to twenty times more than the ordinary bulbs they last ten to fifteen times as much. In fact all this makes it the most energy efficient option for the purpose of lighting.

High intensity discharge lamps or the HID provide the longest service life and the highest quality of any lighting type. They are commonly used for outdoor lighting and in large indoor areas. These lamps and fixtures can save 70-90% of lighting energy when they replace incandescent ones. The three most common types of HID lamps are the mercury vapor, metal halide, and high-pressure sodium lamps.

Low-pressure sodium lamps are the most efficient artificial lighting, having the longest service life, and maintain their light output better than any other lamp type. They work in some ways like fluorescent lights and is used where color is not so important. Its typical applications include highways and security lighting.

TECHNICAL – TIPS ON ENERGY CONSERVATION

Focus Area – Road Transport

- Tests on Indian cars have shown that we can get upto 40% extra mileage at 45-55 kmph against 80 kmph.
- Use of bi-metallic spark plug saves over 1.5 % fuel and reduces exhaust emission too.
- As the driving touches 40-45 kmph shift to top gear. Use of top gear reduces fuel consumption considerably. Wrong gear selection can increase fuel consumption by 10%.
- Clean air filters regularly because cylinder bores are known to wear out 45 times faster in engines without air filters.
- Check tyre pressure regularly. A decrease of 25% in tyre pressure can cost 5-10% more on petrol or diesel and 25% on tyre life.
- Use radial tyres for 3-7% fuel economy, longer tyre life and greater driving comfort.
- Engine oil that is thicker than the recommended oil can cause 2% increase in fuel consumption, so use recommended grade of engine oils.
- Up to 20% more fuel is consumed when the car A.C. is on. Judicious use of A.C. can result in considerable fuel saving.
- Stop leakages because leakage of even 1 drops of oil per second wastes over 2000 liters per annum.
- Keeping the engine on when the vehicle is stationary results in wastage of oil at a rate of about 2 liters per hour.

6 CHAPTER

Fire Protection

IMPORTANCE OF FIRE SAFETY

Considering the importance of fire safety let us stress upon the following:

- history of fire fighting
- fire fighting strategy
- fire fighting personnel
- fire fighting apparatus
- extinguishing fires.

HISTORY OF FIRE FIGHTING

- Ancient Rome is known to have had a fire department by 1st century consisting of 7,000 paid fire fighters.
- The inventor Clesibius of Alexandria devised the first known fire pump 200 B.C. but the idea was lost.
- Fire pump was reinvented about a.d. 1500.

- The only equipment available to fight the London fires in 1666 was two-quart hand syringes.
- The London fire stimulated the development of a two-person operated piston pump on wheels.
- In 1648, Governor Peter Stuyvesant of New Amsterdam (New York City) was the first in new world to appoint fire inspectors.
- About 1672 leather hose and couplings for joining lengths together were produced.
- Boston imported the first fire engine to reach America in 1679.
- Richard New Sham in 1725 devised ten-person pump was the most widely used.
- Thomas Lote of New York built the first fire engine made in American in 1743.
- Rubber treated hose did not came into general use until 1870.
- A steam fire engine was built in London in 1829 but it was not well accepted.
- The aerial ladder wagon appeared in 1870.
- The hose elevator about 1871.
- In 1910 the two functions were combined, propelling the truck and driving the pump.

FIRE FIGHTING STRATEGY

Fire fighting strategy involves the following basic procedures:

- Arriving at the scene of the fire as rapidly as possible.
- Assessing the nature of the fire by determining:
  - It's intensity and the extent
  - The type and abundance of fuel
  - The danger of entering the fire area
  - The most effective techniques for extinguishing the fire.
- Locating and rescuing endangered persons.
- Containing the fire by protecting adjacent areas.
- Ventilating the fire area to allow for the escape of heat and toxic gases.
- Finally extinguishing the fire.

FIRE-FIGHTING PERSONNEL

- In most cities, fire-fighters are trained members of government supported organizations, such as fire departments.
- Elsewhere, fire-fighting organizations are primarily composed of volunteers.

- Fire fighting organizations also help design and implement fire-prevention programs, which may include such measures as:
  - building codes requiring fire alarms
  - regularly located fire extinguishing equipment
  - internal fire walls to help contain a fire
  - sprinkler systems
  - the use of fire retardant construction materials
  - safe electrical wiring
- Educating the public about fire safety and fire-prevention practices is an important part of all fire-prevention programs.

FIRE FIGHTING APPARATUS

- Fire fighting vehicles have involved into highly specialized equipment.
- Ladder trucks provide access to buildings as much as 100 ft (30 m) high.
- Snorkel trucks enable fire fighters to house fires from above.
- In addition, modern fire apparatus includes rescue trucks, mobile laboratories, searchlight cars, double-ended tunnel engines, smoke rejecters, high-pressure spray trucks, foam trucks, and even coffee wagons.
- For fires of long duration there are tanks to bring extra fuel to pump.
- The modern diesel pump delivers about 2,000 gal. per min. (8,000 liters per min.) through lightweight hose 1 in. (2.5 cm) to 2.5 in (6.3 cm) in diameter, reinforced with artificial fibers.
- A fireboat, not limited to hydrant supply, can deliver as much as 10,000 gal. per min. (40,000 liters per min.).
- Airports have specially equipped crash trucks.
- Refineries have chemical applicators.

EXTINGUISHING FIRES

- The commonly seen metal cylinder with a short hose attached is the soda-and-acid extinguisher, in side it, above a solution of soda and water, is a container of acid. When the extinguisher is inverted, the acid mixes with the solution and reacts with the soda to generate carbon dioxide, gas pressure then forces the solution out of the hose.
- A foam extinguisher is a cylinder containing water, sodium bicarbonate, an agent (often licorice powder) for strengthening the foam, and an inner container of

aluminum sulphate powder. Mixed together, these ingredients form foam of carbon dioxide bubbles.

- A carbondioxide extinguisher consists of a tank of liquid carbondioxide under pressure. When released, the carbondioxide forms flakes that vaporize and blanket the fire.

For a fire to occur there must be available oxygen, a supply of fuel, and enough heat to kindle the fuel. Therefore, these three basic ways of extinguishing fire are to smother it, to cut off the fuel supply, or to cool it below the flammability temperature.

Fires are classified into four types:

1. Those in solids, e.g., wood, paper, and cloth.
2. Those in flammable liquids, e.g., gasoline, alcohol, oils, lacquers, and paints.
3. Those in electrical apparatus.
4. Those in flammable metals such as magnesium etc.

These are called, respectively; class A, B, C, and D fires.

FIRE PROTECTION TIPS FOR INDUSTRIES

On Site Emergency Planning

In an on site emergency plan the following are planned:

- Emergency control centre
- Incident controller
- Site main controller
- Other key personnel
- Emergency task force

Emergency Control Centre (ECC)

- Where internal and external communication system are provided.
- Plant layout is displayed along with fire-fighting equipments and other facilities deployed.
- Role of incident controller, site controller, other key personnel are displayed.
- Names and details of task forces are displayed.
- Emergency and important telephone numbers of key personnel.
- Inventories of fire fighting materials and equipments.
- Inventories of safety equipments and PPE.
- Works entrance and road system layout.
- Assembly point.

- Relation of works to immediate surroundings and plans which can be used as emergency develops to show:
  - Area affected by hazard
  - Area evacuated
  - Deployment of emergency teams and equipment.
- Mutual aid schemes
- Medical services
- Fire services
- Local administration
- Voluntary organizations.

FIRE PREVENTION MANAGEMENT

- Fire prevention management emphasize on fire safety first before any other activity.
- Management's primary task is to run a business profitably. A fire can ruin it. Therefore, management must take care to prevent the fire.
- Fire prevention must start from planning, designing and project stage.

FIRE SAFETY IN INDUSTRIES

Common Causes of Industrial Fire

- Leakages and spillages of flammable/combustible materials.
- Electrical short circuiting/overloading.
- Overheated bare surfaces/heaters/electric lamps.
- Welding, cutting, soldering and other hot work.
- Equipment failure.
- Smoking in prohibited areas.
- Chemical reaction/runway reaction.
- Friction heat/spark.
- Spontaneous/combustion sparks/lighting.
- Naked lights.
- Molten substance.

Basic Prevention Measures

- Ensure high housekeeping standards.

- Cover trash containers tightly and empty them regularly.
- Segregate flammable materials from sources of ignition.
- Promptly eliminate oil/gas leaks and clean spillage of flammable materials.
- Strictly adhere to work permit instructions for welding, cutting and other hot work in areas where flammable substances are present.
- Store incompatible chemicals separately.
- Where flammables are used, ensure adequate ventilation, prohibit smoking, and use flameproof electrical equipment. Keep fuses and control boxes clean and closed.
- Avoid multi-socket connection.
- Qualified personnel should carry out electrical repairs.
- Do not use damaged cords and avoid temporary connections.
- Lubricate, maintain and align all machines/equipments to prevent generation of heat.

Tactical Fire Control Measures

- To set a policy and establish a plan.
- Qualified, trained and experienced fire co-ordination.
- Early warning system.
- Effective and efficient first aid fire fighting arrangements.
- Automatic fire control installation, i.e., smoke detector, heat detector, flame detector, sprinkler system, fire hydrant and hose reel system.
- Fire drill on regular basis with records.
- Continuous fire fighting training for all personnel at all levels.

What to do in The Event of Fire

- Raise alarm/bell. Alert all staff and call the fire service.
- Give location, type of fire and action being taken.
- Attempt to extinguish fire with fire equipment provided.
- Evacuate staff/visitors from danger area towards safe assembly point.
- Search as you evacuate – account for all staff and visitors.

FIRE CONTROL MEASURES

Procedural Protection

- Fire emergency procedure
- Disaster preparedness plan

- Mutual aid scheme
- No smoking policy
- Investigation of all accidents
- Hazard identification through safety committee, house keeping committee, safety audit committee
- Conducting plant survey, safety survey
- Work permit system
- Statutory requirement
- Safety promotional activities
- Information notes on unsafe conditions
- MSDS
- Annual medical check up of employees
- Safe start up and shut down procedure
- Regular and preventive maintenance
- Periodic testing of fire fighting appliances.

Physical Protection

- Strict and rigorous approach in following the relevant standards, codes and practices
- Built in safety devices and safety system
- Venting through tall stacks
- Field monitors for different toxic gases
- Burning waste gases in a flare system
- Provision of wind cones
- Fire proofing of steel structures
- PPE
- Passive protection system
- Active protection system
- Automatic protection system
- Improved waste water management.

Educational Protection

- Periodic training program on safety, fire safety and hazardous properties of materials.
- Mock fire drill
- Safety manuals

- Health and safety news bulletins
- Safety motivation schemes
- Plant operating manual
- Educating the public living nearby about the activities in the industry.

Fire: I Know

- Fire accident is in fact a ghastly scene.
- The sufferings of the fire stricken people really know no bounds.
- A person who witnesses the fire scene once can never forget the same in his life.
- It is a lesson for all individuals to handle fire with utmost care.

What Should I Do

- Immediately extinguish the flames by rolling the individual on the ground.
- The rule is "drop and roll".
- A blanket is an efficient extinguisher, but do not waste time if not available.
- Try not to use hands.

What Should You Do

- Cool quickly! Cool the affected area with cool water.
- Remove burned, non sticking clothing.
- Keeps the burned person lying on his/her back and sure he/she can breathe?
- Remove rings and other jewelry before swelling begins.
- Call the doctor or emergency number for anything but a slight burn.
- Burns are deceiving; they often look less serious than they really are.

What You Should Know

- All fabrics burn, but some are more flammable than others.
- The natural fibers like cotton, linen and silk wool burn quickly.
- However cotton blue jeans can be safe since they are tightly woven and cling to the body.
- Synthetic fibers burn less easily, but when they burn sticks on the body causing deep burns.

How Can You Tell

- There are three degrees of burns.
- In the first-degree burns, the skin is reddened.
- In the second-degree burns, the skin is blistered.
- In the third-degree burns, the full thickness of the skin and the tissue is destroyed. The area looks white, brown, bright red or charred.
- First-degree burns usually heal without scarring in six days or less.

- Second-degree burns heal in two weeks or so with scarring.
- Third degree burns of more than two inches in diameter will heal only after months of treatment.

Please Remember

- Whatever burns never returns.
- Fire prevention is everybody's concern.
- Kill the fire before it kills you.

Concluding Note

- Miseries in a life are many. They are to be dealt properly.
- Panics in life are lessons for us.

Action to be Taken in Case of Fire in High Rise Building

- Locate the fire and inform the control room.
- Shout 'fire, fire, fire'.
- Break the glass of manual call point.
- Do not open the doors, windows or other passages, which will let in more air to add to the building fire.
- Look for any one who has fainted or become unconscious and remove him/her from the room to a place of safety where medical aid can be rendered.
- Avoid panic and maintain calm and control the situation.
- In case of fire in electrical appliances, switch off the sources of current.
- Do not use lifts as means of escape when fire is on.
- Use only the staircases for evacuation or reaching to the place of safety.
- Do not attempt to get out through window or other openings, especially at higher floor.
- Beware of fallen or hanging electric wires, which may be live.
- Wrap a wet cloth on your nose while working inside a smoke filled atmosphere.
- Accumulation of large quantities of smoke and heat cause serious asphyxiation and other adverse affect. The occupants, other than those who are engaged in fire fighting, should evacuate the affected area and move to proper assembly point in the same or other floors.
- Render first aid to the injured person, if any.
- Avoid confusion and shouting instructions should be issued through public address system to be heard clearly and followed.
- In case of smoke filled atmosphere always walk along the side of walls and preferably not walk erect (to avoid inhalation of carbon monoxide or toxic gases at upper levels). Escape by crawling on hands and knees.
- In removing/handling records, the procedure laid down for allotting priorities should be followed.

- At night, rouse all occupants of the building and get them out of the building.
- Do not jump from the window of an upper floor, if blankets or bed sheets are available use these to slide down.
- Remember that if you hang at arm length from the window, this will reduce the height of your fall.

BURNS AND SCALDS REALLY HURT

Children are most involved in burns or scalds. Because of their inherent curiosity they often place themselves in situations where they may be severely injured.

Who has not heard of the child that swallowed pills, lit fires, pulled hot cups of drinks from the table or other similar escapades?

It is normal for children to be inquisitive. Special care should be taken to ensure they grow and develop in a safe environment. The observance of certain common sense rules will protect not only the children but also all members of the family.

Keep the handle of pans, pots and kettles away from the edge of stoves where toddlers' grasping hands may reach. Use place mats, not table clothes when serving meals. Young hands may pull the clothes and tip hot food or drinks over the child.

Always have short cords on electric jugs and fry pans. Dangling cords on electric appliance cause many accidents. Never use frayed cords. Use pot mitts or hand protection when touching hot kitchenware.

If fat catches fire in a frying pan, turn off the heat and cover the pan with a lid to exclude the air. Never carry it through the house or try to put it out with water. This will increase the flames.

Always put cold water in the bath first. Never leave a baby or young child unattended in the bath.

Never leave young children alone in a laundry or near a bucket of hot water.

Make sure that the bathroom can be opened from the outside and an alarm bell for an elderly person to call for help is another good idea.

Checklist for Escape in Case of Fire

- Are the exits marked clearly?
- Are the exits suitably illuminated?
- Is the approach to exits (including aisles) clear, free from extra chairs, exhibits, debris, etc.?
- Are the exits kept unlocked during the show?
- Where the doors are double leafed, are both the leaves kept unlatched?

- Is the space outside the exits kept free from chairs or other furniture items, crates of bottles, or other items?
- Are the exit corridors/passages free from encroachments by shops, goods, etc.?
- Are all exits in usable condition, without doors getting jammed?
- Are stairways in good condition, with handrails, non-slippery surface, and free from projections that may cause people to tumble?
- Are there emergency lights in pathways?
- Are there luminous tapes or markings in the escape routes and are they in good condition?
- Are there signs/symbols to indicate direction of exit to outside?
- Is the space outside the exit from the building free from obstruction such as parked vehicles, building materials, debris?
- Is the main entrance to the hall/compound operable?
- Are there caution notices not to use lift in case of fire emergency?

You should be able to answer "yes" to all the questions ; If there are any "No", take action NOW TO set matters right.

CHECKLIST – FIRE PREVENTION

Electrical Equipment

- No makeshift wiring.
- Extension cords serviceable.
- Motors and tools free of dirt and grease.
- Light clear of combustible materials.
- Safest cleaning solvents used.
- Fuse and control boxes clean and closed.
- Circuits properly fused.
- Equipment approved for use in hazardous areas (if required).
- Ground connections clean and tight.

Friction

- Machinery properly lubricated.
- Machinery properly adjusted and/or aligned.

Special Fire-Hazard Materials

- Storage of special flammables isolated.
- Non-metal stock free of tramps metal.

Welding and Cutting

- Area surveyed for fire safety.
- Combustible removed or covered.
- Permit issued.

Open Flames

- Kept away from spray rooms and baths.
- Portable torches clear of flammable surfaces.
- No gas leaks.

Portable Heaters

- Set up with ample horizontal and overhead clearances.
- Secured against tripping or upset.
- Combustibles removed or covered.
- Safely mounted on noncombustible surface.
- Not used as rubbish burners.

Hot Surfaces

- Hot pipes clear of combustible materials.
- Ample clearance around boilers and furnaces.
- Soldering iron kept off combustible surfaces.
- Ashes in metal containers.

Smoking and Matches

- "No smoking" areas clearly marked.
- Butt containers available and serviceable.
- No discarded smoking materials in prohibited areas.

Spontaneous Ignition

- Flammable waste material in closed, metal containers.
- Flammable waste material containers emptied frequently.
- Piled material cool, dry, and well ventilated.
- Trash receptacles emptied daily.

Static Electricity

- Flammable liquid dispensing vessels grounded or bonded.
- Moving machinery grounded.
- Proper humidity maintained.

Housekeeping

- No accumulations of rubbish.
- Safe storage of flammables.
- Passageways clear of obstacles.
- Premises free of unnecessary combustible materials.
- No leaks or dripping of flammables and floor free of spills.
- Fire doors unblocked and opening freely with fusible links intact.

Extinguishing Equipment

- Proper type.
- In proper location.
- Unobstructed.
- Clearly marked.
- In working order.
- Service date current.
- Personnel trained in use of equipment.

Do's and Don't's in Case of Fire

Do's	Don't's
• Raise alarm or shout **'fire'** at the peak of your voice if you notice a fire within your vicinity.	• Do not panic.
• Approach the scene within the quickest possible time. Try to attract others attention on your way to the scene of fire.	• Do not take undue risk.
• If you are first to reach, make sure that no life is entrapped.	• Do not argue or discuss at the scene of fire.
• Try to put off the fire with the nearest appropriate type of fire extinguisher.	• Do not flood the affected area with water unless required.

• Do arrange to switch off the supply in case of electric fire.	• Do not crowd the scene of fire.
• Use appropriate extinguisher.	• Do not use water on oil/gas/metal/electrical fires.
• Dial fire station and give exact location.	• Do not resort breaking/cutting unless required.
• Throw cigarette/bidi before approaching.	• Do not carry lighted cigarette etc. where flammable materials are used/stored.
• Materials should be stored below 3 feet from electrical point.	• Do not stock the materials up to ceiling height.
• Close the main valve and open the door and window for dispersal of the gas.	• Do not check LPG/acetylene gas leakage with lighted match or other flames.

FIRE PREVENTION AND PREPAREDNESS

- Are your premises kept clear of all kinds of refuse or process waste?
- Is waste swept up daily and removed from the building before closing?
- Are metal bins with lids provided for combustible waste?
- Are the waste collection areas safely located clear of buildings and stock?
- Do you control smoking in fire danger areas?
- Are the areas where smoking is prohibited clearly defined?
- Are there adequate receptacles for discarded smoking materials in areas where smoking is not prohibited?
- Do you allow open flame fires or braziers in areas where combustible materials are used or stored?

Do you know where on your premises employees consort for breaks luncheon or rest periods and are you satisfied with the fire precautions

FIRE PROTECTION – MODERN WAREHOUSING

Twenty years ago the fire hazards of warehousing were much less than they are today.

Today's fire problems include those presented by automation, relying heavily on computers instead of people; stacking devices permitting goods to be stored to great heights; and economic pressures producing the need to get the maximum amount of storage into the smallest space. Accesses for fire fighting had become much more difficult and too few warehouses were sprinklers with the commutative results that fire losses have increased substantially.

TYPES OF STORAGE SYSTEMS

Those using pallets range from 50 pallets in a system to as much as 100,000 pallets and they might be stored in a variety of ways:

- Self-supporting blocks.
- Racks if goods were crushable.
- Live storage employing skate wheel conveyors up to 20 m deep.
- Powered mobile storage racks (on rails) which allowed use of 95% of warehouse space compared with the 60 to 80% usages achieved by other systems.
- Post pallet systems (where the steel bases formed fire baffles, others were of cage type).

IN CASE OF FIRE OR OTHER EMERGENCY WHAT TO DO?

- **Keep your head** – avoid panic and confusion.
- **Know the location of exits** – be sure you know the safest way out of the building no matter where you are.
- **Know the location of nearby fire extinguishers** – learn the proper way to use all types of extinguishers.
- **Know how to report a fire or other emergency** – send in the alarm without delay; notify the Chief of Exit Drills.
- **Follow exit instructions** – stay at your work place until signaled or instructed to leave; complete all emergency duties assigned to you and be ready to march out rapidly according to plan.
- **Walk to your assigned exit** – maintain order and quiet; take each drill seriously – it may be the real thing.
- **Remember** – It is part of your job to prevent fires.

LIGHT A FAG, NOT A FIRE

This sermon is for smokers. Since fire is not at all discriminating, we suggest that non-smokers too should lend us their ears.

In the West arson or malicious ignition, careless use of electrical equipment and smoking are the leading causes of fire. By smoking, we mean the use of cigarettes, cigar or pipes and of course, match. Smoking causes a large number of fires, both in households as well as in factories and commercial establishments.

In our country too, smoking must be a leading cause though its position is not certain statistically. Probably smoking at home in our country is not as popular as it is in the West. This assumption, indirectly, is supported by the fact that the respondents in a small consumer research conducted for us did not consider smoking a major cause of fire in households in our country. On the other hand, we suspect that many fires start in our factories owing to irritable throwing away of cigarette butts and lighted matches anywhere and everywhere one feels like.

Cigarettes can start a fire more easily than cigars or pipes as the paper in which tobacco is wrapped in a cigarette prolongs its burning period. The temperatures of a burning cigarette can over 900 degree C, a temperature that can set fire to most combustible materials. When you have a puff or draw air through the cigarette, the glowing tip of it can rise to a temperature of 1200-degree C.

A burning cigarette carelessly thrown down among materials such as pieces of card-board or layers of dust is an unusual sight in mills and factories, and can start a process of smoldering for hours which can eventually start a fire.

Burning tobacco can ignite most flammable gases and vapors and dust of explosible.

Most large fires caused by smoking materials in industry are discovered at night and in areas where goods are stored, packed, loaded and dispatched. It can, of course, also happen during the day when a cigarette end is thrown away in secluded areas or places we do not visit frequently, such as a storeroom.

One could prohibit smoking in areas where it can be dangerous. For example, in areas where you keep flammable liquids and gases or where there are combustible dusts and fibers. But just a sign declaring **'Smoking Prohibited'** can be as effective as those statutory warnings that accompany cigarette advertisements.

If you are serious about your job, you should try to explain the reasons for such a prohibition to all your fellow employees and enforce the prohibition firmly. On the other hand, have some consideration for the smokers. Please try, as far as possible, to provide special areas or smoking rooms where people can smoke freely and safely.

PORTABLE FIRE EXTINGUISHERS

- Is the fire extinguishing appliances at your premises all approved types?
- Can the location of your fire appliances be clearly seen throughout the premises?
- Would a person have to travel more than 23 meters to secure a fire extinguisher or hose reel?
- Are your fire extinguishers located on escape routes from the building?
- Are your fire extinguishers the correct type for the risk?
- Would it be possible to improve standardization of fire extinguisher types within a department or building by carrying out an overall redistribution of existing extinguishers?
- Are all fire extinguishers including hose reels serviced at least annually by competent servicemen?

PROPERTIES OF FIRE FIGHTING FOAM

Expansion: The amount of finished foam produced from a foam solution when it is passed through foam making equipment.

Stability: The ability of the finished foam to retain its liquid content and to maintain the number, size and shape of its bubbles. In other words its ability to remain intact.

Fluidity: The ability of the finished foam to be projected on to, and to flow across, the liquid to be extinguished and/or protected.

Contamination Resistance: The ability of the finished foam to resist contamination by the liquid to which it is applied.

Sealing and Resetting: The ability of the foam blanket to reseal should breaks occur and its ability to seal against hot and irregular shaped objects.

Knock Down and Extinction: The ability of the finished foam to control and extinguish fires.

Bum-Back Resistance: The ability of the finished foam, once formed on the fuel, to stay intact when, subjected to heat and/or flame.

TYPES OF FOAM CONCENTRATES

Protein Based Foam Concentrates

- Protein (P)
- Pluoro Protein (PP)
- Film forming, pluoro protein (PPPP)
- Alcohol resistant PPPP (PPPP_AR)

Synthetic Based Foam Concentrates

- Synthetic detergent (SYNDET)
- Aqueous film-forming foam (APPP)
- Alcohol resistant APPP (APPP_AR)

The performance of fire fighting foams is greatly influenced by:

- The types of foam making equipment used and the way it is operated and maintained.
- The type of foam concentrate used.
- The type of fire and the fuel involved.
- The tactics of foam application.
- The rate at which the foam is applied.
- The equality of the water used.

- The length of pre-burn.
- The most effective and efficient use of fire fighting foam can only be achieved after full consideration of the above factors.

MAN BURNT WHILE DEMOLISHING OLD PIPELINES

Description

Some old pipelines were being demolished. They were cleaned as far as possible and then rested with a combustible gas detector. No flammable gas or vapor was detected and so a burner was given permission to cut them up. While he was doing so, sitting on the pipe 12 ft. above the ground, a tarry substance seeped out from one of the pipes and caught fire. The fire spread to the burner's clothing and he ended up in a hospital with burns to his leg and face.

The tarry deposit in the pipe caught fire when it was heated by the burner's torch. The deposit was not flammable when it was cold, so the combustible gas detector could not detect it.

Preventive Measures

Everyone who has to burn or weld, or give permission to burn or weld, on pipelines or other equipment which may contain heavy oils or deposits should be aware that oil which are safe when cold will burn or explode when hot. It is almost impossible to make pipes which have contained heavy oils or polymers perfectly clean and therefore fires may occur when the pipes are heated. When demolishing pipelines there should be as many open ends as possible so that pressure can not build up. Good access must be provided so that the burner or welder can withdraw from the burning point without difficulty if a fire occurs.

Protecting Workers Against Factory Fires

- Fires in workplace are among the most feared industrial events and left their mark in history.
- Industrial fires have underlined the need for vigilance, planning and preparation for dealing with the unexpected especially in the form of a viable evacuation plan.
- Where large numbers of workers are working, without a proper evacuation plan it is very difficult to save all.

  Example: Because of evacuation plan during devastation of World Trade Center in New York, 25,000 lives were saved though 4,000 lives were lost.

Features of a Viable Evacuation Plan

- There needs to be emergency planning, addressing action to be taken in case of fire.
- There needs to be, bare minimum, two well-lighted, clearly marked, unobstructed ways from the work station to a safe area.
- There needs to be co-ordination among the employees, the in-house emergency service and local emergency service. Adequate back-up generation of power to assure lighting to support the evacuation.
- There needs to be a mechanism to account for workers, visitors, and guests in a safe area and procedure for assessing disabled.
- The ILO fire prevention checklist is a guide towards large factory fires like major fire at Kader Industrial Co. Ltd. in 1933 at Thailand.

Roles of Government and Social Partners

- Government should provide adequate labor inspectors. They must work as per ILO's guideline "Ten steps for strengthening Labor inspectors."
- Workers and employees play equally important role. The ILO guidelines on occupational safety and health are a guide towards that.

Sprinklers and Other Installations

- Is your sprinkler installation checked regularly?
- Are regular checks carried out to ensure that all valves are in the correct positions?
- Do you know the action to be taken when your sprinkler installation is shut off for any reason?
- Does a competent person inspect your installation?
- Does your sprinkler installation qualify for a maximum insurance discount? If not, do you know the reason why it is not an approved system?
- Do you have any other automatically operated fire extinguishing installations? If so, are they checked by competent engineers' quarterly?
- Do you have automatic fire detectors installed? If so, is it an approved installation qualifying for insurance discount?
- Do you have any hazardous process or plant, which could usually be protected by an automatic fire extinguishing installation?
- Does your hose reel installation conform to the approved specification?
- Do you know how much water is available in your hydrant installation and whether or not a fire brigade booster connection is available?

- Have there been any alterations or additions, which would adversely affect the operation of the sprinkler installation?

Sprinklers Douse Fires

Consider the impact of a major fire; the incalculable loss of human lives, devastating property damage, work interruption, loss of business and staggering reconstruction costs. it's important, therefore, to install fire sprinkler systems for these reasons:

It Saves Lives

There have never been multiple fire-related deaths in buildings fully equipped with fire sprinkler systems. In most cases, the fire is out before fire fighters arrive, which eliminates the threat to their safety as well.

It Completes an Overall Fire Protection Plan

Combined with smoke detectors, sprinkler systems increase the chance of survival between 74% and 90%.

It Saves Property

Sprinkler systems contain fires to their point of origin, which retards any fire growth that may cause extensive fire and smoke damage.

It's a Sound Investment

Sprinkler systems raise property value and give you peace of mind, should a fire start, you know it can be contained.

Compared to several cities abroad, in India, there's no such law which insists on fire sprinkler systems in certain structures. However Johnson & Johnson India has installed the systems as one of its many safety measures.

Structural Fire Hazards

- Have you examined your premises for structural defects, which could provide tinder for fire ignition or aid the spread of fire?
- Are there any obvious defects, which come to mind, and could be remedied at little cost?
- If you have combustible ceilings or linings, have any precautions been taken to prevent or limit surface spread of flame?
- Do you have unprotected structural steelwork in area where there is a high fire load? If so, have you considered ways and means of protecting it.
- If you have air conditioning or cable ducting, have you checked the availability of fire dampers to prevent the spread of fire through compartment walls or floors?
- Is there adequate fire separation between manufacturing process areas and storage of combustible materials?

- If you have a computer, are you satisfied with the adequacy of the separation from other fire risk?
- Are all fire doors in good working order, free from obstruction, and closed in idle periods?
- Do you have any external fire exposures to building with non-fire resisting walls?
- Before any alterations or additions are carried out, do you have consultations with your municipal fire department and insurers on fire precaution measures to be incorporated?

WHY ARE THERE SO MANY DEATHS FROM HOTEL FIRES?

Once a hotel is built, a decorator is usually hired or if it is a chain hotel, the hotel itself has its own employee who will select the furniture and the fittings. If you will check you will find that there are virtually no codes by any city government or otherwise that are meaningful with regard to the fire safety of interior decorator. Worse, there is not even any meaningful research that is being done on the problem.

The hotel decorator makes selections according to budget, aesthetics and comfort, durability and ease of maintenance, individual preference.

The public to get the needed protection it is suggested that:

- There should be no carpets, whatever in hotels, even in the hall ways. The floors should be of hard wood, mosaic, tiles or some material that does not burn easily, and put out a minimum of gas if and when it does burn. It is not difficult to make masonry, mosaic or marble floor skid-proof. The technology exists. The only carpets necessary would be rugs in the bed rooms to add some luxury.
- Drapes in public rooms such as ball rooms should be made of fire resistant materials. Several companies have developed reasonable substitutes for asbestos.
- No material that produces hydrogen cyanide when burning should be allowed in any hotel bed rooms or public rooms. Remember this includes foam, rubber and nylon. There are substitute materials that are adequate.
- All electrical insulation tape used in hotels should be of fire proof type.
- Paints and coatings that contain oil, such as linseed oil, should be prohibited. There are some excellent water-based paints and coatings.
- All absorbent material that are not frequently laundered or dry-cleaned (such as curtains, drapes and uphold) should be sprayed or dipped and made fire resistant with some substance that will prevent them from burning.
- A minimum of material that produces carbon monoxide when burning should be used in hotel furniture and fittings.
- In public rooms such as dining rooms, ball rooms, etc., no doors should be installed that open inward. People panic and rush against such a door in a fire. Then no

body can escape because there are so many people pushing against the door that it can not be opened. Sliding doors or doors that open outward must be used.

- Every hotel should have a set of directions like air plans on "what to be done in case of fire" posted in each room.
- Last but not the least, the subject be brought out in the open. When one boards in an airplane, almost immediately there is a demonstration on safety, which is done on every section of the plane. Safety is brought right out into the open and covered as the first topic, and the most important one during the entire flight. This has not hurt the airline business; more people fly today than ever before.

Hotel management should discard the idea that they will hurt their business if they discuss the subject of fire. If they treat it properly, they will find that they will actually gain business, because people will feel more secure staying at hotels.

TREATING BURNS PROPERLY

Knowing how to treat a burn victim depends greatly on what kind of burns he or she has suffered. There is a significant difference in treatment for each varying degree of burn.

According to a report published in The Safety Voice, treatment of first-degree burns – marked by redness, swelling, and mild pain – involves applying cold water to the burn and then covering with a dry bandage.

Second-degree burns, which are deeper and are marked by blistering, should also be placed on cold water, but the blisters should not be broken, and no medications should be used. Immediate medical attention is the best course of action for third-degree burns. If that is not readily available, burns should be covered with clean cloths and burned limbs should be elevated. These burns look white and are frequently caused by burning clothes for electrical shock.

Ten Commandments of Fire Safety in Hospitals and Health Care Facilities

1. Ensure use of fire resisting materials for construction of the facilities.
2. Divide each floor into atleast three main components depending on floor area and subdivide them into smaller ones having fire resisting characteristics to facilitate evacuation of the occupants to safe place.
3. Provide adequate means of egress.
4. Consider protection of all horizontal and vertical openings meant for service lines in walls/ceilings to prevent spread of heat, smoke and toxic gases.
5. Mark the exits, illuminate them properly and ensure emergency power supply arrangement to the premises.
6. Limit the storage of combustible, flammable materials in work area to the minimum.

7. Install a good fire detection, alarm, and communication and protection system and maintain it properly.
8. Maintain a good house keeping standard throughout the premises.
9. Establish an onsite emergency plan for the facilities, conduct mock drill and update the plan if necessary.
10. Train and retrain the employees in fire prevention and basic fire fighting techniques.

YOUR FIRE PROTECTION CHECKLIST

Public Fire Service:

- Do you know the location of the fire station nearest to your premises?
- Do you have the fire telephone number of the public fire service prominently displayed at every telephone likely to be used for calling the fire brigade?
- Do you know how quickly and in what strength the fire brigade can be in attendance at your premises in response to a call?
- Do you have information readily available on hazardous sections of the plant, water supplies and special equipment, for use by the fire brigade in the event of a fire?
- Have the fire brigade ever visited your premises to see the risk?
- Do you discuss alterations or adaptations to your premises or hazardous plant, with the Fire Prevention Officer?
- Could the fire hydrant most likely to be used by the public fire services be obstructed by parked motor vehicles?
- Are you satisfied with the existing liaison with the public fire service?

Fire Defence Organization:

- Do you have a fire defense organization?
- Do you know the person responsible for the organization?
- Do you have any vital plant or material not adequately protected from fire?
- Are responsibilities for fire precautions clearly defined, preferably in writing?
- Is there a closedown procedure for each department?
- Are employees in hazardous areas instructed in safe practices to be observed?
- Do you have a preplanned preventive maintenance program?
- Do you use 'permit to work' for hazardous operations?
- Is anyone responsible for the control of contractors working on the premises?
- Are fire safety inspections frequently carried out?
- Do you have a fire alarm with a distinctive signal?

- Do you have instructions on the action to be taken in the event of fire prominently displayed?
- Do you have an evacuation action plan?
- Do employees receive regular fire training?
- Have security guards written instructions on the action they are to take in the event of a fire?
- Have security guards adequate facilities for calling the fire brigade?
- If you have a works fire brigade are you satisfied that it is adequately equipped and trained?
- Have you any special risks requiring preplanned fire drills?
- Has any provision being made for recovering from the effects of a fire?

Fire Hazards of Materials:

- Do you use or store any materials, which are readily ignitable?
- Do you use or store large quantities of materials, which burn fiercely giving off great heat?
- Do you use or store any materials, which would melt or flow in a fire situation?
- Do you use or store any explosive substances?
- Do you use or store any material, which give off dense smoke or fumes likely to hinder fire fighters?
- Do you store any materials, which absorb water and could endanger the building by increased weight or expansion?
- Do you use or store any chemicals, which could be dangerously reactive in fire conditions?
- Do you use or store any materials which, in fire conditions, could give off poisonous, corrosive or radioactive fumes?
- Do you use or store any oxidizing agents?
- Do you use or store any materials likely to heat spontaneously?
- In the event that you use or store any of these materials are you satisfied that the operators or store men handling them are fully aware of the potential dangers?
- Can any improvements be effected in the existing precautions to minimize fire ignition or rapid speed?

Other Fire Hazards:

- Are your premises kept clear of all kinds of refuse or process water?
- Is waste swept up daily and removed from the building before closing?
- Are metal bins with lids provided for the combustible waste?

- Are the waste collection areas safely located clear of buildings and stock?
- Do you control smoking in fire danger areas? and The areas defined?
- Do you allow open flame in areas where combustible materials are used or stored?

FIRE SAFETY CODE

In order to prevent or reduce the incidence of fire in warehouses and cold storages, the Bureau of Indian Standards has formulated an Indian Standards entitled 'IS 3594: 1967 code of practice for fire safety of Industrial buildings: General storage and warehousing including cold storages'. The standard requires the godowns and warehouses to be so located as to have minimum exposure to external fire, adequate water supply for fire fighting and easy access to public fire services. Whenever possible, the building and open storage sites should be at least 50 meters away from a railway line, siding or yard used by coal-fired locomotives. Buildings within the municipal limits of a city or town should not be used for the storage of fireworks, gun powder and other explosives, nitrocellulose, vegetable fibers and flammable liquids having flash point less than 65.5 degree C without obtaining prior approval from the appropriate authorities. Godowns used for the storage of hazardous and extra hazardous goods are required to confirm to Grade-I fire-resistance gracing of buildings specified in the relevant Indian Standard while cold storage buildings and those used for the storage of non-hazardous goods should confirm to Grade II of the same standard.

Besides laying down essential requirements for the construction of general godowns, warehouses and cold storages, the standards specifies that separating walls should be provided between: a storage godown and packing godown; a storage godown and a processing building; a separate godown and boiler house or where naked flames are used; a non-hazardous storage godown and a hazardous of extra-hazardous storage godown.

As for fire fighting arrangements in godowns and warehouses, the standards stipulates the following:

- An automatic fire alarm system, fire fighting appliances and water buckets fire extinguishers all conforming to the relevant Indian Standards should be provided;
- The godowns and warehouses should be provided with a hydrant system unless they are located within 10 KM of the municipal fire station and have a static water tank of 450,000 liter capacity within the premises, and
- All godowns exceeding 10 m^2 should have an automatic sprinkler system.

To minimize the spread of fire, the standard specifies general storage arrangements, both indoor and outdoors; norms for installation and maintenance of electrical wiring and equipment; and general safety provision and house keeping requirements. Also included in the standards are instructions to the staff regarding the following:

- How to call the nearest fire brigade; and
- What to do when fire does breakout in the premises.

Fire Fighting Foams

- Fire fighting foams have been developed primarily to deal with the hazards posed by liquid fuel fires.
- Water is used for most fire fighting incidents.
- However, it is generally ineffective against fires involving flammable liquids.
- This is because water has a density that is greater than most flammable liquids so, when applied, it quickly sinks below their surfaces, often without having any significant effect on the fire.
- However, when some burning liquids, such as heavy fuel oils and crude oils, become extremely hot, any water that is applied will begin to boil.
- The resulting rapid expansion as the water converts to steam may cause burning fuel to overflow its containment and the fire to spread – this event is known as a slop-over.
- Also, the water that sinks below the fuel will collect in the container and, should the container become full, this will result in the fuel overflowing.
- Finished fire fighting foams, on the other hand, consist of bubbles that are produced from a combination of a solution of fire-fighting foam concentrate and water that has then been mixed with air. These air filled bubbles form a blanket that floats on the surface of flammable liquids. In so doing, the foam suffocates the fire and can lead to the knockdown and extinction of the flames.
- The low density of fire-fighting foam blankets also makes them useful for suppressing the release of vapor from flammable and other liquids. Special foam concentrates are available which allow vapor suppression of many toxic chemicals.
- Water miscible liquids, such as some polar solvents, can pose additional problems for fire fighters.
- These quickly attack finished foams by extracting the water they contain.
- This rapidly leads to the complete destruction of the foam blanket. Consequently, special fire fighting foams, generally known as alcohol resistant foam concentrates, have been developed, to deal with these particular types of liquid.
- Some fire-fighting foam has also been developed specifically for use against class-A fires.

DANGER IN REFILLING FIRE EXTINGUISHERS

This was a potentially lethal accident situation, which occurred at one of the premises.

At that location, many of the staff has been trained in the use of fire extinguishers. The type of extinguisher used was a dry-powder, self-pressuring type. After each training session, a fireman refills the fire extinguisher with dry powder and they are then pressurized to 150 psi using a bottle of compressed air.

During one such refilling operation, there was a loud bang, and after the dust was cleared, the head of the extinguisher was embedded in the ceiling.

The extinguisher manufacturer was called in to investigate. It was noted that the thread of the extinguisher head was worn to such an extent that it was not able to contain the pressure within the extinguisher.

It was estimated that the extinguisher had been refilled approximately 100 times and the continual friction on the thread had caused the thread to wear significantly.

The manufacturer was agreed to replace the extinguisher and suggested the following procedure where extinguishers are refilled regularly.

- Clean the threads on both the head and the body of the extinguisher as meticulously as possible.
- Inspect the threads for signs of wear.
- Take care not to cross thread when assembling.

If, on inspection, the threads show signs of wear, the manufacturer advised us to dispose of the head and he would supply a new one free of charge.

7 CHAPTER

Good House Keeping

"The bigger place than a temple, church, mosque or gurudwara is the place a man works, what better place he needs to show his faith than his place of work."

—Jawaharlal Nehru

DO'S AND DON'T'S OF GOOD HOUSE KEEPING

Do's

- Work place shall always be kept clean.
- Pathways, stairs, aisles should be clean.
- Production materials should be stored at specified places.
- Ensure that any leaks like oil, water, coolant etc., are promptly reported to the concerned for repairs.
- Mark pathways in yellow paint periodically.
- Draw only required quantity of materials at a time.
- Ensure that damaged floors or potholes are reported to the concerned for repairs.

- Avoid congestion around the machines, equipments by keeping the materials away from them.

Don't's

- Do not block pathways keeping materials.
- Do not allow materials to spill on pathways.
- Do not drop cotton waste, refuses, oily rags etc. on floor.
- Do not allow materials to project on pathways.
- Do not keep anything on window edges or hang from wall.
- Do not keep inflammable materials in open containers.
- Do not leave slippery floor unattended.

GOOD HOUSE KEEPING TIPS

- Good house keeping prevents accidents.
- Good house keeping is much more than cleaning.
- Good house keeping is the starting point of TQM.
- Good house keeping is "a place for every thing and every thing in it's place".
- Good house keeping is not drudgery.
- Good house keeping is an investment for user friendly work place.
- Good house keeping is good fire prevention.
- Good house keeping is good anywhere.
- Good house keeping is essential for good working condition.
- Good house keeping can be achieved by participation of all.
- Good house keeping is the first step towards quality.
- Good house keeping can not be achieved without good will.
- Good house keeping is essential to good safety practices.
- Good house keeping can not be ensured by last minute cleaning.
- Good house keeping needs good planning.
- Good house keeping is useful for all actions.
- Good house keeping and orderliness in work are made for each other.
- Good house keeping sets a good example of team spirit.
- Good house keeping can be achieved by implementing 5 S Principles.
- Good house keeping ensures safe working condition.
- Good house keeping increases efficiency and productivity.

- Good house keeping takes care of workplace.
- Good house keeping ensures zero accident.
- Good house keeping builds efficiency.
- Good house keeping ensures proper maintenance.
- Good house keeping produces a sobering effect on the visiting customers.

HOUSE KEEPING PAYS

Many major accidents result from apparently insignificant causes. For example, a major fire erupts from a harmless looking cigarette stub carelessly thrown away the night before. Or a worker slips on an oil-soaked floor and ends up in a hospital. Yes, these hazards sound so commonplace that they are taken for granted. Good house keeping ensures that they are not.

To put in a nutshell: Good house keeping is taking care of your work place and doing it constantly, so that you have a safe, clean and congenial place to work in.

In many factories, a common sight is the accumulation of cartons, rubbish, packing material, gunny bags and other waste material. Let them go into metal bins and be disposed of quickly. Fires love to feed on such materials.

Keep your floors free of spills and leaks. Store chemicals in stable racks in clearly marked containers, kept in designated areas. Label them according to recommended procedures. Clean up immediately in case of spills. Chemicals can react with other substances and lead to an accident.

Good house keeping ensures that machines are cleaned, lubricated and maintained properly, and stocks, parts and tools are always available at their assigned places. This reduces time loss in locating things, every now and then.

Always leave gangways between stacks and between stacks and walls. Stacks should not obstruct the inside view of the store. Keep aisles, stairs and gangways clear at all times.

Form safe habits. Resist the temptation of smoking and tossing matchsticks and cigarette butts all around. Use ashtrays to dispose of such material. Better still; go to smoking zones when you want to have a smoke.

In spite of all precautions, fire may still strike. So be prepared. Ensure that fire-extinguishing equipments are located for easy access. More important, ensure their proper functioning.

Yes, good house keeping builds efficiency. Regardless of the nature of your work you will find that it makes your job safer, easier and better. It also pays dividends in terms of pleasure, lighter and faster work.

Good House Keeping can be Achieved by:

- Participation of all.
- With good will.
- Proper planning.
- Team work.
- Implementation of '5 S'.

5S – A SOUND FOUNDATION FOR SAFETY

The 5S principle focuses upon creating an ideal workplace where in SAFETY can take firm roots. It is, therefore, an important prerequisite and an integral part of any effort directed towards initiating, implementing, intensifying and integrating safety into normal work life.

The 5S principle pioneered by Toyota and now being practiced in many countries. It has become popular as it emphasizes on people orientation and practice orientation. It is based on the belief that every individual can contribute to improve his workplace leading to better environment and safety.

The 5S principle has, time and again proven their effectiveness wherever they have been practiced with devotion and diligence. Although 5S concepts are universally applicable in all walks of life and all spheres of activities, the focus of this concept is on making the organizational work life personally fulfilling and rewarding.

Thus as cleanliness is next to Godliness, a 5S work environment is the hall mark of a sound foundation for SAFETY.

5S

5S is a systematic approach to good house-keeping leading to cleaner, better and safer work-place.

5S

SEIRI – Sort – Sort-out un-necessary items and discard them.

SEITON – Systematize – Arrange necessary items in order.

SEISO – Sweep – Clear your workplace thoroughly.

SEIKETSU – Sanitize – Maintain high standard of house keeping at all times.

SHITSUKE – Self-discipline – Train people to be disciplined in house keeping.

SEIRI

SEIRI means sort out un-necessary items in the workplace and discard them.

5 Questions about SEIRI

1. Do you find items scattered in your workplace?
2. Are there pallets, boxes, papers etc. left in a disorganized manner?
3. Are there equipment, machine, tools etc. placed on floor?
4. Are all items sorted out and placed in designated areas?
5. Are tools and stationary properly sorted and stored?

SEITON

SEITON means arranging necessary items in good order so that they can be easily picked up for use. A place for everything, everything in its place.

5 Questions about SEITON

1. Are passage ways and storage places clearly indicated?
2. Are commonly used tools and stationary separated from those seldom used?
3. Are bricks, pallets, containers and boxes stacked up properly?
4. Are fire extinguishers and hydrants readily accessible and usable?
5. Are there grooves, bumps or cracks on the floor which hinder work and safety?

SEISO

SEISO means cleaning your workplace thoroughly so that there is no dust on floors, machines and equipment.

5 Questions about SEISO

1. Are the floor surfaces dirty?
2. Are machines and equipments dirty?
3. Are wires, pipes and furniture dirty or stained?
4. Are machines and equipments dirtied by lubricants, dust, ink etc.
5. Are shades, electrical fittings and reflectors dirty?

SEIKETSU

SEIKETSU means maintaining high standards of house keeping at work places at all times.

5 Questions about SEIKETSU

1. Is anyone's dress dirty and untidy?
2. Are there sufficient lights?
3. Are the noise, dust and heat at workplace causing discomfort?
4. Is the roof leaking or over flowed from down comers?
5. Do people eat at earmarked places only and throw food waste etc. in dust bin?

SHITSUKE

SHITSUKE means train people to follow good house keeping disciplines.

5 Questions about SHITSUKE

1. Are regular 5S checks conducted?
2. Do people clean up without reminders?
3. Do people follow rules and instructions?
4. Do people use their safety appliances?
5. Do people assemble on time?

OBJECTIVE OF 5S

A Clean Workplace

- Is high in productivity.
- Has high quality.
- Keeps cost down.
- Ensures delivery on time.
- Is safe for people to work.
- Is high in morale of people.
- Enhances company's image.

Potential Benefits

- Clean, safe and better organized workplace.
- Easy, safer and efficient job operation.
- Better use of floor space.
- Less accident rates.
- Better product/service quality.
- Better yield of materials.
- Lower breakdown rates.
- More creativity.
- Better flow of work.
- People become automatically disciplined.
- People become proud of a clean and organized work-place.
- More involvement of employees.
- Visible results.
- Generates good company image.
- Happier employee with high morale.

- Effective condition monitoring of machines prevent a major breakdown.
- Ensure accuracy and reliability of measuring instruments.
- Better life of machines and tools.
- Minimize material handling.
- Less work-in-progress and inventories.
- Foundation for TQM.

Crucial Points for Successful Implementation of 5S

- 5S should be practiced by all employees.
- Everyone should be informed about the significance of the concept through banners, posters, newsletter or pamphlets.
- Concept of the 5S program should be made clear to all employees by imparting training.
- To make this program more effective it can be tied up with quality circle activities.
- Implementation of 5S should go hand-in-hand with other quality improvement program.
- Recognize the best or improved practiced unit/department.

Good House Keeping Inspection Rating Sheet

S. No. (A)	Orderliness and cleanliness	Out of mark	Secured	Cross reference of letter dated	Deficiency observed set right	Remarks
1.	Condition of working floor, door, windows, walls, structures etc.	20				
2	Stairways, ladders, platforms, railings, working tables, racks etc.	5				
3	Machine and machines area	15				
4	Pits, drains, wash basins, drinking water points etc.	5				
5	Spillage, leakage, scrap, garbage	15				
6.	Materials stacked properly or not, badly blocked the passage	10				

S. No. (B)	Other parameters						
1.	Maintenance of first-aid box and fire points	10					
2.	Guarding of equipment, condition of fans and blowers, hand and electrical tools	10					
3.	Condition of safety boards and signs etc.	10					

Details of Good House Keeping Inspection Norms

(A) Orderliness and Cleanliness

1. Condition of Working Floors, Doors, Windows, Walls, Structures etc.

(i) Slippery, oily, dusty, etc.

(ii) Not sweeped

(iii) Dislocated

(iv) Opening on the floor

(v) Marking of path way

(vi) Broken

(vii) Structures cleaned and painted or not

(viii) Rusting of structures

(ix) Doors/windows pan damaged/missing.

2. Stairways, Ladders, Platforms, Railings, Working Table, Racks etc.

(i) Not cleaned.

(ii) Broken.

(iii) Railing, toe-guard, hand rail post not provided.

3. Machines and Machines Area

(i) Not cleaned and painted.

(ii) Safety device kept inoperative.

(iii) Accessories not in order.

(iv) Surrounding area of machine cleaned or not.

4. Pits, Drains, Wash Basins, Drinking Water Points etc.

(i) Not cleaned.

(ii) Drain not covered.

(iii) Pits not covered/barricaded.

(iv) Broken.

5. **Spillage, Leakage, Scrap and Garbage**

(i) Spillage/leakage of solid, liquid and gas from, machines, pipelines, valves, chutes, bunkers, containers, storage tank etc.

(ii) Spilled materials not collected/removed.

(iii) Scraps rejections and garbage kept at several places.

(iv) Spillage container, garbage bin not provided.

(v) Old parts left at site after changing.

(vi) Empty containers/jars/bags not disposed from site.

6. **Material Stacked Properly or Not, Badly Blocked the Passage**

(i) Materials stacked properly or not.

(ii) Walkways, entrance/exit/switch board/fire point/hydrant point's passage kept blocked.

(iii) Staircase/ladder landing passages kept blocked.

(iv) Stacking norms maintained or not.

(v) Unwanted materials segregated and removed or not.

(B) Other Parameters

1. **Maintenance of First Aid Box, Fire Points, Hydrant Points**

(i) First aid box and fire extinguishers kept cleaned or not.

(ii) First aid materials available in the box or not.

(iii) Fire extinguishers inspection due date over or not.

(iv) Fire points and hydrant point's passage kept clear or not.

(v) Sand/water available in the fire bucket or not.

(vi) Sand kept in sand bin or not.

2. **Guarding of Equipments, Condition of Fans, Blowers, Hand and Electric Power Tools, Electrical Installations etc.**

(i) All moving parts and transmission machineries guarded or not.

(ii) Fan, blower and portable electric tools connected properly or not.

(iii) Fans and blowers guard is proper or not.

(iv) Handles fitted with hand tools or not.

(v) Whether hand tools worn out or broken.

(vi) Service cable of portable electric tools is correct or not.

(vii) Switch board/panel board door closed or not.

(viii) Motor cooling impeller cover/motor terminal cover fitted or not.

(ix) Fan and blower working or not.

(x) Naked cables left at works.

3. Condition of Safety Boards and Signs

(i) Cleaned or not.

(ii) Readable or not.

(iii) Obsolete boards and posters removed or not

(iv) Safety campaign board maintained or not.

(v) Required safety boards (emergency phone numbers, First aiders and fire fighters name board) displayed or not.

(vi) Vital equipments Do's and Don'ts board displayed or not.

8 CHAPTER

Historical Development of Safety Movement

INTRODUCTION

The history of safety movement is around two hundred years old as industrial accidents first began to occur in large numbers after the massive industrialization. Industrial techniques began to make possible large scale mechanical production with the factory as production unit. Some of the conditions to which the industrial revolution give rise, were so severe as to create widespread feeling of fear and needed reform.

The movement for reform was led by people who felt that they had a moral responsibility for the well being of their fellows. Accident prevention work has from the very beginning owed much to these public spirited men and women, whose sense of justice was outraged by the exploration of the weak and whose sympathy was stirred by their sufferings. The aim of the reformers was to persuade the government into protecting the factory workers and above all the children and women workers, who often lived and worked under conditions which can not be thought today.

In the U.S. before the 19th century, no industrial system existed. Families usually lived and worked on firms. No record was kept of injuries sustained by the workers.

After 1800, the effects of the industrial revolution were felt in the United States.

During the last half of the 19th century, American expanding their product lines and producing at unimagined rates. While the factories were far superior in terms of production, they were often inferior in terms of human values, health and safety.

In the large industrial centers, the ugly results of industrial accidents and poor industrial health conditions became more and more obvious. Voices of protest were raised. Though there were employers who denied the existence of the problem, wiser management began to try to meet specific aspects of it.

As early as 1867, Massachusetts had began to use factory inspectors and ten years later that State had a law requiring the safe guarding of dangerous machineries.

From 1898 onwards, there were various efforts to make the employer financially liable for accidents. In 1911, the first effective Workmen's Compensation Act was passed in the city of Wisconsin (some authorities give this credit to New Jersey). This was followed by similar laws in many other States.

There had also been progress on the technical side of the problem. The rail-roads, which perhaps, had suffered the most adverse publicity from the accidents, adapted the air break and the automatic coupler well before the turn of the century. Some progress was also made in such matters as guarding and fire prevention.

Then attention was turned to the problem of safety. The increasing power, speed and crowding of machinery were making the factories more and more dangerous. Engel remarked that there were so many cripples in Manchester that the inhabitants looked like an army which has just retuned from a campaign. It is almost impossible today to realize the indignation with which some of the mill owners received the suggestion that they should be responsible for any accident that occurred in their premises. But no matter how stubbornly they resisted, the tide of opinions was running against them, and thanks to the combined and persistent efforts of philanthropists, inspectors, statesmen, members of parliament, journalists and others, some effective safety provisions were incorporated in the Factories Act at that time.

RETROSPECTIVE SCIENARIO OF HISTORY OF SAFETY MOVEMENT

History of safety begins with the history of science. Safety and science are inseparable. A man of an ancient era accidentally invented 'fire' and its uses. Fire safety began from then. Protection of self and family from heat, cold, rain, wind, animals and enemies is an age old concept of safety. Safety is existing with human beings by birth. The safety was existing with earliest civilizations, but earlier efforts were personal and defensive. The modern concept of organized safety started with the machine age.

Plato (BC 427 – 347), Gutenbarg (printing press in 1456), James Watt (steam engine in 1765), Eli Whitney (cotton gin in 1793), Isaac Newton, Thompson, Robert Fulton (steam ship 1807), Stevenson (railway engine, 1814), Michel Farad, Thomas Alva Edison (electric bulb, 1879) are some of the notable earlier scientists who laid the foundation of the machine age.

The oldest code of rule, known to protect the people was between the periods 2000 – 1700 BC.

Hammurabi – A Babylonian king devised a code including safety.

Some points were:

- If a man strike another he shall be responsible for the physician.
- A house constructed by a Mason if collapses and kills the inmates the mason shall be killed.
- A wine merchant who allows the unruly people to create nuisance to public, will be killed.
- If a child is killed, due to the carelessness of a nurse who engages another nurse without the knowledge of the parents her breast shall be cut off.
- Due to the carelessness of a doctor, if a person dies or looses his eye-sight the doctors hands shall be cut off.

In 1804, President Thomas Jefferson delivered his safety message to Captain Meriwether Lewis at the start of the expedition (1804 – 1806), he talked of danger, risk and safety of the people.

In 1833 George Stephenson suggested use of a steam whistle on locomotives. In 1866 first National Board of Fire Underwriters organized. In 1881 first Indian Factories Act was initiated. In 1900 first safety periodical named safety maintenance (formerly Safety Engineering) published. In 1903 demands of industrial workers were considered in Russia. In 1914 first safety of life at sea convention was held in London and in 1918 first air mail service started. First World War (1914) and Second World War (1939) accelerated industrialization and the need of safety.

The concept of safety was significantly explained by the President of USA before the National Conference on Industrial Safety as follows:

"The plain fact is that our Nation can not afford the needless loss of skilled workers if we are to produce for prosperity in this country and for peace abroad."

THE CHRONOLOGICAL DEVELOPMENT OF SAFETY AND ACCIDENT PREVENTION

I. The World Scenario

The first tangible achievement of the reforms was actually the adoption in 1802 of an Act for the preservation of the Health and Morales of Apprentices and others employed in mills and factories.

Engel Dollfas, who in 1867 founded an association in Mulhouse for the prevention of the accidents and for the exchange of the experience in safety problems, was a man of high social principles, which he expressed in the following words:

"The employer owes more than wages to his workers. It is his duty to take care of their moral and physical conditions, and this purely moral obligation, which can not be replaced by any kind of wages, should take prudence over considerations of private interest."

The first piece of factories act in France was made dated the 22nd March 1841 but safety legislation in the strict sense was not introduced until 1893.

In Prussia the first step taken to establish a factory inspection system took the form of regulations issued on 9th March 1839 concerning the employment of young workers in factories. A system of inspection covering industrial health and safety generally was introduced in 1872.

An Imperial Act of 15th July 1878 made factory inspection compulsory in all the German states. The industrial accident insurance legislation, under which the system of mutual accident insurance association was developed, dated from 1884.

In Belgium Industrial Safety and Health Legislation Act concerning mines, smelting works and similar undertakings promulgated on 21st April 1910, created a system of inspection.

Other European countries, including Denmark and Switzerland, had factory legislation on the statute books by 1840.

In the United States, Massachusetts was the first state to pass an act for the prevention of accidents in factories. This act dated the 11th May 1877, provided for guarding of belting, shafting and gearing, prohibited the cleaning of machinery in motion, and required elevators and hoist ways to be protected and sufficient exits to be provided in case of fire.

Massachusetts was also the first state to pass an act requiring accidents to be reported; it was dated 1st June 1836. Similar acts were passed by Ohio in 1888, Missouri in 1891, and Rhode Island in 1896.

Once again in the United States, Massachusetts was the first in the field; there a state incorporate was established in 1867. Wisconsin passed factory inspection legislation in 1885 and New York in 1886. After 1885, too, the principle of employers liability in respect of employment injury began to appear in the legislation of the different states.

With the assistance of medical, electrical, chemical and other specialists the labor inspectors could become a technical consultant to whom employers and workers could turn and in this capacity he could make a better contribution to safety promotion than when he was merely an official responsible for enforcing the law.

A system has been followed in Germany since 1884; it resulted in that country having two different services, one in labor inspection and other in social insurance, both of them responsible to some extent for accident prevention – an arrangement that has given rise to some administrative problems.

In the United States as the number of states to pass laws concerning employers liability in respect of employment injury increased, the employers' liability was gradually taken over by insurance companies. The latter appointed Inspectors to supervise safety measures in the insured undertakings and in this way they entered the accident prevention field.

A number of International Safety Congress were held during same time; in Paris 1889, in Berne in 1891, and in Milan in 1894; which had considerable influence on the legislation of the period. The system of promoting safety by exchanges of experience and the publicizing of suitable safeguards had been shown to be invaluable but not sufficient to arrive at substantial results.

After all these, it was found, that who were responsible for the enforcement of safety measures in the factory itself were not sufficiently independent or had other work to do which prevented them from attending to safety matters; alternatively there was no co-operation between management and workers, or the workers themselves were opposed to the new measures.

It was felt then that these difficulties should be overcome by promulgating safety laws and by setting up state inspection services for their enforcement; in this way safeguarding dangerous places would become a statutory obligation. Moreover, to make sure that the obligation should be a real one, state inspectors, not influenced by local conditions, should be appointed to see that the law was enforced.

To promote the safety and protecting the health of the workers it was proposed that Government should promote safety associations which are organized by private persons. As far as is known, the oldest safety organization in the world is the Mulhouse Accident Prevention Association, founded in 1867. The Belgium Manufacturers Association for the prevention of industrial accident was formulated in 1890 and its Italian counterpart in 1894. The Swedish workers protection Association dates from 1905. The British National Safety First Association (now the Royal Society for the prevention of Accident) did not come into existence until after the First World War. The National Safety Council of United States was founded in 1913. The Cuban National Safety Council, goes back 1936. The first safety association to be founded in Africa seems to have been the Cape provinces Safety First Association, dating from 1936. In Asia the Japanese Industrial Welfare Society founded in 1928, was first to appear; the second was the Safety First Association, founded in 1931. The National Safety Council of Australia and the New South Wales Safety First Association both began activity in 1927. The National Safety Council of India was set up long after on the 4th March 1966.

II. The Indian Scenario

Industries were established in India as early as 1850s. Large scale industrialization, however, started after the country became independent in 1947. Today India is one among 10 most industrialized nations in the world. The country has today all types of industries which are located through out the vast areas, naturally the potential for hazards arising out of industries are also large. In India the dimension of problem are due to a variety and diversity of industries – small and large, old and new, traditional vs. modern and so on. Spread over of the industries throughout the vast area of the nation.

With the coming of the Iron age and the development of use of machines in the manufacturing of articles of utility, the worker came to be regarded as a mere slave of the machines. To his woe the machine became his master and he became a victim to the monotonous and painful life in factories with unhealthy surroundings. In course of time capitalists thrived in the exploration of labor. The laborer was worst than a beast. While the industrialists lived in pomp and luxury, the worker had to pass his monotonous and woeful existence in slums, which were most unhealthy and not fit even for human habitation. Animals and birds of the day were free and happier than the unfortunate factory laborer.

1. Indian Factories Act, 1881 (XV of 1881)

The first comprehensive legislation for regulating safety of laboring factories was the Indian Factories act, 1881. It applied to manufacturing establishments using mechanical power and employing 100 or more persons. Plantation industries being exempted. The Act prohibited the employment of children less than 7 years of age and prescribed the minimum and maximum ages for employment at seven and twelve, 9 hours working day with an interval of rest for one hour and a weekly holiday for children only.

Salient points are:

- Applicability – 100 or more workers.
- To protect children – few health and safety measures.

2. Indian Factories Act, 1891 (XI of 1891)

This Act was an advance of previous Act, applied to all factories employing 50 persons and using power. The lower and upper limits of age of children were fixed at 9 and 14 respectively and their hours of work were limited to 7 hours a day, with rest interval of half an hour. The Act prescribed an 11 hour day with a rest interval of one and half hour for women and restricted the employment of women and one child. Men were to enjoy an interval of half hour rest and holiday every week. The Provicincial Government was empowered to make rules regarding measures of sanitation and conflict.

Salient points are:

- Applicability – 50 or more workers.
- Children below 9 years – prohibited.
- Children below 9 to 14 years – working hours: 7 Hrs./day.
- Children and women – prohibited in night shift.

3. Indian Factories Act, 1911 (XII of 1911)

The Act regulated the hours of work of adult male industrial workers and covered seasonal factories which work for less than four months in a year. The Act limited the hours of work of adult male workers to 12 a day, and of children to 6 a day in textile factories with a rest interval of half an hour. This Act contained extensive provisions regarding health and safety and effective inspection of the administration of the safety in factories.

Salient points are:

- Applicability – 50 or more workers.
- Children working hours: 6 Hrs./day.
- Adult working hours: 12 Hrs./day – 1 hour rest interval.
- Children and women – prohibited in night shifts.
- Inspection made straight.

4. The Factories Act of 1922

First World War (1914 to 1918) brought about a rapid industrial development. The International Labor Organization which came into being in 1920 brought changes in the factory laws to a great extent, with the result the Factories Act of 1922 was passed. It applied to all factories using power and employing not less than 20 laborers. The local Government was empowered to extend its application to factories employing ten or more laborers. The maximum hours of work for adult laborers were fixed 11 per day and 60 per week. Hours of work for children were reduced to 6 per day in all sorts of factories. The minimum age for employment of children was raised from 9 to 12 years and the upper limit was fixed at 15. The employment of women and children in the factories between 7.0 P.M and 5.30 A.M. was prohibited. Sunday or any other day was to be a holiday. All workers were given half an hour rest for work exceeding 6 hours. Provision regarding the safety and health of the workers were extended and the Provincial Government was to provide standard of ventilation, humidification, etc. to prevent injury of the workers. This Act was amended in 1923 and again in 1926. According to the amendment to adult workers for half an hour for those working not more than 8 and half hours, was permitted. Provincial Government was given power to forbid the cleaning of machinery while in motion and to provide for a better reporting of accidents. This Act declared an offence for a parent or guardian allowing a child to work in two or more mills on the same day. The previous laws of 1859 and 1860 making workers liable to criminal penalties for breaches of contract were replaced in 1926 and 1931.

- Applicability – 20 or more workers with power.
- 100 or more workers – provincial government can enforce.
- Adult working hours: 11 Hrs./day – 60 hours/week.
- 1 hour rest interval after 6 hours.
- 1 day weekly off.
- O.T. hours – double wages.

5. Factories Act of 1934

The Factories Act of 1934 is a comprehensive measure amending and consolidating all the previous factory legislations of 1881, and 1911 as amended by the acts of 1922, 1923, 1926 and 1931. The main objectives of the Act are (1) reduction of hours of work, (2) improvements in working conditions within the factory and (3) provision for adequate inspection and strict observance of the Act. The maximum hours of work for adults in perennial factories were fixed at 10 per day and 54 per week while for seasonal factories the limit was fixed at 11 per day and 60 per week. The hours of work for children were reduced to 5 per day. The principle of "spread over" was introduced for the first time. Overtime was required to be paid at the rate of 1½ times of the ordinary wages. This Act created a new class of workers. Called "adolescents" and placed all persons between 15 and 17 years in it. Fencing of machineries, safety devices, humidification etc. were also made. The Provisional Governments were made responsible for the administration of the act. The Provisional Governments were empowered to appoint Chief Inspector of Factories and Inspectors for the purpose. The Act provides a penalty which may extend to Rs. 500 for contravention of any of the major provisions and enhanced penalty for repeated breach. The provision for health and safety were amplified and made more stringent. It covers all manufacturing establishments employing 20 or more persons and using mechanical power. It has made a distinction between seasonal and perennial factories. After the year 1934 many amendments were made during 1935 – 1946.

Fifth Factories Act – 1934 (enacted after the report of Royal Commission of Labor – Whitely Commission 1929 – 31).

Salient points of this Act:

- Seasonal factories workers' working hours: 11 hours/day and 60 hours/week.
- Perennial factories working hours: 10 hours/day and 54 hours/week.
- Children: 12 to 15 years working hours: 5 hours/day.
- Women working hours: 10 hours/day – night duty prohibited.
- Overtime: 1.5 times wages.
- Provisions for health, security, rest house, cradle, first-aid, etc.

1946 Amendment:

- Working hours; 9 hours/day and 48 hours/week.
- Seasonal 10 hours/day and 54 hours/week.
- Overtime: double wages.

1947 Amendment:

- Canteen facility for more than 200 workers.

6. The Factores Act of 1948

The Act of 1934 revealed a number of defects regarding administration of safety, health and welfare of the workers. The provisions were inadequate and unsatisfactory. The protection as was provided by the Act did not extend to a large mass of workers employed in small work places. Hence, the Factories Act, 1948 was passed and it came into effect on 1st. April 1948.

Factories Act 1948 and Amendment 1987

Provision in Factories Act for Safety of Workers

Sl. No.	Provision in Factories Act, 1948 (India) and Amendment to Factories Act, 1987	Ref. Sec. of Act
1.	Fencing of machinery and plant	21
2.	Work in or near machinery in motion	22
3.	Employment of young persons in dangerous machines	23
4.	Striking gear and devices for cutting off power	24
5.	Self acting machine	25
6.	Casting of new machinery	26
7.	Prohibition of employment of women and children near cotton openers	27
8.	Hoists and lifts	28
9.	Lifting machines, chains, ropes and lifting tackles	29
10.	Revolving machinery	30
11.	Pressure plant	31
12.	Floors, stairs and means of access	32
13.	Pits, sumps, and means of access	33
14.	Excessive weight	34
15.	Protection of eyes	35
16.	Precaution against dangerous fumes	36
17.	Precautions regarding the use of portable light	36A
18.	Explosive or inflammable dust, gas etc.	37
19.	Precautions in case of fire	38
20.	Power to require specification of defective part or tests of stability	39
21.	Safety of buildings and machinery	40
22.	Maintenance of building	40A
23.	Safety officers	40B
24.	Power to make rules	41
25.	Definition of hazardous process	Sec. 2 (cb)
26.	Site appraisal committee	41A
27.	Information to be furnished by occupier	41B
28.	Responsibility of occupier	41C

29.	Appointment of enquiry committee	41D
30.	Special emergency standard	41E
31.	Permissible limits of exposure to toxics	41F
32.	Worker participation in safety management	41G
33.	Right of worker to warn about danger	41H
34.	Authority of Inspector to prohibit employment in case of hazardous condition	87A
35.	Condition of employing women	22, 27 66, 87
36.	Conditions for employing children and young persons	CH, VII 67 to 76 23, 27, 87

PHASES IN THE DEVELOPMENT OF SAFETY MOVEMENT

A. Phase I (up to 1920) : Legislations:

Progress in industrial safety before 1911 was practically non existent. With the Workmen's Compensation laws all states handled injuries under the "common law." Under the common law the legal defenses available to the management of industry almost ensured that they would not have to pay for any accidents occurring on the job. Under this common law system employees did not automatically receive payments when injured on the job; as they do to-day. If employer could show any of the four legal defenses he would not have to pay the injured employees for the injuries he suffered:

- The employee himself contributed to the cause of accident.
- Another employee contributed to the accident cause.
- The employee knew of hazards involved in the accident before his injury, and still agreed to work in the condition.
- There was no employer negligence.

In the early years, plant conditions were worse. Light, ventilation and sanitation were almost non-existent. Rest rooms were unthought-of. Two-third of workers were women and children whose work day was 12-14 hours. Machine guards were unknown. Occupational deaths were frequent.

B. Phase II (1920-1935): Guarding and Safety Appliances:

The enactment of the Workmen's compensation law in U.S.A. gave a great moral boost to the safety movement. No company management liked to loose their hard earned funds in paying compensation for injuries. It was therefore created a strong need to find scientific method for counter acting accidents. Fortunately in 1929, H.W. Heinrich put forth his famous theory of "Foundation of a major injury", according to which out of 330 similar accidents to the same person, 300 accidents result in near misses/no injury; 29 result in minor injuries and 1 result in a major injury.

In 1931 a major breakthrough was possible in the solution of safety problems when Heinrich published his famous "Domino Theory" in a book titled 'industrial Accident Prevention'.

This domino theory was a scientific and logical model for analysis and control of accidents. It was therefore immediately accepted by the factory managements as a sure cure for the evils of industrialization. The seeds of a scientific approach to accident prevention were thus shown. Engineers applied their knowledge in designing safer machines. The concept of safety guards and safety appliances take birth at this stage yielding very good results in U.S.A.

There have been continuous efforts from different areas for betterment of working conditions and ensuring safety of workmen. The various factors which have directly or indirectly contributed to this growth are as under:

- Over the years of trade union movement have grown and it is recognized as an integrated part of social system. The trade unions have contributed to safety movements in many ways:
  - Their fight for better wages to workers.
  - Their fight for better working conditions.
  - Bringing of fresh legislations due to link in social and political circles and enforcing existing legal provisions concerning safety and health at work.
  - Involvement in case of compensation to injuries.
- The safety legislation has undergone revisions during past few decades specifying better conditions of work and increased responsibility for safety on the part of the employee.
- Emergence of new theories in the field of management giving importance to 'man'. The safety and health of worker has assumed greater importance.
- The all round consciousness generated and support from management and society have led to the formation of many voluntary bodies to promote safety and health in industry, e.g., The National Safety Council of U.S.A. Royal Society for Prevention of Accidents. Consumer product Safety Commission (CPSC) etc.
- Improvement in the standard of education of workers, which made them conscious of the hazards around and their right for protection.

An off-shoot of this scientific approach to safety was the appointment of safety officers by large organizations. Safety committee was also started functioning during this phase. Unfortunately, the emphasis slowly shifted to safety specialists and safety organizations. As such line management took little or no interest in safety, which was a bad trend cropped up.

C. Phase III (1935 – 1960): Safety Promotional and Propaganda Phase:

Heinrich's Domino Theory clearly indicated that persons and not things caused accidents. Heinrich further shown that only 10% accidents resulted from 'unsafe conditions' are visible and through good house keeping program all unsafe conditions are eliminated. But elimination of all unsafe acts which contribute 88% of accidents are difficult because it is difficult to find out in what way a person does 'unsafe act'. So soon it is realized that the best safety device that can stop accident is a 'safe worker' only.

Safety promotional and propaganda techniques thus received a great boost, its primary objective being to influence the minds of people and orient their thinking such that positive attitudes are created towards safety and interest in safety kept alive on a continuous basis.

D. Phase IV (1960 Onwards): Managing Safety at Work:

Two new significant concepts introduced in this phase were:

(1) Safety can only come from the top management operating through its line management acting as a catalyst for promoting safety and ensuring compliance with all safety requirements.

(2) Line management is directly responsible for safety and they must play a direct and active role to promote and ensure safety of their men.

Two other important conclusions followed from this concept:

(1) That the safety officer may only act as a specialist agency in guiding, assigning and advising the line management in matters related to safety.

(2) That line managers and supervisors must be well trained in the techniques of safety and safety management so as to make their role effective in counteracting accidents and promoting safety.

The philosophy of safety and accident prevention has thus undergone a sea change from the earliest phase when the individual was held responsible for accidents to the present times when it is considered the responsibility of the top management to take initiative for safety and the line management is directly held responsible for ensuring safety of their men.

Some Other Legislations Applicable to Factories in India

Sl. No.	Year	Legislation
1.	1855	The Fatal Accidents Act, 1855
2.	1884	The Explosive Act
3.	1890	Indian Railway Act
4.	1908	The Explosive Substance Act
5.	1923	Indian Boilers Act

6.	1934	The Petroleum Act (as amended till 1997) and Petroleum Rules 1976.
7.	1948	The Factories Act (as amended till 1987)
8.	1952	The Inflammable Substances Act 1952
9.	1952	Boiler Regulations
10.	1956	Indian Electricity Rules
11.	1962	The Emergency Risk (Factories Insurance Act, 1962)
12.	1974	The Water (Prevention and Control of Pollution) Act.
13.	1975	The Water (Prevention and Control of Pollution) Rules
14.	1976	The Petroleum Rules (as amended till 1955)
15.	1977	The Water (Prevention and Control of Pollution) Cess Act
16.	1978	The Water (Prevention and Control of Pollution) Cess Rules.
17.	1981	The Air (Prevention and Control) Act
18.	1981	The Static and Mobile Pressure Vessels (Unified) Rules as amended till 1997
19.	1982	The Air (Prevention and Control of Pollution) Rules
20.	1984.	Indian Explosives Act 1984 and Explosives Rules 1983
21.	1986.	The Environment (Protection) Act
22.	1986	The Environment (Protection) Rules
23.	1983.	The Explosive Rules including amendment rules 1989
24.	1989	The Central Motor Vehicles Rules (under Motor Vehicles Act, 1988)
25	1989 2000	The Hazardous Wastes (Management and handling) Rules including amendment 2000
26	1989 2000	Manufacture, Storage and Import of Hazardous chemicals Rules 1989 including amendment of 2000
27.	1991	The Public Liability Insurance Act
28.	1992	Environmental (Protection) Rules – 'Environmental Statements'
29.	1993	Environmental (Protection) Rules – 'Environmental Standards'
30.	1984	Gas Cylinder Rules, including Amendment Rules, 1993
31.	1994	Environmental (Protection) Rules – 'Environmental Clearance'
32.	1995	The National Environmental Tribunal Act

33.	1996	The Environment (Protection) Second Amendment Rules – 'Environmental Standards'
34.	1996	Chemical accident (Emergency, Planning, Preparedness and Response) Rules
35.	1997	Amendments in the Environment (Protection) Rules, 1994 'Public Hearing'
36.	1998	National Environmental Appellate Authority Act
37.	1998	Environment (Protection) Second Amendment Rules – 'Environmental Standards'
38.	1999	Direction for Use of Fly Ash based products under Environmental Protection Rules 1986
39.	2000	The Bio Medical Waste (Management and Handling) Rules
40.	2000	The Ozone Depletion Substances (Regulation) Rules
41.	2000	The Noise Pollution (Regulation and Control) Rules
42.	2001	Battery Management and Handling Rules
43.	2000	The National Pollution (Regulation and Control) Rules
44.	2001	The Energy Conservation Act
45.	1996	The Building and Construction Workers Act
46.	1996	Comprehensive list of MOEF authorized waste oil/waste recycle/reprocesses
47.	1923	The Workmen's Compensation Act
48.	1950	Factory Rules of the State in which Factory/Plant is located
49.	1948	Industrial Employment (Standing Orders) Act

Managing Safety at Work Should Involve Following Principle

1. **Policy Decision:** The Company should first decide the level of safety it is going to achieve. The attitude of top management, accident liability, profits, relation with employees, government policy, accident records, funds available etc.will influence this decision. Policy decision should include:
   - Targets for performance – targets could be spell out in terms of reduction from earlier results, or maximum limits in terms of accidents.
   - A statement as to what the company proposes to do, to achieve the targets.
   - What it expects from its employees right from manager to the worker?
   - Action required at executive/supervisory level.
   - How it proposes to monitor and evaluate the performance?

2. **Assignment of Responsibility for Safety:** The management should assign the responsibility of safety to its executives in clear terms. Some companies employ a full time manager. If there is no safety manager the job of co-coordinating safety activities is given to an officer as an additional charge. There is also safety committees constituted as per statutory binding. The different departmental heads and other line executives are also involved in the safety program. The safety manager and the safety committees help the supervisor and line executives to achieve safety targets. The responsibilities, duties, and authorities in different levels are clearly spelt out by the companies.
3. **Joint Participation:** Theoretically, the necessity of safety committee does not exist, once a specialist safety organization is installed and it carries out its functions effectively. The committee approach to solving safety problems has taken firm roots all over the world and in India as per the statutory provision, Section 41-G of Factories Act, 1948 has made the formation of safety committees a statutory obligation in factories where hazardous processes are involved.
4. **Communication with Employees:** The Company's safety policy should be made known to each and every employee in clear terms. Employees should be told:
   - That safety of workmen is of importance to the company.
   - That the management has assigned the job of looking after the safety of workmen to the executives.
   - That it expects the employees to work safely, and co-operate with the management in ensuring safety.
   - About annual safety programs and safety organization in the plant.
5. **Overall Management Directions:** Safety management should have the four basic elements of direction and control:
   - **Planning:** Decision for safety targets for performance, setting standards, working out detailed activities, budgeting, assignment of responsibility and procedures, data collection, and analysis.
   - **Activities:** Carrying out activities, which are planned. These include:

     (a) Providing safe conditions of work.

     (b) Directing people to be safe.
   - **Measurement:** To evaluate actions taken to compare performance with standards and targets set, to identify weak areas.
   - **Control:** Using the information from measurements to bring about changes in the next cycle/future plans.

By this time it is established that safety is an organized and conscience effort to prevent accidents and minimize risks. There is a general tendency to forget or overlook the aspect of safety. This may be due to the fact that accidents do not happen every day. As a matter of fact when safety measures work, accidents do not occur; and in absence there of, accidents take place. So as a common human tendency, one quite often neglects 'safety'. One looks at it only when an accident takes place. Occupational health issues are often given less attention than occupational safety issues because the former are generally more difficult to confront. However, when health is addressed, so is safety, because a healthy work place is by definition also a safe workplace. The important point is that issues of both health and safety must be addressed in every work place. The basis of all safety organization is awareness of accident risks and hazards both quantitative (i.e., their frequency and severity rules) and qualitative (i.e., according to the nature of causes of actual or potential accidents). Plant management should have the means to assess their own degree of risk, enabling to make a comparison with other firms. Quantitative analysis is the most important branch, because it examines accident causes directly. Plant managements should not be content merely to investigate and analyze their own accidents. They should draw on the experience of trade organizations, employees and workers' associations, specialized institutions and other firms.

Worker participation in plant safety organization can be planned in many ways depending on National law and practice. Among the many ways and means of providing for worker and trade union participation in plant safety organization the most frequently adopted are safety and health committees. Details concerning the membership, powers and duties of these committees are usually laid down in laws and regulations varying from country to country. Another form of participation undertaken to achieve enhanced safety and all round improvement of working condition is the establishment of research teams. In order to ensure their effective participation, the workers and their organizations should be made aware:

- That safety regulation is enacted to protect workers' life and limb and prevent health improvement.
- They are closer to the production process and have to spend many hours daily in the working environment.
- It is for their safety that safer design of materials and equipment and work safety rules are developed. It is obvious, therefore, those workers and their organizations should be associated with in plant safety and occupational health organizations, and that they should be given every facility for this cooperation. It is desirable that they or their representatives should participate in all systematic investigations of accident casualty, inquiries following accidents and policymaking and implementation of decisions concerning measures to reduce or eliminate hazards.

TEN PRINCIPLES OF PLANT SAFETY AND HEALTH PROGRAM

1. Safety is not a separate subject. It is just another aspect of industrial progress. It should be closely integrated in all production problems and decision making.

2. Top management should communicate its policies and decisions preferably in writing, to all plant personnel at every level, through normal channel of communication.
3. Every representative of top and middle management, engineers and supervisory staff, down to shop floor level should be responsible for plant safety, i.e., at all production levels. It should receive equal importance with other professional skills and performance and taken into account in weighing up promotion possibilities.
4. The safety department should be considered a king-pin service, reporting directly to the top most person. Its role consists essentially in safety promotion, documentation, information, and general training, advisory tasks, coordination and inspection. The department should participate fully in all in plant safety activities, but in no case take over any of the basic responsibilities of management and supervisors in this field.
5. The safety service should devote a considerable part of its time to work place inspections, with special attention to ergonomics and health and safety engineering aspects.
6. The workers and their accredited representatives should be associated in occupational safety and health policy making also in planning and implementation.
7. All actions taken in the field of occupational safety and health should be coordinated as part of an overall rationalized program embracing the following stages: preparation, application, checks and controls regarding implementation, assessment of results, administration, enforcement and application of the results.
8. A safety program should not be based only on the analysis of past accidents, but also on in depth studies carried out before occurrence of accidents and assessment of risks and hazards in production departments. Total loss control methods (employment injuries, material loss or damage, financial aspects) are highly recommended.
9. The improvement of workplace and working conditions, which includes occupational safety and health aspects can be achieved most effectively by work place studies, leading to improvement or better design or machinery installation and production processes; drafting of work routes and so on.
10. Safety training at all levels should be an integral part of vocational training.

Suggestions for Promoting Safety Movement

Some suggestions for promoting safety movement include the following:

- Make the work interesting by using job enrichment and by curbing boredom, fatigue and stress.
- Ensure that all workers are provided with a safe and healthy work process.

- Establish bipartite safety committees and ensure their effective functioning in collaboration with all concerned.
- Encourage safety contests and awards amongst employees who submit good accident prevention ideas.
- Publicize accident statistics.
- Identify the causes of accidents and the conditions under which they are most likely to occur.
- Carry out regular inspections and audits in order to eliminate the risks.
- Organize continuous education and training programs on accident prevention and safety.
- Maintain records listing all dangerous occurrences, their causes and the remedial actions taken.
- Enforce vigorously safety legislation, mechanism to curb work hazards and the penalties on convictions must be sufficiently severe to convince most employees that it is more sensible to implement safety precautions than risk the consequences of failure to do so.
- Provide for rehabilitation of physically disabled in any legislation dealing with health and safety at work place.
- Assign occupational health and safety a greater priority at the national level and concerted government, employer and union action is needed to improve the quality of the working environment.

Some Important Indian and Foreign Origin Concepts and Scientific Inventions/ Events in Historical Safety Movement

- Vedkal: Yajurveda, Rig-Veda, Upanishads etc. Old concept of science and safety in Nation. Our ancient heritage.
- BC 2000: Chanakya Kautilya's Arthshastra dealing many subjects including safety.
- BC 427-347: Plato's teachings of mathematics and globe shapes of all planets.
- BC 384-322: Philosophy of science by Aristotle.
- BC 287-212: Displacement of water, buoyancy and specific gravity by Archimedes.
- 100-178: Ptolemy who discovered that the sun moves around the earth. He gave mathematical models in his book, 'The Great Treatise of Astronomy'.
- 1456: First printing press in Germany by Gutenberg.
- 1473-1543: Nicolas Copernicus who discovered that the sun is the centre and the earth and other planets move around it.
- 1564-1642: Galileo who discovered equal speed of falling bodies, telescope and reaffirmed Copernicus' sun-centered principle.

- 1571-1630: Kepler who stated that the elliptical motion of planet around the sun.
- 1642-1727: Isaac Newton, principles of gravity, rules of light, optics, calculus etc.
- 1732: First spinning machine by Richard Arc Right, pioneer of industrial revolution.
- 1749-1838: John Stevens, Father of American Railway.
- 1761-1828: Nicolas Lul Rober, pioneer of paper industry.
- 1765: Steam engine by James Watt.
- 1765-1825: Aley Whitney produced sawing, washing and other machine.
- 1768-1835: Samuel Sietor, Father of American cloth industry.
- 1771-1852: David Wilkinson, Father of machine tools industries.
- 1796: Dr. Edward Janner, small pox vaccination.
- 1800-1860: Charles Goodyear, father of rubber industry.
- 1801-1874: Gail Borden, father of modern dairy industry.
- 1804: President Thomas Jefferson delivered his safety message to captain Merriweather Lewis.
- 1806-1873: John Stuart Mill, the great contribution in Philosophy of science.
- 1807: Steam ship by Robert Fulton.
- 1809-1884: Sirus Hall McCormick, father of agricultural industry.
- 1813-1818: Sir Hennery Bessemer, father of steel industry.
- 1814: Locomotive engine by James Watt.
- 1819-1880: Edwin L. Drek, father of petroleum industry.
- 1825: Railway usage started.
- 1831-1879: James Clerk Maxwell, electromagnetic waves which led us to radio and TV.
- 1832-1891: Nicholas August Auto discovered internal combustion engine. Father of automobile industry, a great contribution to industrial revolution.
- 1833: England, Government factory inspections established.
- 1833: George Stevenson suggested use of a steam whistle on locomotives.
- 1844: England, law enacted to provide great fencing for mill gears and shafts. Lord Ashley's Great factory act.
- 1844-1929: Karl Benz made first motor car and called father of motor car industry.
- 1845-1923: Wilhelm Roentgen, discovery of X-ray. First Nobel Prize winner in 1901.
- 1847-1931: Thomas Alva Edison, father of electrical industry.
- 1847-1922: Alexander Graham Bell discovered telephone called father of telecommunication.

- 1847-1937: Gugly Elmo Marconi discovered wireless telegraph and called father of wireless telegraphy.
- 1855: Insurance protection against boiler explosion was afforded in England.
- 1858-1932: Dr. Jagdish Chandra Bose – sensation of plant Crescograph to view enlargement of plant movement.
- 1858-1913: Rudolf Diesel discovered diesel fuel and called father of diesel industry.
- 1863-1914: Charles Martin Hall obtained pure aluminum and called father of aluminum industry.
- 1864: First accident insurance policy in North America.
- 1865: Benzene ring structure.
- 1866: National Board of Fire Underwriters.
- 1867: Boiler and machinery insurance started in USA.
- 1869: Germany – acts passed providing that all employers furnish necessary appliances to safeguard health and life of employees.
- 1869: Massachusetts (USA) established the first state bureau of labor statistics in order to determine the kinds and causes of accidents.
- 1869: Periodic Table of Elements by Mendelif.
- 1870: Westing house air break adopted by the rail roads.
- 1872: First electric automatic signal installed on the Pennsylvania rail-road.
- 1873-1961: Lee De'Forest discovered radio and called father of radio industry.
- 1874: France, law enacted providing for special inspection service of workshops.
- 1876-1920: Willis Hevill and Carrier discovered air-conditioning and called father of air conditioning industry.
- 1877: Massachusetts; Law passed compelling guarding of dangerous moving machinery.
- 1899-1955: Albert Einstein, Quantum Theory and Principles of Relativity.
- 1879: Electric bulb by Thomas Alva Edison.
- 1880: American Society of Mechanical Engineers.
- 1881: American National Red Cross.
- 1881: First Indian Factories Act.
- 1885: Germany Alabama, passed employers liability law. Germany, Bismarck prepared and enacted the first compulsory compensation Act for workers. This act covered only sickness. (Germany was the first country to abandon the employers' liability system for that of workmen's' compensation.)

  Massachusetts passed an employers' liability law.

Ervin Schrodinger – Wave mechanics.

Safety department of Joliet works of Illinois steel company formed. This has been called "the birth place of American industrial accident prevention movement." The first safety order was the inspection of all engine flywheels.

Federal safety appliance act required use of standard safety equipment on rail road.

National Fire Prevention Association.

Radioactive elements by Curie couple.

First safety periodical 'Safety Maintenance' published by Alfred M. Best Company.

National Bureau of Standards.

First street passenger car constructed.

Extension of Quantum theory by Einstein.

Quarterly of the National Fire Protection Association published by NFPA.

Transportation of dangerous explosives act passed.

Airplane by Right Brothers.

First National Conference on industrial diseases held.

New Jersey first state workmen's compensation law passed.

California passed the first American law for the compulsory reporting of occupational diseases.

American Museum of Safety.

Ernest Rutherford – concept of nucleus and electron in atom; alpha, beta and gamma rays and many inventions on atomic energy.

- 1912: National Safety Council (USA).
- 1912: Discovery of thorium, polonium and radium by Madam Curie.
- 1913: Bureau of Labor Statistics.
- 1913: 'Safety' published by the American Museum of Safety.
- 1913: Atomic structure, nuclear structure and atomic model by Nisbohr.
- 1914: The first safety of life at sea convention held in London.
- 1915: American Society of Safety.
- 1915: Elliptical motion of electrons by Summerfield.
- 1918: Air mail service started.
- 1919: National railroad accident prevention drive inaugurated.
- 1919: National Safety news published by the National Safety Council. Then many other publications started in the subsequent years by NSC (USA).
- 1919: International Labor Organization (ILO) was established.

- 1929: ILO at Geneva set up a safety service.
- 1922: Greenberg and Smith introduced the impinger, a dust sampling device, which resulted in the impinger method becoming the standard for the U.S. Bureau of mines and the public health service.
- 1925: 'Occupational safety and health' published by the ILO, Geneva.
- 1926: Bensol, poisoning study.
- 1926: 4:1 accident cost ratio presented by H.W. Heinrich.
- 1927: First rocket fly.
- 1927: A study of the relation between safety and production was made by the American Engineering Council 1926 and 1927.
- 1928: First National Aeromatic Safety Conference held in America.
- 1928: American Standard Association.
- 1929: The US Load Line Act passed to prevent overloading of cargo under various conditions.
- 1929: The foundation of a major injury ratio 300-29-1 indicated by H.W. Heinrich.
- 1929: Penicillin by Alexander Fleming.
- 1930: First Greater New York Safety Conference held in New York City. It was a one day session with 900 delegates.
- 1934: Bureau of Labor Standards.
- 1935: The Air Hygiene Foundation was created to conduct scientific studies to prevent occupational disasters and industrial heat.
- 1937: Automotive safety foundation.
- 1937: National committee on films for safety.
- 1938: Nuclear fission of uranium by Farmy and Han.
- 1938: Centre for safety education.
- 1939: American Industrial Hygienic Association.
- 1940 – 1950: Inclusion of modern defense equipments viz, radar jet aircraft missiles, atom bombs, computer etc.
- 1941: Industrial hygienic department was set up in 33 states in USA.
- 1941: The accident case code was compiled by USA. This code introduced an era of accident cause standardization in USA overcoming a weakness in industrial accident prevention that had long existed.
- 1941: National Bureau of Industrial Protection (USA).
- 1945: Solid state transistor by Bell Telephone Laboratories of America. Ultimately this solid state electronics has now come to stage of microelectronics using silicon clad and integrated circuits.

- 1945: August, America threw atom bomb on Hiroshima and Nagasaki of Japan causing around 1,20,000 deaths and more injuries.
- 1945: Tata Institute of Fundamental Research was established in Bombay (Mumbai).
- 1947: Atomic Energy Commission (USA).
- 1948: April 6th Declaration of industrial policy for small scale industries and public sectors.
- 1948: Atomic Energy Commission.
- 1950 – 60: Establishment of Indian Institute of Technology at Khadagpur, Bombay, Delhi, Madras (Chennai), and Kanpur and defense organizations and council of scientific and industrial research and department of technology in our country.
- 1952: Pesticides manufacturing started in India.
- 1954: Atomic battery (giving crores of electrons per second on transistor wafer) by USA.
- 1954: Atomic energy establishment at Trombay in Bombay. This was renamed as Bhaba Research Center in 1967.
- 1955: Dr. Bhabha selected as president of conference on the peaceful uses of Atomic energy at Geneva.
- 1956: Our first nuclear reactor 'Apsara', the first in Asia also.
- 1957: Sputnik the first satellite in the sky by Russia.
- 1958: Defense Research and Development Organization.
- 1966: Electronics committee at the chairmanship of Dr. Vikram Sarabhai.
- 1966: The first tidal electric plant in France giving 5000 KWH electricity per year.
- 1969: Atomic Power Station at Tarapur at Maharashtra.
- 1969: July 21. Apollo – II landed on the moon with three scientists.
- 1969: DAE – NASA Satellite – I TV experiment.
- 1971: Electronic commission under the presidentship of Dr. Menon.
- 1974: Atomic experiment in the desert of Rajasthan.
- 1975: Combination of two space shuttles Apollo (USA) and Soyuz (USSR) in the sky.
- 1976: Landing of Viking I and II (USA) on the Mars.

Concluding Question

How did the Industrial Revolution give birth to the safety and accident prevention movement?

9

CHAPTER

Home Safety

In home we use many useful things which can cause bodily harm or injury. For example, the kitchen is the place where a number of dangerous objects like knives, forks, cutters, openers, etc. are stored for our daily use. Children also handle many objects with sharp edges in their daily work: pencil sharpeners, penknives, geometry instruments, etc. Be careful how you handle them.

We tend to sharpen pencils with used razor blades. This very often leads to bad cuts that are painful and take long time to heal. Use pencil sharpeners. They are clean and easy to use.

Almost every household has for ready repairs, hammers, chisels, screwdrivers, etc. Handle them carefully, use the right tools for the right job and see that they are put back in their proper places after use.

A lot of cutting and chopping work goes on in the kitchen. These cutting implements should be in the good conditions with firm non-slip grips.

Do not do any cutting or chopping work with wet hands – do not use wet surface either. The knife may slip and harm you.

Never try to cut or slice things holding them with your fingers or in the palm of your hand. You are quite likely to slice of your fingers or palm instead. Put back knives, forks, etc. safely after use.

Never use cracked chipped, glass or enamelware. Both can cause bad cuts that may turn septic.

Never put glassware in a sink full of other utensils.

Do not clear up broken glass pieces with bare hands. Sweep up broken pieces with a broom or a brush into a dustpan, wrap in a newspaper and keep apart from other rubbish for disposal. Do not throw broken glass in rubbish bins. Put your shoes and slippers while cleaning up broken glass.

HOUSE FIRES

What to do in Case of An Emergency?

If there is an ordinary fire (e.g., wood, paper or clothes): Pour water on it to put out the flames. Try to fight it only if it is a small fire.

If oil in frying pan catches fire: Shut off the heat source. Cover the pan with a lid.

Incase of electrical fire: Switch off the mains. Put sand on the fire.

If clothes catch fire: Pour water if available or stop where you are, drop to the ground and roll to put out the flames. Do not run. Running would only increase the flames because fire, as you know, loves air (oxygen).

If you are trapped in a smoke filled room: Get down on all fours and crawl to a safe area. Crawling helps you remain in a relatively smoke-free zone that exists 12" to 24" above ground level. Cover your nose and mouth with wet cloth.

Remember that smoke is even more dangerous than fire. Smoke contains poisonous gases like carbon monoxide. In a fire situation, many people die of suffocation long before the flames actually reach them.

For burns: Pour water till the burning sensation stops. Never apply ghee, butter, oil or any greasy substance. If the burn is serious, consult a doctor. Never apply ointment or any other substance before consulting the doctor.

In case of big fire, call the fire brigade: When you call the fire brigade you must tell the fire officer clearly the exact location of the fire (complete address along with some prominent landmark, in the area), your name and address and wait to answer questions.

If you are trapped in a multistorey building: Use the stairs and not the lift, for going down. Fires do funny things to metal and cables, twisting and warping them out of shape, so elevators often get stuck or tend to go straight to the fire floor.

Fire Safety at Home

Here are some fire prevention pointers for home:

- Keep your home and yard clear of loose flammable debris, including rags, papers and dried leaves. Store all gasoline, kerosene and other flammable liquids in their original containers or in listed or approved containers. Never use these flammable liquids to start a fire in a stove or oven.

- Kitchen appliances should also carry the label, or that of another reputable testing agency. Keep them free of grease and other food build-up. Do not overload your electrical circuits by using multiple attachment plugs.
- Make sure that space heaters and stove are placed well away from drapes, curtains, and furniture. Have the chimney and flue connections checked out by a qualified service person at least once a year.
- Keep the matches away from children.
- Do not allow smoking inside the house.

KITCHEN IS FOR COOKING, NOT FOR FIRES

Follow these safety rules:

- Always cook on the platform and not on the ground.
- Do not leave cooking unattended on the stove. Always turn the stove off when you have to do something else away from the kitchen.
- Heat cooking oil slowly, and watch carefully. A fire can easily start if you keep the burner too high and then leave the pan unattended.
- Turn pan handles in for safety. A pot handle hanging over the edge of your stove can be bumped in passing or grabbed by a child, causing serious burns.
- Unplug electrical appliances such as heater, mixer, toaster etc., when you have finished the work. Do not overload electrical outlets, plugging in too many appliances in one socket may cause a fire. Use only one appliance in one socket.
- Never wear loose clothing while cooking. Loose clothing or flowing sleeves can easily catch fire.
- Never use a cloth piece to remove pans from the stove, always use tongs.
- Do not store, crackers or other items above the cooking stove or in a place which might entice children to climb or reach over the burners.

Every year many fires originate in the kitchen. Generally these fires occur, when burners are set too high and or people are not paying attention to what they are doing. For example, in cities, people sometimes leave the stove unattended to attend or make a phone call, or watch TV or even visit neighbors. This sometimes results in big fires. Do not let this happen to you.

Kitchen Quiz

- Is your stove and sink areas well lit?
- Do you wipe up spills immediately?

- Has your kitchen adequate wiring to carry the heavy load needed to operate electrical appliances such as toasters, waffle irons and grills?
- Do you make sure your hands are dry before operating electrical appliances?
- Are you in the habit of using a step stool or utility ladder when reaching into high cupboards?
- Do you turn pot handles away from the stove front but not over another burner?
- Have you a special rack, compartment or tray for storing sharp knives?
- Do you use pot holders and make sure they are dry?
- Are emergency phone numbers – police, fire, doctor, and utilities – kept handy by your telephone?
- Do you replace cracked or frayed electrical appliance and extension cords?
- Are house hold cleaners, disinfectants and insecticides kept in their original containers and separate from food and out of reach of children?
- Do you know that water should not be poured on a grease fire?
- Do you shield yourself from hot steam when removing covers from hot pans by lifting the far side first?
- Do you avoid wearing loose, flimsy garments around sources of flame?

LPG Safety at Home

When leak is noticed:

- Never panic.
- Do not operate any electrical switches.
- Keep open the shutters.
- Inform the dealer about the leak.
- Ask the persons to be away from the place.

Safe Procedure in Handling LPG

- Open the window shutters before lighting the LPG stove.
- Close the regulator after use.
- Do not have any naked flame near the LPG cylinder.
- Remove the regulator and keep the safety cap while going on long vacation.
- Never tilt or put it into hot water to drain out the LPG.
- Roll the cylinder on its bottom ting for transportation.
- Replace the rubber tube once in a period of 2 years or whenever defects are noticed.
- Keep the phone numbers of the dealer and the emergency services at the correct place.

- Handle the valves and knobs gently.
- Use only quality stoves and rubber tubes.

Handle LPG Carefully and Correctly to Avoid the Serious Consequences

Avoid Kitchen Fires

Make sure all the cooks in your family follow these kitchen precautions:

- Never leave cooking food unattended.
- Do not store combustible items on or over the stovetop.
- Turn pot handles inward or toward the back of the stove, but never over another burner while in use.
- Keep sleeves rolled up or tightly wrapped to avoid dragging them over the heat.
- Never pour water on a grease fire.
- Always keep a pan lid and hot pad close by while you cook. If you have a fire confined to a pan, carefully slide a lid over the pan and then turn off the heat.

Learn how to use a fire extinguisher and store one near the entrance of your kitchen. Also, remember that the safest option to extinguish a kitchen fire may be to escape and call the fire department from neighbors home.

Precautions in Handling LPG Cooking Gas

- Cooking gas or LPG is invariably used in the kitchen of almost every household.
- It is high heating effect and easy to handle, but needs safety measures to avoid accident.
- Always the burner of the stove should be at higher level than the cylinder head.
- While installing cylinder ensure leak proof connection.
- Although LPG is odorless an odorizing agent is added to detect the leaks.
- It yields carbon dioxide during combustion for which adequate ventilation of the room is required.
- While using LPG first open the cylinder valve then light the match sticks and there after open the stove knob allowing gas to flow to light the burner. Match stick is always preferable than a lighter since any time lighter fails to give required spark and allows excess gas to flow thereby warrants explosion, unless extraordinary care is maintained.
- While switching off the stove first turn the cylinder knob off and then close the stove knob by which no gas remains in the connecting tube.
- Rubber connecting tube should regularly be checked and when any sign of deterioration is noticed, should be replaced immediately.

- Cotton saris should be donned while using cooking gas.
- By following the above guidelines occurrence of accidents will be rare. However, despite that if one small leakage it should not get panicked.
- All doors, windows, ventilators in the room should be opened as quick as possible.
- No electrical switches should be touched since a light spark from it will cause explosion.
- The cylinder should be kept upright to avoid liquid leakage.
- If the cylinder is already on fire try to cool the top of the cylinder by water spray if possible shot-down the cylinder valve.

Learn Not to Burn, Cultivate Fire Safety Awareness

- If the cylinder valve is damaged and there is no possibility to shut down the leakages the gas should be allowed to burn and continuing the cooling of the cylinder.
- If possible, the cylinder shifted to open space and assistance of fire service sought for.

Electricity at Home

Electricity is a wonderful servant in the house and the numbers of electrical accidents are very small considering its widespread use. Unfortunately however, an electric shock can very easily be fatal. There is a lot you can do to help prevent electrical accidents.

Modern electrical installations and appliances are controlled by regulations and the safety standards applied by electricity authorities. But old or badly maintained flexible cords and appliances can be dangerous, as can any "do-it-yourself" wiring or repairs.

Electrical repairs are for the electrician, not for the home handy person. Each year wrongly wired extension cords; house wiring and appliances kill several "do-it-yourself" and their family members.

You need to inspect plugs, cords and appliances to see if they are in good condition and make arrangement for all necessary repairs immediately. If you feel a tingle or electric shock from an appliance, immediately switch off the power and remove the plug. Have it checked out by an electrician before using it again.

An earth leakage circuit breaker can be installed at a moderate cost to protect against electrocution.

Microwave Safety

If you are one of the microwave oven users, you may want to make sure you operate your machine safely. Microwave-oven users to exercise the following precautions:

- **Avoid Burns:** Use potholders to remove containers from your microwave oven. Burns are the most common microwave-oven accidents. The problem is that people fail to realize that even though the air inside the oven does not get hot, the food gets hot and that temperature will conduct to the cooking dish. Burns can result from escaping steam. Remove the lid or plastic wrap away from your face to avoid contact with steam.

- **Use Aluminium Foil Properly:** Flat pieces of aluminum foil can be used to cover drumsticks and other areas that defrost or cook too quickly. However, do not cover containers with foil and do not use crumple foil, because you can trap the microwaves and cause arcing, which could lead to a fire.
- **Supervise Children:** If you allow or encourage your children to use the microwave oven, you should supervise them at least until there is no doubt that they clearly understand how to use a microwave oven.
- **Beware of Chemical Migration:** Do not let plastic wrap touch the food.
- **Prevent Food Explosions:** Pierce the skin of unpeeled potatoes, sausages, frankfurters and similar foods to allow steam to escape.
- **Follow Instructions:** Severely overcooked food can catch fire. Make sure you follow cookbook or manual directions for appropriate cooking times.
- **Keep Your Oven Clean:** Arcing can occur when food residue is in the oven. If food is left in the oven, microwaves are going to cook that food, too.
- **Watch Baby Bottles:** Remember to only use glass bottles and to avoid any bottles with plastic liners or holders.
- **Take Care with Meat and Poultry:** Make sure meat, poultry and fish are cooked thoroughly to avoid salmonella and other types of bacteria.
- **Use Microwave** – Safe utensils.
- Address the damage immediately.

Cell Phone Alert

Mobile phones the symbol of communication revolution, are immensely useful and extensively used. All is well when every thing goes right. But careless usage may cost one dearly.

Take the case of Mr. C. Pondyselvaru: The 33 year old Textile company owner was admitted to a private hospital here with partial loss of hearing in the right ear and damage to his taste nerves.

Reason: His mobile phone was suddenly on fire even as he was speaking-when the phone was on charging mode.

Mr. Pondyselvaru was at his factory at Pethappampatty near Udumalpet.

Around 4 P.M. workers were piloting a huge lorry that carried parts of a wind turbine. Clearing the electrical cables with lengthy poles they made way for the vehicle. Suddenly two wires crossed and high voltage electricity shot through the near by areas. Three workers felt the heat.

Loses Consciousness

"Immediately lost consciousness and developed fits – like condition. When regained consciousness, I felt unbearable pain in the ear. Slowly I realized that I had burns in my right ear. My hearing has been affected and I can not feel taste on the right part of the tongue." Mr. Pondyselvaru said.

V. Anand who is treating him said the partial burns on the pine were due to the excess energy radiated by the mobile. "If the fits lasted more than five minutes it would have cost his life. There is a possibility that the right side of his face may lose mobility. Our treatment is to prevent it."

If the hearing does not improve he should undergo a minor surgery to apply medicine in the inner ear. "In that case, I feel it is necessary." the ENT surgeon said.

Irony of the story: the mobile phone is still working.

Asked whether he spoke over his mobile after the incident, Mr. Pondyselvaru nodded with a wry smile. But this time the phone was not on the charging mode.

Child 'CO' Poisonings Rise

Carbon monoxide poisoning to children less than 5 years of age have increased sharply over the last decade, says the American Academy of Pediatrics.

Dr. Regina Aronow, director of the poison center at the children's hospital of Michigan in Detroit, says that because of economic hard times, many families have put off repairs to furnaces and cars. As a result, gas leaks are not being detected and children are being slowly poisoned. Children are more readily affected by carbon monoxide because their brain tissues are still developing. Dr. Aronow says.

Some families are using unvested space heaters in tight, insulated homes with closed windows to save heating costs. This combination depletes the oxygen in a home while producing carbon monoxide, Dr. Aronow says.

Children who are being slowly poisoned have symptoms often mistaken for flue; intestinal disorders, headaches and lack of energy.

To avoid poisonings, Dr. Aronow says space heaters should always be vented to the outside, ovens and gas ranges should not be used for heat, and a window should be opened slightly when a car's heating system is used.

Child TV Addicts Think Less

Is your child glued to the idiot box? Remember that excess TV viewing is responsible for loss of eyesight, disinterest in schoolwork, decreasing creativity and reduced thinking abilities in children.

A national survey conducted by the Media Research Group on behalf of the UNICEF has also brought to the fore that a majority of them also ascribe rising crime, rape, murder and unsociability to the TV culture.

41% of children interviewed agree that due to watching violence and crime-related programs, their friend's behaviour are turned aggressive and violent.

Only 17% of children disagreed. 53% of parents and 62.6% of teachers agree that it has increased vulgarity and obscenity in society.

An equal number of parents and teachers suggested that it had increased crime in society and that the glamour shown had also had its ill effects.

About 38.5% of parents suggested that their children had picked up abusive language to which 49.6% teachers and 39.1% of children agree as against those who disagreed for these categories, i.e., 10.4%, 26.7% and 20.8% respectively.

The general view was that feature films and film-based programs and western culture based programs especially MTV and V channels could be one reason. The respective percentages for those who thought that it caused irritability among children when they were watching TV and were asked to do other work was a high 65.1%, 67.7% and 51.9% for children.

The survey also pointed out that heavy viewers were sleeping less, i.e., 480 minutes and spending on an average of 14% of their waking time before the TV.

Of more concern is the finding that TV is also causing health-related problems with 68.9% parents and 82.8% of teachers vouching for it.

They co-related it with the growing number of children using spectacles these days.

'Common' Cold can Become Serious

The enterprising scientist, doctor or chemist who develops (1) a vaccine to prevent the so-called common cold, or (2) a medicine which kill the virus when it first manifest itself, would undoubtedly earn the undying gratitude of millions of cold sufferers around the world and an equal number of employers losing money through absenteeism.

However in the absence of any panacea, cold sufferers should be encouraged to take whatever treatment is recommended immediately. Cold can lead to a multitude of more serious illness. Tonsillitis, sinusitis, and laryngitis, while non-fatal, can be responsible for the need for several days' bed rest. More serious – and possibly life threatening – are pneumonia, emphysema, tuberculosis and, in young people particularly, whooping cough.

The cold virus attacks when the body's defenses are down, caused by exposure to a draught, chilly or damped weather, or sudden immersion in cold water. The old adage of "three days coming, three days here, three days going" appears to be fairly valid, despite the application of modern over the counter remedies, which for the most part, only diminish the symptoms of runny nose, cough or sneeze; they do not cure the causes.

The average cold sufferer should go to bed at the outset for two reasons: one, the body's defenses can work best when no other energy is being expended, and two, by isolating the sufferer in his own bed, the risk of infecting other is reduced.

Old Medicines

Too many home medicine cabinets are cluttered with old bottles of prescription medicines and tablets, which should be discarded. It is false economy to save old medicines, because medicines, like food can get stale and lose their potency and even become dangerous.

Any medication with a lost or illegible label should be promptly disposed of. Never trust your memory to recall with accuracy what those strange little pills in the brown bottle are; you might be tragically wrong.

Never place half-empty bottles of medicine in the kitchen tidy or in the rubbish bin. A curious toddler may find them and drink the contents by mistake.

When disposing of old drugs and medicines or any other poisonous substances, flush the contents down the toilet (not if a septic tank system). Rinse the container with water, then dispose of it correctly.

Unused medicines and tablets may be taken to a pharmacist for disposal. Ideally you should discard the "deadwood" from your medicine cabinet once in a month. After the cleanup, put the remaining items – properly labeled and marked with a "poison" sticker – out of reach of children, locked up if possible. If you keep toiletries in the medicine cabinet, they should be kept distinctly separated from medicines. (Too many cases have been reported of people mistaking hair tonic, for cough medicine in the dark.)

Finally, be prepared for the time when that one mistake might happen:

Get a poison antidote chart and paste in on the inside of the medicine chest door.

In the event of a poisoning accident telephone your doctor, or local hospital, or poisons information center. Give all details and they will advise what action to take.

Put Poison in its Place

Properly store household cleaning products and chemicals to keep yourself and your family safe from accidental poisonings.

As a general rule, keep hazardous products in their original containers. Always use safety latches or combination locks to keep children out of cabinets and drawers. And do not let children watch you open them; they learn quickly. Remember children are likely to taste almost anything. So, keep the phone number of your local poison-control center, family doctor and hospital emergency room posted near your telephone.

Handle even everyday cleaning products safely to minimize the risk of accidental poisoning. Here are some precautions to follow:

- Choose products packaged in child-resistant containers.

- Store cleansing products in cabinets out of a child's reach; secure cabinets with a lock or child-resistant latch.
- Do not turn your back on a child while household cleaning products are in use or accessible.
- Always read and follow any label instructions before you use household cleaners.

Take strict precautions when handling such common household chemicals as automotive products (waxes or engine fluids), petroleum products (benzene, kerosene and light fluids), paints and varnishes, paint thinner, charcoal starter, glues, rodent and insect poison, pesticides and herbicides, and lie.

- Store these products in their original, labeled containers in a locked cabinet.
- Use these products only in well-ventilated areas.
- Discard containers carefully; call your local public health or sanitation department for advises on safe disposal. Store these containers off the ground, away from children and pets, until they are collected.

Precautions while Using Pesticides

- Never use any pesticide to alkali solutions for simultaneous control of diseases and insects. In this solution the property of insecticides diminishes.
- Never use insecticides like DDT, BHC, Gamaxine or Linden in the Cucurbit plants like Cucumber, Pumpkin, and Ridge Gourd as these chemicals damage the leaf surface of these categories of plants.
- Never use Gamaxine in the soil for control of termites in tuberous crops like potato, sweet potato etc. as it leaves toxin substances in the fruit it self. It is better to use Aldrin dust instead of Gamaxine.
- Never use the insecticides like Folidol dust, TEPP, Dimeton, Trithion, Mevin phos in the kitchen garden of the quarter. The grasses emitted from these chemicals are harmful for the inhabitants.
- Never use the insecticides like DDT, Aldrinchlordane, and Dieldrin like chemicals over the plants in fruiting stage.
- Synthetic granular insecticides like Thimet should be used at least 6 weeks before harvesting of the crop as the insensity of the poison remains up to three weeks of application of insecticides.
- When the plants are spread with pesticides like Malathion, Carbaryl, Endosulfan, Endrine then the fruit should be plucked at least after 3, 7, 5, 21 days respectively after spraying. The toxicity of these chemicals remains for these specified periods.
- Never use the pesticides having sulphur content in scorching sun.

Categories of Toxic Pesticides

Sl. No.	Category of insecticides	Color of identification band on the label	Symbol and warning on upper portion of square
1.	Extremely toxic	Bright red	Skull and cross bones and the word **Poison** printed in red
2.	Highly toxic	Bright yellow	Word **Poison** printed in red
3.	Moderately toxic	Bright blue	Word **Danger**
4.	Slightly toxic	Bright green	Word **Caution**

Super Toys for Each Age Group

Choose toys appropriate for the age and development of the child. Look before buying or even accepting toys as gifts for your children.

Check for the following hazards:

- Small loose parts smaller than a ping pong ball that could choke a child under the age of three years.
- Pointed, sharp parts that could cut or pierce.
- Toxic paint or chemicals that could poison.
- Flammable materials that could burn.
- Electric currents that could electrocute.
- Projectiles that could be fired.
- Labels that indicate they are not suitable for the age of the child.

Use Medicines with Care

All of us take medicines when we fall sick. Misuse of medicines can cause damage to your body. When you fall sick, always keep in mind the following guidelines:

- If you fall sick, do not take any medicine on your own; consult a doctor. Do not take medicines prescribed for someone else who is suffering from the same type of disease.
- Inform your doctor of any other medicines you may be taking because some medicines, when taken together can be harmful. Always ask your doctor for possible side effects, if any.
- Buy medicines from a reputed chemist only. Insist on a bill even if you are buying a simple headache tablet. Examine the medicines thoroughly, paying special attention to the seal and expiry date.

- Carefully check the name of the medicine you buy. At times spurious drugs are available in the market with similar sounding names.
- Medicines with almost similar names can be for totally different diseases. Check carefully that you are buying what the doctor prescribed.
- If a particular medicine prescribed by your doctor is not available, do not purchase an alternative medicine on the advice of the chemist; consult your doctor.
- After opening the bottle if you find any disorder, do not use the medicine, report it to the manufacturer.
- At night always switch on the light when you give/take medicines.
- Never take medicines on an empty stomach, unless otherwise advised by doctor.
- Do not transfer medicines to unmarked bottles, keep it in original container.
- Store medicines out of reach of children.
- Take full course of medicines as prescribed by the doctor.

Use your Television Set Safely

- Study carefully the manufacturer's operating instructions and safety precautions provided in the T.V. manual. Learn how to use the set properly and explain it to all members of your family.
- Do not cover the ventilation openings in a T.V. set with cloth, papers, or by placing it against a wall or piece of furniture or any other thing. This can cause heat to build up inside the T.V. set and create a fire hazard.
- Never leave a T.V. set on, when you are going out of the room for more than a very short period of time, especially those T.V. sets that have the "instant on" picture tube feature. The set may start or even catch fire.
- Always leave sufficient space between the T.V. set and the wall.
- Do not keep plants, glasses of water, or other liquids, on the cabinet of the T.V. sets. Liquid may spill and cause fire or electrical shock.
- Always keep the T.V. set on a stable base-one appropriate for its size and weight.
- Do not turn a T.V. set on and off from the wall switch ; make use of the T.V. switch instead.
- Caution your children never to insert any object into the openings of the T.V. set. This could lead to a fire or shock hazard.
- Never try to repair the T.V. set yourself; call the authorized representative of the manufacturers.

Going on Vacation, Check Your House

When you go out on vacation, your mind is plagued with worries whether everything is safe at home. Sensing the house is empty, thieves become active. Take a few precautions and have a holiday without hassles. Here are some guidelines:

- Stop newspaper delivery before you leave. Piled up newspapers outside is a sure sign for a thief that you are not at home.
- Never discuss your itinerary with others in public.
- Leave a key with a trusted friend/neighbor/relative who can contact you in an emergency. Leave your telephone number and address with your trusted ones.
- Remove all food items from the refrigerator/shelves; clean up at spilt food particles, which might attract pests. Clean the fridge thoroughly, dry it and unplug it.
- Make sure that all electrical appliances are unplugged. Disconnect the antenna/cable connection from your T.V. set. Switch off the mains.
- Lock all grills, windows and doors.
- If you use LPG, disconnect the gas supply.
- If you are not taking out your car, leave it in a locked garage. Either disconnect the battery or request your neighbor to start it periodically.
- Install a mailbox outside your house so that the postman can put your mail in it.
- Ensure that all the water taps are properly closed.
- Keep all costly items like jewelry in the bank locker.
- If you are going out on a trip by car, take your family, but do not take the entire home with you. Travel light with the barest essentials. An unnecessary heavy load can make the vehicle unstable and prone to rolling over; luggage may also obstruct your vision and hinder safe driving.
- Put out diyas and aggarbattis when you are step out of the house.
- Finally, before you get out of the house check your house once again, to see every thing is safe.

The Role of Housewives in Building a Safe Culture

Safety is a major concern not only for the industries, government, media and the public but to the house wives as well. Individual house is the unitary point of the society. So long improvement of safety in house front has not taken place it is difficult to develop safety culture as a whole. Here lies the importance of house wives for the development of safety culture. Reacting after happening of an accident is not a good culture. In the matter of safety prevention is always better than cure. It is to be remembered that accidents are always caused. The investigation reveals that causes are careless action. Attitudinal change is an important activity for the development of safety culture. It is suggested that safe habits to be inculcated at young age at home itself.

Children are innocent and easy believing. They do not know the danger posed by various items and situations. Hence, they need protection and guidance in all their activities during their formative years so as to avoid any major accidents that may leave a mark for the whole life.

Presenting toys is an extension of parents love to the children. Before buying the toys the house wives should give a thought as to the types to buy so that the toys are safe also. Items to guard against such as sharp edges and corners, small pieces, screws that comes loose, rust prone materials, etc. types of toys to be avoided such as bows and arrows, guns that shoot anything, match boxes, toys made of flammable materials, those containing paints, etc.

Old people in the house need special care by the house wives due to their poor vision, hearing, sense of smell, physical strength, etc.

Electricity is a good servant but bad master. The house wives must give emphasis on using good quality three-core wires, fixtures etc.

House wives spend maximum hours in the kitchen. For several hours each day fire is used in the kitchen for heating and cooking. Further, inflammables such as gas, kerosene, matchboxes, cooking oil etc. are stored there. Then there are sharp knives that can hurt, boiling water or hot eatables that can scald a person, and water spills or fruit spills on which a person can slip.

A household contains a large variety of items. It has chemicals like cleaning agents, detergents, kerosene, cooking gas etc. Oils such as cooking oil, butter, hair oil etc. sharp items such as knives, needles, razor, scissors etc. tools like screw drivers, hammer, electric tools etc. appliances such as oven, refrigerator, mixie etc. entertainment items like T.V., VCR, games, toys etc. dry areas, wet areas (bathroom), stair cases, garage and garden tools, etc. It may have pets. Then there are children and adults of different ages and visiting guests. With such a large variety of things, accidents are bound to happen and here lies the challenge to house wives how they can maintain full safety in the house.

Many households have cats and or dogs as pets. Pets are just like infants. They can bite the children or others, so all safety precautionary measures have to be taken by house wives if pets are kept.

Though medicines are essential now a days but it should always be kept away from children's reach. Many serious accidents have been occurred due to this.

The air within homes can sometimes be more polluted than the out side. The house wives, the old, the children and the sick people spend more of their time indoors and are more susceptible to indoor air pollution. Hence the wives must use agarbattis, mosquito coils etc. very judiciously.

A lawn or kitchen garden gives the body some exercise, and contributes towards the ecological balance too. Like any other hobby, gardening also requires one to take precautions because of sharp tools and chemicals involved as fertilizers and pesticides. The house wives must know the handling methods of gardening tools like lawn mowers, edge trimmer's etc. Avoidance of loose clothes while using such tools, application of insecticides, etc. must be known to them for safety.

Everybody enjoys swimming, kite flying and takes pleasure in organizing picnics; specifically children's enjoy those most. But in all these activities special care must be taken to see that everything is done in a safe manner to avoid any unwanted happening.

Road safety is an important area wherein house wives can play an important role. They can pressurize to their children, husband, brother, friend, etc. for the use of crash helmets while driving two wheelers, because by not using a crash helmets so many untimely deaths are occurring every day.

No body knows when a natural disaster can strike. However, by proper planning and training by house wives the loss of lives and property can be reduced.

Safety is the act of remaining safe. This is an attitude. Towards development of safe attitude house wives have major roles to play. We all know that accidents are unplanned and unwanted happenings. Hence, planned actions should be initiated in all activities which at the long run can lead to a safe culture. Building of accident free families, accident free societies, accident free Nation and accident free Industry is possible and has already been said it is to be done initially by house wives. They can very well help in building a safe culture.

Make Home Safe

Home safety is largely a responsibility of house occupants and their perception of individual needs. Everyone has different attitudes, ideas, and interests and engages in different activities in and around the home.

So much depends on the leadership and example given by responsible adults who, after all, do tend to relax a little when they are at home. Certainly if parents adopt a careless approach to protecting and training their family this will have an adverse effect upon their children.

On the other hand, even with the best of guidance, accident still happens. So adopting an awareness of hazards and a positive approach to prevention can save lots of injuries and even fatalities.

The statistics for fatalities resulting from accidents at home show that falls are by far the greatest single factor. The most vulnerable age groups are adults over 65 years of age and children under the age of five years.

Falls can be prevented in most cases by a little attention to floor surfacing, lighting, worn mats and carpets and clear walkways, steps and stairs should have handrails.

It can be said that in general a tidy home is a safe home – and a safe home is a happy home.

Grip rails or handles in the shower, bath and toilet will help elderly people. Garden paths and drive way should always be free of obstacles like children's play things, hoses and work materials.

10

CHAPTER

Importance of Industrial Safety

INTRODUCTION

The importance of industrial safety was realized because every year millions of industrial accidents occur which result in either death or temporary or permanent disablement.

Safety is the state of being 'safe'.

S	Spot the hazard	Stop
A	Asses the risk	Accident
F	Find the safer way	For
E	Every year	Ever

So, safety is the state of being certain that adverse affect will not be caused by some agents under defined conditions.

'Safety' denotes continuing and healthful living without injury. Safety is freedom from harm. Life and health are most precious. The word safety also refers to the precautions people take to prevent accidents, harm, danger, damage, loss and air/water/environment pollution. Safety also deals with improvements in working conditions for better health.

Safety is important to everyone and at every stage of activities and at all times 'safety first'.

Safety is necessary everywhere and at all times, in homes, or at roads, in offices, public places, while travelling, in working in industry.

Industry has more hazardous situations and activities than home or an office. Many persons work as a team in an industry and safety is of interest to every individual, group of individuals and the total organization. Every individual in the society and an industrial organization has obligation to organize and establish safety disciplines. Safety management is an essential and important part of industrial management.

Management is responsible to provide safe working condition and individuals' safety. Lapse on the part of management and individuals may result in an accident or disaster.

Safety management is an essential and mandatory function of industrial management. Accident and unhealthy situations in industry must be prevented by appropriate actions by management in advance. Safety should be the way of life and work.

SAFETY INTERFACES

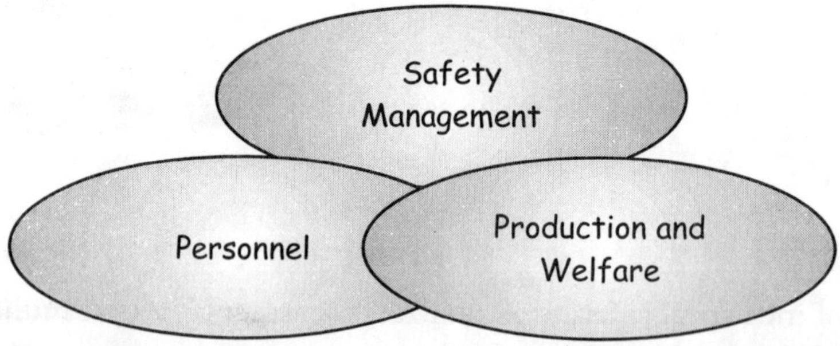

Several thousand lives are lost and properties are destroyed due to accidents and fires. A casual glance at industrial workplaces reveals the lack of essential safety measures and casual approach to safety by management and workers. Such happenings can be prevented by implementing safety management techniques at every stage.

Industrial accidents are leading cause of death throughout the world and in India. Vast money are incurred in medical expenses and lost income by accidents.

Safety management and safety precautions are necessary at every stage, right from design, manufacture of equipment, testing, dispatch, site construction work, operation and maintenance of industrial plants/equipments.

Mother and parents protect the child, supervise and train the child till it grows up safely. Same applies to management of industrial safety.

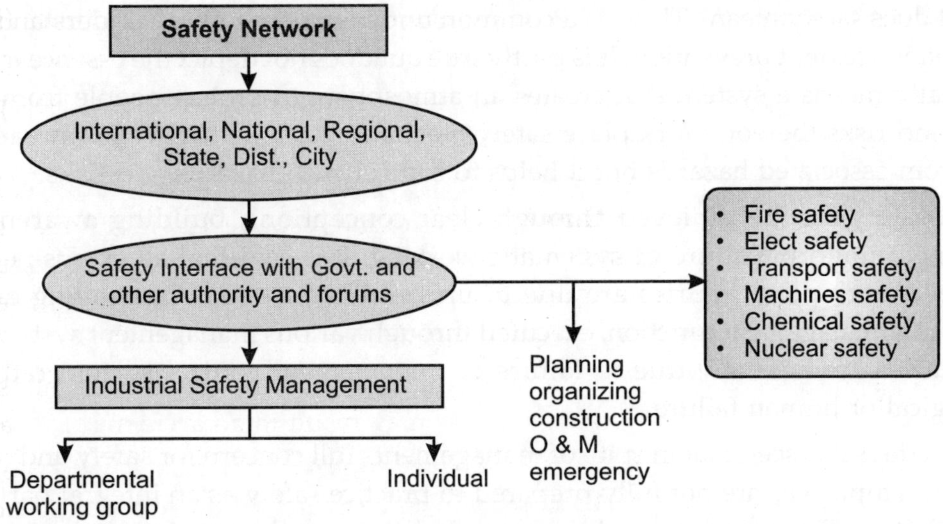

Industrial safety is the science and art of identifying, evaluating and controlling workplace hazards. It includes measures to prevent human exposures to chemical and physical agents as well as faulty or unsafe work practices. It is connected with the safety of people's life and property as well as the general situation of development and stability. Safety is not a matter of chance; it is something that the employees and their families have a right to expect from their employers.

Industrial safety is mainly concerned with minimizing hazards. Hazard is a state of physical or chemical having the potential to injure the person. Any method or technique or process which can minimize unwanted events in an industrial concern may be referred to as a method, technique or process of industrial safety.

Industrial work is full of hazards. It is necessary to take precautions with a view to ensure safety of the plants, machinery and the human beings.

Most industrial operations are safe if they are performed in a right way without clumsiness or awkwardness. There are correct and efficient methods of doing things which must be so well mastered that there is no chance for bodily movements, which can unsafe. The inexperienced workers are most likely to be involved in accidents. They make unsafe movements because of their work habits. If the employees are not taught the right ways of performing their operations, they may acquire some unsafe habits which would expose them to accidents. It is in this sense that right type of training acquires a great importance in accident prevention. If good working habits are integrated in the workers at the time of their training, they become an inseparable part of their behaviour, and they observe the necessary safety precautions without repeated warnings. It is necessary, therefore, to place enough emphasis on safety training, when entrants in the organization are trained in their respective trades.

Work place safety is an essential pre-requisite for the industries to remain fit, productive and competitive. Only a safe and healthy work place can achieve the desired goal.

What does safety mean? There is a common under standing or misunderstanding that safety means accident prevention. It is partly true but does not depict the essence in totality. Safety really means a system that creates an atmosphere to protect people from various hazards and risks thereof. Work place safety means a system, which not only safeguards people from associated hazards but it helps to control such hazards and risks.

Total safety can be achieved through clear conceptions, building awareness and developing a uniform culture of systematic working. It is said that all events need to be controlled. Work place injuries are due to uncontrolled events. Controlling events or activities is a management function, executed through various management systems. Work place injuries are basically due to failure of management control system rather than technological or human failure.

Now a days it is seen that in spite of managements full concern for safety and statutory provisions, employees are not fully prepared to practice safety as an integral part in their work activities. Researches have been revealed that employee motivation is primary requirement in achieving the safety and health goals in the industry.

Everything people do originate from their attitude. Behaviour is the window of attitude. Behaviour can be observed/measured and therefore amended. It is established that more than 85% of accidents do happen due to unsafe behaviour of human beings and about 155 due to unsafe condition at work place. In spite of all these information unsafe conditions are always present in the work place and people are allowed to behave (work) unsafe. The following points may help us to understand the reality.

- Most accidents occur when things look all right.
- Some occur due to unsafe working condition.
- Many a time accidents are not linked with specific hazards.
- Frequency/severity largely depends on luck.
- Near miss/fatality differ in millimeter/mille-seconds.
- At-risk behaviour is a warning for accident.
- Accident can be avoided by personal care.
- Telling people to take care does not always work.
- Progress through legislation is difficult.
- Behaviour influences accident potential.

Basic components that help us in imparting our safety performance are:

- Working place environment, i.e., means of access, physical conditions, house keeping and safe place of work etc.
- Training and competence building.
- Motivational and behavioural influences.

Why People Behave Unsafe?

Basically behaviour is a function of two elements – activators and consequences. There are many factors that activate our behaviour. Due to these activators the same man is seen to behave in different manners at different point of time. So activators are inputs. Once we behave, in any way, it has its consequences too. Consequences are the outputs. Consequences may either be in our favor (positive) or may go against (negative). The positive consequences encourage repetition of similar behaviour while the negative consequences discourage such repetitions.

Activator ⟶ Positive ⟶ Encourage Repetitive Behaviour
Activator ⟶ Negative ⟶ Discourage Repetitive Behaviour

Basically there are two types of activators:

- Management expectation and behaviours are the most powerful activators.
- Personal activators, related to personal needs. Personal activators may often go beyond other activators.
  - Basic need related to food, shelter etc. reflect the need to remain employed.
  - Esteem needs are for self worth and recognition.

All these activators together decide the way we behave whether at house or at work place.

There is a natural reward for every behaviour – even for unsafe behaviour. Those natural rewards are comfort, convenience and expediency. Let us now compare the two aspects, i.e., natural reward for unsafe behaviour vs. negative consequences for unsafe behaviour.

Unsafe behaviour, although it carries risk of accident/untoward incident, its short term benefits are generally positive (in favor), certain (without fail) and immediately available. On the other hand, negative consequences of unsafe behaviour are of course negative, uncertain it's a matter of probability and considered as an after effect, i.e., in future terms. Positive, certain and immediate consequence have more influence than negative, uncertain and future.

Unsafe Behaviour

Natural Reward	Negative Consequence
• Reward is positive • Reward is certain • Reward is immediate	• Consequence is negative • Consequence is uncertain • Consequence is for future

Therefore, unless otherwise controlled by the three E's, i.e., Engineering, Education, and Enforcement, people may often be tempted to behave unsafe (taking unnecessary risks) for it's positive, certain and immediate rewards.

To change behaviour, therefore, is a complicated task. We have only two options:

1. Intervene at activator stage or
2. Intervene at consequence stage.

By imparting training and education it is possible to intervene at the consequence stage which can ultimately promote safe behaviour. After all human being is human being only: telling people do not work always. It is essential therefore that monitoring of task of workers should be done in each step to ensure safety.

It is possible to intervene in the consequence stage by two ways. The first is increasing positive consequences of safe behaviour by giving rewards and the second is increasing negative consequences of unsafe behaviour by imposing penalties etc. however, it is to be remembered that negative consequences rely on enforcement and lead to negative attitude. Positive consequences lead to self-ownership. Also, positive reinforcement or recognition is most convenient, inexpensive, and readily available and at the same time most powerful motivator.

Some important guidelines to exercise the positive reinforcement are given below:

- Be sincere and genuine
- Make it timely.
- Apply on an individual basis.
- Explain need for safe behaviour.
- Give personal praise and thanks.
- Pay attention to suggestions/actions.

At the same time we must remember that:

- It takes time to change habits. Changing culture takes much longer time.
- Individual recognition to follow group recognition.
- Application of positive reinforcement to be facilitated.

INCULCATING THE SAFETY CULTURE

Safety culture at the shop floor is the need of the hour. The question then arises that what should be done in this regard? The correct way is to review the present safety practices for the deficiencies in management system, process system and finally the compliance system. Written safety policy is to be formulated and the top executive force should see that these policies are implemented. Shop floor managers should render all help in creating safe working conditions for the employment. Finally, the workforce should review their habits and amend them if required.

12 – Safety Habits for Development of Safety Culture

1. He is cautious.
2. He is safety minded
3. He ensures safety.
4. He is vigilant.
5. He loves cleanliness.
6. He has sportsmanship.
7. He is loyal.
8. He is time conscious.
9. He is reliable.
10. He is a leader.
11. He believes in continuous learning.
12. He is stick to the safety principles.

Cultivating a safety culture within an organization is vitally important to the long term success of the organization. It can literally mean the difference between life and death. Creating and nurturing a culture of safety ingrains safety into every aspect of the organization. In creating this culture, safety became second nature of every member of the organization at every level involving and empowering every one toward accomplishment of the organizations goal and mission with the best possible risk to benefit ratio. The organization that cultivates a positive safety culture will reap huge benefits such as greater mission accomplishment rates, lower personal injury related costs, lower equipment damage costs, increasing morale, increased productivity, increased ability to accomplish a greater range of mission or tasks and increased overall health of the organization.

The culture of an organization consists of the characteristics, beliefs, feelings, attitudes, and accepted norms for behaviour of the numbers of the organization. Some key points to mind about safety culture are:

- Everyone in the organization maintaining a good, safety focused attitude.
- Safety must be the highest priority for everyone in the organization from top management to the bottom most employee.
- Safety must be considered as the core value by the organization.
- Safety must not be a stagnant affair; it must be continually assessed and changed as per the new demands of the organization.

The key elements that have been proven well to work safely are:

Setting up of the standards: Management must set the standard they want to become and accordingly the norms of behaviour for all categories of employees in the organization.

It means much more to be done than lip service to safety. They must demonstrate the behaviour by examples.

Sound safety program: This means all regulatory safety programs are fully developed and established. Everything including mishap reporting and investigation, employee training, policies, procedures, use and procurement of personal protective equipments, hazard reporting and an investigation system etc. must be established.

A learning organization: The organization must be focused on learning. It must see every new challenge, failure, short comings or mistake as an opportunity to learn. This includes determining the root causes of every mishap no matter how minor to fully understand and act on the lessons learnt. The organization must analyze and apply this information to everyday operations and share the lessons with other organizations.

Recognition: Recognition for promoting safety should be given freely on the spot. On the spot awards – even a handshake and thanks from a supervisor – will go a long way in promoting the culture of safety within the organization. Also, the recognition and the reason and reason for recognition should be made public.

Punish as a last resort: Punishment is also necessary for long term success of promoting a good safety culture but it should always be used as a last resort.

Building a safety culture in any organization does not happen overnight. At the root of a safety culture is behaviour, and changing human behaviour requires education. To develop a safety culture, organizations should integrate their written safety and health programs into daily operating procedure that influence employee behaviour. By focusing on unsafe behaviours, an organization may be able to generate an immediate and tangible reduction in accident frequency and severity. The organization must adopt proactive and not the reactive approach towards safety. It is therefore important not only to identify the cause of accident but to change the behaviours that generate the accident.

11 CHAPTER

Personal Protective Equipment (PPE)

BODY PPE MUST PROTECT

There is nothing stylish about personal protective clothing. It must do the job: guard against hazards and be comfortable to wear.

But how do you select what works best against specific hazards?

Many hazards can threaten the worker's body. These include:

- Heat
- Splashes from hot metals and liquids
- Impacts
- Acids and other corrosive materials
- Radiation
- Sparks
- Toxic dusts
- Vapors and gases.

A variety of protective clothing currently available include:

- Aprons, bibs, leggings, vests, sleeves, capes, coats and cover alls for partial or full-body protection.

- Full body suits to protect against extremely hazardous or corrosive chemicals or to prevent contamination from being spread.
- High visibility and night hazard clothing to protect against traffic hazards.
- Lead line clothing to protect against X-rays and gamma radiation.
- Thermal and quilted clothing for low-temperature work.
- Heat-reflective or other specialized clothing for work in a hot environment.

OSHA says wool and specially treated cotton is natural fibers that are fire-resistant and comfortable, since they adapt well to changing work place temperatures. Duck, a closely woven cotton fabric is good for light-duty protective clothing. It can protect against cuts and bruises on jobs where employees handle heavy, sharp and rough material.

Heat-resistant material, such as leather, often is used in protective clothing to guard against dry heat and flame. Rubber and rubberized fabrics, neoprene, and plastics give protection against some acids and chemicals. If the substance is extremely toxic, a completely enclosed chemical suit may be necessary, OSHA (Occupational Safety and Health Administrator) says.

PPE MANAGEMENT

Industrial hygienists recognize that engineering, work practice, and administrative controls are the primary means of reducing employee exposure to occupational hazards.

Engineering controls minimize employee exposure by either reducing or removing the hazard at the source of isolating the worker from the hazard. Engineering controls include eliminating toxic chemicals and substituting non-toxic chemicals, enclosing work processes or confining work operations, and the installation of general and local ventilation systems.

Work practice controls alter the manner in which a task is performed. Some fundamental and easily implemented work practice controls include:

- Changing existing work practices to follow a proper procedure that minimizes exposure while operating production and control equipment.
- Inspecting and maintaining process and control equipment on regular basis.
- Implementing good house keeping procedures.
- Providing good supervision.
- Mandating that eating, drinking, smoking, chewing tobacco or gum, and applying cosmetics in regulated areas to be prohibited.

Administrative controls includes controlling employee's exposure by scheduling production and tasks, or both, in ways that minimizes exposure levels. For example, the employee might schedule operations with the highest exposure potential during periods when the fewest employees are present.

However, when effective work practices or engineering controls are not feasible or while such controls are being instructed, appropriate personal protective equipment (PPE) must be used. Examples of PPEs are gloves, safety goggles, helmets, safety shoes, protective clothing, and respirators.

To be effective PPEs must be individually selected, properly fitted and periodically refitted, conscientiously and properly worn, regularly maintained and replaced, as necessary, the PPE committee has provision for followings:

- Identifying new PPE for usage.
- Raising request for PPE.
- Approval of the request.
- Check availability status.
- Check condition of PPE.

STEPS INVOLVED IN THE SELECTION OF PPE

Once the need for PPE has been established, the next task is to select the proper type. Two criteria need to be determined:

- The degree of protection required.
- The appropriateness of the equipment to the situation (including the practicality of its being used and kept in good repair).

The degree of protection and the design of PPE must be integrated because both affect its overall efficiency, wear ability, and acceptance.

The following are guidelines for selection:

- Match PPE to the hazard
- Obtain advice
- Involve workers in evaluation
- Consider physical comfort of PPE (ergonomics)
- Evaluate cost considerations
- Review standards
- Conduct training
- Obtain support from all departments
- Audit the program.

PROMOTING 'PPE' PROGRAM

The overall goal of a safer workplace is supported by a careful promotional strategy. This strategy focuses on:

- Commitment by management and workers to the program and a sense of responsibility for it.
- The reasons for the program.
- How the program will work.

The success of the PPE program depends upon winning the cooperation and support of all those concerned. This can best be achieved by helping workers understand the need to wear the PPE, and by encouraging them to want to wear it rather than demanding that they do so.

PPE programs are often plagued by the belief that once a piece of equipment is put on, the worker is totally protected. This is a false sense of security. Basic safety principles, such as house keeping and environmental controls, must not be ignored.

Since the goal of an occupational health and safety program is to prevent occupational injury and illness, PPE can not be the first protection option. The use of PPE does not prevent an accident from happening. It does not eliminate the hazard. It only minimizes the exposure or reduces the severity of injury or illness. In practice, PPE is only to be used as the last line of defense.

DESIGN FOR HUMAN USE

The layout of the equipment at work station (it may be a crane cabin, a control room, a computer terminal, or any other) must ensure proper reachability, good postures, and quick responses. The design of controls must be based on an understanding of what the operator is trying to control, as well as how he can control it. Power, speed, accuracy are each achieved by different types of controls. Easy identification of the controls is very important, e.g., shape, size, position, etc. the design of displays may be analog or digital, qualitative or quantitative. The nature and design of displays must be based on a clear definition of the task and on an understanding of the way it is performed. The same type of display can not provide maximum speed, maximum attention, and maximum precision.

The direction of a movement of a control in relation to effect (or movement in display or controlled object) which are expected by the majority of the population are called **stereotypes,** and controls of displays which conform to these expected patterns are called **compatible.** Incompatibility can lead to longer response times, greater error rate, longer training times, and quicker fatigue. In an emergency, people tend to revert to their natural stereotype and this may lead to an accident if the critical control is incompatible.

Illustration: The stereotype of taps/valves is close when moved in a clockwise direction. A valve with an opposite control action (anticlockwise to close) was well labeled and working well for many years until, in an emergency the nearest operator turned it clockwise, which resulted in a major accident.

DESIGN FOR SAFETY

Ninety-five percent of all road accidents are thought to involve human error. Indian railways attribute two out of every three-railway accident to human error. These include alcohol, inexperience, tiredness, illness, stress and cleanliness among other reasons. Ergonomic design is to design assuming that the user may make a mistake, i.e., design with human error as a given design constraint. Examples include 'child resistant containers' – containers which can not be opened by children, or requiring industrial pressing or cutting machines to be operated by pressing two widely separated switches simultaneously, so that the hands can not be in the danger zone.

DESIGN OF SAFETY EQUIPMENT

In any hazardous equipment, the use of personal protective devices (PPD) should be considered as a last line defense. Unergonomic design of PPDs has been established as a major reason for their non-use. An ergonomic evaluation of three non-respiratory PPDs (helmet, gloves, and goggles) compared the existing dimensions with the users anthropometry. The helmets were the closest to the recommended dimensions, and the goggles had three maximum divergences. Most of the gloves varied widely on both sides of the recommended dimensions. Based on these results, PPDs now in use were critically examined and design recommendations made for future procurement specifications. A spillover effect is that the benefit would also accrue to other smaller industries in the region that procure their PPDs from the same source.

PERSONAL PROTECTIVE EQUIPMENT (PPE)

PPE is equipment worn by a worker to minimize exposure to specific occupational hazards. Examples of PPE are respirators, gloves, and aprons, fall protection, and full body suits, as well as head, eye and foot protection. Using PPE is only one element in a complete safety program that would use a variety of strategies to maintain a safe and healthy occupational environment. PPE does not reduce the hazard itself nor does it guarantee permanent or total protection.

ROLE OF PERSONAL PROTECTIVE EQUIPMENT

Hazards exist in every workplace so strategies to protect workers are essential. The priority should be the elimination and control of hazards at their source or along the path between the source and the worker. Many methods are available, and those most appropriate to the specific situation should be used.

Controlling a hazard at its source should be the first choice because this method will eliminate it from the workplace altogether or isolate it from the worker. This 'safe place' approach may require substitution of a material with non-hazardous ones, isolation of hazards, addition of safety features to existing equipment, redesign of the work processes, or purchase of new equipment. When the hazard can not be removed or controlled adequately, personal protective equipment (PPE) must be used if the work process is to continue.

PLANNING A PROTECTION STRATEGY

Before any decision is made to begin or to expand a PPE program, it is important to understand the underlying principles of protection strategies.

There are three elements that must be considered:

- Protection of workers
- Compliance with applicable laws/regulations and internal company standards
- Technical feasibility.

In practice, only a few strategies are available

These include:

- Engineering controls
- Material substitution
- Process change
- Revised work practices
- Equipment change
- Administrative controls
- Use of personal protective equipment.

A good comprehensive strategy considers the hazards, evaluates all possible control methods, integrates various approaches, and reexamines them frequently to ensure a safe work operation. It does these things by requiring that conscious decision making, evaluation, and reevaluation be done at various stages throughout the program.

PERSONAL PROTECTIVE EQUIPMENT (PPE)

- PPE is not a substitute for safe working arrangement.
- Do not discard PPE.
- Wear your helmet.
- Shoes first, steps next.
- Develop habit of using PPE.
- Wear your ear defender.
- Protect your eyes-wear goggles.

- Always use safety protection.
- Wear your protective equipment.
- Safety provide secured life, like a helmet on the ride.
- Be wise, save your eyes, use goggles, the best device.
- To see tomorrow, wear eye protection to-day.

USE OF PERSONAL PROTECTIVE EQUIPMENT (PPE)

PPE is used to reduce or minimize the exposure or contact to injurious physical, chemical or biological agents. A hazard can not be eliminated by PPE, but the risk of injury can be eliminated or greatly reduced. For example, wearing hearing protection reduces the likelihood of hearing damage when the ear plugs or muffs are appropriate for the kind of noise exposure and they are used properly. However, hearing protection does not eliminate the noise.

PPE should only be used:

- As an interim (short term) measure before controls are implemented.
- Where pre-contact control technology is not available.
- During activities such as maintenance, clean up, and repair where pre-contact controls are not feasible or effective.
- During emergency situations.

Design of a PPE Program:

A PPE program must be comprehensive. It requires commitment and active participation at the planning, development, and implementation stages from all levels: senior management, supervisors, and workers. A good PPE program consists of these essential elements:

- Workplace survey
- Selection of appropriate controls
- Selection of appropriate PPE
- Fitting
- Training
- Management support
- Maintenance
- Auditing of the program.

The organization's occupational health and safety policy should be a statement of principles and general rules, which serve as guide to action. Senior management must be committed to ensuring that the policy and procedures are carried out. PPE program must be, and must be seen to have equal importance with all other organizational policies, procedures, and programs.

PROTECT YOUR HANDS

Hands are two busiest, most important, invaluable, indispensable and at the same time vulnerable tools the human body has at its disposal. We use them all the time for so many diverse jobs that we tend to take them for granted. A lot of people injure their hands while performing various jobs. A few vital first aid measures for controlling hand injuries are given below:

Cuts: Put direct pressure on the wound and keep the injured hand elevated above the shoulder to stop the bleeding. Clean up wound and apply sterile dressing.

Minor heat burns: Soak in cold water immediately and continue soaking till pain subsides. If skin is broken, cover with sterile dressing. Do not apply ointment or grease. Seek medical help.

Sprains, Blows: Put on cold compresses to reduce pain and swelling. Get medical help immediately.

Blisters: Leave blistered skin unbroken; clean up and apply sterile dressing if broken. Get medical help.

Chemical burns: Flush injured area thoroughly in cool running water for at least 10 minutes to dilute and wash away chemical. See a doctor immediately.

Amputation: Put amputated limb in a bag of ice and rush victim with it to the nearest emergency unit of a hospital. Severed limbs can be reattached in many cases if proper procedures are promptly followed.

Prompt first aid can reduce the severity of injury.

CHOOSE THE RIGHT GLOVE

Assess each job to determine which gloves will best protect your hands. Types of gloves and hazards they protect against include:

- Rubber, vinyl, neoprene and other specialty synthetics – use with caustic chemicals (e.g., acids, cleaners, and petroleum products) to keep hands dry. Should have a liner to protect hands in case the glove punctures or snags.
- Leather – general use for heavy-duty work, protect against sparks, rough surfaces and scraping objects – especially good with highly abrasive materials. Provide minimal cushioning against blows.
- Metal mesh – protect hands from knives, blade and other sharp instruments. Often used to cut meat.

- Plastic film – also called coated fabric gloves. Keep hands dry from moderately concentrated chemicals. Often used in food processing, canneries and food-handling industries. Can be used instead of a rubber gloves and offers greater comfort and flexibility.
- Cloth – provide traction to hold slippery objects. Protect against chafing, insulate against moderate heat or cold and protect hands from sharp edges. Easily laundered and re-used.
- Aluminized – protect hands from intense heat or molten materials.
- Lead-lined – mainly for protection against radiation exposure. Do not use for other jobs because they are cumbersome.
- Insulated – often used by electricians and line workers to protect against electrical shock and burn. Often made of rubber and worn under leather gloves. Rubber gloves should extend above the wrists so that there's no gap between the coat or shirtsleeve and the glove.
- Gauntlets or wristlets – made of plastic, neoprene or coated fabric. These slip over the hand and keep sleeves out of the way to protect forearms from scrapes or burns.
- Barrier creams – protect against corrosive substances and make cleanup easier. Use water- soluble creams for work with oils, paints or varnishes and water-resistant creams for oil or lubricants with more than 10% water content.

EYES ARE GOD'S GREATEST GIFT, PROTECT THEM

There are somethings that we always take for granted. One of them is eyesight. But thousands of people injure their eyes in accident every year. Only then do they realize that eyes are one of our most precious possessions – something which one can not afford to replace.

Protect your eyes against mechanical hazards arising out of flying objects at the work place/sparks, flying chips, particles, dust etc. Chemical hazards can result in splashes or spillage's : especially when powders and liquids are splashed, agitated or shaken. Heat, glare, ultra-violet and infra-red rays originate from radiation or thermal hazards. Learn to identify these hazards and protect your eyes.

Some of the accepted safety rules are:

- Wear your safety glasses when working.
- Wear close fitting safety goggles or cup sided shields while grinding.
- Scratched, pitted or damaged safety glasses should be replaced immediately.
- Wear properly shaded lenses when welding and cutting.
- Do not look directly into open containers of hazardous materials.

6. Make sure power tools have been turned off before you remove goggles.
7. Be sure hands or handkerchiefs are clean before wiping face and eyes.

Prevent Eye Injuries by following the above Simple Precautions.

SAFETY THOUGHTS FOR YOUR EYES ONLY

At the workplace, there is generally a reluctance to wear protective eyewear, such as safety goggles. But one is rarely aware of the numerous hazards around – waiting to strike the eyes. Mechanical, chemical and radiation hazards – to name a few – are some, we should learn to recognize and control.

Learn to identify these hazards and provide appropriate eye protection equipment. Yes, it must be assigned top priority in your safety policy.

More importantly it should be ensured that people use their protective eye wear. A good design and a comfortable fit would ensure greater acceptance. This should be supplemented with periodic eye checks.

Yes, it pays a lot to be concerned with the safety of your eyes. And we will give you two very important reasons for being extra careful: first, your left eye, and second, your rights eye.

CONTACT LENSES COMPLICATE EYE SAFETY

In a document published by the Canadian Center for Occupational Health and Safety, (CCOHS) called contact lenses in the workplace: The pros and cons, the issues surrounding contact lens use in the workplace are clearly spelled out.

The booklet states that "It is impossible to say with absolute certainty whether or not contact lenses are safety hazards in the workplace…Put very simply, the problem is that contact lenses complicate eye safety. Contact lenses have the potential to entrap a substance (vapor, chemical, dust) and hold it against the eye, possibly damaging the eye".

"Conversely, some contact lenses may prevent some substances from reaching the eye, thus minimizing or even preventing an injury. Both types of situation have been documented, leading to the diversity of opinion about the safety of contact lenses in workplace."

At the time this document was published, British Columbia was the only Canadian jurisdiction that had legislated the subject of wearing contact lenses.

It's Industrial Safety and Health Regulation says that no worker shall wear contact lenses where:

- Gases, vapors or other materials are present that could harm the eye; or
- Where dust or other materials are present that could harm the eyes or distract the worker, thus exposing the worker to other injury.

The CCOHS concludes that a universal ban of contact lenses in the workplace is unwarranted.

As for reports claiming that contact lens wearers exposed to welding arc flashes or sparks have suffered eye injury and even blindness, the CCOHS has this to say: "Most recently it has been alleged that workers exposed to welding arc had suffered eye injury, resulting from drying of fluid between the eye and contact lens. Which cause the contact lens to be bonded to the cornea. When the contact lenses were removed, it was claimed, the cornea was damaged…

"According to the basic laws of physics, it is impossible. Heat from a welding arc or electrical spark is not intense enough to dry up the eye's tear fluid. Nor could a contact lens concentrate rays to intensify the heat."

The CCOHS adds that all welders, whether they are wearing contact lenses or not, must wear the appropriate eye protection (e.g., welding helmets and spectacles with side shields).

SAFETY HARNESS AND LANYARD

Why do I have to wear a safety harness and lanyaed?

- To arrest a fall from height.
- Because it has been provided by your employer-for your safety.
- Because you have a legal obligation to wear it – The Health and safety Executive can prosecute you.

Do I need to check my harness and lanyard before use?

Your lanyard and harness need to be checked and inspected regularly. Things to be checked include:

- Knots in lanyard other than those provided by the manufacturer.
- Surface abrasion across the face of webbing and at webbing loops.
- Abrasion at the edges of webbing.
- Cuts to webbing, rope or stitching, particularly at the edges, e.g., where the lanyard may have been choke hitched around steel work (this practice is not recommended).
- Areas that have been subjected to chemical attack, which can result in weakening and softening-often indicated by flaking of the surface. There may also be a change to the color of the fibers.
- Heat of friction damage indicated by fibers with a glazed appearance, which may feel harder than surrounding fibers.
- Damaged or deformed fittings (e.g., carabiners, screw link connectors, scaffold hooks).

- UV degradation which is difficult to identify, particularly visually, but there may be some loss of color (if dyed) and a powdery surface.
- Partially deployed energy absorber (e.g., short pull out of tear webbing).
- Contamination (e.g., with dirt, grit, sand, etc.) which may result in internal or external abrasion.

Limitation of Safety Belt:

- Harness should be the personal property of the user.
- The strength of the anchor device should be greater than 10 KN and the anchor point be situated above user's head.
- It should not be used in highly acid or basic environment.

Checklist at the Time of Purchase:

- Confirming to the ISI standard.
- Identification of the manufacturer.
- Type of product code.
- Batch No./Lot No.
- Year of manufacture.
- Material.
- Size.

OSHA (OCCUPATIONAL SAFETY AND HEALTH ADMINISTRATOR) ON PROTECTIVE CLOTHING

Check manufacturers' selection guides for the effectiveness of specific materials against specific chemicals. Whatever the clothing, it should be inspected to ensure proper fit and function for continued protection, OSHA says.

An OSHA standard on protective clothing for electrical workers became effective Nov. 1, 1994. It prohibits employees exposed to flames or arcs from wearing clothing that could make their injuries worse because of the nature of the clothing itself. But the rule has sparked disagreement in the electrical industry and among manufacturers over what types of fabrics are suitable and how to test them effectively.

Two other key issues to consider:

Comfort: When you put somebody into protective clothing, you create a new set of problems that may include discomfort, the possibility of heat stress, and lessened mobility and dexterity.

Manufacturers are trying to lighten the weight of protective body clothing to help reduce stress but still guard against hazards.

Reuse or Throw Out: OSHA says disposable suits of plastic-like or other similar synthetic materials are particularly important for protection from dusty materials or splashes. But in industries such as pharmaceuticals, with heavy use of protective clothing, buying disposable suits can be costly. Some companies are turning to garments that they can safely decontaminate after use so can be worn again. They cost more to purchase, but their reuse saves money.

PPE Program Checklist

Designing a PPE Program:

- Ensure engineering controls are considered first, PPE is the last line of defense.
- Secure the active participation of all parties.
- Ensure that a program coordinator has been appointed.
- Observe the gradual phasing-in of the PPE program on a pre-arranged time schedule.
- Reevaluate program on an ongoing basis.

Promotional Strategy:

- Publicize commitment to the program.
- Ensure a clear concise company policy has been formulated.
- Examine the educational program.

Workplace Survey:

- Review work practices, job procedures, equipment and plant lay out.
- Use job hazard analysis techniques to integrate accepted safety and health principles and practices into specific operations.

Selection:

- Choose PPE to match the hazard.
- Obtain advice on proper selection.
- Institute to workplace trials.
- Consider the physical comfort of PPE.
- Evaluate cost considerations of PPE usage.
- Ensure PPE meets standards/certification (e.g., ISI, NIOH).

Fitting and Wearing:

- Ensure program includes the individual fitting of PPE.
- Survey users to ensure PPE are worn properly.

Maintenance:

- Ensure that workers know how to perform regular maintenance and inspection of the PPE.

Training:

- Verify that all users, supervisors, selectors, buyers, and store keepers are trained.

Support:

- Ensure that education programs are ongoing.

Auditing the Program:

- Review the program at least annually.
- Review and compare production and safety performance records.

12

CHAPTER

Risk Management/Emergency Preparedness Plan

CONCEPT OF RISK MANAGEMENT

In the rapidly developing field of Scientific Management most useful and unusual branch is Risk Management. It is useful because it provides a flexible framework for estimating, planning and controlling the impact of the risk. Risk management attempts to identify and manage threats that can severely impact or bring down an organization. It creates a strategy to reduce financial loss, physical injuries, and property damage. It analyzes the costs and benefits of those programs and strategies, Albeit estimated cost and probable benefits.

Levels of Risk Management can be as below:

(a) Crisis management calls for plans to be in place if and when the crisis occurs.

(b) Facilities Management calls for one long-term planned development of buildings, offices, and computers manufacturing plants and their planned operation and maintenance.

(c) Security management calls for guarding of physical properties against theft, fraud, and forgery.

(d) Safety management is about plans against workplace accidents.

(e) Insurance management calls for planned transfer of risks.

Types of Risks to be Managed

(a) Financial risks related to involvement of funds.

(b) Industrial risks related to hazards in factory, and stores.

(c) Transportation risks for raw materials, finished goods, and machinery.

(d) Technology products like software data and programs, and hardware like data storage, computers and peripherals, cable network, and Internet etc.

HISTORICAL DEVELOPMENT

Risk management is our tool for survival and growth. Conquerors who have gone on a campaign and taken risks, have won the laurels are the survivors. Losers have lost out and ceased to exist in history. Successful application of risk management started around 1955 through concept of scientific management by Taylor came about in 1930. Concept of risk management grew out of insurance buying and selling. Product risk analysis followed development of system reliability analysis used greatly in Space Sciences and by Defense Departments. Quantitative Risk analysis grew exponentially into tools of Financial Risk Analysis.

RISK CONTROL MEASURES

Procedural Protection

- Fire emergency procedure
- Disaster preparedness plan
- Mutual aid scheme
- No smoking policy
- Investigation of all accidents
- Hazard identification through safety committee, house keeping committee, safety audit committee.
- Conducting plant survey, safety survey
- Work permit system
- Statutory requirement
- Safety promotional activities
- Information notes on unsafe conditions
- MSDS
- Annual medical check up of employees

- Safe start up and shut down procedure
- Regular and preventive maintenance
- Periodic testing of fire fighting appliances.

Physical Protection

- Strict and rigorous approach in following the relevant standards, codes and practices
- Built in safety devices and safety system
- Venting through tall stacks
- Field monitors for different toxic gases
- Burning waste gases in a flare system
- Provision of wind cones
- Fire proofing of steel structures
- PPE
- Passive protection system
- Active protection system
- Automatic protection system
- Improved waste water management.

Educational Protection

- Periodic training program on safety, fire safety and hazardous properties of materials.
- Mock fire drill
- Safety manuals
- Health and safety news bulletins
- Safety motivation schemes
- Plant operating manual
- Educating the public living nearby about the activities in the industry.

RISKS IN RURAL AREAS AND ITS PREVENTION

Environmental Risk

- Ozone layer depletion by methane formation from animal dung.
- Low ground water level resulting in high fluoride content in drinking water.
- Wastage of water by using it in unscientific way and excessive use.
- Land degradation because of excessive use of pesticides/fertilizers.

- Tree cutting for domestic use.
- Use of energy (electricity) in unscientific way, i.e., by using non ISI appliances.
- Using open space for human discharges.
- Excessive use of plastics by rural masses.
- Smoke pollution due to use of woods/raw cokes in chulas for cooking/other purposes.

Prevention Methods

- Gobar plants can be constructed on cooperative basis which can facilitate use of methane for domestic cooking purposes.
- Check dams can be constructed to raise ground water level and awareness can be created for economic advantage of using ISI motors instead of assembled motors.
- Scientific methods can be employed by agriculture sale and credit co-operatives to recover from land degradation.
- Community tree plantation can be encouraged by combined efforts of co-operatives and government.
- Community toilets can be constructed for use of public.

EFFECTIVE COMMUNICATION AND RISK MANAGEMENT

Role of 'IT' in Health and Safety Management

Timely communication is essential for the HSM (Health Safety Management) to produce result. The development in IT (Information Technology) and communication technology can help in the following:

- Seamlessly collection, tracking and reporting key performance indicators with respect to already defined health and safety goals.
- Display graphical analysis of important Health and Safety metrics through digital dashboard.
- Enable active communication between professionals, through automated e-mail and SMS alerts, workflow based task allocation, progress tracking, and completion of scheduled health and safety activities.
- Alerts can be generated for timely submission of reports to regulatory bodies.
- Ease of communication with regulatory bodies through e-mail. Selective access can also be given to the regulatory bodies, eliminating the need for document submission.
- Tracking location of workers and equipment through RFID.
- Monitor adherence to safety procedures through Web camera.

- Remote expert guidance for first aid and other emergency procedure by use of web camera.

Risk management is an essential part of health and safety management. Identifying the risk, assessing the risk, planning for risk mitigation and monitoring the risk are essential part of the risk management. There are two ways by which this can be achieved. One is by carrying out regular audit for adequacy/effectiveness of the system, and the second for compliance and by carrying out inspection of workplace for safety and hygiene.

IT can help organization in a big way and will save valuable time and money, using point and click technology in the following:

- Prepare checklist for audit.
- Planning for audit.
- Assigning Auditor.
- Scheduling audit.
- Capturing audit details and printing report.
- Follow up of audit recommendations.
- Raising request for worksite inspection.
- Approval for worksite inspection.
- Schedule worksite inspection.
- Generate report of worksites exceeding the limits.
- Follow up planning, scheduling, and tracking corrective actions and to-do's.
- Managing all data.

SOCIAL DIMENSION OF RISK-CONTEMPORARY THINKING

Definition and usage of risk is under continuous change over ages. In fact, we can trace the journey of 'risk' from fate to contemporary understanding of risk as manufactured uncertainty. Traditional theories on risk, which were based mostly on actual estimation, would be now slowly but steadily yielding to certain social theories. Focus of analysis is shifting from individual/unit to the group and to the society. From late 90's certain new paradigm of risk has appeared. The reasons are to be believed broadly:

- The certainties of modernity's knowledge are challenged.
- The traditional social welfare provisions are under threat.
- The life enhancing promise of modernity is showing signs of failure.
- There is loss of faith, trust accentuated by doubt about existing social reforms.
- Giddiness suggests that, "In a society such as ours, oriented towards the future and saturated with information, the theme of risk unites many otherwise desperate

areas of politics; welfare state reform, engagement with world financial markets, responses to technological change, ecological problems and geopolitical transformations."

Actually, contemporary understanding of risk is to be examined against transformation of modernity to post modernity. The reason may be that modern agenda of free society shuns the traditional time tested welfare provisions. Therefore, we are talking about safety net, which in essence is distribution of risk. Now, the most important question, is asked, whether we would, pool the risk or pool the resources. Again, some sociologists think that risk is replacing need to a great extent.

At the end, whatever may be the debate over risk, we are to live with risk for all the time to come and as rational human being we must keep watch on dynamics of risks, innovate measures seeking maximum protection against probable loss, and try to find opportunity out of risk.

POST LOSS FUNCTIONS OF RISK

So long we have dwelt upon mostly on planning for taking guard to protect us from adverse outcome of any event. Now, let us take a peep into the real world when an event takes place and its outcome affects our lives – social, corporate or otherwise. In fact, acid test of risk management process lies during the post loss period. These activities demand critical look.

- **Survival:** After any major loss due to viz. earthquake, tsunami, air-crash etc. survival is not only to be ensured but to be seen as such. For risk management, 'survival is not only exactly legal oriented but operational. An organization survives when its production integrity remains intact, its marketing force is seen on road and finance does not emit any public signal of crunch. Examples are galore when many reputed concerns have ceased to exist after a calamity whereas few others carry on without any visible interruption.
- **Continuity of Operation:** To make the continuity visible despite a major loss following measures are necessary:
  - Pull up the stand by resources immediately and put into the essentials of operation at the most unlikely and difficult times.
  - Plant gate/front office should be kept as normal as possible. This can only restore confidence in the market.
- **Humanitarian Conduct:** An accidental loss does not only affect a plant/factory/ establishment physically but makes dent into all stakeholders including the society at large. Risk management should handle all these human resources to ensure continuity of their contribution towards the enterprise value.
- **Initiate and Conclude the Recovery Process:** Recovery from insurers, debtors and other agencies where the risk stood transferred and spread should be completed

at the earliest and the resources to be handed over to management to prevent volatility of resources.

IDENTIFICATION OF HAZARDS AND THEIR MONITORING, MONITORING HEALTH ASSETS, CALIBRATION OF MEASURING INSTRUMENTS

(Role of 'IT' in Health and Safety Management)

Identification of Hazards and their Monitoring

In order to ensure safe and healthy work place, one need to identify, evaluate and control occupational exposures to chemical agents and other physical, biological or ergonomic hazards at the work place. This requires assessing potential risks, planning regular inspection, interpreting sample results and implementing strategies to limit exposure. All these have to be done with limited time and resources.

IT can help organization to protect employees from occupational exposure, evaluate the effectiveness of the safety program and do it in less time at lower costs. From planning through reporting, this easy-to-use software provides the tools you need to:

- Tracking workplace conditions round the year.
- Collect, document and analyze exposure-monitoring results.
- Communicate monitoring results to employees and management.
- Identify opportunities to further control exposures.
- Assure compliance with occupational health standards.

Monitoring Health of Assets

One reason of accident is breakdown of equipment. Breakdown takes place by surprise and may lead to accidents with damage to people and property. Timely maintenance of equipment can definitely reduce, if not eliminate, the chances of breakdown.

Asset management application is used for tracking the entire lifecycle of equipment, including the preventive, predictive, and breakdown maintenance. Based on the commissioning date and manufacturers' instruction, the maintenance is planned. Asset management application schedules the maintenance automatically and keeps track of status of the same. HSM application can be integrated with the application to monitor the health of assets and ensure that assets are maintained in good health to prevent incidents/accidents.

CALIBRATION OF MEASURING EQUIPMENT

In order to control the exposure, we need to know the actual level of exposure. To know the actual level, we need to have measuring equipment, those are accurate. Inaccurate measurement will lead to erroneous resulting in unwanted consequences.

IT can help in keeping track of measuring equipment and their calibration dates, validity date, date of recalibration etc. and help users to manage their work better. This will help in monitoring the work place exposure in a more effective manner.

EMERGENCY PREPAREDNESS AND RESPONSE PLANNING (EPRP) IN MAJOR ACCIDENT HAZARD (MAH) FACTORIES

I. Major Accident Hazard Factory

Major accident is defined as an accident involving loss of life inside and outside the installation, or ten or more injuries inside and/or one more injuries outside or release of toxic chemicals or explosion or fire or spillage of hazardous chemicals resulting in on-site or off-site emergencies or damage to equipment leading to stoppage of process or adverse effects to the environment. The major accident hazard (MAH) factory is defined as a factory handling including transport through carries or pipeline of hazardous chemicals at a site equal to or in excess of the threshold quantities specified under the law.

II. Emergency

An emergency is an unplanned event that can cause deaths or significant injuries to employees, customers or the public; or that can shutdown an industrial activity, disrupt operation, cause physical or environmental damage and it includes fire, explosion and hazardous material incident. Emergency management is the process of preparing for, mitigating, responding to and recovering from an emergency. The emergency planning and response planning are the documents prepared to facilitate emergency management in industries.

III. Emergency Preparedness Plan (EPP)

An emergency preparedness plan describes the actions to be taken by the employees to ensure their safety in case of an emergency and its purpose is to facilitate and organize employer and employee actions during work place emergencies. The elements of emergency plan includes evacuation procedures, and emergency escape route assignments, procedures to be followed by employees who remains to operate critical plant operations before they evacuate, procedure to account for all employees after an emergency evacuation, rescue and medical duties, means of reporting fire and other emergencies and name or job titles of persons who can be contacted for further information or explanation of duties under the plan.

It consists of on-site emergency plan or off-site emergency plan. The on-site emergency plan details explicitly what actions should be taken in the event of a major accident occurring on-site and should cover all reasonably foreseeable incidents, which is prepared by the employer. The off-site emergency plan deals with these incidents identified in the on-site emergency plan, which has the potential to harm persons or the environment outside the boundary of the premises, which is prepared by the district authority, or the Government.

Emergency preparedness plan provides and details on preparedness of the industry to tackle an emergency.

Emergency Preparedness and Response Planning

Emergency preparedness and response planning (EPRP) is an important procedural document for a MAH factory by way of preparedness for handling accidents and emergencies, and it incorporates both preparedness of the organizations to tackle emergencies, and response planning for such emergencies. It includes the following:

- As assessment of risk scenario leading to spills and probable impacts.
- Installation and maintenance of warning signages.
- Continuous access to the site incident response manual.
- Staff training in incident response protocols.
- Availability of equipment to mitigate the effects of any chemical spill.
- Planning for containment of contaminated water if there is a spill and /or fire.

On-site Emergency Response Teams

Emergency response teams are the first line of defense in emergencies and emergency response team member should be physically capable and mentally alert to perform the duties that are assigned thereto. Different emergency response teams in an industry are as follows:

- Use of fire extinguishers.
- First aid, including cardiopulmonary resuscitators.
- Shut down procedures.
- Evacuation procedure.
- Chemical spill control measures.
- Use of self contained breathing apparatus.
- Search and emergency rescue procedure.
- Trauma counseling.

Off-site Emergency Response Teams

The off-site response team of an emergency consists of the following agencies or government department:

- Fire brigade
- Ambulance service
- Poison centers
- Mutual aid
- Local administration
- Police
- District authority
- Occupational health services
- Non-governmental organizations
- Community.

Entrapment Defined

A local population is demographically trapped if it has exceeded, or is projected to exceed the combination of:

- The carrying capacity of its own ecosystem.
- Its ability to obtain the products, and particularly the food, produced by other ecosystems except as food aid.
- Its ability to migrate to other ecosystems in a manner which preserves (or improves) its standard of living.

Item (b) and (c) describe the links that a population has with other ecosystems, and are crucial. They are most easily thought of as "connectedness", and its opposite "disconnectedness". A severely trapped population faces the four tragedies of entrapment in varying combinations. Depending local cultural, political and ecological factors it can:

- Starve;
- Die from disease;
- Slaughter itself or its neighbors;
- Be supported indefinitely by food aid (if food is available).

Since endangered populations are growing rapidly, the critical part of the above definition is "is projected to", and concerns the ultimate size of a population at the end of its demographic transition, in relation to its carrying capacity and its connectedness. The major constraint is time, and particularly whether such measures as female education, etc. have time to bring the birth rate down before carrying capacity and connectedness are exceeded.

Confined Space

Confined space is a space of any size, which has certain characteristics include:

- Limited opening for entry and exit
- Unfavorable natural ventilation
- Often an atmosphere which is contaminated or oxygen deficient.

Examples: Gas tanker, silos, degreasing baths, drains and sumps, sewerage man holes.

It is also a space, which is not intended as a regular workplace. There are many hazards, which may exist in a confined space. These include the risk of explosion, electrocution, engulfment, oxygen deprivation or being overcome by toxic gases and vapors.

Many tragic accidents have occurred because the dangers of working in a confined space are often underestimated, ignored or not clearly understood.

The most common confined space hazard is that of an oxygen deficient or contaminated atmosphere. One of the most dangerous aspect of such an environment is that the hazard is invisible. It is therefore essential to ensure correct entry, exit and testing procedures are carried out prior to entry.

In normal atmosphere the oxygen content is 21% approx. The minimum oxygen level for safe entry into confined space is 18%. Once the level falls below this, a person in the confined space is like to develop serious symptoms of oxygen deprivation or starvation. These symptoms of oxygen deprivation are:

- headache
- difficulty in breathing
- ringing in the ears
- loss of muscle control
- feeling of euphoria.

Oxygen starvation often leads to death because the person experiencing euphoria has no appreciation of the danger.

Flammable – Liquid Hazards Stem from Vapors

We call them flammable liquids, but it's not the liquid that we must worry about. It's the vapor that these liquids release.

This vapor and the air in a room form a mixture that threatens to explode at the first spark from a light switch, faulty electrical equipment or static electricity. Even high temperatures or simple friction can set off an explosion. Flammable vapors are especially dangerous because you can not see them and, often, you can not smell them either.

What are some flammable liquids you use on the job? Solvents, cleaning fluids and fuels are a few that come to mind. The following covers the keys to handling flammable liquids safety.

Keep the Lid on:

Keeping the lid on is a matter of good house keeping. Keep flammable liquid in safety cans, stored away from other chemicals. They should be kept in a well ventilated, temperature – controlled areas. Dispose of flammable soaked rags and other waste materials in oily waste cans designated for this purposes.

Avoid spilling the liquid on yourself, check with your supervisor about how to properly dispose of flammable liquids.

Ventilate the Area

Each flammable liquid reaches a peak of explosiveness when enough of it mixes with the oxygen in the air. Prevent buildup of vapors to this level by using flammables only where there is enough ventilation to clean the vapors out. Areas surrounding the work area should be either sealed off or ventilated as well.

HANDLE CHEMICALS SAFELY

Chemicals when not handled properly can cause fires, explosions or toxic exposures. Remember the following tips while handling them:

- Persons handling the chemicals should know the fire and toxic hazards.
- Transferring chemicals from bigger to smaller containers should be done in well ventilated place ear marked for the purpose. Hand operated pumps are suitable.
- Avoid using pressure transfer method.
- Safety cans and containers with proper caps for the openings should be used when small quantities of chemicals are handled.
- For transporting chemicals within the factory premises, use hand trolleys with proper securing arrangements. Never carry the containers in hand.
- Spilled liquids should be promptly mopped up using non-combustible absorbents like chalk powder, sand etc. and disposed off in a safe place.
- Persons handling chemicals should wear appropriate personal protective equipment.

HAZARDS IN MANUFACTURING INDUSTRIES

In the metal manufacturing industries, large amounts of materials are processed, transported and conveyed by massive equipments.

A hazard in any existing or potential condition in the workplace which, by itself or interacting with other variables, can result in unwanted effects of death, injuries, property damage, or other losses. Those responsible for maintenance may sometimes cause hazards in the workplace. Examples include:

- Improperly identifying high and low pressure steam lines, compressed air, and sanitary lines;
- Not detecting or replacing worn or damaged machine and equipment parts;
- Failing to adjust or lubricate equipment and machinery on a scheduled basis;
- Failing to inspect or replace worn hoisting equipment;
- Failing to replace worn and frayed belts on equipment;
- Over-oiling motor bearings, resulting in oil being thrown onto insulation (fire hazard) and onto the floor (fall hazard);
- Failing to replace machine guards after maintenance;
- Failing to tag or lockout unsafe equipment.

Such failures are not intentional. Often maintenance management does not have safety standards in place, or has not trained their workers in safe maintenance practices. Or, the maintenance workforce may be overburdened with corrective maintenance or even paperwork related to work-orders, and their preventive maintenance schedule of activities is ignored or delayed.

Tools needed for certain adjustments may not be available; parts (e.g., replacement hoist or conveyor belts) may not be available, at least at the time of scheduled replacement; or there may not even be a preventive maintenance program in place. In the last case, it's easy to see how examples 1-8 could in fact occur; many of the actions called for would, in fact, be 'elective' or performed only when 'time is available'. Unfortunately, if production supervisors and workers begin to believe that 'safety work orders are the last priority of the maintenance department', they may stop sending such work orders, creating a vicious cycle.

HINTS ON HANDLING OF HAZARDOUS CHEMICALS

For safe storage, handling and transportation of hazardous chemicals like coal tar, chromic acid etc., here are few safety hints:

- All containers containing hazardous materials, chemicals should be clearly labeled.
- Keep chemicals in cool and dry place away from heat. Avoid storage in open sun.
- Store in compatible materials separately.
- Check containers for leaks and open carefully with right tools.
- Prohibit eating, drinking and smoking in areas where hazardous materials and chemicals are present.
- Never leave the chemical containers in open condition.
- Limit the quality of flammable, corrosive and toxic chemicals in storage to minimum.
- Attend immediately to leaking containers to shift them away or to stop the leak.

First Aid

- No matter how small the injuries get first aid first and then get medical aid.
- Never administer the first aid of your own, if you do not know.
- Take the assistance of the first aid trained persons.

Fire – "Kill Fire before it Kills You"

- In case of fire, no matter how small it is, try to control the fire by using the extinguishing media.
- Raise alarm when you notice a fire.
- Immediately report to the concerned for future action.
- Use right type of extinguishing media for specific type of fire.

TIPS DURING EMERGENCY

- Be calm, do not get panicky.
- Decide wind direction. Move away perpendicular to wind direction.
- Do not run, walk quickly.
- Cover your nose with wet cloth and breathe through it.
- If possible, use any available vehicle to move away.
- Try to save lives, do not bother about properties.
- Set the live stocks free.
- Extinguish any open flame.
- On hearing siren during emergency, switch on the media for any important message.
- Communicate to everybody about the emergency.
- Extend full co-operation to those who come forward to help and rescue.

Identification and Grouping Persons Need to be Educated in Emergency Preparedness and Response Planning (EPRP)

EPRP on-site

The following are the persons involved in on-site EPRP; works incident controller whose duty is the direction of the efforts of the works emergency team to control the situation and he should take decision involving the operation of other plants, the works main controller is the one who is vested with the authority to make decisions on behalf of the works and the key personnel includes senior manager responsible for production, engineering, technical services, medical personnel, transport, safety and security. The essential workers constitute the task force required to perform specific functions in case of emergency and the non-essential workers are not involved in these plans.

EPRP off-site

It includes all groups of persons identified in the on-site EPRP as well as all the other persons identified in the off-site emergency preparedness and response plans.

Design of the Safety Education Modules for Effective EPRP

The safety education modules were designed for conducting the safety education program for the identified group of persons. Two modules can be prepared for the safety education program on EPRP.

IMPLEMENTATION OF THE DESIGNED SAFETY EDUCATION MODULES

The designed capsule of modules should be implemented to all the group of persons as per norms.

Feedback

The feedback from the participants of all the groups should be obtained after conducting the designed safety education program and the suggestions, recommendations and views should be analyzed and if necessary they must be incorporated in the original EPRP to make them more effective.

Legal Requirements of EPP

In India, Section 41B (4) of the Factories Act 1948 provides for the preparation of an on-site preparation plan by the occupier of hazardous processes listed in the first schedule of section 2(cb). Under this Act, the type of the chemical and its threshhold quantities are not considered for applying this provision. Rule 13 and 14 of the Manufacture, storage, and import of Hazardous Chemical Rules 1989 provides for preparation of on-site emergency plan and off-site emergency plan, respectively. These provisions would be applicable only if an industrial activity involves a quantity of a hazardous chemical listed under the schedule with a quantity equal to or more than the value specified in schedule. Further the manufacture, storage, and import of hazardous chemicals Rules 1989 states that on-site emergency plan should be prepared by the occupier and off-site emergency plan by the concerned Authority (District Administration). The response plan is not mandatory in India, till now the law enforces only the preparation of emergency plans and not response plans, even though few components of response planning is incorporated in these plans.

Major Shortfalls in the Existing EPP

The major shortfalls in the existing EPP are as follows:

- Response planning is not provided in on-site emergency plans.
- Emergency response procedures alone covered in off-site emergency plan instead of complete response planning.
- Safety education program is not designed and incorporated explicitly in the plans to make it effective.
- Awareness of these plans among workers, management, key persons, visitors, government authorities, outside services and the community has not been ensured.

Need for Response Planning and Safety Education Programs

The emergencies in MAH factories could be due to the accidental releases of toxic gases, chemical spills, fires and explosives. The success of emergency planning squarely depends on the effectiveness of responses, which can only determine the level of employee and community protection minimized property loss and reduced environmental degradation. This underlines the need for the incorporation of response plans in EPP. These emergency preparedness and response plans can only be successful if necessary awareness is created among all the concerned persons and proper attitudinal change takes place, which are achievable only by safety education.

List of Legislations Relating Chemical Disaster Management

- The Environment Protection Act, 1986.
- The Factories Amendment Act, 1987.
- The Manufacture, Storage and Import of Hazardous Chemicals Rules, 1989 (amended in 1994 and 2000).
- The Public Liability Insurance Act, 1991 and Rules.
- The National Environment Tribunal Act, 1995.
- The Chemical accidents (Emergency Planning, Procedure and Response) Rules, 1996.
- The Central Motor Vehicle Rules, 1989 (amended in 1993).
- The Environmental Clearance of Project Notification, 1994 (ECP Notification).
- The Hazardous Wastes (Management and Handling) Rules, 1989 (amended in 2000 and 2003).
- The Bio-Medical Waste (Management and Handling) Rules, 1998 (amended in 2003).
- The Explosives Act, 1884:
  - The Explosive Rules, 1983.
  - The Static and Mobile Pressure Vessels (unified) Rules, 1981 (amended in 1993, 2000, and 2002).
  - The Gas Cylinder Rules, 2004 (replaces the Gas Cylinders Rules, 1981).
- The Petroleum Act, 1934:
  - The Petroleum Rules, 2002 (replaces the Petroleum Rules, 1976).
  - The Calcium Carbide Rules, 1987.
  - The Cinematograph Film Rules, 1948.

On-site Emergencies in Petroleum Product Pipeline

Leak

Causes

- Corrosion, internal/external
- Equipment failure
- Operator error
- Other

Consequences

- Oil spillage
- Fire hazard
- Casualties

Control Measures

- Prevent ignition
- Safeguard personnel
- Stop oil spillage by closing the sectionalizing valves near the leaking area.
- Contain the spread of oil
- Clean the area

Fire

Causes

- Ignition short circuit, static electricity of spark generation
- Equipment failure
- External source of ignition
- Damage due to normal calamity (lightning etc.)
- Other

Consequences

- Damage to equipment
- Injury to personnel
- Casualties

Control Measures

- Extinguish oil fire by foam, DCP and electrical fire by CO_2
- Cool neighboring equipment by water by running fire-fighting pumps
- Safeguard personnel
- Isolate the section
- Take the help of other communities' fire wing and municipal fire brigade as per the requirement.

SAFETY EDUCATION UNDER 'EPRP'

(Emergency Preparedness and Response Planning)

Safety can be defined as a condition or state of being resulting from the modifications of human behaviour and/or designing of the physical environment to reduce the possibility of hazards, there by reducing accidents. Safety education is the proactive development of knowledge, attitude, behaviour and skills of the employee on safety. Safety education meets a basic social need of society as it develop an awareness of the role of safe human behaviour in advancement of social and material progress. Through the development of safe habits, attitudes, awareness and knowledge, safety education plays a pivotal role in ensuring safety by preventing and reducing accidents. The establishment of a successful program of safety education requires proper identification of needs, motivation, objectives, employee attitudes, planned instruction, management support and environment for training. Safety education programs are developed in various subject fields depending on the need and the safety program of these individual instructional areas must be integrated with the other safety programs for their effective functioning in industries.

Identified Group of Persons for the Safety Education Program

Group of persons	Module	Periodicity
Works incident controller Works main controller` Other key personnel	Module I	Once in six months
Essential workers Non-essential workers Visitors	Module II	Once in every year
Fire brigade Police District authority Ambulance services Poison centers Occupational health Services Mutual aid members NGO's and experts Local administrators Community	Module III	Once in every year

Implementation of the Designed Safety Education Modules

- Study and analysis of EPP of MAH units in India.
- Legal requirements for EPP.
- Major shortfalls in the existing EPP.
- Need for response planning and safety education program.
- Emergency preparedness and response planning (EPRP).
- Identification and grouping of persons need to be educated in EPRP.
- Design of the safety education modules for effective EPRP.
- Implementation of the designed safety education modules.
- Feedback.

STUDY AND ANALYSIS OF EPP OF MAH FACTORIES IN INDIA

The on-site emergency plans in India generally contain the following:

- Name and address of the persons furnishing information.

- Key personnel and their responsibilities.
- Details If the outside organizations involved for assisting.
- Liaison arrangement between organizations.
- Information on the preliminary hazard analysis.
- Site details.
- Description of hazardous chemicals at the plant site.
- Likely dangers to the plant.
- Warning, alarm and safety and security system.
- Communication facilities.
- Fire fighting and other facilities available.
- First aid and hospital services availability.

The off-site emergency plans in India generally contain the following:

- Types of accidents and releases.
- Key personnel and responsibilities and liaison arrangements between them.
- Information about the site.
- Chemical and physical characteristics and dangers of the substances and plant.
- Identification of facilities and transport routes.
- Contacts for further advice.
- Communication facilities.
- For fighting materials, damage control and repair items.
- Emergency response procedures.
- Notifying to the public.
- Evacuation arrangement.
- Press and other media interests.
- Clean up.

The notified MAH industries get their on-site emergency plan prepared and approved by the directorate/inspectorate of factories. The off-site emergency plans in India are in developing stage as this concept is not fully comprehended and lot of improvement has to be done for their effectiveness.

On-site Emergency Plan

Checklist for Assessment of Preparedness

I. General

- Name and address of the factory

- Industrial activity
  - Main products manufactured
  - Hazardous materials stored on the premises and the quantities in metric tonnes
  - Hazardous processes conducted on the premises
  - Nature of identified hazards (please tick the relevant hazards) fire, explosion, release of toxic vapor, release of toxic/corrosive/flammable/dangerous liquid
- Total number of workers
  - employed in a day
  - present during the visit
- Number of shifts
- Number of entry and exit points of the factory
- Condition of approach roads
  - to the factory
  - to the plant inside the factory
- – Number of safety officers
  - Name and address of chief safety officer
- Whether adequate safety equipments available? Yes/No

  If yes attach list.
- Fire fighting facility certified by (please tick the relevant ones) state/local Authority/tariff advisory committee
- Whether adequate emergency equipment available? Yes/No

  If yes attach list.
- Whether adequate first-aid and medical facilities available? Yes/No
- Type of training given to:
  - First aider
  - Fire fighter
  - Essential persons
  - Key persons
  - General public
- Techniques adopted to assess the hazards (please tick the relevant ones) Hazop, Safety Audit, Any other.
- Provision for emergency power supply for essential services
- Whether mutual aid scheme exists?
- Number of factories included in mutual aid scheme

  - fire fighting
  - first aid and medical management
- Does the emergency plan incorporate a directory of external technical support?
- Does excavation procedure exist?

II. Alarm System

- Type – Electrical/Mechanical/Manual
- Total number of alarms installed
- Alarm signal for general public
- Whether distinct alarm signals adopted for different types of emergencies?
- Are all the alarms in good working condition.

Control Room and Communication System

- Whether control room exists?
- Number of control rooms and their sizes
- Is the control room(s) in minimum risk area?
- Facilities available in the control room (please tick appropriate ones)
  - telephones
  - public address system
  - vehicles
  - clear access
  - wireless sets
  - list of important phone number
  - plan of the factory
  - on-site emergency plan
  - plan of the area
  - hot line to district magistrate
  - hot line to police control room
  - hot line to emergency/casualty
  - ward of the hospitals
  - hot line to fire brigade
  - non stop power supply
  - meteorological information.

Assembly Points at the Time of Emergency

- Assembly point details

- Whether there is any board/display to indicate the point of assembly?
- Is it a safe place?
- Whether the place is under the charge of a person?
- Whether roll call arrangement exists?
- Arrangement of keeping details of visitors at site

Emergency Shut-Down Procedures

- Does the emergency plan provide for the emergency shutdown of operating system?
- Have specific individuals been designated to be responsible for shutdown implementation?
- Have procedure checklists been developed for each individual operations, equipment or area?

All Clear Signal

- Is the code for giving "all clear signal" established? Yes/No
- The person responsible for giving "all clear signals".

Recommissioning

- Whether proper assessment is made for safe operation of the plant before recommissioning after the incident?
- Whether start up procedure in clear terms established?

REHEARSAL OF EMERGENCY

Fire Explosion Toxic Gas Release

- Date
- Time
- Place of rehearsal

A. Information given to:

Name and Telephone Number

- Officers of the factory department
- Pollution control board
- Police
- District medical authority/local hospital

- Fire brigade
- Civil defense
- District emergency authority

B. Alarm System

- Was alarm audible in all work area?
- Confusion, if any, noticed

C. Wind Direction Indicator

Whether the indicator for wind direction visible from all places in the plant?

D. Control Room and Communication System

- Were the communication system and their maintenance adequate?
- Communication system available in the case of power failure including the name of the messenger

E. Assembly Points

Reporting Time	Confusion detected in their reporting

- Whether people assembled in the designated area?
- Whether roll call taken?
- Whether evacuation procedure followed?

F. Reporting of Key Personnel

- incident controller at site
- site controller at control room
- communication officer at control room
- other key persons at control room
  - transport
  - medical
  - security
  - safety
  - fire fighting
  - assisting teams at the control room, e.g., Electrical/mechanical crew, salvage team, drivers, rigger runners, volunteers, home guards etc.

G. Were the Site Controller and Incident Controller in Desired Clothes, Helmet or Colored Appron?

Yes/No

H. Number of Mutual Aid Factories Participated in Rehearsal

- Fire fighting
- First aid and medical management
- Any technical support utilized during rehearsal?

I. Fire Brigade

Sl. No.	Name of fire brigade	Name of fire station	Distance from plant	Contact name	Contact person telephone No.	Person concerned	Time of first information	Reporting time at incident site	Whether equipment worked	If not, reasons
1	2	3	4	5	6	7	8	9	10	11
(i) (ii) (iii)										

J. Police

Tel. no.	Person contacted	Distance in kms.	Time of first information	Reporting time
1	2	3	4	5

K. Ambulance/Transport

Sl. No.	Name of organization	Contact person name	Contact person Tel. No.	Person contacted	Distance in kms.	Time of first information	Reporting time at accident site
1	2	3	4	5	6	7	8

L. Assessment

- Whether timely information given to concerned authorities? If not, indicate the discrepancies.
- Did alarm system work properly? If not, state the reasons.
- Whether the facilities available in the control room were adequate? If not, indicate short falls.

- Was there any confusion in the assembly point?
- Did the key persons report within minimum response time at the appropriate places? If not, indicate short falls.
- Was mutual aid assistance available in time and adequate?
- Indicate response time and adequacy of fire fighting system.
- Did police arrive at site in time?
- Indicate response time and adequacy of ambulance/transport facilities.
- Whether any improvement noticed from the previous rehearsal?
- Whether the emergency plan is updated in view of the previous rehearsal and copy given to concerned?
- Adequacy of training of key persons.
- General remarks.

Place:

Date: **Signature, name and designation of the Inspector**

THE DISASTER MANAGEMENT

The disaster management research has evolved through four distinct steps as given below:

- Emphasis on relief.
- Contingency planning for disaster preparedness.
- Emphasis on hi-tech tools and techniques.
- Vulnerability analysis and hazard assessment.

Types of Disasters

- **Natural:** Flood, drought, cyclone, earthquake, volcanic eruption, heat waves, cold waves, tidal surge, and landslides etc.
- **Manmade:** Explosion, stampede, industrial accident, building fire, pressure on infrastructure declining quality of life, traffic accidents, terrorist atrocities, contagious diseases, bio-terrorism, chemical and nuclear warfare.

Disasters Categorization

- Water and climate related hazards
- Geological related hazards
- Chemical, industrial and nuclear related disasters

- Accident related disasters
- Biologically related disasters.

Factors Affecting Disasters

Various factors contributing for the increased number of natural disaster are as given below:

- Population growth and urban development.
- Development practice – industrial development and high tech.
- Shortage of water.
- Effects of environment degradation – rise of global temperature/retreat of mountain glacier etc.

There is a need to integrate disaster mitigation strategies for pre-disaster, during disaster, and post disaster periods. The integrated approach during relief, rehabilitation and reconstruction should be considered as a part of long term plan, which should eventually constitute preparedness for a future disaster. Team spirit may be a key word. The challenges before us is to find the right mix of actions that will manage the natural disaster risk as an integrated strategy with the application of science and technology we can evolve mitigation measures to reduce the impact and minimize the loss of lives and property.

MAJOR DISASTERS (INDIAN SCENARIO)

Year	Types of disasters	Effects
3rd December 1984	Bhopal gas tragedy Leakage of MIC gas	10,000 people died
October 29-30, 1999	Super cyclone in Orissa	Villages affected – 14,586 Population affected – 1,56,81.072 Human casualties – 9,893 Livestock perished – 4,44,531 House destroyed – 16,61,683 Crops area damaged – 18,43,047 ha.
27th January, 2001	Earthquake in Bhuj, Gujrat	Population affected – 16.04 million Persons killed – 20,086 Persons injured – 1,66,836 House damaged – 1.2 million Industrial units affected – 10,000

26th December, 2004	Earthquake and tsunami in Indian ocean (Affected in South East Asia)	India – 13,000 Indonesia – 1,00,000 Sri Lanka – 30,000 Thailand – 4,500 Miamar – 90 Maldwip – 75 Malaysia-62

LIST OF WORLD WIDE TSUNAMI DISASTERS

Year	Place	Number of Lives Lost
1692	Port Royal, Jamaika	3000
1703	Honshu, Japan	5000
1707	Japan (38 Feet Waves)	30,000
1741	Japan (30 Feet Waves, following voncanic eruptions)	1400
1753	Lisbon, Portugal	50,000
1783	Italy	30,000
1868	Chile and Hawaii	>25,000
1883	Indonesia (Krakatoa Volcanic Explosion, Indonesia)	36,000
1896	Sanrika, Japan	27,000
1933	Sanrika, Japan	3000
1946	Hilo, Hawaii (32 Feet High Waves)	159
22nd May 1960	Chile	Aprox. 3000
1946	Honsu, Japan Kodoak, Alaka (195 Feet Waves Engulf)	2000
1964	Philipines	131
17 Aug. 1976	Indonesia	8000
19 Aug. 1977	Indonesia	189
18 July 1979	New Guinea	540
12 Sep. 1979	Columbia	100
12 Dec. 1979	Sea of Japan	500
26 May 1983-1998	Papua New Guinea	Approx. 100
26 Dec. 2004	Bay of Bengal (India, Indonesia, Sri Lanka, Thailand, Maldives, etc.)	Approx. 1,70,000 (+1,30,000 Missing)

LIST OF HISTORIC TSUNAMIS

Rank	Death toll	Event	Location	Date
1.	230,210	2004 Indian Ocean Tsunami	Indonesia, Sri Lanka, India, Maldives, Malaysia, Somalia, Bangladesh Thailand	26 December 2004
2.	123,000	1908 Messina earthquake/tsunami	Messina, Italy	1908
3.	100,000	1755 Lisbon earthquake/tsunami/fire	Portugal, Spain, Morocco, Ireland, and the United Kingdom (Cornwall)	1755
4.	36,000	Caused by 18838 eruption of Krakatoa	Indonesia	1883
5.	30,000	1707 Hoei earthquake	Tokaido/Nankaido, Japan	1707
6.	25,674	1868 Arica earthquake/tsunami	Arica, Chile	1868
7.	22,070	1896 Meiji-Sanriku earthquake	Sanriku, Japan	1896
8.	15,729 to 20,368	2011 Tohoku earthquake and tsunami	Iwate/Miyagi/Fukushima, Japan	11 March 2011
9.	15,030	1792 Mount Unzen eruption in southwest Kyushu/ tsunami	Kyushu, Japan	1792
10.	12,000	1771 Great Yaeyama Tsunami	Yaeyama, Okinawa, Japan	1771
11.	Unknown	Kaveripattinam (Poompuhar) Tsunami	Poompuhar, Tamilnadu, India	400 AD

LIST OF WORLD WIDE DEADLY EARTHQUAKES

Rank	Death toll	Event	Location	Date
1.	830,000	1556 Shaanxi earthquake	China	23 January 1556

2.	242,419–779,000	1976 Tangshan earthquake	China	28, July 1976
3.	316,000	2010 Haiti earthquake	Port au Prince, Haiti	12, January 2010
4.	250,000	526 Antioch earthquake	Antioch, Byzantine Empire (now Turkey)	May 526
5.	235,502	1920 Haiyuan earthquake	China	16, December 1920
6.	230,210	2004 Indian Ocean earthquake	Indonesia	26, December 2004
7.	230,000	1138 Aleppo earthquake	Syria	11, October 1138
8.	200,000	856 Damghan earthquake	Iran	22, December 856
9.	150,000	893 Ardabil earthquake	Iran	23, March 893
10.	142,000	1923 Great Kanto earthquake	Japan	1, September 1923
11.	123,000	1908 Messina earthquake	Italy	28, December 1908
12.	110,000	1948 Ashgabat earthquake	Turkmen SSR, Soviet Union (now Turkmenistan)	5, October 1948
13.	100,000	1290 Chihli earthquake	China	27, September 1290
14.	100,000	1755 Lisbon earthquake	Portugal	1, November 1755
15.	100,000	1667 Shamakhi earthquake	Azerbaijan	November 1667

16.	79,000	2005 Kashmir earthquake	Pakistan (Pakistan-administered Kashmir)	8, October 2005
17.	77,000	1727 Tabriz earthquake	Iran	18, November 1727
18.	70,000	1970 Ancash earthquake	Peru	31, May 1970
19.	70,000	1932 Changma earthquake	Gansu, China	25, December 1932
20.	68,712 (18,392 missing)	2008 Sichuan earthquake	China	12, May 2008
21.	60,000	1268 Cilicia earthquake	Armenian Kingdom of Cilicia (now Turkey)	1268
22.	60,000	1693 Sicily earthquake	Italy	11, January 1693
23.	60,000	1935 Balochistan earthquake	British India (now part of Pakistan)	31, May 1935
24.	50,000	1783 Calabrian earthquakes	Italy	1783
25.	50,000	1990 Manjil-Rudbar earthquake	Iran	21, June 1990
26.	45,000	1999 Izmit earthquake	Turkey	17, August 1999
27.	40,000	1498 Meio Nankaido earthquake	Japan	20, September 1498
28.	40,000	1797 Riobamba earthquake	Ecuador	1797
29.	40,000	1927 Gulang earthquake	Gansu, China	1927
30.	32,962	1939 Erzincan earthquake	Turkey	26, December 1939

31.	30,000	1202 Syria earthquake	Syria	20, May 1202
32.	30,000	1939 Chillán earthquake	Chile	24, January 1939
33.	28,000	1949 Khait earthquake	Tajikistan	10, July 1949
34.	26,271	2003 Bam earthquake	Iran	26, December 2003
35.	25,000	1988 Spitak earthquake	Armenia	7, December 1988
36.	23,700	1293 Kamakura earthquake	Japan	27, May 1293
37.	23,000	1976 Guatemala earthquake	Guatemala	4, February 1976
38.	22,066	1896 Meiji-Sanriku earthquake	Japan	15, June 1896
39.	20,000	1812 Caracas earthquake	Venezuela	26, March 1812
40.	20,000	1905 Kangra earthquake	British India	4, April 1905
41.	19,727	2001 Gujarat earthquake	India	26, January 2001
42.	15,621	1970 Tonghai earthquake	China	4, January 1970
43.	15,269	2011 Tohoku earthquake and tsunami	Japan	11, March 2011
44.	15,000	1960 Agadir earthquake	Morocco	26, February 1960

45.	15,000	1978 Tabas earthquake	Iran	16, September 1978
46.	12,225	1962 Bou'in-Zahra earthquake	Iran	1, September 1962
47.	12,000–15000	1907 Qaratog earthquake	Tajikistan	21, October 1907
48.	12,000	1968 Dasht-e Bayaz and Ferdows earthquake	Iran	31, August 1968
49.	10,500	1934 Bihar earthquake	British India	15, January 1934
50.	10,153	1985 Mexico City earthquake	Mexico	19, September 1985
51.	10,000	1509 Istanbul earthquake	Istanbul, Ottoman Empire (now Turkey)	10, September 1509
52.	10,000	1703 Apennine earthquakes	Italy	1703
53.	10,000	1703 Genroku earthquake	Japan	31, December 1703
54.	10,000	1854 Ansei-Nankai earthquake	Japan	24, December 1854
55.	10,000	1944 San Juan earthquake	Argentina	15, January 1944

13

CHAPTER

Road Safety

AFTER A ROAD ACCIDENT

Obstructing traffic after you have had an accident can be dangerous for other motorists, particularly at night or when visibility is limited.

If your car can be driven, pull over to the side of the road as soon as you have marked the point of impact to help determine liability. If your car is blocking traffic or is a hazard to other motorists, move it out of the way if you can. Unless you do, you may be charged with causing an obstruction.

However, if police attend the scene they may ask you to leave your vehicle where it is, while they work out how the accident happened.

If the accident has happened over the crest of a hill or around a bend, try to have someone go to a spot where warning can be given to approaching traffic so that no accident occurs. At night, use a torch to minimize the danger to other road users by directing them around the accident scene. It's useful, too, to operate your hazard warning lights.

Before you move your vehicle mark its position on the road by drawing around its four wheels. In doing so, try to show the direction your vehicle has come from. These procedures – known as 'marking the point of impact' – will help later to determine liability.

Drivers are responsible for cleaning the roadways of any dangerous matter – such as broken glass or pieces of metal – which could be left lying about as the result of an accident.

ACTION DURING ROAD ACCIDENT

Assess the Situation

- Locate the victim.
- Examine the victims quickly.
- Prevent further risk of fire, explosion, road traffic.
- Keep the vehicle stationary.
- Switch off engine, fuel and battery connection.
- Display warning signals.
- Send for help.

Care of the Victim

- Rescue the trapped casualties.
- Look for breathing, heart function and consciousness.
- Care for the unconscious cases first.
- Take care of bleeding and fractures.
- Use car first aid kit if available.
- Transport the casualty to nearest hospital.

Care of the Vehicle

- Keep the vehicles immobilized and in safe custody.
- Protect the property from damage.
- Take help of local people.
- Inform police.
- Isolate vehicles carrying dangerous goods.

Driving Crazy: Heavy traffic, poor infrastructure and absence of a road culture bring out of worst in drivers.

- One hand on horn
- One hand on gearing
- One ear on cell phone
- One ear listening to loud music
- Foot on acceleration

- Eyes on female pedestrians
- Overtaking from left, right and centre that is a highway code.

India's automobile population grown heavily while the road infrastructure has not extended correspondingly.

Be Careful When on the Road

- Never play near or on a road. Play in a park, playground or the backyard of your house, away from the road. Never chase a kite or a ball onto the road – a passing vehicle may hit you. While learning to ride a bicycle, never venture out onto the road. Practice in an open space, like a play ground, away from traffic.
- Do not ride a tricycle or take a baby carriage out on the road.
- Do not play around or behind parked cars or other vehicles you may get hurt, if they suddenly start.
- Be more alert during the rains, as visibility is often reduced by rain and clouds, drivers of vehicles can not always see you clearly, hence chances of an accident are high. Moreover, roads are slippery and waterlogged and you may not be able to see open manholes, potholes, etc.
- At night, it is difficult for vehicle drivers to see you. Wear bright light-colored clothes so that drivers can easily spot you in the dark.
- Always help younger children, the handicapped and the old in crossing the road.
- Be alert and watchful for other people who may make a mistake.
- Be very careful at railway level crossings. Never cross railway tracks. Always use footover bridges. If overbridges are not provided, never cross when a train is expected to come.

Roads enable us to travel from one place to another. We can go on foot or on a bicycle, motorcycle, in cars, buses or auto rickshaws. Most of the vehicles travel at high speed. You should therefore, be very careful when you are on the road-whether you are on foot or in a vehicle.

Causes of Road Accidents

- Driver's fault – 70%
- Bad roads – 3%
- Vehicle fault – 3%
- Passenger's fault – 2%
- Pedestrian fault – 2%
- Other causes – 19%.

When we look in detail at the possible causes of road accidents we find that they can be caused by a wide range of factors but they can be grouped together under seven categories:

- The driver
- The vehicle he is driving
- The vehicle load
- The road he is driving on
- The driving environment
- Other road users
- Driver management and route planning:

For each of these topics there are many sub-topics which need to be considered for example:

The Driver

- Driver competence – education, training
- Driver attitudes
- Driver fatigue
- Driver distraction
- Driver eye-sight
- Driver inappropriate or reckless behaviour
- Driver under influence of drugs, alcohol or medications
- Driver under stress or pressure.

The Vehicle

- Vehicle not appropriate for the task
- Vehicle not properly maintained
- Vehicle-poor tires
- Vehicle-mechanical failures
- Vehicle-lacks safety equipment.

The Load

- Overloaded
- Unstable loads or weight distribution
- Unsecured loads
- Passengers not secured.

The Road

- Poor design of road
- Poor construction techniques
- Poor maintenance of the road
- Poor signage

- Road works
- Lighting
- Warnings
- Traffic calming.

The Driving Environment

- Poor visibility- fogs, mists and dusts
- Rain, ice, snow
- Flooding and standing water
- Darkness
- Excessive light
- Excessive heat or cold.

Other Road Users

- Traffic conditions
- Pedestrians
- Animals
- Other drivers condition – drunken etc.
- Other vehicle conditions
- Trains.

Driver Management and Journey Planning

- Managing drivers hours
- Rest periods
- Planning journey with realistic times
- Driving at night
- Emergency plans
- Driver supervision
- Driver standard setting
- Driver checks – medicals, eyesight, licenses.

Cell Phones Can Be Dangerous While Driving

Distraction in any form while driving is dangerous. Using a cellophane while driving makes attention wander and accidents can result. It is difficult to restrict or curb the use of cellophane while driving despite legal enactment's but it should be used with responsibility.

The best option in the interest of safety is to switch off your cellophane while you are at the wheel. However, in case use of cellophone is unavoidable, follow these suggestions:

- When you have a co-passenger, let him/her handle the calls.
- Get to know the features of your cellophane-speed dial, redial and answering facility.
- If traveling alone, position your cellophane within easy reach so that you do not have to take your eyes off the road.
- Let the voice mail facility take messages for you while you are driving. You can call back latter.
- In case you are invariably required, stop the car at the nearest safe point and get out of the car to converse.
- Do not engage in stressful talk that may take your attention off the road.
- Let the person you are speaking to know you are driving. As a driver, your first responsibility is to pay attention to the road.
- Making notes while driving should be a NO, nor should you look up for phone numbers. Wait till you can pull over.
- Use abbreviated speed dialing and program frequently called numbers. Install a hands free kit in your car, this is much safer.

Prevent Road Accidents by Following these Simple Precautions:

Commuting to Workplace Safety

If due care is not taken, accidents may happen while traveling to and from the workplace and also within the workplace.

Here are some safety tips to be followed while commuting.

Be a Safe Pedestrian

- Always walk on the footpath.
- Keep your eyes open for pot holes, fruit skins and other obstacles.
- For crossing the road, use zebra crossing or choose a safe point along the road from where the traffic is clearly visible on both sides.
- Cross two-way road in two stages.
- Never cross at a blind curve or from behind a parked vehicle along the road side.
- Use sub-ways or footover bridges wherever available.

The Bus Ride

- Do not jump on to or off a running bus.
- Do not catch or get down the bus at signals or unauthorized stops.
- Do not stand on the doorway.
- Do not lean out of a running bus or let your arms out of the window.
- Do not distract the driver by shouting or making noise.
- Hold on a support bar while standing.

Travelling by Rail

- Do not cross the track when the level crossing gates are closed.
- Do not stand at the door and lean out of a running train.
- Do not jump on to or off a running train.
- Do not travel on the roof of a train or by standing on the door.
- Do not keep your legs hanging out of the train.
- Do not get in or down at unscheduled halts.

Driving Cars/Two Wheelers

- Do not overload your vehicle beyond its capacity.
- Keep safe distance from the vehicle in your front.
- Keep to proper lane and do not change it without due care.
- Overtake only on the right. Never overtake on turns.
- Signal your intentions clearly well before you slow down, stop or turn.
- Do not over speed while turning.
- Avoid intake of alcohol or other intoxicants before driving.
- Park vehicles only at authorized and safe spots.
- Pull off the road if you feel drowsy.
- While driving at night, dip your head lights for on coming traffic.
- Check the rear before reversing.
- Use footpath side for getting in or out of a car.
- Open the door only after the car stops completely and making sure that it is not likely to hit any passer-by or vehicle coming from behind.
- Make sure that the doors are properly locked before the car moves.

Additional Guidelines to Two-wheeler Riders

- Always wear crash helmet and avoid excessive speed.
- Do not indulge in racing and showing off (avoid acrobatics).
- Avoid riding on the painted markings on the road to prevent skidding.
- Always use rear view mirrors.

Cycling

- Remember, cycle is a vehicle for one person.
- Before moving out, check tyre inflation, brakes, bell and light.
- Do not catch another moving vehicle while riding.
- Keep to left. Ride close to the curb.
- Keep both hands on the handle bar. Do not take anything in hand.

- Be careful about a open man hole at road side.
- Always ride in a single file.
- Keep safe lateral distance from fast moving heavy vehicles.
- Always wear light colored clothes while riding at night. Also ensure provision of reflector on rear mudguard.

At the Work Place

- Never trespass the prohibit areas.
- Never take ride in industrial trucks/forklifts.
- Observe speed limits.
- Do not walk through or a cross any operating plant unless you are authorized to do so. Avoid shortcuts.
- Use designated routs for crossing the work areas/shops.

START EARLY REACH SAFELY

Defensive Driving: Safe Driving

When was the last time your car got involved in an accident for no fault of yours? Did you recently have a narrow escape in one of those close encounters on the road, even though you were in the right? If the answer is yes, you ought to know about the art of defensive driving. And if it is no, then too read on, because you may become a victim soon.

Defensive driving is anticipating situations and factors that can possibly lead to accidents when you are behind the wheels; so that you prevent accidents in spite of the wrong actions of others, or the presence of adverse conditions. If you are a defensive driver, you think ahead and anticipate the trouble that the other fellows are going to create, and be ready with an added margin of safety. For example, some drivers may overtake from the left; others may simply screech to a halt on a busy road; some others may take a turn abruptly without signaling. And their errors put you in a tight spot.

Likewise, there may be errant, ignorant and unpredictable pedestrians on the road. Worse is the band of cyclists, handcart pullers, animal driven vehicles and what-have-you.

So if you have to be safe, you have to be on the "defensive", i.e., adopting a defence against all these hazards. Defensive driving, however, is much more than adapting to the negative behaviour of other road users. It calls for a positive approach to your driving also.

Observe lane discipline. Always give right of way to all vehicles on your right at all times. Keep to the left; and overtake only on right. Do not go crazy when the other fellow is overtaking you. You are not competing for the grand pix, anyway! Let him pass. Slow down when approaching intersections, road junctions or road corners.

Keep safe following distances. And never drink and drive. Drinking and driving do not mix.

To sum up, as a defensive driver, you just can not have complete faith in the other fellows on the road. So develop your skill to make allowances fore their lack of skill and knowledge. Well, some may brand you a pessimist. But never mind. Tell them you are practicing the art of staying alive! Happy driving.

Do not Drive Yourself Crazy Driving to Work

An article in health reports that going to work can be harmful to your health – if you have to drive to get there.

A researcher from the University of California at Irvine who has studied the effects of driving on health and personality since the 1970s says that the daily commute by car can result in "driver stress".

The characteristics of this highway syndrome include the following:

- The longer the commute, the higher the blood pressure.
- Employees who drive to work show a greater incidence of absences – usually cold or flu.
- Stressed-out drivers suffer "Inter domain transfer". They tend to carry negative emotions from their home life into the office, or take out job frustrations on their families.

Here are some ways to avoid driver stress:

- Limit the time you spend in traffic; for example, avoid rush hour by planning an after-work activity.
- Once you are on the road, make your car a pleasant place to be; for instance, play music' language tapes or books on tape.
- Keep anger from building by not letting other drivers or situations get to you; realize that you have little control over such things as red lights and roadblocks.

Driver's Checklist in Rainy Season

Some Life Saving Questions

When Approaching a Junction

- Can other drivers see me?
- Am I sure they have seen me?
- Do I have an escape route if they have not?

If You are Approaching a Bend

- How sharp is it?
- Is my speed right?
- Am I in right position?

When Approaching Green Lights

- Are they about to change?
- Do I have to time stop?
- Can the vehicle behind me stop?

Driving Hints

Cut back your maximum speed if you want to save money. In most cars petrol consumption skyrockets once you go above about 80 km/hour. If you have got overdrive use it, particularly on the open road and aim to keep the accelerator at no more than half to three quarter throttle.

Drive smoothly and sensibly, avoid jack-rabbit starts and tyre burning stops, the extra energy used on in fuel is just washed, so aim for a more gradual build up and slow down.

Change down for going uphill and round corners, rather than trying to make it by struggling through on a wide-open throttle.

When starting do not use the choke to excess, only use it long enough to keep the engine running smoothly; avoid prolonged engine idling. When stopping do not rev the engine before switching off. It only wastes fuel and can dilute the oil on the cylinder walls causing extra water.

Get your car serviced regularly, checking spark and distributor gaps and renew them about every 10,000 to 15,000 km. Ensure the timing is set accurately while you are at it. Flush the cooling system at least every 12 months and replace the inhibitor, check the condition of the radiator hoses and drive belts.

Use only the correct grade engine oil for your car. Heavy grades of oil can increasing engine drag and increase petrol consumption.

Under-inflated tyres also can cause more resistance to overcome, so keep your tyres at the specified pressure. Remember, when buying new ones that radials also have less rolling resistance than conventional tyres.

Do not ask your engine to do more work than necessary. Your boot's not a store for old spares; clear out the heavy junk from it and remember that an air conditioner used unnecessarily also can add your petrol consumption.

Drunken Drivers Risk Other Lives Besides their Own

Findings from many studies made in recent decades seem to be universally applicable; the relative risks to drivers who drink are the same whether in Bangladesh, Belgium, Botswana or Brazil. The absolute number of accidents involving drinking in any one country will depend on other factors, including driver training, experience and attitudes and the general road traffic solution. Nevertheless there was now an accepted yardstick by which the accident risk due to alcohol could be judged.

For legal purposes, two approaches emerged; in one the use of alcohol by drivers was effectively forbidden, and in the other a maximum allowable level of 0.8 per mill became the most popular choice. The 0.8 per mill received support from international organizations, such as WHO, and from various country groupings.

To-day, enforcement procedures are relying more upon accurate breath test machines, simple enough to be used by trained policemen but which provide legally acceptable evidence, rather than blood testing which involves medical attendants and costly analysis.

The use of alcohol by road users is the largest single identifiable contributory factor to road accidents and in theory should be relatively easy to prevent. In practice, the problem is surprisingly robust and resistant to treatment, especially in the developed countries, where both drinking and driving a car are integral social features of long standing.

The developing countries may be in a much better position, and most of them have either imposed a complete ban on alcohol when driving, or have set maximum alcohol levels for drivers at about 0.8 per mill or lower.

The experiences of the developed countries are being studied with some advantage and important lessons have been learned to benefit the third world.

If You Drink, Do Not Drive; If You Drive, Do Not Drink

If you are a drinker, whether habitual or occasional, you would be familiar with situations where you drink "just one more" or have "one for the road". We are not sure whether you should refuse that "just one more" but if it is meant to be "one for the road", we would strongly recommend that you say a firm "NO".

Our reason is simple. It is always the safest policy not to drink before driving. Many of you know your limits and have a responsible attitude towards drinking and safe driving. This, however, does not apply to problem drinkers and many of us often do not know that we have problems.

We could give you the sentimental line "before you drink and drive, think of the others waiting for you at home."

This would not work because you have heard it before. So, if you must drink and drive, we would suggest a few precautions:

Eat something before you drink. This helps to slow down the rate of alcohol absorption. Drink slowly and space out your drinks evenly. Know what you are drinking and how strong the drink is and how it is likely to affect you. Set a limit to the number of drinks and stop in time. Do not mix your drink.

Better still follow the maxim: "If you drink, do not drive; if you drive, do not drink." Be honest with yourself. If you have any doubt do not drive.

In-plant Truck Drivers

Fork trucks, tractors and other internal vehicles can be very valuable assets to the company. Drivers of the equipment are generally professional drivers who take a pride in their capabilities, but somehow we still have accidents.

The most common types of accidents involving in-plant vehicles are:

- **Carrying unsafe loads:** Occasionally we can see the containers being transported with side members loose or missing. Drivers must check for this condition before moving a load.
- **Pedestrians walking in front of vehicles without looking:** Pedestrians have a certain responsibility to look where they are going. After all we look both ways before crossing a road, why not also do these in the plant?
- **Drivers reversing without looking:** There is a temptation for drivers who go forward into an area to lift a pallet and to reverse out without looking back. This is a highly dangerous act and drivers must always look in the direction in which they are traveling.
- **Drivers pushing containers along the floor:** Under no circumstances should non-wheeled containers be dragged or pushed along the floor. This action damages equipment, the floor, and on occasions it has trapped operators.
- **Carrying passengers:** Most trucks have single seats for the driver only. Passengers must not be carried unless proper seating has been provided. There are several cases on record of persons sitting on the sides of trucks and tractors, then falling off and getting caught under one of the wheels.

INTERESTING INFORMATIONS ON ROAD SAFETY

- **The old driver,** to pass a driving test is Mrs. Gerty Edwards Land, born on September 9, 1897, she was granted the license in Colne, Lancs, on April 27, 1988, when she was nearly 90 years.
- **It is easy in Egypt,** where you can drive 6 meters forward and an equal distance in reverse, it is sufficient to make you an eligible driver.
- The driving license system was first introduced in the year 1903 in great Britain. The driver was required to pay one pound towards registration and five shillings for driving license. Interestingly, there was no driving test; the license could be obtained by making the payment at a post office.
- **Auto devastation in 1980,** it was estimated that motor cars in the United States annually estimated 60 million tons of carbon monoxide, 6 million tons of nitrous oxide, 12 million tons of hydrocarbons and 1 million ton of smoke. According to research at the University of California, pollution from cars kills up to 30,000 people

a year in U.S.A. alone. It affects the lung capacity and aggravates heart disease, bronchitis and emphysema.

- **The first automobile accident** occurred on May 30, 1896 in New York City when a car collided with a bicycle and broke Ms. Thoma's leg.
- **The first fatal accident,** however, was reported in London on February 26, 1899 when the driver of a car met with an accident while negotiating a turn on Grove Hill.
- **The first fatal accident** involving a pedestrian was reported in New York city on September 3, 1899 when a man stepping off a street car was run over by a car.
- **Windscreen wiper:** The credit of inventing the wind screen wiper goes to a woman, Ms. Marry Anderson of Birmingham (England). She made a drawing of a gadget that was a simple manually operated arm to clear rain, snow, etc. from the windscreen. It was patented in 1903.
- **The worst driver:** A 75 year old male driver (name withheld) from Texas (U.S.A.) received ten traffic tickets, drove on the wrong carriageway four times, committed four hit-and-run offences and caused six accidents, all within 20 minutes, on 15 October, 1966. He got his notoriety enshrined in the Guinness book of records.
- **Ist speeding ticket** was given on 28th January, 1896 to Mr. Walter Arnold of Kent (U.K.) by a tough cop who chased his car on a bicycle and apprehended him for exceeding the speed limit by nearly 4 miles per hour. Walter was speeding away at a break-neck speed of 6 m.p.h., while the speed limit as per the Red Flag Act of 1878, was notified as 2 m.p.h. The speed limit was raised to 12 m.p.h. in 1896, and to 20 in 1903.
- **Old is gold:** Speeding is not a temptation for youngsters alone. Mr. Roy M. Rawlins of California (U.S.A.) was apprehended and warned for driving at 152 km/h in June 1974, when he was just 104 years old. What a way to go.

  The Golden Rule:
  - Descend a gradient in the same gear as would have been used for ascending it. Control the speed by staying in the correct gear to avoid excessive use of brakes, which can lead to 'brake-fading'. (The brakes fade as a result of excessive heating leading to temporary brake failure.) When allowed to cool, the brakes will function normally again.
  - Is that you must maintain a minimum distance of one car length from the vehicle in front for every 15 km/h of your speed. Thus at a speed of 60 km/h, you must keep a minimum distance of 4 car-length from the vehicle you are following.

Place where Speed Breakers are Justified

Use of speed breakers is justified primarily under the following three circumstances:

- T-intersections of minor with trial truck highways, characterized by relatively low traffic volumes on the minor road but very high average operating speed and poor sight distance. Such locations have a high record of fatal accidents and as such a speed breaker on the minor road is recommended.

- Intersections of the minor roads with major roads, and mid-block sections in urban areas where it is desirable to bring down the speeds.
- Selected local streets in residential areas, schools, college or university campus, hospital etc. Also in areas where traffic is observed to travel faster than the regulated or safe speed in the area.

Other places where they may be used include:

- Any situation where there is a consistent record of accidents primarily attributed to the speed of vehicles, e.g., when hazardous sections follow a long tangent approach;
- Approaches to temporary diversions;
- Approaches to weak or narrow bridges and culverts requiring speed restriction for safety;
- On the minor arms of uncontrolled junctions and at railway level crossings;
- Sharp curves with poor sight distance;
- Places of ribbon development, where road passes through built-up areas and vehicles traveling at high speeds are a source of imminent danger to pedestrians.

Unmanned Level Crossing

By simply adhering to the already available provision of the Motor Vehicles Act, 1988, standard specified by the Indian Road Congress and the railway subsidiary rules, accident can be avoided. Section 131 of the M.V. Act. 1988 clearly explains the duty of motor vehicle drivers to take certain precautions at unmanned level crossings.

"Every driver of a motor vehicle at the approach of any unmanned level crossing shall cause the vehicle to stop and the driver of the vehicle shall cause the conductor or cleaner or attendant or any other person in the vehicle to walk up to the level crossing and ensure that no train or trolley is approaching from either side and then pilot the motor vehicle across such level crossing, and where no conductor or cleaner or attendant or any other person is available in the vehicle, the driver of the vehicle shall get down from the vehicle himself to ensure that no train or trolley is approaching from either side before the railway track is crossed."

- Better be late than lose your life.
- The train is speeding at the rate of 25 meters/sec.
- In 20 secs., the train will cover a distance of half a kilometer.
- A second's delay in crossing the line and it will end the journey of your life.
- Do not try to out beat this speeding train approaching the level crossing.
- Stop – think – watch out.

Safety While on the Move

- Know your routs and choose the correct lane.
- Change lane well in advance and after giving a proper signal and making sure through the rear-view mirror that no vehicle is closely following you.
- Keep foot off the clutch and drive in correct gear.
- Always keep both hands on the steering wheel.
- Never turn around to talk to another passenger or allow your attention to be distracted.
- Never race on public roads. A gentleman would never resent being overtaken. A personal challenge can result in a sight to the ultimate finish – **Death.**
- Never coast downhill with your gears or transmission in neutral.
- Never switch off the engine while stopping at traffic signals. Apart from being an offence, frequent states adversely affects the life of the battery and the starter motor.
- Never exceed speed limits.
- While on long distance travel, it is advisable to have at least ten minutes rest for every two hours of driving in the plains and every one and half-hours in hilly terrain. If you feel drowsy or uncomfortable, stop the vehicle off the carriageway and walk for a while. Opening the window to let in fresh air will also help.

Telltale Signs of Intoxicated Drivers

Each year many people die in alcohol-related accidents, including drivers, passengers and pedestrians.

To avoid becoming a victim, watch for drivers who:

- Drift or weave
- Speed or drive too slowly
- Give inconsistent signals
- Brake erratically
- Stop without apparent cause
- Accelerate or slow down rapidly
- Drive with his or her head out of the window or with the window down in cold weather
- Drive into opposing or crossing traffic
- Drive with tires on lane marker
- Respond slowly to traffic signals
- Almost strike an object or another vehicle

- Make unusually wide turns
- Drive on the shoulder or the roadside
- Tailgate
- Turn abruptly or illegally
- Drive with the headlights off in the dark.

If you a driver under the influence take these precautions to protect yourself and your passengers:

- If the driver is ahead of you, follow at a safe distance. If the driver is behind you, turn right at the nearest intersection and let the driver pass before resuming your trip.
- If the driver approaches you, quickly slow down as you move to the right and stop. This will help you avoid a head on collision. If possible, sound your horn or flash your lights.
- When you approach an intersection, slow down and be ready for the unexpected. Look both ways and be prepared to take evasive action, especially at night.
- Above all, make sure you and your passengers are buckled up, small children are in approved safety seats and your doors are locked.

Travelling Safely by Bus

A large number of people have to travel by buses to places of work, for shopping, etc. There are certain safety precautions that one should keep in mind while traveling by bus. For your safety, follow these guidelines:

- Stand in a queue while waiting for a bus. Stand on a footpath or at the bus stop, not on the carriageway.
- Do not get in until passengers have alighted.
- Once inside the bus, keep your head and arms inside the window; a passing vehicle may brush against your body and injure you.
- After getting into the bus, move forward so others may get in easily. Do not crowd the entrance and exit.
- Never get into or out of a moving bus. You may lose your balance and have a nasty fall. Traveling on the footboard is dangerous.
- After getting off the bus, wait till the bus leaves before crossing the road ; look for a safe place to cross and while crossing the road, follow the five point curb drill:
  - Stop at the curb
  - Look to your right
  - Look to your left

- Look to your right again
- Walk straight across the road if no approaching vehicle is nearby, do not run.

Do not get into arguments with the driver; it can disturb and distract him and cause accidents.

You can get involved in an accident when you are traveling in a bus, you should, therefore, learn the safe way of getting into/out of buses and be safe.

Two Wheelers are Saffer Than One

Mopeds and motor scooters are more powerful than bikes and less costly than motorcycles. They continue to grow in popularity. But the authors of "Drive right" suggest several reasons why you must take special care when you interact with mopeds or motor scooters in traffic.

Since the engines in mopeds and motor scooters are smaller than those in motor cycles, they lack the speed and acceleration of the more powerful two wheeler. Leave a large space in front of you when you are following a moped or motor scooter.

Because mopeds and motor scooters weight less than motorcycles, drivers can maneuver them more easily. However, their narrower tires give them less contact with the roadway. In adverse weather conditions, especially, this can result in sudden loss of control.

Mopeds and motor scooters are smaller, quieter and less noticeable than their noisy big brothers. So automobile drivers must be extra careful to check blind spots before maneuvering in traffic.

Mopeds and motor scooters attract young drivers – many of them untrained and inexperienced. Be prepared for the unexpected when you are near these vehicles.

TRAFFIC LAWS ARE FOR YOUR SAFETY

No moving vehicle is ever completely free of the possibility of involvement in an accident. Even a vehicle being driven on a straight dry road on a clear day risks an accident. That's why it is important to recognize potential accident situations in time and adjust to them and avoid an accident.

Here are some fundamental traffic laws that can help you to drive safely and prevent an accident.

- Keep left. Allow traffic in the opposite direction to pass you on the right.
- Overtake only on the right.
- Overtaking on the left is permitted only when the car in front is about to turn right.
- Overtaking is not permissible if it is likely to cause inconvenience or danger to the other traffic or where the road ahead is not visible.

- When being overtaken or passed by another vehicle do not increase your speed or try and prevent the other vehicle from passing you.
- Slow down when approaching intersections, road junctions or road corners. Enter the intersection or junction if it does not endanger any one.
- When entering a main road from a junction gives way to the vehicle proceeding along the main road. Give way to all traffic approaching the intersection on your right hand. If there is a 'Dead slow-major road ahead' signs, yield right of way to the vehicles on your left also.
- Drive slowly when passing a procession or when passing road repairs. In any case your speed should not exceed 25 km/h.
- When turning to the left, drive close to the left-hand side of the road.
- When turning to the right draw to the center of the road, stop, if necessary, at the intersection, then move to the left half side of the road you are about to enter.

Obey traffic laws and build a safe zone around you.

ROAD SAFETY TIPS

- Have care, courtesy and consideration for other road users.
- Make safe driving a way of life.
- See and be seen on the road.
- Drinking and driving do not mix.
- Practice defensive driving for safe motoring.
- Do not drink if you have to drive.
- Safety first, speed next.
- Proactive action is accident prevention.
- Speed thrills it also kills.
- Life is precious, save it.
- Joy ride on the road is dangerous.
- Traffic planning is key to road safety.
- Watch all blind corners.
- Do not drive in excess speed.
- Use crash helmets while driving two wheelers.
- Do not allow children to play on the road.
- Be alert to the bumps on the road.
- Start early, drive slowly, reach safely.

- Wait for signals before overtaking vehicles.
- Follow the traffic disciplines and rules.
- Avoid unhealthy competition on the road.
- Always keep your documents while using the vehicles.
- Driving with care makes accident rare.
- Keep more attention, to avoid collision.

TEN COMMANDMENTS OF SAFE DRIVING

Before Commencing Journey

- Ensure that the driving license is with you.
- Check tyre pressure, radiator water and fuel.
- Keep separate wheel, fan belt, hosepipe and toolbox in the vehicle.
- Ensure that lights are clean and operating properly.
- Make sure that number plates are clean and clearly visible.
- See that windows are clean and obstructions to clear vision are removed.
- Adjust rear-view mirrors and release hand brake.
- Ensure that all doors are closed and locked.
- Make sure that there is no object or animal under the vehicle, and the area to the front and rear of your vehicle is clean.
- Check foot brake on start.

Conclusion

Road safety can be increased by the use of the following five E's:

- Proper engineering of the vehicle and the road.
- Proper education on road safety to all.
- Proper enforcement of all rules without any discrimination.
- Proper enthusiasm with everybody to follow road safety rules.
- Proper evaluation by all to follow road safety rules.

14

CHAPTER

Safety Rules in Industries

CAUSES OF ACCIDENT

All unsafe acts and conditions can be eliminated by gaining a better understanding of the common causes of accidents and thereby decrease the possibility of accidents. The following list represents the principal causes of accidents:

Improper Tools of Equipment

Know your tools and use the proper tool for the job.

Method Not Suitable

A safe workman knows the correct method of performing his job. Beware of shortcuts. Take time to be safe. Lift weights correctly. In case of doubt, consult your supervisor.

Protective Equipment Not Used

Every employee must use all safe guards and protective equipment required for his protection.

Rules and Instructions Not Observed

Rules and procedures are essential for smooth and effective company operation. Suggestions are always welcome; but before deviating from the established rules, consult your supervisor.

Lack of Proper Inspection and Maintenance

Machinery, tools and operating equipment should be inspected before and during use. Necessary repairs should be reported to your supervisor immediately.

Contributory Negligence

Think about the other fellow. Do not allow your carelessness or neglect to endanger somebody else.

Inattention

Keep your mind actively on the job. Daydreaming, worry and horseplay have no place on any job.

Mental and Physical Condition

Poor mental or physical condition which may not allow you to be alert can contribute to accidents.

Poor Judgement

Safety is usually a matter of common sense. Use it always.

Walkways and Roads

Where walkways are provided, use them instead of taking shortcuts through process or working areas. Shortcuts often result in slips and falls.

House Keeping

A large percentage of unsafe conditions can be classified as "poor house keeping". A clean plant is a safe plant.

Lack of Communications

Poor communications often cause accidents. You must communicate effectively with every employee connected with the job you are doing to prevent accidents specially signs for cranes.

SAFETY RULES FOR EMPLOYEES

The Supervisor's Safety Responsibility

Each supervisor has personal and individual responsibility for the safety of all employees who report or are assigned to him.

While the supervisor may make use of the assistance provided by staff groups, this in no way reduces his own obligations to assure that his personnel execute their assignments safely. Each supervisor must make a careful study of the material in this manual, because adequate knowledge of safety rules and procedures is an essential part of good supervision. Safety rules and procedures require follow-up, and as part of this follow-up, supervisors have the responsibility for initiating action when there is a need for different or improved safety requirements.

Supervisory responsibility is indicated but not limited by the following activities:

- Supervisors must make certain that any unsafe conditions are identified and that adequate safety precautions have been taken.
- Supervisors must take immediate corrective action whenever unsafe conditions and unsafe practices are discovered.
- In case of doubt about the safety of personnel, equipment, procedure, operation, or material, the supervisor must consult with his immediate supervisor for an appraisal of the situation. Where conditions justify it, the supervisor shall discontinue operations until corrective action has been taken.
- Supervisors will develop safety awareness in the minds of all employees (by making safety contacts, and conduct employee safety meetings as required).
- Investigate thoroughly all accidents that take place in their area of responsibility to determine the causes and take required corrective action. A written accident report must be promptly submitted to proper company authorities.
- Supervisors must enforce safety rules and procedures. It is each supervisor's responsibility to see to it that employees under his direction are capable of performing their jobs safely.
- It is the supervisor's duty to provide instructions when necessary, in the safe method of doing a job.
- Supervisors are required to make periodic contacts with employees assigned to work in isolated locations.

It is the duty of each supervisor to strive for results in safety just as in production, quality control and cost reduction. This must be done on a day-to-day basis as an important part of his supervisory responsibilities.

Existing safety rules and procedures must be followed and whenever employees ignore them, on the spot corrective action must be taken to assure future conformance. Supervisors must take corrective action whenever rules are not observed because a single violation can place the safety of the individual or a work group in jeopardy.

The Employee's Safety Responsibility

- Any questions or comments concerning safety practices or specific unsafe conditions are to be directed to your supervisor.
- Report all accidents and injuries to your supervisor.
- Get instructions from your supervisor before starting work with which you are not familiar.
- Each employee must use protective equipment required for performing his work safely and ensure it is in proper working condition.
- If conditions arise which make it unsafe to proceed with your assigned job, stop and immediately notify your supervisor.
- When you work alone in an isolated location, keep in contact with the other person working near by.
- Prior to commencing maintenance work in any unit which is in operation, contact must be made with the operating personnel in the area.
- Do not indulge in any kind of horseplay or practical jokes or quarrel with any body.
- In case of sickness immediately inform your Shift-in-charge.
- Before running any machinery ensure by visual checking:
  – That there is no foreign material inside;
  – That belt guards, fly wheel guards or any other moving part guards are properly secured in their position.
- Do not go near the unguarded moving parts or work on the moving parts of the machinery.
- In case of power failure, except the push button switches put the other switches in off position.
- Inform the deviations occurred in your shift at the time of handing over to the reliving shift in writing.
- Follow the steps in sequence before taking any **cleaning job or maintenance job** where entry is necessary or where chances or accident prevails though working outside.
- Handover the key and the electrical permit to the man who will attend the job actually work.
- After completing the work ask Electrical Department in the "Clearance from" for putting the fuse.

- Before putting the local switch "ON" also check inside the machinery that there is no foreign material inside or no body is working.

N.B.: Caution Board: **MEN AT WORK**
DO NOT START THE MACHINE

- Maintain a Safety Register mentioning the above points for attending any maintenance or cleaning jobs.

Fire Prevention

- Smoking is prohibited in specified areas inside the Factory properly posted with signs or/and symbols.
- Should employee like to smoke he/she should check whether the area where he/she likes to smoke is not a prohibited area.
- Smoking in unauthorized locations or in motor vehicles within the premises is forbidden.
- Fire and safety equipment must be kept unobstructed in its designated location.
- Dry chemical and/or carbon dioxide extinguishers only must be used on fires on or around electrical equipment.

House Keeping

- Good house keeping is an important part of any fire prevention programme.
- Each employee must maintain good house keeping in the area in which he works.
- Oil or chemical spills must be washed up or cleaned up promptly. If spills are overhead, warning must be given to any men below.
- Oil rags, rubbish and papers must be placed in covered metal containers. Debris and waste material must be removed.
- Materials must not be placed where they will obstruct doors, aisles, passage ways, stairs, platforms and ladders or where they will create tripping hazards. Store material in an orderly manner.
- Report oil leaks or any other leaks promptly to your supervisor.
- Floor must be kept clean and in good repair. Remove or bend down all protruding nails.

Traffic

- Only authorized personnel having a valid driving license are permitted to operate motor vehicles. Passengers must never board or leave vehicles that are in motion. They must be seated inside the vehicle body when in transit.
- Stop and warning signs at all street and railroad crossings must be obeyed.

- Speed limits must be obeyed. Speed not to exceed 5 kmph.
- Vehicles must be parked only in designated parking areas.
- Vehicles must not be stopped on railroad tracks.
- Drivers of company vehicles on public roads must never pick up or offer rides to any one.

Equipment Safety Rules

A. Confined Spaces Rules:

A confined space is any vessel such as a tower, drum, tank, large line, manhole, sewer, or valve box, sump or excavation more than four feet in depth.

- Adequate means of entrance and exit must be provided.
- Proper ventilation must be providing to get minimum 20% oxygen.
- A standby person must be assigned and immediately be available to assist in the event of an emergency.
- Emergency equipment if required must be readily available and in good operating condition.
- When entering from the top, and if this is the only means of access, a life line must be readily available.
- There shall be no carbon monoxide or other toxic gases present.

B. Compressed Gas Cylinders:

1. ***Identification:***
   - A compressed gas cylinder should not be accepted unless its content can be quickly determined by the wording on it or by a tag securely attached to it. Cylinders without protective caps should not be accepted.
   - Tags and labels often get lost, torn during transportation and handling. In such cases, the only means left for the identification of cylinder contents is the ground color of the cylinder body.
   - Under no circumstances, the means of identification should be removed or tampered with.
2. ***Storage:***
   - Gas cylinders should be stored in a cool, dry and well ventilated place, away from sources of heat such as furnaces, steam pipes, welding-shop battery charging rooms etc.
   - When cylinders are stored in the open, they should be protected from direct sunlight and rain.
   - If a large number of gas cylinders are to be stored, a separate storage facility should be provided. They should be segregated in at least three groups:
     - Oxygen and inert gases.
     - Toxic but non-flammable gases.
     - Flammable gases.

Unless stored apart, oxygen cylinders and flammable gas cylinders should be separated by a fire resistive partition.

- Smoking should be strictly prohibited and "NO SMOKING" sign should be displayed, especially in the flammable gas storage area and electrical fittings if any should be of the flame proof type.
- Cylinders should be kept away from the highly combustible materials in order to reduce the fire hazard.
- Round bottomed cylinders should be laid on the floor and stacked in pyramid style, not more than 4 high with substantial wooden wedges retaining the bottom layer on each side. Outlet valves of all cylinders should face the same way.
- Always cylinders of acetylene and liquefied gases should be kept vertically.
- Full and empty cylinders should be stored apart with notices "FULL" and "EMPTY".
- Do not keep the cylinders in wet floor, to avoid corrosion of the cylinder body.

3. ***Transport:***
   - Whether full or empty, valve caps should be in position. Adequate precautions should be taken to prevent them from falling of the vehicles or being subjected to rough usage, excessive shocks or stresses.
   - Specially designed holders or cradles should be used for moving cylinders by hoist crane. They should not be lifted with any slings or electro-magnets.
   - Cylinders should not be dropped from height while unloading. Each cylinder should be slide down over cushioning materials such as coir mattress of 6" thick or used tyres. Raised platform also can be used for lowering down gas cylinders from trucks.
   - Cylinders should be properly chained or braced while in storage, transit or use. Suitable hand trolley with a chain or belt should be used for transporting cylinders. Rolling, dragging or sliding should be avoided.
   - Safety shoes are worn while handling cylinders to prevent injury to feet.
4. ***Use:***
   - Parts of valves and other fittings should be made of such materials which are not affected by the contents of the cylinder, e.g., with acetylene, copper lines should not be used, as copper acetylides formed are explosive compounds.
   - Only standard key or a proper spanner should be used to operate the valve spindle. Leverage should not be increased by other means, nor should excessive force, e.g., as by hammering. The valves should be opened slowly.

- Compressed gas cylinders should not be used without a pressure reducing regulator attached to the valve. Cylinder valve should not be used to dispense the gas directly.
- The valve outlets of cylinders are provided with standard connections:
- Left hand threads for flammable gases.
- Right hand threads for non-flammable gases.

  So that hazardous interconnections cannot be made. Connections that do not fit should never be forced.
- Before fitting the regulator, any loose dirt lying inside the valve socket should be removed by cracking the valve. Valves of flammable gases should not be cracked because there is possibility of the gas catching fire.
- Gas should not be allowed to enter the regulator suddenly. When the cylinder is not in use, the valve should be closed and pressure from the regulator released.
- Non-return valves should be provided in lines connected to the hydrogen cylinder to prevent flashback of fire.
- Cylinder valve and fittings should not be lubricated except under specific advice from the supplier. On no account oil or grease should be used on Oxygen cylinder because of the risk of fire and explosion.
- Oxygen should never be used as a substitute for compressed air for any purpose whatsoever.
- Safety plug in the valve of chlorine cylinder fuses at 69°C. And special care should be taken to see that it is not exposed to steam, hot water etc. which could produce this temperature.
- Sparks, hot slag or flame should not be allowed to contact with the cylinders.
- Valve of acetylene cylinder should not be opened by more than 1½ turns of the spindle. Acetylene should not be used at pressure in excess of 1 kg/cm^2 (15 lb/in^2) gauge.
- Practically all cylinders and outlet valves have safety devices of various types fusible plugs, relieve valves and combinations. These devices should not be tampered.
- Cylinder and its fittings up to use point should be regularly checked for leaks, using simple tests like soap bubble tests or approved type leak detector. Never tighten a leaky connection without first closing the cylinder valve.
- Do not attempt to repair leaky valves on cylinders or regulators. Remove the equipment to an open space away from fire or workmen by using proper breathing apparatus.

- All cylinders should be tested at stipulated intervals of time. For this purpose, they should be returned to the supplier.
- If nitrogen cylinders are used for liquid transfer, a non-return valve should be installed on the line. Never allow the cylinder pressure to drop down so low as to equalize with the system pressure. This is to avoid liquid backing up into the cylinder in case the vessel to be pressurized is full of liquid.
- Oxygen or acetylene cylinder must not be taken inside tanks or vessels where work is to be performed.
- Damaged connectors or faulty seats may cause backfire or flashback. Always check them.
- The valves on empty cylinders should be closed and the protective caps should be replaced. They should be marked empty before returning to the supplier. Empty cylinders should be handled with as much care as full ones.

5. ***Emergency Procedure***

- In the case of accidental leakage of toxic or inert gases from cylinders, efforts should be made to stop the leak after wearing proper breathing apparatus. If the leak is large, the area should be evacuated.
- If gas cylinders are involved in a fire which has originated in other materials, efforts should be made to remove the cylinders which are involved in the fire after ensuring that the valves are properly closed. The cylinders which have become heated should be cooled with fine spray of water.
- Where flammable gas leaking from a cylinder is burning at or near the source of leak attempts should not be made to extinguish the flame at the leak. The gas should be allowed to burn, but the cylinder should be kept cool with a spray of water.
- If a flammable gas cylinder is found to be leaking even after closing of the valve, it should be taken into the open space away from any source of ignition and slowly drained off the gas.
- Cylinders involved in emergencies should be tagged accordingly and the supplier notified.
- In case of any fire in the connecting hose, immediately stop the cylinder valve.
- An accident caused in the use of gas cylinders involving loss of life or serious injury, has to be reported to the Chief Inspector of Explosives in accordance with the provisions of Gas Cylinder Rules, 1940. This requirement is in addition to the similar requirements under the Factories Act.

C. Electrical Equipment:

- Before working on any electrical equipment make sure that the circuit is dead and switch is properly tagged.

- Only authorized employees shall start electrically driven equipment. In the event that it does not start or run properly they must not tamper with it. In case of emergencies duly authorized and instructed individuals are permitted to change cartridge-type fuses up to and including 440 volts.
- All electrical equipment, stationary or portable, must be properly grounded before energizing.
- On portable electric equipment with an outside ground wire, the ground connection must be made before making the electrical connection. Rub the ground clamp back and forth at the point of connection so that rust, paint, etc. will be scraped off, thus insuring a good contact.
- All portable electric tools and equipment, except office and laboratory equipment, shall be inspected at intervals by an electrician.
- Never open or close a switch without full knowledge concerning the circuit.
- No electrical apparatus capable of causing a spark is to be placed in locations or areas where volatile flammable material is confined or likely to be present except with specific permission.
- When working with 440 volts or more two experienced men are necessary. One man must keep himself in the clear and in position to aid his working mate when necessary.
- Do not paint on switch boards or near electric equipment until an O.K. is secured from the Electrical Supervisor.
- Properly inspected rubber gloves must be worn when working near "live" wires carrying 440 volts or more.
- An electric extension cord should not be used if it is in bad condition. Check each cord before using it for bad insulation, broken grounds, or cracked or broken protecting gloves. Avoid wrapping the cord around the arms or any part of the body. Avoid standing in water while using the cord.
- Employee should regard all wires as live and dangerous and are warned against permitting any object being handled to come in contact with electric lines. The insulation on the wire should not be assumed to be complete insulation. Any wire found dangling from a pole or other electrical equipment should be reported immediately to the supervisor.
- When working on overhead lines where there may be danger to pedestrians passing beneath, place a sign in a prominent place reading "Danger-men working above".
- Cover plates that have been removed from lighting and power cabinets, electrical manholes or other electrical enclosures must be replaced immediately after the completion of the work.

- Never use carbon tetrachloride to clean electrical equipment.
- Any defective electrical equipment should be reported to your supervisor.
- Wherever possible, portable cords should be hung overhead so that the insulation cannot be damaged by foreign objects or by workmen walking on them.
- If anyone should come in contact with live wires or cables and be unable to release his grip on the wires, do not attempt to pull him off with bare hands. Shut off the current if possible, and protect the hands with rubber gloves or if they are not available, use thick folds of dry cloth to cover the hands before attempting to release the victim. If the wires are directly on top of victim use a dry stick to remove them.

D. Guards, Barricades, Warning Signs:

- Tools, machinery and equipment safety guards and devices must always be operable and in place before such equipment is used.
- Excavations must be adequately guarded by covering them with planks or by erecting guards. Covers or guards must be in place before leaving excavations.
- Covers removed from manholes, pits in floor or in the ground must be replaced, or these openings must be handled as excavations.
- Permanent handrails and guard rails temporarily removed to facilitate work must be replaced promptly after the need for the removal is ended.
- Suitable barriers and warning signs must be erected whenever road repairs are to be made or when other work is in progress which would necessitate closing the road.
- Suitable barriers and warning sign "Men Working Overhead" must be erected at ground level whenever work is being performed above a road, a walkway, machinery, or whenever an emergency condition exists overhead.
- Barricades must be adequate.
- All warning signs must be obeyed.

E. Hoists Cranes:

- Men are not allowed to ride on blocks, hooks, balls or suspend loads.
- A warning signal must be sounded before rotating the cab of the crane.
- When operating cranes or doing rigging work within ten feet of electric wires call the Electrical Supervisor and request the necessary protection.
- Drums on hoists are to be checked for sufficient turns of rope at all times and in no instances, when under strain, should the number of turns of the rope on the drum be less than three.
- When operating traveling hoists see that no one is in the path of the load. Keep yourself in the clear at all times.

- It is important that no unauthorized person is allowed to operate the Crane.
- When on duty, remain alert in the Crane Cabin.
- Never allow any unauthorized person to go to top of the crane.
- Lift the mixer bucket to required height and definite not beyond to hook it by the hooks provided in the crane and then only moves the crane.
- Normally do not permit your crane to bump into another crane.
- Examine the crane at the start of every shift for railings, warning bells, switches, hooks of the crane. Initially run the crane without any load.
- Never pick up a load beyond the rated capacity.
- Whenever the rope is too loose than the normal operating condition check the proper seating of the rope in the sheaves and on the drum prior to further operation.
- Never move the load or the crane unless you are sure that you understand the floor signal.
- Do not allow the load to swing against the trolley man.
- Never leave a load suspended. In case of power failure, wait for 5 minutes, clear the man under the load. Release the brake slowly and mechanically to lower down the load.

F. Hooking the Load:

- At the beginning of the shift, check hooks, visually.
- Never overload a sling or wire rope. For abnormal lifting consult the Supervisor concerned.
- Distribute the load equally on the legs of the sling as far as practicable.
- While hooking or un-hooking a load, keep hand out of pinch points.
- Before giving the hoisting signal, make sure the load is safe and warn everyone to stay well out of the way in case the load swings or falls.
- Never walk under a load or permit other to do so.
- When releasing slings, make sure that they are entirely free from the load.
- Learn the crane signals and use them.

G. Ropes, Chains and Slings:

Special safety precautions are essential for using and storing ropes, wire rope, chains and slings. Manila or nylon ropes give the best uniform strength and service among the ropes but their uses are limited to cold service conditions only. Nylon rope has over 2½ times the breaking strength of manila rope and about 4 times its working elasticity. While nylon rope is wet on frozen, its breaking strength is reduced by 10 to 15%.

Wire rope is used widely instead of fiber rope because:

- It has greater strength for the same diameter and weight.
- Its strength is constant when wet or dry.
- It has constant length under varying weather conditions.
- It has greater durability.

Causes of Deterioration of Wire Ropes

Deterioration of wire ropes is due largely to the following factors, which very considerably in importance, depending on the conditions of service.

Wear, particularly on the crown or outside wires, from contact with sheaves and drums.

Corrosion, particularly of the interior wires, indicated by pitting. This condition is difficult to detect and highly dangerous. Wear is accelerated by corrosion.

Kinks, acquired in improper installation of a new rope, hoisting with slack in the rope, and so forth. A kink cannot be removed without creating a weak place.

Fatigue, indicated by a square break of a wire break showing granular structure and particularly due to excessive bending stresses from sheaves and drums with small radial, whipping, vibration, pounding, and torsion stresses.

Drying out of lubrication, often hastened by heat and operating pressure.

Overloading, including dynamic overloading, if acceleration and deceleration are factors of importance.

Over winding, which is drum crushing caused by uncontrolled multiple wrapping.

Mechanical abuse, such as pinching down and cutting wires or dragging ropes.

Alloy steel chain has become the standard material for slings because it is at least twice as strong as wrought iron chain. A link-by-link inspection should be made to detect the following:

- Bent links.
- Cracks in weld areas, in shoulders, or in any other section of link.
- Transverse nicks and gauges.
- Corrosion pits.
- Elongation caused by stretching can only be caused by overloading. The best way to detect such elongation and also link wear is by a visual link-by-link inspection.

Safe Practices

In the use of chains, recognized safe practices will do much to prevent failures.

- Never splice a chain by inserting a bolt between two links.
- Never put a strain on a kinked chain. Workmen should be trained to take up the slack slowly and see that every link in the chain seats properly.

- Do not use a hammer to force a hook over a chain link.
- Permanent identification tag is usually attached to chain slings by the manufacturer. Tags should never be removed.
- Remember that decreasing the angle between the legs of a chain sling and the horizontal increases the load in the legs.
- Use chain attachments (rings, shackles, couplings, and end links) designed for use with the chain to which they are fastened.
- See that the load is always properly set in the bowl of the hook. Loading on or toward the point (except in the case of grab hooks or others especially designed for the purpose) overloads the hook and leads to spreading and possible failure.
- Chains not in use should be stored in a suitable rack. Do not let them lie on the ground or floor for extended periods.

H. Laboratory Rules:

- Never put food in or eat or drink from laboratory apparatus.
- Never exceed pressures and temperatures which have been designated as safe upper limits for the apparatus in question.
- When siphoning or pupating harmful liquids, suction should be started with an aspirator bulb and never with the mouth.
- Use gloves, rags or specially designed equipment when boring holes in corks, or when inserting glass tubing in stoppers, rubber bungs or tubing. Lubricate tubing with water or glycerin.
- Ether and carbon disulphide shall be used with care in a room in which there is an open flame or glowing electric heater.
- Oil or gasoline soaked rags should not be left on or under work benches, or in lockers, but should be placed in containers provided for this purpose.
- Only the minimum amount of flammable liquids necessary for making tests shall be kept on work benches.
- Rubber gloves and goggles and/or face shield should be worn while handling acids and other corrosive liquids.
- Laboratory bottle washers shall wear a rubber apron, rubber gloves and goggles when handling strong chemicals, or corrosive liquids.
- Draft fans should be running constantly to carry off vapors and prevent accumulation of toxic flammable mixtures or dusts.
- Damaged glassware shall not be used.
- The pouring of mercury into a sink or drain is strictly prohibited.
- Spills should be wiped up immediately and used rags properly disposed of.

- Acquaint yourself with location, type and limitations of all fire extinguishing equipment, and be sure you know how to use it effectively.
- Do not wash spots from your clothes with gasoline. This is a definite fire hazard. Moreover, it may cause skin irritation.
- Hot equipment, such as flash cups, melting point pans, etc. should be cooled before cleaning.
- When pouring inflammable liquids from one metal container to another is certain that containers are all grounded. This should be done out of doors.

I. Ladders and Stairways:

- Ladders must be visually inspected by the user for defects prior to commencement of the job. Defective ladders must not be used and must be tagged as defective and put out of use until repaired.
- A straight ladder must be placed with its feet approximately 1/4 of the ladder length away from the line that is vertical with the top support.
- Straight ladders must be secured at the bottom to prevent slipping.
- When ascending or descending ladders, the user must face the ladder and keep a fire grip on the RUNGS.
- Only non-metallic ladders or legs insulated shall be used in electrical substations and when working in close proximity to exposed electrical circuits.
- Ladders must not be placed in front of doors, in passageways, or in the vicinity of vehicular traffic unless appropriate.
- Portable ladders must be taken down and stored when the job is done.

J. Manual Material Handling:

- Do not attempt to clean pipe threads on flanges with your bare hands. Use a brush or cloth.
- When lifting, moving or carrying pipe keeps the hands and fingers out of the ends of the pipe. Keep feet and hands from underneath pipe when it is lowered.
- In backing off flanges, catch them with bar or pipe, never with the hands the motion or weight of flange may cause severe laceration.
- When two or more men are lifting an object together they should agree on a given signal to pick up or let down, to avoid placing a strain on man or throwing the load on him. Coordination is essential in lifting, lowering, or carrying objects.
- Avoid back injuries by using the correct method of lifting loads. Bend your legs and never your back to lift loads.

The Principles of Correct Lifting:

Correct Grip:

A full palm grip not only makes for security, it enables the arms to be kept straight and permits the load to be distributed over the whole of the body and it will also prevent injury to fingers.

Arms Close to the Body:

When lifting or carrying, this keeping of the arms close to the body is of vital importance. The whole body can now be employed to carry the load and the framework can support tremendous weights without stress.

Flat Back (Straight Back):

This is the important part of the whole instruction. The adoption and maintenance of a flat back during effort of lifting eliminates compression of back muscles are not being employed in severe and dangerous fashion. In conjunction with the next principle, this position provides a definite mechanical advantage that reduces the work done to an absolute minimum and even heavy jobs can in safe and easy fashion.

Foot Positions:

When performing any action the body needs to be balanced, the position must be comfortable; the ability to move must be facilitated. The strong muscles of the legs must be employed to the best advantage because they form the strongest part of the body mechanically intended to do the work of lifting, pulling, pushing and carrying very safely.

There have been many cases of serious damage to the spinal cord and to the vital disc, due to wrong method of manual lifting.

Use the Body Weight:

This means that the strongest muscles are employed to over come the inertial of the object, and then they relax and permit the momentum of the object to complete the work safely without any strain on the back bone spine.

- Be careful about the adages of the refractory which can cut the hand.
- At the time of stacking, see the proper bonding and stability of the particular stack, so that it should not collapse.

K. Machinery Safety Rules:

- The operation of any machine, except by an authorized employee, is prohibited.
- Wear proper eye, face and hands protection on all jobs requiring them.
- Do not work on any machinery while it is in motion, if it is practical to shut it down. All guards must be kept in place while the machinery is in motion and not being worked on.
- No repair work should be done over moving machinery. When working close to moving machinery a guard must be provided between the machinery and the men working.

- Tool rests on abrasive wheels must be kept adjusted to 1/8″ from the wheel and above the centre of wheel.
- Only authorized employees shall be permitted to change or replace grinding wheels on permanent installations.
- In machine sawing, small pieces should be pushed with a stick.
- Never reach over a moving saw to get material from the other side.
- Ensure all guards in place when sawing, and do not go away leaving a saw running.
- When opening a machine, keep hands and fingers in the clear.
- When using a drill press the work should be securely clamped to the table or in a jig or chuck. When part is held in hand, an accident is likely to occur should the drill catch or stick.
- Do not attempt to operate a machine until you have acquainted yourself with the operating switches.

The common causes of personal injury occur while operating the following machineries. Be careful to avoid the same.

Grinding Machine:

- Failure to use eye protection in addition to the eye shield mounted on the grinder.
- Holding the work incorrectly.
- Incorrect adjustment or lack of work rest.
- Using the wrong type of wheel or disk or a poorly maintained or imbalanced one.
- Grinding on the side of a wheel.
- Taking too heavy a cut.
- Applying work too quickly to a cold wheel or disk.
- Grinding too high above the centre of a wheel.
- Failure to use wheel washers (blotters).
- Vibration and excessive speed which lead to bursting of wheel or disk.
- Use of bearing boxes with insufficient bearing surface.
- Using spindle with incorrect diameter or with the threads cut so that nut loosens as spindle revolves.
- Installing flanges of the wrong size, with unequal diameters, or unrelieved centers.
- Incorrect dressing of wheel.
- Contacting unguarded moving parts.
- Using controls that are out of operator's reach.
- Using an abrasive saw blade instead of a grinder disk.
- Using the disk after the expiry period.

Lathe Machine:

- Contact with projections on work or stock, face plates, chucks or lathe dogs, especially those with projecting set-screws.
- Flying metal chips.
- Hand braking of the machine.
- Filing right-handed, using file with unprotected tang, or using the hand instead of a stick to hold emery cloth against the work.
- Callipering or gauging the job while the machine is in operation.
- Attempting to remove chips when machine is in operation.
- Contact with rotating stock projecting from turret lathes or screw machines.
- Leaving chuck wrench in chuck. Using a spring-loaded wrench can eliminate this hazard.
- Catching loose clothing or wiping rags on revolving parts.

Drilling Machine:

- Contacting the spindle or the tool (Do not touch the tool which using a quick-change clutch).
- Breaking a drill.
- Using dull drills.
- Being struck by insecurely clamped work.
- Catching hair or clothing in the revolving parts.
- Sweeping chips or trying to remove long, spiral chips by hand.
- Leaving key or drift in chuck.
- Being struck by flying metal chips.
- Failing to replace guard over speed change pulley or gears.

Milling Machine:

- Failure to draw the job back toes safe distance when loading or unloading.
- Using a jig or vise which prevents close adjustment of the guard.
- Placing the jig or vise locking arrangement in such a position that force must be exerted toward the cutter.
- Leaving the cutter exposed after the job has been withdrawn.
- Leaving hand tools on the work table.
- Failure to clamp the work securely.
- Reaching around the cutter or hob to remove chips while the machine is in motion.
- Removing swarf by hand instead of with a brush.

- Adjusting he coolant flow while the cutter is turning.
- Callipering or measuring the work while the machine is operating.
- Using rag to clean excess oil off the table while the cutter is turning.
- Wearing gloves, ties, or loose clothing.
- Using cutters incorrectly dressed.
- Storing cutters incorrectly.
- Attempting to remove a nut from machine arbor by applying power to the machine.
- Striking cutter with hand or arm while setting up or adjusting stopped machine.

L. Safety Rules in Pipe Fitting Work:

- Do not remove blanks or break open lines or equipment until the unit supervisor/ operator in-charge has inspected the lines and approved the work.
- In repairing chemical lines or equipment wear goggles, protective gloves and where necessary rubber aprons and gum boots.
- Use a wire brush to remove cuttings from a pipe. Do not attempt to clean pipe thread on flanges with your bare hands. Threads and rough edges are sharp. Do not handle pipe or fittings with hands inside.
- When lifting, moving or carrying pipe keeps the hands and fingers out of the ends of the pipe.
- In lifting, lowering and carrying pipe, coordination is essential. Keep time with the others. Broken toes have resulted from falling pipe.
- Lift and lower pipe at a given signal. Work together. Accidents occur when one man lifts or lowers a load before others are ready.
- Keep feet and hands away from underneath the pipe when it is lowered.
- In supporting pipe for make-up, keep hands clear of threads. Pipe too heavy to handle by hand should be securely blocked up.
- Line up holes in flanges with studs, drift pins or flange wrenches. Keep fingers out of flange holes.
- Do not use pipe on wrenches for extension handles. Wrenches are designed for the leverage provided by their handles and the use of extension causes slipping and damages the wrench.
- Be watchful in operating travelling hoists and see that no one is in the path of the load. Keep in the clear at all times.
- Stand clear of the pipe bending machine, when it is in operation. Every pipe line should be treated as if it were under pressure when working on it. The general procedure outlined below should be adhered to:
  - Loosen the bolts that are the most difficult to remove first, always leaving at least two bolts tightened opposite from each other on the flange.

- Wear goggles and loosen the last two bolts and break the seal before completely removing the nuts and bolts.
- Never completely remove all nuts and bolts before breaking the seal.
- Before assembling pipelines and connection, make sure that the lines or equipment is free of foreign matter such as dirt, rocks or tools.

- Pipe fitters should work from a stable platform when breaking or pulling up of flanges. Do not work from an insecure ladder.
- Never use air pressure for testing piping or fittings unless proper authorization has been given.
- Keep material off the floor as far as is practicable and out of the aisle.
- Do not wear loose clothing, rings or jewellry around moving parts.

M. Safety Rules for Fork-Lift Trucks:

1. ***Safety and the Truck:***
    - Have an overhead guard and backrest. The overhead guard can save any falling of object over the driver while raising the load above head level.
    - Before beginning a work shift give your truck a complete going over. Check the oil, coolant, battery water, fuel level. Test brakes, front and back light, steering, horn and everything else you can think of. Follow the instructions given in the truck operating manual.
    - Make sure trucks are given regular maintenance, as per the schedule, given by the operating manual. Parts in the steering system, and in the brake system, which are critical to proper operation can wear and suddenly breakdown causing any number of dangerous situations. Make sure all systems get thorough maintenance checks regularly. Also be constantly conscious of how your trucks are operating while you drive.
    - At first sign of poor truck performance notify your supervisor. Have every sign of poor performance out.
    - Take refueling cautiously. Never leave the truck running, do not smoke, watch for spills, and assure adequate ventilation. Refuel only in assigned safety areas. For battery operated truck a fully charged battery will give a specific gravity reading of 1.280 and should never be allowed to discharge below 1.140 gms/cc.
    - Check that all battery plugs and terminals are tight and the caps of the cells are closed properly.
2. ***Safety and the Load:***
    - *Lifting a load:* Drive the truck as close to the load as possible and turn the vehicle so that the forks are in line with the load. Check that the forks are correctly

spaced and confirm with the width of the pallet entry. Raise the forks to the required height. Push the tilt lever forward until the masts are vertical. Drive slowly forward until the forks are fully entered into the pallet. Raise the fork carriage until the weight of the load is just taken up. Tilt the masts back. Ensure the way is clear, back slowly away from the stock. Lower the load to within 6" of the ground and proceed to the destination.

- Back down inclines. Always keep the load on the uphill side of the truck. In case of descending an incline move with the load behind, i.e., the vehicle will move backward.
- Travel in reverse for better vision when carrying bulky loads. Never move your truck if you cannot clearly see where you are going.
- Never travel with the load elevated. Your load is more stable when it is kept as close to the floor as possible. There is a great temptation especially on the short run, to keep a load taken from the top of a stack and destined for the top of another stack up high. Avoid it.
- Avoid raising or lowering a load while the truck is in motion.
- When raising a load, lowering it or carrying it, always keep the mast vertical or tilted back to keep the load against the carriage.
- Never overload than the capacity.
- Make sure the load is balanced. Never handle unstable or poorly stacked loads.
- Use extra care in handling long loads. See that the passage is clear especially in the corners.
- Use the widest fork spread possible for better stability.
- Always watch the load closely while rising, lowering, under all similar unstable situations like rough flooring and incline. Any movements a ride over, rough floors, rising, lowering can loosen the load.
- Use special care when stacking high, watch out for falling stock.
- Never use forks as a personnel elevator unless properly equipped. A fellow worker is the most unstable load you can put on your forks, and he is fragile and irreplaceable. Do not give him a lift on the forks.

3. ***Safety and the Driver:***

The driver, of course, is the most important safety factor in the lift truck operation.

- Always make sure the coast is clear before moving the truck.
- Obey the rules of the road.
- Slow down for corners and blow horn.
- Never try to turn on an incline.

- Never try to drive with wet or greasy hands or shoes.
- Keep a clean rag on the truck if necessary. Always keep hands and shoes dry and free of anything that can cause slipperiness.
- Always cross railroad tracks diagonally and at a flow speed. Look to the sides before crossing.
- Ignore everything except your driving.
- Always be aware of rear and swing. Driving a life truck forward is like driving a car backward. When you turn, the portion of the truck that's behind you makes a bigger arc – covers more territory – than the portion that's ahead. It's easy to neglect this fact about your truck and end up slamming a 2000 pound counter weight into walls or stacks or even a fellow worker.
- Avoid holes, sharp bumps, loose obstacles, oil sticks grease and water on the floor.
- Always start and stop the truck smoothly. Avoid jerking. Never use reverse as a brake, while the truck in forward motion.
- Do not show off. No matter how good you are – no matter how good it makes you feel.
- Report all accidents immediately – even the minor.
- Keep legs, arms, feet, hands, and head within the dimensions of the truck, so that it should not be dragged by any protruding objects on the way.
- Stay out from under forks and loads, and do not let any one else under.
- Do not give anyone a ride.
- Never operate in insufficient light.
- Always park your truck on a flat area, away from traffic, with the engine off, brake set and forks flat on the floor. Block wheels if necessary. Avoid leaving a loaded vehicle anywhere for any reason.
- Always be alert expect the unexpected.
- Watch out for overhead obstructions. Beware of electrical wires.
- Never bump or brush any object with your truck.
- Never run the vehicle more than 10 kmph.

4. *Emergency Stop:*

- For an emergency stop, fully release the accelerator pedal and press hard on the foot brake.
- While you come to know that due to certain problems without pressing the accelerator, the vehicle is moving immediately disconnect the plug from the battery and press hard on the foot brake.

N. Rules for Use of General Tools:

- Use the right tool for the job.
- Use tools in good condition. Split handles, worn teeth, chipped edges do poor work and cause injuries. Keep tools clean, free from grease, oil and ground metal.
- Use tools correctly. You can do better and safer work. There is a right and safe way to use even the simplest tools.
- Keep tools in a safe place. Place them in tool boxes, trays, cases, or hang them on wall. They cause injury, and are damaged when they lie around in a haphazard manner.
- Machine tools should never be left running unattended.
- Operators should not wear jewelry or loose fitting clothing, especially loose sleeves or cuffs of shirts or jackets and neckties. Long hair, which could be caught by moving parts, should be covered.
- All operators should wear eye protection, as should others in the area (such as inspectors, stock handlers, and supervisors).
- Throwing refuse or spitting in the machine tool coolant should not be allowed, such actions foul the coolant and may spread disease.
- Manual adjusting and gauging (callipering) of work should not be permitted while the machine is running.
- Operators should use brushes, vacuum equipment, or special tools for removing chips.

O. Safety Rules for Welding:

The various welding involved in the industries are of four types, namely: Oxyacetylene gas welding, Arc welding, Metallic inert gas (MIG) welding and Tungsten inert gas (TIG) welding. Out of these four types we are mainly related to the Oxyacetylene gas welding and Arc welding which are carried, out in our day to day work.

The various safety rules to be observed for them are as follows:

Gas Welding:

- Follow the safety rules for compressed gas cylinders.
- Oxygen in contact with oil or grease may cause a violet explosion. Keep them away from Oxygen.
- Oxygen is bottled under extremely high pressure (2200 psig). The cylinders must be handled carefully.
- Acetylene is highly inflammable. Keep the cylinder away from heat source.
- Acetylene has a strong, disagreeable odor resembling garlic which indicates leakage.

- Acetylene is very unstable over 15 psig which can explode also. Hence do not raise the pressure more.
- Acetylene valve should never be opened more than 1½ turns. In this way it can be turned off quickly in case of fire. From the same reason the key should always be left on the valve.
- Always keep the acetylene cylinder in upright position.
- Oxygen equipment is identified by green marking and has right hand thread whereas acetylene equipment is identified by red color and has left hand threaded connections. Do not interchange one with another.
- Sudden release of Oxygen pressure may damage the gauges. Open valve very slowly until a slight pressure registers. Do not stand in front of the gauge face. Pressure may blow face outward.
- An oxidizing flame is harmful to the weld. It is never used for welding. Unless specified always use neutral flame.
- Do not hang the hoses on the gauges. The weight may damage the gauge.
- First shut off the acetylene gas, so that escaping of oxygen will blow any soot or impurities from the tip.
- Provide proper ventilation while welding inside a confined space to remove the fumes.
- Never weld a close container. It will burst at higher temperatures.
- Bronze contains zinc, which gives off poisonous fumes when it is heated. Inhaling these fumes causes stomach cramps, vomiting and shortness of breath. Do not breathe brazing fumes. Avoid them with proper ventilation.

ARC Welding:

- Avoid striking an arc when the persons are close.
- Electric shock is always a possibility. Be sure the floor is dry. Use an insulated electrode holder. Use leather gloves.
- The danger of burns is always present. Do not handle hot metal with the hands. Use tongs or pliers.
- Never use welding machines which are not properly grounded. Ground all power circuits prevent accidental shock. Stray current can cause a fatal shock. Do not ground the welding machine to any pipes which carry gases or flammable liquids.
- Check welding cables frequently. Do not overload the capacity of the cable. Do not use cables which have breaks in the insulation. Be sure that all cable connections on the machine are tight.
- Check the electrode holder frequently. The gripping surface of the jaws must be clean to ensure a tight hold on the electrode. Never touch two electrodes

together when they are connected to two different machines, because the operator can receive an electrical shock and the machines can be seriously damaged.

- Do not change the polarity while the machine is under a welding load. The operator who changes the polarity switch while welding circuit is in use can be seriously burned.
- Never weld on containers which held explosive or combustible materials.
- Do not touch any exposed or non-insulated parts of cables or clamps.
- Face shield or goggles with proper lenses should be used to avoid infrared or ultraviolet rays which can cause blindness. It will also prevent the sparks going to the eye. Use hand gloves to protect from sparks.

P. Compressors:

- Make sure the flywheel is properly blocked so that it will not turn when making internal on engines at operating units.
- Leave at least two nuts and bolts loose in place when trying open valve covers.
- Never place the hands inside compressor cylinders or valve parts until it is made certain that the pistons will not move.
- While working on engines and when it is desired to turn the fly-wheel to reposition engine parts, make sure that all other employees working on the engine are notified and are standing clear.
- Upon completion of repair work on a compressor, it must be turned over by hand at least one revolution to assure that the machine will run clear. When turning, make sure that the cylinder vent is open to prevent kick backs.
- Compressors should not be tested or run above recommended speed limit.

Q. Portable Electric Light:

- No portable electric light or any other electric appliance of voltage exceeding twenty four volts shall be permitted for use inside any chamber, tank, vat, pit, pipe, flue or other confined space.
- If any inflammable gas, fume or dust is likely to be present in such chamber, tank vat, pit, pipe, flue or other confined space, no lamp or light other than that of flame-proof construction shall be permitted to be used therein.

R. Scaffolds:

- When erecting a scaffold, proper consideration must be given to load requirements, location and the protection of other employees or equipment below such scaffolding.
- Empty drums or barrels must not be used as a scaffold or as supports for built-up scaffolds.

- Scaffolding material, wood, bamboo or metal, must be inspected prior to the commencement of the job. Care must be taken to use only sound materials, and to follow established procedures for erection.
- Handrails must be 42 inches or more high. All scaffolds must be provided with a firm footing.
- Scaffold planks must be battened together and wired or nailed down with no nails protruding. Scaffolds must be constructed at least 10" width and plank thickness of 2".
- Scaffolds must not be overloaded.
- Before erecting scaffolds near any electrical lines or near exposed electrical equipment, electrical supervisor must be consulted to determine what special precaution needs to be taken.
- The horizontal centre distance between transoms and putlogs carrying 32 mm. Thick boards, shall not exceed 1.5 M.
- Scaffolding shall be inspected by the Supervisor-in-charge at least once every week irrespective of the length of time the scaffold is expected to remain in position.
- Avoid shock loads such as dropping heavy objects or jumping on platforms or scaffold members.
- Do not leave bolts, pieces of pipe and any other object likely to create a slipping or tripping hazard on platform.
- Under no circumstances must excavation work be allowed at or near to the base of scaffolding.
- The vertical distance between ledgers may vary between 1.3 M to 2.1 M depending upon whether access is required under platforms.

Height Work:

- Worker suffering from Hypertension, Epilepsy, and Vertigo etc. should not allow working at height.
- While working at unsafe height of more than 2 meters, the use of safety belt is a must which should confirm ISI specification.
- A worker must wear safety belt before climbing for work place/temporary platform.
- Before use, the life line and clamps of safety belt must be checked for soundness.
- The diameter of rope should be more than:
  - Manila rope-19 mm
  - Nylon rope-15 mm
- The life line of safety belt must be tied to a permanent stationary and fixed structure.
- The life line must not be rubbed against any sharp edge while working and it should not be tied to sharp edged structure.

- Suitable access to the work place/platform like ladders, ramps, stairs etc. must be provided.
- Openings on the platforms and walking must be covered or barricaded.

S. Office Safety Rules:

- Keep desk and file drawers closed when they are not being used.
- Do not use waste basket as an ashtray.
- Never stand on drawers, folding and rolling chairs or similar objects.
- Do not run electric cords for office equipment through walkways. Electric cords must be in good condition.
- Wipe up all spills and pick up objects that fall on the floor.
- Never hurry or run around blind corners, past doorways, on stairs, or in corridors. Use caution in approaching closed or swinging doors.
- Be cautious in opening file drawers. Opening too many on one unit at the same time may cause the cabinet to overturn.
- Beware of pointed office equipment such as pencils, pens, scissors, etc. they can cause puncture wounds. Pencils should be placed in the shift pockets with points downwards.
- All guards must be in place when operating office machines.
- Running is prohibited to prevent injury from slipping, tripping or collision.
- When going up and down stairs, walk never run; when carrying supplies keep one hand free and use hand rail to prevent falling.
- Keep good house keeping at all times.
- Know what to do in case of fire.

15 CHAPTER

Safety Slogans

- 'Be safe' be your watch word.
- 10 fingers, 10 toes, if you are not safe who knows?
- A bad workman quarrels with his tools.
- A casual attitude towards safety is equal to CASUALTY.
- A cat has nine lives, but you have only one, observe safety always whether you work or have fun.
- A cleaner place is a safer place.
- A closer call reported today, is the accident that does not happen tomorrow.
- A danger foreseen, is an accident prevented, follow this advise, it is time tested.
- A happy man at home will be a safe man at factory.
- A harness is better than a hearse.
- A little attention towards maintenance will increase the life of the equipments to work safely.
- A man who is peaceful at home will be careful at factory.
- A man, who is peaceful at home, with love and affection, will win the awards in the factory.

- A new broom sweeps clean.
- A safe man at home will be a safe workman at factory.
- A safe worker feels happier in his job satisfaction than money.
- A single death is a tragedy; a million deaths is a statistic.
- A small leak will sink a great ship.
- A wound neglected is a wound infected.
- Accident brings tears, safety brings cheers.
- Accident can be prevented by common sense; unfortunately the commonsense itself is not common among many people.
- Accident can strike any time.
- Accident do not just happen, they are caused.
- Accident investigation details and other statistics must be recorded and maintained.
- Accident may occur even in a well regulated factory, work safely.
- Accident prevention your number one intention.
- Accident shatters lives, safety makes life better.
- Accidents do not have any choice.
- Action speaks louder than words.
- Actions which are hasty, may not lead to safety.
- Adopt fire prevention and save destruction.
- Affection binds reason.
- Alcohol reduces performance, impairs judgements and increases the willingness to take risks.
- Alert ever accident never.
- Alertness always avoids accidents.
- All human activity is promoted by desire.
- Always look after number one and if you need help just ask.
- Always think safety no matter what the task.
- An accident can cripple your income.
- Anger is one letter away from danger, drive gently.
- Apply your good intention to accept prevention.
- Are you part of the safety team…together employees accomplish more.
- At work, at home, let safety be known.
- At work, at play, let safety lead the way.
- Awards should be meaningful and with motivating effect, even at family.

- Be a leader, follow safe procedure.
- Be a safety hero – score an accident zero.
- Be aware of slips and trips.
- Be aware take care.
- Be proactive and not reactive towards safety.
- Be safe – be your watch ward.
- Be safe and secured.
- Be safe at work or you might miss welcome home, a hug, a kiss.
- Be safety smart right from the start.
- Be sure being safe.
- Be wise, save your eyes, use goggles, the best device.
- Before commanding understand to obey.
- Before starting any work understand the safe method to proceed.
- Before using any new equipment, read and fully understand the manufacturer's instructions.
- Before you go boating, leave a float plan with a friend or marine operator.
- Before you start, be safety smart.
- Being safe is like breathing, you never want to stop.
- Best be safe today.
- Best time for safety; every second, every minute, every hour, every day.
- Better be safe than be sorry afterwards.
- Better to arrive let than never, drive carefully.
- Better to be safe than sorry, do not be unnecessarily hurry.
- Beware of your tongue because loose talking leads to many accidents.
- Broken tools can be replaced, you can not.
- Careful ways brings happy days.
- Careful, careful its better to be careful a thousand times than careless once
- Caution is the parent of safety.
- Check and have safety management control on all operations.
- Check for safety then recheck.
- Check wires, avoid fires.
- Check your shoes and do not let your day slip away.
- Clean safety habits prevents troubles.
- Combine your will and skill, to make accident nil.

- Common sense is not so common.
- Conserve environmental resources.
- Convey correct information to fire station.
- Depend on safety, not on fate; adopt safe ways before it's too late.
- Diet cures more than doctors so is safety saves so many losses including lives.
- Difficulty is a severe instructor.
- Discuss with the workers and take ideas and suggestions. Make them to feel their importance.
- Do a pre warm-up and stretch prior to participating in any sport.
- Do accidents happen to others only? It's time you sit down and think seriously.
- Do not gamble with accident.
- Do not be a fool! Inspect the proper tool.
- Do not be a fool! Inspect your electrical tools.
- Do not be a fool, because safety is cool, so make that your rule.
- Do not be a medical case, keep the guards in place.
- Do not be hasty to miss safety.
- Do not be rash, end in crash.
- Do not believe in miracles, use safety articles.
- Do not break the pair use safety wear.
- Do not fix the blame, fix the problem.
- Do not forget safety off the job too.
- Do not get caught in the web of unsafe acts.
- Do not get caught with your guard off it could be disarming.
- Do not just talk about safety, practice it.
- Do not just talk, practice safety.
- Do not learn the heard way, do it the safe way.
- Do not run, walk.
- Do not twist when handling things.
- Do not work alone watch for others.
- Do not work for somebody's satisfaction but for your own satisfaction.
- Dress for weather, in cold weather, it's better to wear several layers of clothing than one bulky item.
- Driving faster can cause a disaster.
- Each one teaches one, safety is the best one.

- East or west safety is the best.
- Eat to live and do not live to eat.
- Educate your kids and do your bit, inculcate healthy and safe habits.
- Electricity does not accept the mistakes.
- Endangering environment must be avoided; enduring environment must be created to work safely.
- Engage professionally experience people to solve the occupational disease problems and to have a good environment.
- Environments change the attitude of the person, try to maintain good environment.
- Equipments and machines do not speak of their illness – check them.
- Eternal vigilance is the price of safety.
- Even in a hi-tech world your eyes are still your greatest asset.
- Even strongman practice safe lifting.
- Every accident – every time, if it is predictable it's preventable.
- Every near accident is warning.
- Every pleasure has a pain.
- Everyone pays for work accidents but the injured worker pays more, avoid accident losses.
- Expect the unexpected.
- Extremity of right is wrong.
- Falling objects can be brutal if you do not protect your noodle.
- Falling to prepare = prepare to fall.
- Falls hurt stay alert.
- Fear is the foundation of safety.
- Fire and electricity are good servants but bad masters.
- Fire easy to prevent, difficult to control.
- Fire easy to start, hard to stop.
- First creeps then go.
- Flesh and bone is no match for a grinding stone.
- Follow the safety rule, do not just preach it.
- Fools do not follow instructions.
- For all the parts of our body we can not get spare parts, if we loose them by accident.
- For our future 'safety' both the heads 'family head' and 'factory head' should be safe.

- Forget your hearing protection? Forget about hearing.
- Get a grip, to prevent a slip, use hand rails.
- Get a medical check up before starting any exercise routine.
- Get in S.T.E.P – safety takes every person.
- Get involved with safety.
- Give safety some time it gives you life time.
- Go places, but go safely. It will make a happy family.
- Good habits will normally keep you out of bad troubles.
- Good health and environment will increase the efficiency of the worker.
- Good house keeping is everybody's responsibility.
- Good supervision is the key to safety.
- Guard against man eating machines.
- Habit, if not resisted, soon become necessity.
- Haste makes waste.
- Hasty climber has sudden falls.
- Have you an eye for safety or are you blinded by bad habits.
- He makes no mistakes makes nothing.
- Health and safety, words to live by.
- Health is not valued till sickness comes, so is safety and accident.
- Hear to-day gone tomorrow – use your hearing protection.
- Hearing protection is a sound (intention) investment.
- Help protect environment.
- Humans merely share the earth. We can only protect the land, not own it.
- Hurry will burry you.
- I am not an environmentalist, I am an earth warrior.
- Idle brain is the devils workshop.
- If everything goes all right, electricity will be slave to us, and if something goes wrong, we become slave to electricity.
- If you are aware of it take care of it.
- If you do not know what is going to happen, there is no way to stop it.
- If you fight with safety, your chance of remain alive fifty – fifty.
- If you smell something bad, get out of the lab.
- In an underdeveloped country do not drink the water; in a developed country do not breathe the air.

- In any language safety is important! Read, heed and bread safety.
- In case of injury, remember 'RICE' – Rest, Ice. Compress and Elevate.
- In society ladies first, in industry safety first.
- In case of an accident, you can change the helmet but not the head! So are with other parts of the body.
- Integrate safety and environmental protection.
- It is better to lose one minute in life than to lose life in one minute.
- It is not how long, but how well we live.
- It is not working that kills, but worry.
- It is not pollution that's harming the environment.
- It's better to be careful a thousand times than careless once.
- It's better to correct an unsafe friend than to bury one.
- It's not pollution that's harming the environment; it's the impurities in our air and water that are doing it.
- Job of any kind, plan with safety in mind.
- Keep cables clear of gangways.
- Keep your mind/heart on the job or wherever you work.
- Kill fire before it kills you.
- Kill pollution and save destruction.
- Kill pollution and save environment.
- KISS – Keep It Safe and Sound.
- Know safety no accidents.
- Know safety, no pain – no safety, know pain.
- Land, sea or air, safety is needed everywhere.
- Learn safety, teach safety and practice safety.
- Learn to give signal before taking a turn.
- Less care less safety makes duty danger, more care more safety makes duty pleasure.
- Let safety be a sponge – soak it up.
- Let's resolve no ACCIDENTS, any where, any time.
- Life is precious being safety conscious.
- Life is rare – live with care.
- Life is short; an accident makes it further short.
- Lifting is a breeze when you bend at the knees.
- Loaded with safety ideas? Turn them in!

- Look sharp do not get caught.
- Luck saves once a time, safety saves all the time.
- Machine and tools do not have feelings and do not understand your feelings.
- Machine guards keep you on your side.
- Maintain balance while talking, while walking, and while working avoid accidents.
- Make everyday a safe day.
- Make haste slowly
- Make safety a reality and do not be a fatality.
- Make safety a thing to remember – from January to December.
- Make safety a way of life.
- Make shift arrangement – invitation to an accident.
- Make your plant the best – safer than all the rest.
- Man is a selfish goal seeking animal. He uses different yard stick for different people, but not for himself.
- Man who is wise, guards his eyes.
- Management must make the people to know their responsibilities as per the safety rules and regulations.
- Management must publicize their safety policy to all.
- Management should have safety control at all area.
- Many accidents can be avoided by common sense.
- Many people are yet to understand their duties as per Factories Act.
- Memos, punishments will not solve the problems. Personal contact will solve the problems.
- Men, machine and material if not maintained properly get rusted and ruined.
- Merely using helmet safety is not completed. We have to follow the safety rules and regulations religiously.
- More consciousness in safety brings more confidence in work.
- More waste prevention plus more recycling is equal to less waste and less land fill.
- Motivate by supplying good PPEs, good equipments and workplace etc.
- Near accidents are warnings!
- Near-misses are warnings, heed them.
- Never forget about safety.
- Never give safety a day off.
- Never relax on safety.

- Never take anything for granted.
- Never think working safe is in vain when it could save a life time pain.
- New Year resolution – if it's unsafe, let us find a solution.
- No accident is our aim try to achieve the same.
- No goggles! No ear plug! No mask! We are not monkeys/animals! Hence we should use PPEs regularly to avoid accidents.
- No hurry, no worry.
- No safety without inspection and no happiness without safety.
- No safety, know pain, know safety, no pain.
- Normal speed meets every need.
- Observe safety every where.
- Observe safety in all walks of life.
- Observe safety round the clock.
- One bad day at the grinder could ruin your whole life.
- One rung too high and you could die.
- One safe act can lead to another.
- One split second of carelessness could change your entire future.
- Open the door of safety: awareness is the fey!
- Operational risk management prevents accident.
- Others are depending on you, do not take chances.
- Our commitment – safe and green environment.
- Our motto, safety in to-to.
- Our prestige depends on our friends! Our family prestige depends on our children, our office and factory prestige depends upon our safe working, our country's prestige depends upon our export and import! To save our prestige let's work safely.
- Over … speeding…. Causes … accidents …
- Pay it safe.
- Personal protective equipment is self defensive.
- Plan ahead for safety.
- Practical jokes with compressed air will kill you.
- Practice makes a man perfect.
- Practice safety every day safety has no holiday.
- Practice safety on the job and off the job too.
- Prepare and prevent instead of repair and repent.

- Prevention is better than cure.
- Price of an accident is always high.
- Proactive action is accident prevention.
- Production must – safety first.
- Productivity increases with safety.
- Protect your back use a jack.
- Provide proper facilities to monitor the environment.
- Put safety first and a better day is sure to follow.
- Put safety on the top your list.
- Put your helmet, driving defensively; take to your destination safely.
- Put your money on safety, it's a blue-chip investment.
- Quench the thirst – safety first.
- Remember A (Always) B (Be) C (Careful) of safety.
- Remember fire can engulf a home in 60 seconds.
- Risk – is it worth?
- Safe operators are smooth operators.
- Safe to do? Ask.
- Safe today – alive tomorrow.
- Safe today is the reward of safety of yesterday.
- Safe way is the only right way.
- Safety – a good friend to take home.
- Safety – it's a tool for life.
- Safety – it's in your hands.
- Safety begins with number one.
- Safety benefits all.
- Safety comes before schedule only in the dictionary.
- Safety comes in cans, I can, you can, and we can.
- Safety committee can solve many safety and health problems.
- Safety committee members should have a cordial relationship with the management.
- Safety costs you nothing.
- Safety developments can not grow unless we weed out hazards.
- Safety ever, accident never.
- Safety everyone's full time job.

- Safety first and lasts longer.
- Safety gear – 2 minutes … risk assessment – 5 minutes … a mishap that takes a life – forever.
- Safety glasses – all in favor say eye.
- Safety in – we win.
- Safety in action and mind will leave accident behind.
- Safety in mind, safety in action, provides complete protection.
- Safety inspection by hands and safety verification by eyes.
- Safety is a catalyst for production.
- Safety is a frame of mind get the picture.
- Safety is a frame of mind, so concentrate on it all the time.
- Safety is a full time job – Do not make it a part time practice.
- Safety is a key to progress.
- Safety is a mission not an intention.
- Safety is as simple as ABC – Always Be Careful.
- Safety is everybody's business.
- Safety is free using it generously.
- Safety is no accident.
- Safety is not just a slogan, it's a way of life.
- Safety is our business too.
- Safety is our goal what's yours?
- Safety is our motto; achieve it in to-to.
- Safety is savior, develop safe behavior.
- Safety is something you can not live without.
- Safety is success by purpose – not accident.
- Safety is the great guide to human life.
- Safety is the key to accident free.
- Safety is the most productive business.
- Safety leads to prosperity.
- Safety makes good dollars and sense.
- Safety management is a great service to society.
- Safety needs team work.
- Safety officer is not a superman to be present every where, every body should co-operate for safety activity.

- Safety officer is sandwiched between management and worker in the industry and at home he is sandwiched between mother and wife.
- Safety pays always.
- Safety pays with happy days.
- Safety policy includes safe system of work, safe equipment, safe workplace, safety training and proper PPEs.
- Safety provides secured life, like a helmet on the ride.
- Safety records do not happen by accident.
- Safety rules and regulations should be practiced religiously.
- Safety rules are there to follow, so take care and we will see you tomorrow.
- Safety saves ensure safety.
- Safety saves, safety pays and safety protects life.
- Safety should start from home only.
- Safety starts with 's' but begins with you.
- Safety the measure of success.
- Safety's intention is the accident prevention.
- Safety…does it for family.
- Safety…it can charm you, or ALARM you.
- Save tomorrow, think safety to-day.
- Saving a life is a great service to the society.
- Second thoughts are better.
- Shoes first, steps next.
- Short cuts may make you feel you are brave, but it may lead you to your grave.
- Shortcuts cut life short.
- Slogan, shouting, quoting rules and rights will not solve the problems. Present your case in a skillful manner. Everything can be solved by talking across the table only.
- Small hazards cause big fire.
- Small sector or large sector, safety is the common factor.
- Speak up for safety.
- Speed thrills, it also kills.
- Spot a hazard and stop an accident.
- Stand up for safety.
- Stay alert; do not get hurt.

- Step by step the ladder is ascended.
- Stop accidents before they stop you.
- Stop unsafe acts now.
- Stop! Think! Then act!
- Take care of equipments as you take care of your children.
- Take care of the earth and she will take care of you.
- Take care working with chemical baths or you may end up taking a shower.
- Take time to be safe.
- Talk more about safety, hear less about accident.
- Target to-day to prevent accident tomorrow.
- Teach or preach safety should reach.
- Team up to safety.
- Tell me – I forget, show me – I remember, involve me – I committed.
- Thank God men can not fly and lay waste on the sky as well as on the earth.
- The art of life is the avoidance of pain.
- The best safety device is a safe worker. The right way is the safe way.
- The chance taker is the accident maker.
- The door of safety swings on the hinges of common sense.
- The earth belongs to the living, not to the dead.
- The first three letters in workplace safety – you.
- The goal must be zero accidents.
- The greatness of nations can be judged by the way its animals are treated.
- The hotter it gets out side, the more water you need inside.
- The key to long life is to live safely.
- The safest RISK is the one you did not take.
- The safety risk is the one you should not take.
- The safety route always bears fruit.
- The strength of the trade unions depends upon the vivid participation of the workers.
- The system of nature, of which man is a part, tends to be self-balancing, self-adjusting, self-cleansing, not so with technology.
- The worker knows where the shoe pinches.
- There are hundreds of people for your factory but you are the only person for your family – work safely.

- There are so many causes to make an accident, find out causes and take remedial actions.
- There he lies some 6 feet under, did not heed the roaring thunder!!
- There is always an alternate method for every work find out the right method that is safe method.
- There is nothing more frightful than ignorance in action.
- There is sufficient in the world for the man's need but not for man's greed.
- There's so much pollution in the air now that if it were for our lungs there would be no place to put it all.
- Think before you smoke. No smoking – thank you for not being a fire hazard.
- Think positive an accident is only an attitude away.
- Think safety – it could not hurt.
- Think safety always, everywhere.
- Those precious fingers do not ignore…or they could end up on the floor.
- Those who work the safety way; live to work another day.
- Time runs out on luck…do the job the safe way.
- Timely attended first-aid will save a life.
- To avoid a scene keep your workplace clean.
- To be safe, understand people and environment.
- To err is human, to forgive is divine.
- To save the head use the helmet. Gods use helmet why not you?
- To save tomorrow; think safety to-day.
- To see tomorrow wear eye protection today. You must observe safety rules everyday.
- Trade union must maintain a balance and act like a bridge between the employee and the employer.
- Trade unions are the weapons to defend the human rights at work.
- Trade unions prime aim is to achieve the goals by collective bargaining.
- Try to engage deaf and dumb persons in permanently noisy areas.
- Two wrongs do not make a right.
- Understand yourself to avoid accidents.
- Union officials have the key role to play in guiding the people.
- Unsafe menu, accident venue.
- Use ear plug and ear muff in a noisy area.
- Use the PPE's to suit the environment.

- Vigilance to everyone is safety to all, negligence of anyone, brings danger to all.
- Watch your step – it could be your last.
- Watch your step! Floor should be free from oil, grease, water etc.
- Watch your steps where you are going.
- Water plus molten aluminum results in explosion.
- We can not transfer your pain and injury due to accident to somebody; use proper PPE's to avoid injury.
- We learn by seeing 80%, hearing 14%, smelling 2%, touching 2%, testing 2%.
- We need you – work safely.
- We never know the worth of water till the well is dry.
- What you do not know about safety, it could hurt you.
- When disconnecting cords, pull the plug rather than the cord.
- When gamble with safety you bet your life.
- When putting away a chemical shipment, remember personal protective equipment.
- When walk ways freeze – walk safely please.
- While demanding your rights, remember your responsibility also.
- Why learn the hard way? Obey safety rules.
- Wipe up and avoid a slip up.
- Wise men guard his eyes.
- Wishing won't keep you safe; safety will.
- Wishing you a happy, safe, prestigious and accident free life everyday.
- With your skill and will, you can make accident nil.
- Work safely all the while, go home with a smile.
- Work safely or hurt greatly.
- Work safely, live longer.
- Work smarter not harder.
- Work to be safe, be safe so you can work.
- Work together for safety, it is everybody's responsibility.
- Work with confidence.
- Work with utmost care to make accident rare.
- Working safely each day will keep the doctor away.
- Working together gets the job done safely.
- Working together in health and safety.
- Working without safety is a dead-end job.

- You always have time to do things right after mishap.
- You can change the gloves and goggles but not the hands and eyes due to accident.
- You can eat with false teeth, you can see with a glass eye.
- You can never overdo safety.
- You can not transfer your pain and injury due to accident use PPEs.
- You come to this world tied off, so stayed tied off.
- You get the level of safety that you are prepared to walk past.
- You have a duty to give safety training to your staff.
- You may like or dislike, safety is my way of life.
- You need firm footings for pulling, pushing and lifting.
- You will achieve the level of safety excellence that you demonstrate you want.
- Your family is waiting for you at home return home safely.
- Your family wait for your safe return, let your work follow a safe pattern.
- Your future depends on your safe working.
- Your good health is your greatest wealth.
- Your neck on the block, safety officer becomes an escape goat.
- Your safety gears are between your ears.
- Your safety is everyone's responsibility, especially yours.
- Your safety means the safety of your family.
- Zero compromise towards safety.
- Zero in on safety.
- Zero tolerance on safety.

16

CHAPTER

Safety Thoughts

THE CONCEPT OF SAFETY

Safety of the life and limbs of human beings is not a new idea or concept; it is an integral part of Indian thought, literature, philosophy and culture and is as old as mankind. I would quote a small story from Mahabharata to illustrate my point. On the 10th day of the battle of Mahabharata, Bheesma Pitamaha fell and was lying on the bed of arrows writhing in physical and mental anguish. At this historic moment of his life, Yudhisthira, the eldest of Pandavas approached him and asked him 'O Pitamaha' what is the supreme truth in human life. Quick came the reply "man is the finest and the best in god's creation and there is nothing great than man."

The battle of Mahabharata, Bheesma Pitamaha, Yudhistira are nothing but figments of imagination of poet Vyasa who composed Mahabharata. The massage contained in the words of Bheesma Pitamaha about the primary and centrality of human life is an eternal one and is of eternal worth and relevance to all human beings regardless of difference in geography, topography, and demography, regardless of differences in religion, caste, community, creed and color.

The central massage behind the safety of life and limb of human beings is to be perceived and internalized in this perspective. Safety is not merely a statutory requirement to be complied with by producing or performing organizations; nor is it a compendium of codal provisions such as laws and regulations. The concept of safety is undoubtedly embodied in all this but it goes beyond. It is basically a recognition of the dignity, beauty and quality of human existence which is the finest and best in god's creation. It is only when we learn to treat life with dignity.

HOW DO YOU DEFINE SAFETY?

Safety is control of accident loss. This definition takes into consideration:

- That safety is a relative thing.
- That the objective is to prevent all accidents.
- That safety includes consideration of reduction of loss as well as elimination of risk and prevention of loss.

Safety Pays
Always
All the Time

WHAT IS SAFETY?

Safety means free from danger, injury, or giving protection, involving no risk process.

Basic of Safety

In order to improve safety performance one has to have a clear understanding of the basic of safety like.

ACCIDENT

An accident is an unplanned and unexpected or unforeseen event, which causes or could conceivably have caused an injury.

"Accidents do Not
Happen,
They are Caused"

Studies have revealed that accidents are caused by the combination of the following:

- Unsafe personal acts
- Unsafe physical or mechanical condition.

Each of the above causes is further divided into two groups:

A. Proximate or direct cause

B. Contributing or indirect cause

H.W. Heinrich a pioneer in the field of safety established a theory that 88% of industrial accidents result primarily from unsafe acts, 10% from unsafe condition and 2% by the act of God (non-preventable accidents). So out of this 98% which are preventable accidents, unsafe personal acts are responsible for the majority cases.

1. Unsafe Acts:

A. Direct Unsafe Acts:

- Operating without authority
- Failure to secure
- Failure to warn
- Operating at unsafe speed
- Bypassing safety devices
- Using wrong tool/equipment
- Unsafe loading
- Unsafe placing
- Taking unsafe position or posture
- Working on dangerous or moving equipment
- Failure to use personal protective equipment
- Horse playing.

B. Contributing Causes to Direct Unsafe Acts:

- Inadequate safety instruction by supervisor.
- Lack in supervision on operators.
- Incomplete understanding of tools, machines and equipments with respect to their danger.
- Forgetting to use safety guards.
- Physical or mental unsuitability's like poor eyesight, hard of hearing, underage, intoxicated, crippled, oversensitive etc.

2. Unsafe Conditions:

A. Direct Unsafe Conditions:

- Unguarded or inadequately guarded machines or equipments.
- Defective condition of machines, equipments, tools etc.
- Unsafe design or construction of machines and equipment.
- Hazardous waste arrangement and methods – it includes unsafe methods of storing and piling etc.
- Inadequate or incorrect illumination.
- Inadequate ventilation.
- Improper house keeping.
- Non provision of safe personal protective equipment.

B. *Contributory Causes to Direct Unsafe Conditions:*

- Lack of adequate safety training to employees for accomplishing a job safely.
- Lack of safety awareness.
- Negative attitude towards safety.
- Slackening of enforcement of safe working rules amongst employees.

ACCIDENT PREVENTION

- Engineering revision – to prevent unsafe condition.
- Education and training – to prevent unsafe acts.
- Enforcement – to follow safety rules.
- Enthusiasm – to maintain interest.
- Example – to lead all to the correct way to ensure safety.
- Evaluation – after certain specific intervals.

WHAT IS AN ACCIDENT?

"Accidents do Not Happen, They are Caused"

Accident is an unplanned, unexpected event, which causes interference to the work, may or may not result in injury, damage to property or equipment.

Main causes for accidents are:

- Unsafe Actions – 80%
- Unsafe Conditions – 18%
- Natural Calamities – 2%

Cost of Accident

Visible Costs:

- Loss or damage to equipments and assets
- Loss of production
- Medical cost
- Compensation
- Legal costs
- Insurance cost
- Loss of lives or limbs
- Cost of man days lost of injured employees.

Invisible Costs:

- Production loss of linked departments
- Loss of earning power of injured
- Economic loss to injurer's family
- Loss time by fellow workers
- Cost of bringing in new workers
- Spoiled work
- Failure and delay to fulfill orders
- Overhead cost
- Lowered employee morale
- Increased labor conflicts
- Cost of investigations
- Unfavorable public relations
- Cost of processing reports
- Time lost from work by engineers and supervisors
- Time lost by senior managers
- Product spoiled by accident
- Man hour spent in cleaning up accident area
- Loss of functions and of operations income
- Loss of prestige
- Loss of bonus payments of forfeits
- Expenditure of emergency equipment
- Cost of time spend on the case by the first aid attendant and OHS
- Recovery and salvage of damaged equipment and vehicles
- Corrective action to prevent recurrence of an accident
- Obsolescence of parts of equipment destroyed
- Loss of public confidence and therefore of revenue
- Slow downs or stopping operations while accident causes are determined and corrective action taken
- Loss of skilled manpower
- Funeral expenses
- Social costs and liabilities
- Degradation of efficiency of operations because of loss of experienced and trained personnel

- Cost to employer under employees welfare and benefit scheme
- Cost of employer of counting to pay the wages of the injured employee in full, after his return, even though services of the employee (who is not fully recovered) may be worth half to their normal value for a time
- Penalties for failure to take actions to correct hazards or defects or conditions that violate statutes
- Cost of meeting with statutory authorities
- Cost of training a new employee for the position falling vacant
- Time spent on repairs
- Punitive damages
- Rehabilitation of the injured employees
- Settlement of dependents
- Transport costs

Notes:

1. *Visible costs of accidents are only tip of an iceberg, huge costs are invisible.*
2. *Only 1/10 of the iceberg is visible.*
3. *Ratio of visible cost to invisible cost may be taken as 1:9 or 1:10.*
4. *There are at least 100 other items of costs.*
5. *The number of elements of costs may vary from case to case.*

ACCIDENT HURTS

Accident hurts, safety not

Nothing is more important than the health and safety of the employees. It needs your commitment to;

- Integrating health and safety practices into all aspects of work. Continue to incorporate these practices into product and process design, manufacturing and business planning;
- Providing innovative and preventive health and safety programs. Continuously optimizing the effectiveness and integrity of programs through communications, comprehensive training and education, audits and work place assessments;
- Developing understanding among those in leadership of their responsibilities and their accountability to provide a safe and healthy workplace;
- Developing understanding among all employees of their personal responsibility to work safely, their accountability for individual performance and the assignment of appropriate authority to implement these responsibilities; and

- Meeting or exceeding the requirements of applicable legislation and regulations for performance in health and safety matters.

Consequences:

- Pain due to injury.
- Loss of life or limbs.
- Loss of earning capacity.
- Medical expenditure.
- Mental worries to the family.
- Frustration in life.
- Future plans upset.
- Widow finds it difficult to maintain the family.
- Children and dependents become orphans.
- Loss of skill.
- Loss incurred to training.
- Loss of production and profit.
- Loss of morale amongst the workmen.
- Extra cost of recruitment, training.
- Esteem of the company goes down.

A FRIENDLY ADVISE

- There is no magic in safety.
- Safety provides the atmosphere in which one can earn.
- Safety provides the information from which one can learn.
- Safety provides the opportunity to understand, to see, to have the light bulb illumination.

The rest is up to you my friends.

Remember your safety is in your hands.

You must provide the opportunity:

- For the employees to remain safe.
- That allows the employees to ask for advice.
- For the correction when employees make an error.

If you do not or can not or would not do this then do not rely on safety.

Because there is no magic in safety.

SAFETY TIPS

- Make safety as a way of life.
- Be safe stay alive.
- Learn not to burn.
- Do not depend on fate, Depend on safety straight.
- A **"no smoking"** sign is a life saving warning.
- Hand rail provides safety every time.
- See, falls can be fatal, Be safe-stand on firm base.
- Overloading can lead to a disastrous fire.
- Protect against caving-in during excavation is a must.
- Storage of gas cylinders properly enhances fire safety.
- Even minor unsafe conditions should be rectified.
- Do not feed fire, remove the waste.
- Ensure safety of contractor's workers also.
- Publicizing safety is not enough, practice it.
- Safe habits save lives. Yours too.
- Manhole covers and valves when loose can cause disasters.
- Fire easy to light, hard to fight.
- Avoid short cuts.
- It is better to be careful a hundred times than to get killed once.
- Let us resolve to work determinedly for the cause of safety.
- Accidents results in loss of production.
- Color coding system for pipelines save mishandling.
- Report the hazard you spot.
- A cleaner place is a safer place.
- Safety brings cheers.
- Accidents donot happen, they are caused.
- Hasty action may not lead to safety.
- Everybody's goal total accident control.
- Expect the unexpected, be adequately protected.
- Falls hurt stay alert.
- Fire feeds on careless deeds.
- Know how to stop it, before you start it.

- Habit to pay good attention, Relieve you of your tension.
- Safety at each foot step, Give accident a fool stop.
- Do not just work, work with safety; Be an example while doing duty.
- Let your helmet break, not your head. With all safety equipment you work ahead.
- Safety at work means safety in life, Otherwise life is on the edge of knife.
- Follow safety rules and do your duty, Avoid accident and increase productivity.
- Safety is the stepping stone for successful production.
- In business customer first, In plant safety first.
- When you are out, we are out-think safety.
- Do not get carried away by carelessness.
- Safety is a year round job.
- You are key to safety.
- Safe working practice saves our lives.
- Speak up-report hazards.
- Rectification in time saves life.
- Eternal vigilance is the price for safety.
- Look for safety-work safely.
- Safety begins with self.
- Do not close your ears and eyes on safety.
- Always use safety protection.
- Our goal-zero accident.
- Wear your protective equipment.
- Clean up spills to avoid falls.
- Overloading and over speeding are dangerous.
- Insurance is not a substitute for safe working.
- Best safety device is your brain-use it.
- Safe habits save lives.
- Nip the danger in the bud, to avoid a disaster.
- Attitude is the biggest help or hindrance to safety.
- A happy driver is a safe driver.
- Safety objectives are achievable.
- All injuries are preventable.
- Body's spare parts are not available, safety can save it.

- For safety conviction and compulsion both are required.
- The safety route always bears fruit.
- Make safe driving a way of life.
- See and be seen while on the road.
- Drinking and driving do not mix.
- Practice defensive driving for safe motoring.
- Safety first speeds next.
- Speed thrills it also kills.
- Life is precious, save it.
- Joy ride on the road is dangerous.
- Traffic planning is the key to road safety.
- While driving watch all blind corners.
- Alert ever, accident never.
- Do not drive in excess speed.
- Use crash helmet while driving two wheelers.
- Do not allow children to play on the road.
- Be alert to the bumps on the road.
- Start early, drive slowly, reach safely.
- Wait for signals before overtaking vehicles.
- Follow the traffic discipline and rules.
- Avoid unhealthy competition on the road.
- Always keep your documents in the vehicle.
- Keep more attention to avoid collision.
- Go places, but go safely, it will make a happy family.
- Driving with care makes accident rare.
- Safety secures your future, make it part of your nature.
- This is not just another day, today is national safety day.
- Safety in every section, high production less tension.
- Safety is everybody's own business.
- Safety can save (you) for all time to come.
- Safety is our birth right.
- Safety in mind and action, provides complete protection.
- Safety in action and mind, will leave accident behind.

- Safety is savior, develop safe behaviour.
- Safety pays always.
- Safety needs team work.
- Safety is our motto, achieve it in to-to.
- Safety provide secured life, like a helmet on the ride.
- Safety first, production must.
- Safety is the kit, that keeps you safe and fit.
- Safety is a way of life follow it.
- Safety at every turn, ensure happy return.
- Safety starts from house.
- Safety always-all ways.
- Safety improves labor productivity.
- Safety is a prime concern.
- Safety play a vital role to achieve our goal.
- Safety needs involvement.
- Safety has no quitting time.
- Safety is not mystery, just common sense.
- Make safety a thing to remember from January to December.
- Practice safety everyday safety has no holiday.
- Our aim this year, no accident for ever.
- I love safety not for a day, not for a year, but for ever.
- Sign of quality, work with safety.
- Alert to-day, alive tomorrow.
- Never settle for cheapness at the cost of safety.
- Never compromise at the cost of safety.
- Short cuts may cut short the life.
- Accidents do not just happen, they are caused.
- You hold the key for safety.
- Put safety on the top of your list.
- Cultivate the safe habits, it pays.
- The chance taker is the accident maker.
- Attend first aid first.
- Foresight saves eye sight.

- Look to your safety and your fellow workers.
- Do not neglect any injury however small.
- Accident occur when least expected.
- Poor judgment results in accidents.
- Do not excuse accidents.
- Overconfidence breeds accidents.
- Safety has no quitting time.
- You have not a life to spare, look for hazards every where.
- Your life is at stake, with every chance you take.

ACCIDENT TIPS

- Accident happen because of a fraction of judgment of error.
- Accident disrupts the harmonious relationship.
- Accidents are unwanted phenomenon for human beings.
- Accidents are social and economic evils.
- Accidents take away a lion's share of the profits.
- Accident is about one-tenth of overall cost.
- Accident prevention is a laudable goal for all.
- Accidents are the result of failure to act properly and timely.
- Accidents are attributable to human failures.
- Accident prevention is essentially a human problem.
- Accident prevented is a bonanza, Accident compensated is an apology.
- Accident do not just happen, they are caused.
- Accident occur when least expected.
- Accident strikes when you are not alert.
- Accident is a symptom of something wrong somewhere.
- Accident and injury are distinctively different.
- Accident has only one root cause and many contributory causes.
- Accident results in loss of production.
- Accidents do not have any choice.
- Accident is an unforeseen or an unexpected event.
- Accident usually produces injury.
- Accident is an unplanned and uncontrolled event.

- Accident is unconscious deviation in work activity.
- Accident means wasteful effort, prevent them.
- Accident is a repetitive problem if not taken care.
- Accidents are avoidable-forget alibi.
- Accident bring tears, safety brings cheers.
- Accident shatter lives, safety makes it better.
- Accidents are someone's fault.
- Accidents have no closed season.
- Accidents interfere with the orderly progress of work activities.
- Accident will not spare you for your excuses.

AN APPEAL

All of us are aware of the effect of the accident. We are citing some of the case studies where by not using personal protective equipments, heavy losses are incurred not only the employee but also to the management and the society.

- For not using helmet on the head in a metallurgical plant, a flying object hit a worker's head and injured his brain permanently despite treatment needing Neuro-surgery. The man lost one of his eyes and also lost the memory power.
- A man not wearing safety shoes on his leg was injured by a forklift for which the right ankle was amputed. In this there was a strike in the plant for 20 days costing the management few crores on account of production per day and the subsequent loss of good will of works; can we give a natural leg to any one, can any compensation make him walk and fit to earn as before?
- For not using chemical safety goggles, several persons have lost eyesight; due to a acid or alkali splash. Even faces have been burnt and both eyes lost. Let us compare the cost of goggles with the cost of accident?
- For not using simple dust masks, we find people suffering from silicosis and many die because of ailment every year.
- For not using self-contained breathing mask while attending to chlorine and ammonia leakages several persons have lost their eyes and some died.
- For smoking in no smoking areas, 5 workers have died due to bi-hexane in one secondary solvent extraction plant in Orissa 20 years back.

Thus we earnestly appeal one and all to use all applicable "safety appliances" while on work provided by the company as it is rightly said that 'remember, somebody is waiting for you at home' and thus we have a greater obligation not only to our family, but also to our employer and to the nation at large.

ARE INCENTIVES MOTIVATORS FOR SAFETY?

Many people still believe that workers can be motivated by cash incentives to cultivate safe-working behaviour; yet some management experts have doubts about this. Some researchers have found that 'one-time reward' or an occasional 'time bound incentive scheme' may motivate the employees to achieve high target or set goal, once, twice or thrice in succession but not continuously for a long period of time because the motivating force of incentives weans away gradually and becomes a matter of habit.

People cannot be motivated if safety and quality are viewed separately from production for which a person is employed in the industry. In fact in any organization, more motivated employees are available than most managers think. It is the role of managers (and the management team) to motivate the employees under their care by sound management to produce quality goods through safe operation. Some of the management principles are applicable in general, but some come from the environment in which people work. Once the employees are dissatisfied with the managers and try to sort out their grievances, (wages, perks, bonus, and promotion) by applying external pressure, safety of men and machines is the first to be affected in a cycle of events.

The following factors to be considered in lieu of monetary benefit to establish long-term effect:

- Inculcating a feeling of pride or self-esteem of working for a good company, building self-confidence among all employees.
- Providing reasonably good safety, health and welfare support for every individual need.
- Taking care of the work-environment.
- Two-way effective communication between the managers and the workers.
- Job enrichment to avoid monotony.
- Adopting standard and safe operating practices.
- Self-searching and autosuggestion by employees themselves.

To conclude, sound management system should be applied for motivating employees to adopt safe practices and not through incentives or compensations. Hence good safety management is long-term solution and incentives are short-lasting palliative measure.

BASIC ELEMENT OF SAFETY ORGANISATION

1. **Management Leadership:**
    - Assumption of responsibilities.
    - Declaration of policy.

2. **Assignment of Responsibility:**
   - To operating officials.
   - Safety Director Supervisors.
   - Committees.
3. **Maintenance of Safe Working Conditions:**
   - Inspectors.
   - Engineering Revisions.
   - Purchasing.
4. **Establishment of Safety Training:**
   - For supervisors.
   - For workers.
5. **An Accident Record System:**
   - Accident Analysis.
   - Report on injuries.
   - Measurement of results.
6. **Medical and First Aid System:**
   - Placement examinations.
   - Treatment of injuries.
   - First Aid services.
   - Basic health examinations.
7. **Acceptance of Personal Responsibility:**
   - By employees training.
   - Maintenance of interest.

FORMING SAFE HABITS

Have you given a thought to the importance of habits in your day to day life? One often hears parents or elders chiding children for forming bad habits. Parents usually expect their children to shun bad habits and acquire good ones. But should these be confined to children alone? Are not adults' susceptible to bad habits?

Habit forming is inevitable. That is human nature. A child makes a lot of effort when he first learns to walk bit as he grows up, he does so effortlessly. He does not have to tell himself: "lift your left foot, take it forward, put it down, and now raise your right foot…" This is so, because it has become a habit.

Habits are very important for your well being – both at your home and at your work place. Good habits acquired over the years are an asset. You realize this only when you go through an accident because of a careless act. For example, when you are driving, you are instinctively guided by the changing traffic signals to do what is right. You do it without thinking because it has become a habit. However, if you are in the habit of ignoring signals you very well know what is in store for you.

Have you watched the womenfolk chopping vegetables? They do it with ease and very little effort, making the entire routine appear so easy? Yet if someone tries doing it the first time, it will require a lot more patience and effort. What is the reason? It is just that they have learnt the right way of doing the job, and now it has become a habit.

You can get into the habit of doing any job safely. The safe way can become something you do matter-of-factly-without stopping to think about it. For example, if you get into the habit of striking a match before turning on the gas burner knob, it will prevent you from doing the unsafe thing-fumbling with the match after the gas is released.

If you are in the habit of switching off electrical appliances immediately after use, you will never leave your iron 'on' to perform some other job and forget all about it.

Good habits help you remain safe. You will never ignore first aid for any injury, no matter how small it might seem. You could stay away from injuries if you make it a habit of wearing protective equipment when you work.

Always remember, just as there is safety in good habits there is danger in bad ones. Stay clear of bad habits and try to form good ones. Here are a few tips:

- Start the job the right way. Learn safe job habits.
- Practice the right habits. Every time you do the job, do it properly and safely.
- Never let the habit slip. Always do the job the way you are supposed to do it. Never try short cuts.

Whether good or bad, you are bound to form habits. Since it is just as easy to form good habits, as it is to form bad ones, be smart and learn the good habits. Learn the right way of doing any job and continue doing it the right way. That is how good habits are formed. After all, these good habits will help make your life a lot easier and safer.

GOOD HABITS CAN OVERRIDE BAD ONES

- What are your healthy, winning habits?
- What habits would you like to replace?
- Do you believe people can learn a new set of skills or habits if they have been "like they are" for a long time?

But the good news is that you can change your life by changing your habits. Psychologists have done scores of studies of how habits are formed. We can now track a habit from the time sensory nerves carry messages to our fertile brains from our organs for hearing, touching, seeing, tasting, and smelling. The brain uses this information to make decisions, then sends working orders through motor nerves to the body parts needed for action.

It should come as no surprise, then, that habits are formed after the body responds the same way twenty-five or thirty times to identical stimuli. But here is an interesting discovery: After a certain amount of this repetition, the message from the sensory nerves jumps directly to the conditioned motor nerves without a conscious decision by the brain. So while a mere twenty-five or thirty repeats can forms a habit. I am happy to report that the same number is involved in developing good habits, depending on input practice and supporting environment.

If twenty-five or thirty repeats can form a new habit, you may wonder why making it permanent requires at least a year of practice. The reason is that the old patterns remain underneath. If you slip back even if your association with them – a links immediately recalls and tries to reassert them.

GUIDELINES FOR INDUSTRIAL SAFETY

- Designed safety features
- Policy
- Industrial safety and fire section
- Fire protection engineering
- Safety performance indicators and award schemes
- Safety incentive schemes
- Training
- Work permit system
- Safety committee
- Emergency exercises
- Accident investigation and reporting system
- Audits
- Reporting of unsafe conditions
- Management system
- Use of personal protective equipments
  - Radiation areas
  - High noise areas
  - Chemical areas
  - Height areas

- Fatal accident reports
- Safety promotional activities
- Monitoring of work environments
- Observation of special days
- Observation of year long campaigns
- Medical examinations.

IDENTIFYING SAFETY STRATEGIES

In achieving the results of safety efforts in the work organizations much depends upon the strategies or how to attack accidents at the workplace. Accident prevention seems remote to achieve until the right areas have been properly designed or identified. The identification of safety input requirements in industry becomes a priority area in order to safeguard against accidents. The generation of such data is the first requirement for prevention of mishaps at workplace.

SAFETY STRATEGIES ADOPTED/PROPOSED

- Training and education in safety.
- Health and safe working conditions.
- Clear-cut safety procedures.
- Developing safety interest through incentives/training/motivation.
- Proper selection and placement of personal.
- Machine maintenance.
- Acceptance of safety suggestions.
- Good quality tools.
- Positive supervisory behaviour.
- Support from top management.
- Proper work distribution.
- Improved interpersonal relations between workers and supervisors.
- Availability of personal protective equipment.
- Improved technology.
- Assigning responsibility for safety.
- Safety competition between departments.
- Appreciation of work through newsletter, recognition etc.
- Job experience.

- Status of safety officer in the organization/role clarity.
- Opportunity for learning new things.
- Welfare activities/facilities (canteen, medical, get-together etc.)
- Small work groups.
- Feeling of job safety.
- Emphasizing job standards/norms.
- Quality circle/quality and safety corners/participation and involvement.
- Development of Safety Committee/Group Safety Committee/JDC etc.
- Safety incentives (monetary).
- Timely promotion.
- Job rotation.
- Housing accommodation for employees.

OBSERVE SAFETY RULES

- Follow safety rules.
- There is no relaxation on safety rules.
- Alibis do not excuse.
- Work procedures are applicable to all at all times.
- Make shift methods are dangerous.
- Avoid short cuts.
- Take rest only at approved locations.
- Concentrate on the job you are doing.
- Follow safe procedure.

ABC MODEL OF SAFETY CULTURE

Attitude (What we think): Attitude, ability and awareness shape our action which give rise to behaviour, which is observable.

Ability (what we can): Behaviour results in injury due to lack of attitude, awareness, and ability.

Reported behaviour becomes habit, which is translated into culture of behaviour, and habits of majority people are similar.

Action (What we do)

Awareness (What we know)

Behaviour (Habit): Collective behaviour of individuals within the organization.

Culture: The basic elements of culture are 5 Cs.

- **Consciousness:** All individuals within the organization are conscious and they have right to a safe and healthy workplace.
- **Commitment:** To protect the safety and health of others.
- **Compliance:** Each and every individual complies with the safety procedures, rules and follows safety instructions.
- **Credibility:** Trust between management and employee in the matter of safety. Safety can not thrive in an atmosphere of miss-trust.
- **Continuity:** As safety has no holiday the commitment and compliance is required to be continuous.

ETHICS AND SAFETY GO HAND IN HAND

A general policy can not cover all situations. Commonsense and judgment should be used, as and when required. Here are some SHOTS, which might help you.

Shot One

- Is the action legal?
- Is it fitting with our values?
- If I execute this, will I feel bad?
- If it comes as a headline in the newspaper, can I honestly defend my decision?

Shot Two

- Am I being honest and fair?
- Can my action stand the test of time?
- Can I sleep in clear conscience tonight?
- What lessons will my subordinates/children learn from my action?
- Am I sacrificing long term benefits for short term gains?

Unethical Symptoms

These may be tempting, but will cause problems. Be careful. Take proper SHOTS, before getting infected.

- May be only this time.
- No one will come to know.
- Every one does it.
- Tear the document.
- Hide it.

- I do not think anyone will get hurt; even then, why should I bother? Let him take care of himself.
- What's the gain in it for me?
- Forget about how it gets done, get it done somehow.

SAFETY AS A COST SAVING TOOL

It is universally accepted truth that industrial accidents do not just happen, they are caused. With the improvement of ideal physical conditions, best methods, perfect training, well motivated employees, the finest supervision and the safest machinery only it is possible to achieve perfect safety record. A well organized and effectively directed programme of safety management in the plant is bound to improve company's financial performance.

Companies impelled by the economic facts of running a business are to be on a constant alert for cost savings possibilities. This just happens to be another potential area for cost reduction. To explore this area, the exercise of a certain amount of discipline is necessary. The method that offers the best and most lasting results is the use of persuasion. This can be implemented by using emotional appeal and by monetary incentives.

The practice of sound finance system in companies dictates the need to examine and analyze closely all operating expenses. Accidents in the plant dictates a recurring cost in both direct and indirect or hidden costs. It is already proved that for each rupee paid in direct cost four rupees are lost in indirect cost.

Now-a-days insurance companies have several types of merit rating plans in which monetary savings on insurance premiums can be achieved by reducing losses due to accidents.

Efficient production methods and safety can not be separated. Effective accident prevention is much more than pasting bulletins, issuing rules, and holding periodic meetings. It is a problem that must be approached by the same logical manner that he increases production efficiency, reduces cost, and eliminates waste.

Now a days safety, health and environmental affairs are gaining its strong footage in the industries. It is mainly due to enactment of stringent laws and Acts in these areas and partly due to the statutory authorities. Much impact could not be created by the company's safety, health, and environmental professionals ; because the status of safety officers and safety department as a whole is considered (till date by many) to be statutory imposition on the company. For such status, in my opinion, we safety professionals are responsible. We always demand our status as per the Factories Act. If we shift our thinking pattern without demanding any status, only by doing our job in a different manner, automatically status will be earned.

Safety is first, but for this we have to organize our safety systems with profit saving motive. Companies run on profit not by safety alone. Once the safety professionals are able to do this automatically other things will follow.

Top bosses understand every thing in terms of money. Hence organizing safety systems with profit saving motive is essential. We have to convert our activities to the monetary form and forward the same to the top executive. The examples are:

- Money lost due to lost time of accidents.
- Money lost due to exact man days lost due to accident.
- Money lost due to medical expenses born for treatment.
- Money saved from less premium through better house keeping, suitable fire fighting arrangements.
- Money saved from dust reducing.
- Money saved from reducing leaking chemicals, fumes, steam, compressed air and various other gaseous products.
- Money saved through fuel saving.

In this increasingly competitive world, there can be no doubt that the most important assets of any organization are the employees and their skills. Protecting assets and promoting industrial productivity can be achieved simultaneously by realizing the value of safety in an organization.

How to successfully compete? That is the continuously nagging question for executives to-day. Price is certainly critical, but, as those chief executives know, price is nor all and in fact is usually the result of many other factors. Competitiveness can be defined – "the ability of a company to proportionally generate more wealth than competitors in the world markets." It is clear that many of the truly successful companies in the world to-day, have achieved their status because they have continuously and jealously protected and invested in their core strength ; their people, and the infrastructure around them. Price will always be important but the future will be different. Those companies well positioned for that different future most likely know that, they must invest in their people to generate more wealth per person than their competitor. In short, they must successfully add value where others could not. This ultimately brings us to safety.

SAFETY, WHOSE JOB

Whose job is safety?

Why this question? Certainly it is safety department's job or else, what for is this department?

This is the normal comment you hear from production department and maintenance people of an industry. Also you find some people who generalize the responsibility saying "safety is everybody's job".

In management, it is a proven experience "everybody's job is no body's job". Then safety is safety department's child or nobody's child, i.e., orphan. If we look at shop floor situation, either way safety is ineffective, then what is effective safety?

Let us answer it on the basis of similar situations in other areas of shop floor activities.

What is safety? It is not something concrete to be produced with hammer and chisel. Safety adds quality, luster, and dignity to the production process, brightens the image of the company and raises the morale of employees. Safety activities are comparable with quality control, cost control, energy management, and internal audit functions of an industrial undertaking.

Quality control officer can not and does not add quality to the product independent of production department. Production means quality production. An internal auditor can not save wasteful expenditures himself, he can only suggest. Production department is the king. All others are advisors. Advice can be accepted, rejected or modified in the best interest of an overall situation. Each and every activity on the shop floor is carried out under the direct control of the production department, be it maintenance, white washing and painting, quality control, cost control etc. therefore safety is not separate from production – it is safe production just as it has to be a quality product or a cost effective product.

There is nothing like 'production first' or 'safety first'. It is **Safe Production.**

Every body knows that if there is a quality improvement or cost reduction, production department takes the major credit so also in case of accident free periods. Safe production is the job of production people.

What then is the job of safety department? Same as internal auditor or quality inspector. They are guides and advisors of the management and shop floor employees.

THE NEW COMMANDMENTS

Most of you are familiar with the Ten Commandments. Well, here we have a new set of edicts – The Ten Commandments of Safety Management. These are not meant to replace Moses' version. But if your company believes and follows the new commandments, you will certainly help create a safer environment for us to work and live in.

- Thou shall have safety graven in thy management philosophy.
- Thou shall not relegate safety to the bottom rung of thy priorities.
- Thou shall not dismiss accidents as Act of God.

- Remember that thou propagate safety everyday and not just on National Safety Day.
- Honor thy commitment to the safety of thy employees.
- Thou shall not pollute the environment with damaging effluents from thy plant.
- Thou shall not hesitate in giving due importance to thy safety professional and his profession.
- Thou shall not flout the safety laws of thy land.
- Thou shall not shirk thy responsibility towards society for thy own parochial gain.
- Obey the real Ten Commandments.

TIPS FOR HABIT FORMATION

- Identify your bad habits. When, where, and why did you learn and develop them? Are you unconsciously imitating peers or negative role models? Do you use them to cover fear or feelings of inadequacy-emotions that would cause you to seek (false) comfort in tension relieving instead of goal-achieving activities?
- Learn what triggers your bad habits. Identifying your unwanted patterns makes replacing them easier, beginning with triggers – which are often stress, criticism, guilt, or feelings of rejection. Identify the situations that cause you the most frustration and tension and plan ways to avoid or reduce them as much as possible.
- List the benefits of new habit that would replace the old. Self-esteem, improved health, longevity, improved relationships, more professional productivity and respect, better focus, enhanced promotion potential, accelerated financial security...each helps lead to your ultimate goal of lifelong improvement and growth.
- Say farewell forever to excuses for mistakes and failures. Accept your imperfection when an old habit begs for attention. Instead of "There I go again," say, "Next time I will be strong enough to do what's right." Instead of thinking "I am too tired", say, "I've got the energy to do this and more". Change, "It's too late" to "As I get organized, I know I'll have time".
- Visualize yourself in the new habit patterns of a positive new lifestyle. It takes many simulations and repetitions to spin new cobwebs on top of your old cables. If you want to give up smoking, intentionally sit in nonsmoking areas and request nonsmoking hotel rooms. A clean environment, with hands and teeth of normal, healthy color, will help you feel in control. And if you can keep the new habits going, fresher breath, cleaner smelling clothes, furnishings, and a steadier heart will augment that control.

You deserve as much happiness and success as anyone. You are worth price – which is effort, training, practice, and courage. You control your thoughts, and your thoughts control your habits.

Your mind can not distinguish a vividly repeated simulation from a real experience. It stores as fact whatever you rehearse. The software drives the hardware-, which is true for ducks, eagles, and humans.

WHY ACCIDENT INVESTIGATION ?

It is from statics we learn:

- How many accidents occur?
- What kind of accidents they are.
- How serious they are.
- What class of worker incurs them?
- What machines and other equipment's are involved in them.
- What sort of behaviour is associated with them?
- At what times and places they occur most frequently.
- About the situation, estimation of needs/judging results.

Statistics of accidents are essential for planning accident prevention activities and for assuring their effectiveness.

ACCIDENT INVESTIGATION

Accidents may be investigated for two purposes:

- To ascertain who is responsible for them.
- To find out how similar accidents can be prevented.

Accident investigation is concerned with both responsibility and prevention.

Accident investigation is a basis for safety success. When an accident happens, it just is not enough to "fill out the forms" and leave it as that. The accident investigator must dig out for the understanding causes of the incident. This information is vital for dealing with the hazards that must be eliminated to prevent reoccurrence.

The traditional approach of only recognizing and correcting the immediate causes of accident does little to get to the real causes. An investigation should be made of all accidents, not only those which causes injury, but damage as well. With through investigation, management can pin-point the causes of those incidents, and that is what forms the basis of a sound accident prevention program.

ACCIDENT INVESTIGATION PRINCIPLES TO BE OBSERVED

- **Use Common Sense:** Stick to the facts and weigh their value to reach justified conclusions.
- **Investigate Each Clue:** An apparently reasonable conclusion will often be changed by exploring factors which may not appear to be important.
- **Check for Unsafe Conditions and Acts:** Both are involved in the great majority of accidents.
- **Investigate All Accidents:** Chance is often the sole difference between a trivial accident and a serious one. Results can not be predicted.
- **Make Recommendations:** No investigation is complete unless corrective action is suggested.
- **Prepare Report:** Written reports are helpful tools for study and analysis to determine specific areas of operations where accidents are occurring and for follow up action on recommendations.

A TO Z OF SAFETY

- Aim at zero accident targets.
- Better safe than sorry.
- Cultivate safety habits, it pays.
- Do not neglect any injury however small.
- Every worker's goal, total accident control.
- Falls hurt stay alert.
- Good housekeeping prevents accident.
- Handle sharp objects with caution.
- Injury neglected infects.
- Join hands for total safety.
- Keep guards in position.
- Lost limbs do not grow.
- Make every day a safe day.
- Near accidents can be real accidents.
- Oil on floor can break bones.
- Poor judgment results in accident.
- Quality comes along with safety.
- Report every accident at once.

- Shortcuts may cut short your life.
- Tools and fools handle with care.
- Use safety appliances religiously.
- Vision is our priceless possession, protect it.
- Work safely and live happily.
- (e) Xtempore action leads to accidents.
- Your family expects you to return home safe.
- Zero accident our ultimate aim.

SAFETY MANAGEMENT

Safety is defined in the dictionary as freedom from harm. Thus complete safety is an ideal condition. The society expects a fair degree of safety to life and health of workers. The industry has a legal responsibility towards the safety of its employees. The degree of safety varies with the legal requirements in different countries. In case of serious accidental cases, besides being liable for paying compensation for any harm to the employees in course of company's work, the 'occupier' and 'manager' of the company can also be sued for criminal negligence.

The statutory regulations by the Government of most of the countries play an important part for the development of safety aspects in general and safety management in particular. For example management responsibilities, responsibilities of different levels in the organization, safety in engineering design aspect, occupational health exposures to toxic chemicals, responsibilities in handling hazardous chemicals, etc., are generally defined in the legal requirements. The legal responsibilities imposed on the occupiers and managers of the industries are only bare necessity towards maintenance of safety. The industries should strive to work much beyond the legal requirements to achieve a reasonable degree of safety standard.

Various elements of safety management are:

- Commitment and accountability.
- Leadership and administration.
- Management system
- Employee participation.
- Process safety information.
- Process hazards analysis.
- Hazards assessment.
- Operating procedures/Safe working procedures.

- Training.
- Managing contractors.
- Pre-start up safety review.
- Maintenance/mechanical integrity.
- Hot work permits.
- Management of change.
- Accident/incident investigation.
- Emergency planning and response.
- Safety audits.
- Trade secrets protection.
- Risk management planning.
- Planned inspections.
- Materials management/purchasing controls.
- Hiring and placement.
- Occupational health control.
- Off the job safety.

With the commitment to safety the management will able to create a safety culture which will give ultimate benefit to the company only.

17 CHAPTER

Tool Safety

DO NOT FOOL WITH TOOLS

When was the last time you hit the nail right on head? Remember, the day you did not, and ended up nursing a bruised finger. Painful memories are not they?

Once a while we always have to get down to using hammers, screwdrivers, wrenches, pliers et al. at home. After all for minor jobs it may sometimes look unnecessary to call a skilled worker. But these minor jobs could result in major consequences, if taken lightly.

Many nasty accidents can be avoided if certain precautionary measures are followed. Take the hammer, for example, which is found in most homes. Hold the hammer firmly at the end, so that it does not slip out of your hand. If it does, it may injure tender fingers holding the other object; it could also fly out of your hand and cause grievous injuries. While hammering nails, use a gripping tool or piece of cardboard and turn it into a stop-gap nail holder. So even if your aim takes a near miss, your limbs are still intact. Heavy hammering may result in flying chips, which could get scattered all over the place. A curious toddler may gulp it down; someone could even stamp over a sharp piece. So mop up the place after the job is over.

Who has not used a screwdriver? But did you know that for every job the same screwdriver may not be appropriate? Match the screw with the proper screwdriver so that the tool's blade does not slip out of the screw's slot and, cut your finger. Desist from using screwdrivers which have blunt or chipped points – they may slip and hurt you unawares.

We are in an age of dismountable fixtures and furniture items – which means that the use of nuts and bolts. While using a spanner or wrench, it should fit snugly on the nut and bolt so that it does not slip. Pull the wrench towards you – do not push.

You never require tools on a day-to-day basis; this in turn may make you complacent while buying them. The craze for "cheap stuff" may drive you crazy later. Be wiser. Buy known brands which assure a certain standard of quality and safety. And in any case, it is a lifetime investment – so why not pay a few bucks extra and choose the right tool?

Like all kits, your toolbox also should have a designated place for safekeeping. If tools are scattered around all over the house, retrieving one of the right time may become a pain in the neck.

In brief – learn to handle tools safely; use the right type of tool; insist on buying standardized tools. And the message, which should always be hammered home: Do not fool with tools.

DO'S AND DO NOTS IN USE OF HAND TOOLS

Large numbers of injuries are caused from hand tools. The main causes for these accidents are use of unsuitable and damaged tools.

DO'S

- Use hand tools for specific purpose for which they are designed.
- Inspect hand tools before use.
- Heads of hammers, chisels should be dressed periodically to avoid mushroom heads.
- Store hand tools in cabinets or toolboxes.
- Use only quality tools.

DO NOT'S

- Do not use spanner as a hammer or knife as a screwdriver.
- Never use oversize spanner with packing between nut and spanner.
- Do not leave hand tools carelessly, while working at heights as it is a source of danger to persons working below.
- Do not leave hand tools on floors, on machines, and on pathways.
- Do not misuse tools.

Use Right Tool for Right Job

HANDY HINTS FOR SAFETY WITH HAND TOOLS

Axes

Use thin bladed narrow axe for hard wood and a thick-bladed wide axe for softwood. Keep the axe sharp and check the handle regularly for splits or looseness around the blade. Make sure that there is a clear circle in which to swing the axe. Always use eye protection.

Chisels

Replace the chisel as soon as it begins to crack or mushroom. When a mushroomed head is pounced, there is danger that the chips will be knocked off the damaged head and will fly into the eyes.

A cold chisel will buckle or bounce if it is not large or strong enough for the metal being cut.

Wear safety glasses when chipping or shearing with a cold chisel. Protect the sharp edges of the chisel by storing them in a rack, workbench or slotted section of a toolbox.

Kinves

When worked with knives, wear hand guards, mesh gloves or other types of protective equipment. If it is not possible, keep your body clear off the stroke and wear protective clothing.

Cutters

Use heavy-duty cutters when cutting thick wire or reinforcing wire or bolts. Never use cutters near live electrical circuits. Apply the force at a right angle to the cutting edge. Wear approved eye protection when using cutters.

Spanners and Wrenches

Spanners and wrenches should always be of the right size and well maintained. If not, they could cause injury, or damage the equipment being repaired or adjusted. Tube extensions on spanners and wrenches may mean too much leverage, which may cause the tool to break.

Saws

Use smooth, downward strokes to help the saw cut directly across the material. Keep the saw sharp and free from cracks and broken teeth.

Do not crowd or force a saw through the cut because the saw may buckle or fly out. Do not hang saws overhead or leave them lying around. They can cause nastily scrapes and cuts.

HANDLE POWER TOOLS WITH CARE

While using power tools a large number of accidents occur, largely due to human error and deficiencies in earthing. If proper precautions are followed, these accidents can be minimized considerably To protect yourself, follow the following guidelines:

- Familiarize yourself with the tool before using it.
- Always follow manufacturer's instructions for operation and maintenance.
- Make it a habit to inspect the tool before using it and ensure that it is not in damaged condition.
- While using power tools, wear close fitting clothes and cover your hair, if it is long.
- Wear correct type of personal protective equipment such as safety glasses.
- If the power tool is fitted with a guard, never remove it.
- Never leave power tools unattended, if they are plugged in.
- Ensure that power tools are properly grounded.
- Never use any power tool that has cracks or defective wires.
- It could lead to fire or electrical shocks.
- After use, clean and store the tools properly.

Your safety depends on using power tools with caution

PORTABLE ELECTRIC HAND TOOLS

Irrespective of whether a portable electrical tool is of single insulated, double-insulated or all insulated type, it is essential to observe some general safety rules.

The casing of the tool should be free of breaks or damage. Brush caps should be intact and firmly in position. Sheathing of flexible cord should be securely held at the tool with no exposed conductors.

A flexible cord should be in good condition and free of joints of any kind other than through plugs and cord extension sockets. The plugs and extension sockets should be free from cracks and damages and all screws tight. Any defect should be remedied before the tool is used.

Be sure to wear adequate insulating footwear and avoid standing on wet or damp surfaces. Do not overload the tool so that it stops or over heats. Take care not to damage the flexible cord.

If anything unusual happens – a blown fuse, failure of the tool to operate, excess sparking or heating – switch off the power, pull out the plug and have tool and cord examined by a qualified electrical tradesman.

Unfortunately, electrical accidents sometimes occur and immediate action must be taken to rescue the victim.

- Immediately switch off the electricity where practicable and release the patient from source of shock. Do not use any metal object or anything moist when releasing the patient.
- Commence resuscitation without delay and continue without interruption for hours if necessary.
- When assistance is available send for a doctor and an ambulance.

To protect the user of an electric appliance from the risk of electric shock, all accessible metal parts must be insulated from current carrying parts.

A double insulated appliance relies on an in built sound barrier of protective insulation and hence no earthing is required.

Sometimes it is possible for an appliance to be totally enclosed in a casing made of insulating material and have no external metal whatever. This form of construction embodies the principle known as "all insulation" and eliminates the need for further earthing or a second internal barrier of protective insulation.

Effective earthing may be achieved when:

The main earth wire of the electrical insulation is insert. It must not be broken or disconnected.

Properly earthed three pin outlets are used. Not all three-pin outlets are earthed. Lamp holders and two pin power outlets do not provide earthing.

All exposed metal parts of the tool are electrically bonded to the earthing terminal. This can be check tested by an electrical tradesman.

The three core flexible cord of tough rubber or plastic sheathed type is used for the main lead and any extension leads.

Approved three-pin plugs and cord extension sockets, correctly wired, are used. Because they must not be earthed, portable electrical tools of the double insulated and all insulated types are fitted with two-core flexible cord.

A three-pin plug is fitted to a two core flexible conductor attached to the tool but no connection is made to the ear thing terminal of this three-pin plug.

When an extension lead is used, it should comprise an approved core extension socket, three-core flexible cord and three-pin plug.

Extension leads should never be assembled using two core flexible cords because they could be used inadvertently to supply single insulated appliances.

POWER TOOL SAFETY

The equipment rarely causes power tool accidents itself, because manufacturers have designed in a verity of safety features – blade guards and workplace guides, for example – to prevent injuries. But manufacturers cannot design out the "human factors".

There are number of errors people make that lead to injuries.

One common mistake is not dressing right for the job. If you are using a power tool, do not wear loose clothes that could be caught in a whirling blade and pull you into it. You should wear short sleeves, remove all jewelry and tie your hair back if it is long.

You should also wear protective equipment. Safety goggles or glasses will prevent wood chips from flying into your eyes, and ear protection will keep a noisy tool from injuring your hearing. But do not wear gloves when working with tool that have rotating part or accessories – the tool could snag the glove and draw your hand in.

HELPFUL HINTS

- When using a joint/planer, feed the wood with the grain wherever you can. Feed very slowly and to take very light cuts if you must feed against the grain.
- When you are using a table saw, you want to keep your hands away from the blade as much as possible, so feed the wood with a pushtick when you can.
- A portable grinder can kick and glance off the work if not properly controlled, so make sure you have a secure footing and keep a safety grip on the tool.
- If the blade of a circular saw is pinched, the tool can kick back. To prevent these, support large panels so they do not bend into each other.
- When using a circular saw, make sure the workpiece is securely clamped. For best control use both hands and keep a firm grip on the saw.
- When cross cutting, pull a radial arm saw toward you just for enough to complete the cut, or the blade can toss the cut piece.
- When using a drill press, securely clamp the workpiece and back-up material that can not be braced against the left side of the column.
- Adjust grinder tool rests to provide a maximum clearance of 1/8 inch to prevent the work piece from being caught between the wheel and the rest.

POWER POINTS ARE DANGEROUS

- Modern houses are designed with all amenities in mind. Electric power points are usually placed within an arm's reach. However, points of televisions and decorative lamps are sometimes placed at lower levels.
- Toddlers find such plug points very interesting. They crawl and insert their fingers into the points. Occasionally, youngsters may insert clips, pins or even screwdriver into the socket. If the point gets switched on accidentally the child may get a severe shock. Unused plug points should always be kept covered. Some companies manufacture sockets, which have a protective cover and it, slides up only when the plug is inserted. Install such sockets if there is a little child in your house.

- If the sockets in your house are of older variety, see that a plug is always inserted in the point to keep it covered. It may be a matter of life and death.

SAFETY IN HAND/POWER TOOLS

(Hazard identification and preventive measures)

Hazard	Consequences	Preventive Measueres
Unguarded moving part in grinding wheel and drill bit	• Serious injury	• Use proper guard • Ensure tightening mechanism of the tool
Supply of power without earthing	• Electrocution	• Use three-pin plug • Avoid loose connection • Ensure good ear thing

SAFETY PRECAUTIONS IN USE OF COMMON HAND TOOLS

The Vice

The vice is a very innocent looking tool but it is comparatively easy for a man to get an accident if he is not careful. It can cause accident by:

- Getting fingers caught between the jaws and work.
- Getting fingers caught between the knob on the end of the handle head, and the head of the screw.
- Dropping of heavy work loosely fitted on to the foot.

Hammers

Before using the hammer the operator should see that:

- The hammer is free from grease and oil to avoid accidents due to slippage.
- The hammer face is not mushroomed. This will cause chips to fly and injure the operator.
- The hammer is properly wedged to prevent it from coming out and causing injury to somebody.

Chisels

- Do not use a chisel with mushroom head.
- Put a chipping screen in front of you while chipping.
- Chisel head or hammer face must be free from oil or grease.

- Swing the hammer in the right manner to avoid striking the hand.
- Hammer handle should not be loose.
- Use goggles if someone is chipping in front of you, on the other side.

Files

- Never use a file without a handle.
- Always keep the file handle tight.

Hacksaws

The chief danger in the use of a hacksaw is injuring the hand when a blade breaks. Breaking is caused by one of following two things:

- Either the operator is bearing too hard on the blade.
- The operator is not pushing the saw straight, thereby twisting the blade which causes it to break. When this happens the hand may sometimes come against the work and thus cause an injury.

Drills

While working on the drilling machine, the following safety precautions must be observed:

- Hold the job tightly either in a vice or clamp it securely. Unsecured work may revolve dangerously if the drill binds on the work.
- Use brush or air hose to remove chips from table and work. Do not use fingers or waste to remove chips. Keep waste and rags away from revolving drill and chips.
- Do not wear necktie, long sleeves, loose hair, loose gloves or anything that might get caught in the drill. Wear such clothing that fits well and fits comfortably.
- Remove chuck key from chuck and drift from sleeve of drill before starting the machine. These things may fly from the machine and cause injury to the operator.
- Use proper ground drills for each metal. Do not use a drill ground for steel when drilling brass or copper. The drill may bend in the work and break, causing possible injury to the operator.
- Always keep tools, etc., where they can be easily found on the machine.

Scrapers

When using scrapers of any kind the following precautions should be observed:

- Keep both hands clean from grease, oil or respiration.
- Hold the blade of scraper firmly in one hand using the other hand to push the scraper over the work.

- Keep the hand high enough from the work to prevent striking the corners of the piece that is being scraped. The corners are often sharp and might cause serious injury to the hand.
- When scraping bearings keep the hands away from cutting edges of scraper. These edges are sharp and will readily cut the hand.

18 CHAPTER

Training in Safety

IMPORTANCE OF SAFETY TRAINING

Success of any safety plan depends largely on the attitude of individual towards safety. The first introduction to safety during the apprenticeship/training period has a lasting affect. With the development in technology, safety is an integral part of each element of operation and any training in operations must include instructions on how to operate without accidents. The basic purpose is of making the apprentice understand that accidents just do not happen but are caused due to some unsafe conditions or unsafe acts and both these factors can be controlled if not completely eliminated.

A systematic plan to cover safety training has to be evolved as part of apprenticeship training and this should be given a high priority. Depending on the organization the broad outline of the plan could have following coverage:

- Initial introduction.
- Off the job instructions.
- On the job safety practices.
- Supervisor's role in safety and conclusion.

- **Initial Introduction (Half or Full day)**
  - Importance of safety in industry.
  - Growing concern of hazards with advanced technology.
  - Hidden cost of damages due to accidents.
  - Self discipline and attitudinal change.
- **Off the Job Instructions (Two to Three Days)**
  - Causes of accidents (basic, contributory, bad house keeping and maintenance).
  - Identifying the cause group.
  - Safety with machines and equipment.
  - Raw materials, properties, storage and transport requirements.
  - Process control safety.
  - Safety in manual lifting, mechanical lifting tackles, working at heights, ladders, chain pulley blocks, chains, wire ropes etc.
  - Fork lift trucks, conveyor systems safety.
  - Safety in constructions.
  - Electrical safety – power source, transmission, usage, portable electrical tools.
  - First aid and fire fighting, fire causes and prevention. Use of fire fighting equipments and appliances – dos and do nots.
  - Statutory rules and regulations.
  - Hazardous jobs, working in confined places, permit to work system.
  - Accidents, consequences, reporting investigation, follow up, safety statistics.
  - Safety organizations.
  - Introduction to pollution causes and control, waste management.
  - Occupational health.
- **On the Job Safety (Learning by Doing)**
  - Safety features of each process, machine, activities, location and in-process materials.
  - Operation code, rules and regulations for safety – examine what are to be followed.
  - Starting and stopping machines.
  - Safety in repair and maintenance of plants, safety fittings, instrument's verifications, understanding of warning devices.
  - Taking part in fire drill, joining a safety inspection team.
  - Accident investigation procedure – completion of one exercise on site under guidance.

  - Locating information on safety from codes, statutory rules, standards etc.
  - Correct use of protective equipments.
- **Supervisor's Role in Safety (During Concluding Session of Apprenticeship)**
  - Instructing and training workers.
  - Keeping up-date on safety.
  - Check lists.
  - Working in a safety committee.
  - Hazard spotting exercises.

Training can be rounded off by working under guidance on a useful exercise such as classifying various activities and safety interface as applicable. In fact a project on safety can be carried within a year.

Safety is integral part of operation. Training in operation and maintenance can not be complete without training in safety.

TRAINING IS AN INVESTMENT

Training is an investment, not a cost, is validated by the market, but only if its effectiveness can be ascertained. Training is now seen as money well spent. Companies with high growth rates have no time to train their employees. The solution: automated training management. Organizations have many levels where training and education are needed:

- Top management;
- Core corporate strategic fundamentals – developed internally;
- Technical skills (i.e., new technology training) – usually sourced from outside;
- Regulatory compliance and documentation;
- Continuing education and certification.

Rapid change has increased the need for effective training and its management. Liberalization has made development of the Indian Executive/manager a key task for top management. Placing training and development at the heart of a business strategy enables an organization to build its collective international competence and create a learning organization.

In India the acceptance of training, in comparison to foreign countries is frightfully low due to a conventional training approach.

The conventional training approach suffers severe limitations such as:

- All managers are treated as if they have the same problems.
- Most training programs are designed and conducted by persons who have never been trained as trainers, which often results in making transfer of learning difficult or impossible.

- Training programs are often treated as holidays or paid holidays and, therefore, lack the required response from participants.
- Top management as a cost constraint looks upon training and so is never a priority.

However, it must be realized that training and development shall implement new standards and empower managers with new skills and attitudes. In fact, this new orientation must lead to some fundamental change in the training and development function itself.

- There must be a clearly articulated mission, which has to be directly linked to the company's business strategy.
- Training programs should have specific objectives, which will contribute to the company's competitive challenges.
- All training must be tailored to meet the needs of the individuals and the organization.
- High priority issues faced by Indian organizations today are leadership, market orientation, formulation and implementation of strategy and management of change etc. must be addressed in training.
- There must be a more systematic assessment and analysis of training needs objectives and output.
- The training and development function must become independent of HR/HRD/ PERSONNEL and must run like a business, professionally resourced and managed, and held accountable for its results.

Lack of training leads corporate to question its value. Traditional training methods are not producing effective results. Resistance to training comes primarily from perception of effectiveness. Many executives distrust the effectiveness of training with no ability for ROI (Reviewing Operational Instructions) assessment. Two issues cause the gap:

- Operations departments have little control over training. Training departments often do not concentrate on more complex operations. Operations executives complain that they are unable to receive the critical operational training they need.
- Feedback for evaluation and improving effectiveness is poor. Instructor – based training is highly variable.

Training has two costs: direct cost of training assets, and opportunity cost of trainees in training. Technology infrastructure now supports the large market of technology-based training and its automated management. Computer Based Training (CBT) replicates exact copies for training and CBT distribution eliminates costs. With CBT, lesson quality is controlled and trainers concentrate on improving course content. It enables detailed, interactive learning, which increases retention. While, Instructor led training depends upon the rare teacher – charisma, CBT replicates it infinitely.

CBT Helps:

- Reduce schedule problems for attendance of large audiences;
- Increase presentation consistency;
- Increase student achievement;
- Reduce high staff costs and focus on training development, not delivery;
- Students with uneven learning skills to cope better;
- Increase safety through simulation of risky conditions;
- Reduce data entry required for training documentation.

How should a company's human resource strategy ensure that its managers are empowered with such attributes in a way that reinforces the organization's global spirit and builds its collective competencies?

First and foremost, the Indian organizations must recognize its long-term competitiveness that depends on its ability to develop fully and utilize the expertise and talent of all its employees. Next, it must evolve into a knowledge based organization whose major asset is know-how and whose goal is to become a "Learning Organization", where continuos training and development is a way of life.

Indian organizations must move from fragmented or conventional approach in training and development to a more focused approach.

- **The Fragmented Approach is:**
  - A cost not an investment.
  - Not linked to organizational goals.
  - Perceived as luxury.
  - Directive.
  - Primarily knowledge-based courses.
- **The Focussed Approach is:**
  - A continuous learning process.
  - Essential for business survival.
  - A competitive weapon.
  - Linked to organizational strategy and individual goals.
  - On-the-job plus specialist courses.
  - Using creative, non-directive methods.
  - Line manager's responsibility.
  - Tolerance.

Under the focused approach, training and development is seen as a necessity for survival, it is regarded as a competitive weapon and learning to organizational and individual goals. This approach is emphasized through job development, so that learning becomes a totally continuous activity.

Organizations realize their assets walkout the door every night and know they must improve them or lose them. That training is an investment, not a cost, is validated by the market, but only if its effectiveness can be ascertained. In a tight labor market for skilled employees' organizations must train, develop, track and monitor their employees on the job. New methods and structures for business now exist, but few are trained in these. Indian enterprises are witnessing such rapid change that the impact at times is catastrophic within the business and in the industry. Thus training is now seen as money well spent.

OUTCOMES OF TRAININGS

One can list the following as the possible outcomes of trainings when it is implemented patiently over a reasonable period of time.

- Employees in the organization should start taking more initiative (and become more pro-active).
- The employees should be able to solve problems on their own and refer them less frequently to higher levels.
- There should be more team spirit and collaboration.
- There should be a stronger identification with the organization and increased involvement in the work.
- There should be more and more creative ideas coming from employees with an increase in innovativeness at various levels.
- The top management should become more sensitive to the problems and processes due to increased openness in communications.
- People feel involved to work and contribute as these are recognized and rewarded whenever possible by the top management.
- Employees become more prepared to face any challenges or crisis situation the organization faces as they have competencies to handle the game.

COURSE MODULES

Fire Prevention and Protection in Industries

Common Topics:

- Fire losses and concept of loss prevention.
- Understanding fires and fire behaviour.
- Principles of fire and principles of extinguishment.

- Fire safety principles in design, layout and construction of process facilities.
- Ignition sources.
- Statutory requirements on fire safety.
- Selection, care and use of fire extinguishers.
- Fighting fires at incipient stage – demonstration and hands on training.
- Work permits systems.

Industy Specific Topics

- Fire hazards in the specific industry and feasible control methods.
- Bulk storage and handling of hazardous substances.
- Fixed fire protection systems.
- Case histories and case studies.

Fire Safety in Computer Installations

- Loss scenario of fire incidents involving computer centers.
- Sources of ignition and fire spread possibilities.
- Fire segregation requirements for computers, peripherals and utilities.
- Fire detection and protection arrangements.
- Planning for fire emergencies.

Safety in the Use of Cranes

- Introduction to safety in crane operations.
- Regulatory and recommendatory provisions in use and care of lifting machines and lifting tackles.
- Safety in crane and slinging operations.
- Inspection and care of cranes and associated gear.
- Case studies and films.

Sasety in Forklift Truck Operations

- Types and causes of accidents in the use of forklift trucks.
- Safety features of the forklift trucks.
- Checks at the time of taking charge.
- Inspection and maintenance.
- Safety in operations.
- Case studies, quiz.
- Field exercise and safety performance rating.

Conveyor Safety

- Injury and health hazards in conveyor operations and health hazards.

- Fire and explosion hazards and protection systems for conveyor belts.
- Inspection and maintenance requirements for conveyor safety.
- Case studies.

Safety Training Tips

Try these tips, contributed for the operations service division and for safety.

- Think of the learner first. How can he or she understand and absorb the training? (not how comfortable are you with presenting it your way)
- Understand the objectives before you begin.
- Find out where the participants want to go and help them to get there.
- Reduce your concern over your presentation skills – concentrate on the learner.
- Review your visual aids. Make them active, not passive: people will remember them the most if they can participate.
- Make learning interesting by making it interactive.
- Vary your presentation techniques.
- Learn to use repetitions to reinforce information, but vary the form of repetition.
- Try to let people experience the skill or activity you want them to learn. Do not just tell them.
- Keep visual aids simple: show the main points only.

The Management of Knowledge

It would be easy to dismiss "knowledge management" as yet another abstract marketing tag that the information technology industry coins regularly to sell more computers. But while the InfoTech industry is certainly driving the campaign to highlight the benefits of knowledge management, technology is only one of several elements needed to take it work.

In practice, knowledge management requires a combination of many disciplines, from human resources and personal development to corporate re-engineering and infotech. Technology is, of course, important. Without it, knowledge management would be impossible. InfoTech provides the mechanisms for capturing, storing and retrieving the raw data that form the basis of "knowledge." The emergence of the web browser and Internet communications infrastructure as standards makes it simple and inexpensive to access data. But while the technology infrastructure has evolved to make knowledge management possible, the real benefits can only come from applying knowledge.

Undoubtedly, it is the potential benefit of applying knowledge management that has attracted the attention of senior executives. A recent survey found that 95% of executives saw knowledge management as an essential ingredient for the success of their companies. Many also admitted that their knowledge management programs could be improved.

There is good reason. Businesses can only survive and thrive by exploiting every possible advantage in an increasingly competitive market. It followed that any special knowledge that an organization might have – from ownership of intellectual property in the form of patents and copyrights to special skills and innovative business processes – is an asset worth protecting and nurturing.

Knowledge management is a combination of disciplines and technologies, which aims to do exactly this. The disciplines have evolved from several areas, including business process re-engineering and human resource management. The technologies spring from the universal communications medium of Internet and established software technologies such as information retrieval, document management and workflow processing.

This complex pedigree does make knowledge management hard to define-with each area of academic, industry or constancy offering its own variation. InfoTech people see it as an extension of technologies such as data warehousing and information retrieval. Human resources experts see it as part of recasting the corporation as the "learning organization."

WHAT IS KNOWLEDGE MANAGEMENT

Let's start with what managing and sharing knowledge is not:

- Knowledge management is not a new religion or a spiritual calling.
- It is not an attempt to rally disgruntled employees around an appealing philosophical concept.
- It is not an existentialist search for the truth. (Actually, it's about the entirely worldly task of making money.)
- It is not a science or a 'discipline' – yet.
- It is not the latest management fad.

When explicitly managed, organizational knowledge is used to accomplish the organization's mission. Knowledge management is therefore a conscious strategy of getting the right knowledge to the right people at the right time and helping people share and put information into action in ways that strive to improve organizational performance.

Fortunately most companies have some experience already in managing knowledge. Indeed, KM is not a radical departure or a methodology in and off itself. Rather, it is a framework, a management mind-set that includes building on past experiences (libraries, databanks, smart people) and creating new vehicles for exchanging knowledge (knowledge-enabled intranet sites, communities of practice, networks).

For most organizations, KM represents a continuation of efforts begun in other times with other names (or acronyms), all of that have likely yielded valuable learning.

- Radical re-engineering may have not delivered sustainable success, but it has "delivered" the mind-set of the process-oriented organization. Processes can be transferred.
- Total quality management (TQM) may not always have yielded big time change, but it had the foundation for a corporate-wide, systematic initiative for measurement and change and cross-functional teaming, all of which are critical to the successful management of knowledge.

Not surprising, newly trim and lean, re-engineered companies like Amoco, Chevron, and Texas instruments have been at the forefront of the KM "revolution". Companies like these have been among the first to realize that to accelerate growth-again – they must adopt new approaches that leverage their internal expertise.

WHO FOCUSES ON WHAT FOR KNOWLEDGE MANAGEMENT

A Snapshot of Some KM Pioneer' Early of Value Proportions

Organization	Customer Intimacy	Product to Market	Operational excellence
Amoco			PF
Arthur Andersen	PF		SF
BP			PF
Buck man Labs	PF	SF	
Chevron			PF
Cigna			PF
Dow Chemical		PF	
Hewlett-Packard		SF	PF
Hoffmann-La Roche			PF
Huges S and C		PF	SF
IBM		PF	
Kiser Permanente			PF
NSA		PF	
Price Waterhouse		PF	
Sequent	PF	SF	
Skandia			PF

TI	SF		PF
USAA	PF	SF	
World Bank		PF	

PF = Primary Focus

SF = Secondary Focus

TEN TIPS TO CONDUCT A BETTER SAFETY MEETING

How often have you walked out of your safety meeting and felt you could have managed it better?

"Such meetings can be stressful for safety managers," says Dr. C. Brady Wilson, a clinical psychologist from Phoenix who specializes in work environments. "Safety managers may already know how to prepare for the meetings and give a successful presentation. Yet they take the skills necessary to feel confident in a session."

Plan the meeting carefully. Determine why you need a meeting and write an agenda for it. Before the meeting, preview visual aids to be used and check all equipment and exits to make sure everything works. Make sure handouts are clear, concise and plentiful. Ask speaker to rehearse and time their talks. Give employees atleast one day's notice so they can prepare questions.

Safety meetings should not be longer than 30 minutes. If you have unnecessarily long and frequent meetings, they become ineffective. Once per month is usually enough. If you have no clear reason to have a meeting, either find a reason or do not have the meeting.

You may not be able to use all the points listed below at your next safety meeting, but try to use at least three. You can add others at future meetings.

- Keep the session friendly. Before you start your presentation, let everyone know their participation is important to you. Encourage them to ask questions and voice ideas.
- Do not be judgmental. Before you answer any questions, tell your team that there are no wrong questions. Tell them they will not be judged on either their questions or ideas.
- Do not rush your answers. Speak slowly enough for everyone to understand and loudly enough for people to hear. Do not play with a pen, doodle on paper or fiddle with your water glass. Look directly at your audiences.
- Do not allow anyone to ramble. If an employee starts to ramble, ask, "Is this what your question is?" If an employee speaks too quickly, politely ask them to slow down. Remember that they may be nervous.

- Avoid debates. If someone makes a critical statement, accept it as just another point. Do not treat it separately. If you do, you may start a debate. When another person makes the next point, do not view it as an opposing statement. Just treat both comments as different points that can stand on their own merit.
- If do not have an answer say so. Do not panic. Tell employees you will look into it and come back to them with an answer.
- Recap what was said. To stay on track, summarize what was said in the meeting. This helps reinforce important ideas.
- Keep the "Controllers" under control. Prevent people who try to control the meeting. Limit comments to a few minutes each. Insist equal time for everyone.
- Recognize hostility. If people seem hostile, acknowledge their feelings and their comments. This lets everyone know that you take their opinions seriously. Chances are, if one employee is angry, so are others.
- End on a positive note. Summarize relevant points. Give employees atleast ten minutes to ask questions.

FREQUENT SAFETY MEETINGS – A MUST

Company safety meetings should be holding on a regular basis in all operations. Accepting this responsibility to communicate accident prevention knowledge is stressed more in some operations than in others.

In some instances, safety meetings are not held for such reasons as "we have just been too busy this past month". Opinions may also be offered that a program of individual contacts between the supervisor and the worker to discuss safety is more effective than group meetings. "We all believe in safety", it is said, "but we just do not have time for meetings, or for inspections to correct unsafe acts and conditions".

Is not it also true that it's up to each worker to assume responsibility for his own safety? Is not he the one who has to decide if he's going to follow rule and wear his hard hat and seat belt? A supervisor can not watch everyone all the time!

These are just rationalizations for not holding safety meetings or for holding them occasionally. Stating that there is a good program of worker contacts is usually just an excuse for not holding safety meetings. The truth is that those operations that have effective worker contacts are the ones that also have good meetings. The two things go hand in hand.

A busy production schedule, working overtime, and difficulty in getting people together (as with drivers and small construction crews) are reasons for paying more, not less, attention to prevent accidents. A failure to do those things which has been found to be effective in preventing accidents will eventually lead to a higher frequency of accidents than is desirable.

A number of people injured in accidents were under 20 years of age. An even large number were newly hired employees. Are we giving enough attention to safety training and indoctrination of new employees? Good safety meetings are training sessions; useful and potentially life-saving information should be provided.

Supervisors have been heard to declare, "I can not think of anything to say in a safety meeting!" Others complain because meetings become forums for complaint or opportunities to loaf.

There is a great deal of safety materials available, but is important that this be supplemented with information pertinent to the specific site. Much safety material is distributed in the fond hope that it will be used. Too often, it is not.

A superintendent might call on someone else to conduct a safety meeting, but it is inexcusable if he does not attend and participate in the meeting. His absence can indicate that his regard for workers health and safety is not as sincere as it should be.

EVERYTHING ON SAFETY POLICY

- Safety policy is mandatory as per Factory's Act.
- Safety policy is the starting point of safety activities.
- Safety policy should be reflected at the shop floor.
- Safety policy provides guidelines for accident prevention.
- Safety policy demonstrates management's commitment to safety.
- Safety policy leads to effective and efficient team work.
- Safety policy is not a safety manual.
- Safety policy is same for regular and contract labor.
- Safety policy statements should be sufficiently extensive.
- Safety policy should be clear and explicit.
- Safety policy should also focus on human aspects.
- Safety policy should aim to promote total safety.
- Safety policy provides definite guidelines for safety.
- Safety policy should be broad in scope and general in nature.
- Safety policy should proclaim management's commitment.
- Safety policy should be widely discussed.
- Safety policy should be translated in regional language.
- Safety policy must spell out general duties at each level.
- Safety policy should also stress on use of PPE.
- Safety policy should be made in joint consultation.

- Safety policy should be fully implemented from the date of declaration.
- Safety policy should be explained to each and every employee.
- Safety policy should be signed by the occupier.
- Safety policy is not prepared only to comply the law.
- Safety policy should not be too short or too long.
- Safety policy is better implemented through joint forums.

EMPLOYEE SAFETY TRAINING

Statistics indicate that most accidents are preceded by unsafe acts rather than unsafe conditions. However, many times an unsafe act would have been committed if the employee had been shown the hazards involved in a job as well as safe procedures to avoid them. Employee safety training is the answer for controlling unsafe act.

WHO NEEDS TRAINING?

Everyone needs training at one time or the other. New employee needs training in order to get acquainted on the job. Existing employees who are changing the job require training in order to perform their new jobs more efficiently and safely. Employees assigned to any activities where lifting and handling are performed need training, even when relatively light loads are involved. Supervisors need training in safety management techniques, such as how to analyze the job to identify unsafe acts and conditions. Retraining all employees at various times is necessary to reinforce safety procedures.

HOW TO PREPARE SAFETY TRAINING?

- Have a plan.
- Know the job to be taught.
- Break the job.
- List the major steps.
- Highlight key points.
- Have everything ready.
- Prepare the right materials and equipments.
- Have the workplace properly arranged.

HOW TO CONDUCT SAFETY TRAINING?

- Put the employees at ease.

- Determine what knowledge the employee already has.
- Stress key points.
- Cover one point at a time clearly and completely.
- Have the employee perform the job.
- Have the employee tell and show you safety procedures.
- Have the employee explain key points.
- Ask the employee questions and correct the errors.
- Continue until you know they know.
- Encourage questions.
- Strengthen training with little reminders.

19

CHAPTER

Work Place Safety

HEALTHY WORKPLACE TIPS

Office workers are finding difficulty in sitting one position (particularly in front of a computer) for long periods of time. Sore back and necks, eyestrain, impaired circulation in the legs, and painful arms, wrists, and fingers are common, but can be prevented by following these tips:

- Vary task during the day to break up repetitive motions and injuries. Take small, 10 to 30 seconds breaks every 30 minutes, and longer breaks every two hours.
- Reduce sources of environmental stress, such as heat, glare, and noise.
- Discover the features and functions of the work space those enable workers to adjust their environment for safety and comfort.
- Use supplementary support of limbs when necessary, such as armrests. Supports should be well padded with round edges.
- Align monitor and keyboard in front of you.
- Educate workers on the value of ergonomics and how to recognize aches and pains that may be related to their work and work environment.

HEPBURN'S 25 GROUPS OF DANGEROUS PARTS OF MACHINERY

1. Revolving shafts, spindles, mandrels, and bars, machine shafts, drill spindles, drills, reamers, chucks, boring bars, stock bars, vertical travel shafts on milling machines.
2. In running nips between pair of revolving parts, gear wheels, friction wheels, calendar bowls, mangle rolls, metal manufacturing rolls, rubber washing rolls, breaking and mixing rolls etc.
3. In running nips of the belt and pulley type belts and pulleys, plain flanged or grooved chain and sprocket gears, conveyor belt and pulleys, metal coiling drums.
4. Projections on revolving parts – key heads, set screws, cotter pins, couplings, belts, etc.
5. Revolving open arm pulleys and other discontinuous rotating parts, pulleys, fan-blades, spur gear wheels, etc.
6. Revolving beaters, spiked cylinders and drums, scorchers, rag flock teasers, cotton openers, laundry washers etc.
7. Revolving miner arms in casing, dough mixer, rubber extruders, spiral conveyors etc.
8. Revolving worms and spirals in casings, meat mixers, rubber extruders, spiral conveyors etc.
9. Revolving high speed cages in casings, hydro extractors, centrifuges etc.
10. Abrasive wheels, manufactured wheels, sand stones etc.
11. Revolving cutting tools, circular saws, milling cutters, circular shears, wood splitters, chaff cutters, etc.
12. Reciprocating tools and dies, power press, drop stamp's relief stamping, hydraulic and pneumatic presses, blending presses, hand presses, revolution presses etc.
13. Reciprocating knives and saws, guillotines for metal, rubber and paper cutting, trimmers, perforators, etc.
14. Platen motions: letter press platen printing machine, paper and cardboard cutters, and similar adaptations etc.
15. Projecting belt fasteners and fast running belts, belt and nut fasteners, wire pin fasteners and the like, wood working machinery, belts, centrifuge belts, textile machinery side belting and the like, etc.
16. Nips between connecting rods or links and rotating wheels crank or disc, side motion of certain flat type printing machines, jack guard and other automatic looms, etc.
17. Pawl and notches wheel devices for intermittent feed motions, planner tools feed motions; power press dial feed tables, etc.

18. Nips between reciprocating and fixed parts, other than tools and dies, metal reversing steps, sliding tables/planner tables and fixtures, cotton spinning mills carriage and back steps, pillars etc, shaping machines table and fixtures, tools steady guide and steady arm on turret lathe, etc.
19. Nips between revolving central handles and fixed parts, transverse gear handles of lathes, millers etc.
20. Moving balance weight and dead weights, hydraulic accumulator, counter balance weight on large slotting machines.
21. Nips between revolving wheels or cylinders and pans or tables, sand mixers, edge runners, crushing and incorporating mills, dough breathes mortar mills, leather carrying machines, etc.
22. Cutting edges of endless band cutting machines, wood working, log cutting metal and store cutting band saws, cloth cutting band knives, etc.
23. Nips between gears and rack stripes, ink roller driver on lithographic presses, some planning machines drivers, etc.
24. Revolving drums and cylinders, un-ceased rumblers in the foundry, dough mixers, rag digesters, etc.
25. Nips between fixed and unidirectional moving parts, buckets or hoppers on conveyors against tipping bars, stops or parts of the framework, etc.

GUIDELINES FOR MILLWRIGHTS

- The millwright should possess versatile knowledge and skill in different jobs and should have more thorough training in accident prevention than other workers.
- Know-how to use not only ordinary tools but also ladders, protective equipments, chains, slings, ropes and other tools and equipments.
- Be ware of hazards and receptive to proper training. This is necessary to protect them and also others in the maintenance area.
- Be well trained in firstaid and life saving techniques.
- Familiarize with properties of substances with methods of controlling their hazards in industries where irritating, toxic, or corrosive dust, gases, vapors, fumes etc. are present.
- Dress properly for their specific job; wear snug-fit clothes with a few small and covered pockets. They should not wear rings, wristwatches etc.
- Keep loose rags clear of moving machinery.
- Use tool kit/bag, which should contain explosion proof flash light and safety goggles.

- Wear appropriate gloves when handling rough or sharp jobs.
- Wear fall protection devices if they have to climb and work at heights.
- Be trained in confined space procedure if they have to enter the manhole, tank etc.
- Indicate by proper notice boards that the machines or equipment are being repaired and also isolate electrically.
- Understand the contents of pipes. If standard color codes are used for piping they should be able to interpret the contents.
- Take special safety precautions in maintenance of pipelines and follow appropriate safety procedure.
- Care must be taken while carrying out repairs of cranes.
- Turn the machines first by hand after it has been repaired to discover mislead tools and materials in the time of preventing them from reckoning the machine or causing injury.
- Replace and secure furnace guards pick up tools and leave the work in good condition.

GAS CUTTING AND WELDING

Do's

- Wear protective like goggles, hand gloves, shoes and face shields.
- Acetylene cylinders should always be kept in an upright position.
- When the cylinders are in upright position, they should be strapped or chained.
- Gas cylinders shall be kept, maintained under shelter and in ventilated area.
- Use lighters to light the gas torches.
- For moving gas cylinders use only cylinder trolleys.
- Never drop the cylinders nor permit them to strike against each other.
- Ensure gauges on the cylinders are functional.
- Handle the valves gently and smoothly.

Material Handling (Manual)

- Bring the load close to your body for more power and less effort.
- Grip firmly with your hand not just from fingers.
- Make sure you can see where you are going, move slowly with small steps.
- Do not twist your body with the load.
- To unload, face the spot you have chosen and lower the load slowly.
- Use safety shoes.

Health Hazards Associated with Welding Fumes

- The light emitted by an electric arc contains a high proportion of Ultra Violet (UV) radiation, which may cause Photo-ophthalmic known as arc eyes.
- The fumes from welding and flame cutting arises from a variety of sources:
  - From the metal being welded or the metal in the filter rod, e.g., iron, aluminum.
  - From the constituents of various types of steel such as nickel or chromium.
  - From any paint, grease, debris, etc., on the article being welded, e.g., carbon monoxide, carbon dioxide smoke and other irritant breakdown products.
  - By the action of heat or ultraviolet light on the surrounding air, e.g., nitrogen dioxide, ozone, form the inert gas used as a shield, e.g., helium, argon.
  - This from the flux used for welding – fumes and gases should be removed at source by means of local exhaust ventilation or with respiratory protective equipments.
- During electric arc welding a reliable system of earthing of all units and control cabinet is necessary to prevent from electrical hazard.
- Burns of the eyes and exposed parts of the body may occur due to spattering incandescent metal particles.

SAFE PRACTICES IN ARC WELDING

Following safety precautions should be observed during carrying out electric welding jobs.

- Use plug of proper rating while connecting welding machines to AC mains.
- Earth the metallic body of welding machine and the job (work place).
- Use welding return (work cable) of same length as welding cable.
- Do not earth negative terminal of welding machine in case of straight polarity to eliminate welding return.
- Do not use bare conductor in place of welding return cable.
- Maintain welding cables in good condition (without joints and insulation damage).
- Never change electrode in bare hands or wet hand gloves.
- Shock hazard persists even with open circuit voltage of 50-70 V DC, which can even be severe.
- Welding by qualified welders only.
- Use of hand gloves and hand shields essential.
- Face shield with correct filter and cover plate to protect against spark/rays of arc.
- Entire body protection required against burns from spatter, spark, slag etc.

- Adequate ventilation to prevent accumulation of welding fumes.
- Hot work permits and fire fighting equipment essential in hazardous work areas.
- Welding operation away from flammable materials.
- No welding permissible on closed containers; explosion may occur.

Do's of a Turner

- Know your machine thoroughly well, especially the control levers and their operations.
- Check the machine at the beginning of the shift work. If you notice any abnormalities, report them.
- Know safe work procedure for each operation and follow them.
- Use splashguards, shields on the machine.
- Use chip guards (plastic or small mesh screen) or get the chip breakers installed or use hooked rod to remove chips.
- Use face plates and chucks without projections wherever possible otherwise a simple shield formed to the contour of chuck/face plate and hinged at the back should be installed to prevent contact with revolving projections.
- Use safety dogs, i.e., a circular dogs having set screws of the sunken type.
- Ensure that the lathe centers are true and sharp.
- Ensure that the work piece is securely held. Start the machine after checking and ensuring good fastening of the work piece.
- Keep close attention towards the job being machined.
- Keep the machine clean, and the space around the machine clean, neat and tidy.
- Stand clear off the file while filing.
- Cover lead screw with a guard to avoid catching of the clothes.
- Store chucks and accessories on racks only.
- Support long stock.
- Balance jobs correctly on faceplate otherwise excessive centrifugal force may result in flying off or bursting.
- Use closely fitting clothing. The shirts should be half sleeved and properly tucked in boiler suits are best in this regard.
- Wear eye protection against flying metal chips.
- Provide guard to the rotating stock projections of turret or screw machines.
- Wear safety shoes.
- Use lifting devices to lift heavy faceplates, chucks and stock on engine lathes, turret lathes or screw machines.

- Maintenance/repair work is carried out by trained personnel or under supervision.
- The machine be locked out from electricity to avoid accidental start.
- Use proper speed, feed and depth of net.
- Use proper coolant.

Do nots of a Turner

- Do not leave the machine running unattended.
- Do not use jewelry, watch, and bracelets while working on the machine.
- If you have long hair, cover it while working.
- Do not break the machine by hand.
- Do not file with unprotected tang.
- Do not use hand instead of a stick or cloth holder against rotating work.
- Do not caliper/gauge while the machine is in operation.
- Do not attempt to remove metal chips while the machine is in operation.
- Do not leave chuck-key in chuck or on bed.
- Do not use defective/worn out tools or hand tools.
- Do not put hand near rotating chuck, faceplate or job to inspect it.
- Do not fiddle with electrical system, get the service of the specialist.
- Do not take short cuts.
- Do not guess, get guidance of the expert.
- Do not overlook even the minutest abnormality.
- Do not clean the machine when it is in motion.

SAFETY RULES FOR THE USE OF INDUSTRAL LPG HANDLING

- Cylinders must not be dropped from lorry, trailer etc.
- Cylinders must not be rolled on their sides but must always be carried or rolled on their foot rings.
- Before cylinders are handled or transported the safety cap should be properly fixed.
- Cylinders must not be handled in any way which will cause the seal to break before the cylinder is required to be connected up.

Storage

- Not more than 4-LPG cylinders should be stored at one single location.
- Cylinders must be stored in a covered, well ventilated and dust free place, away from direct sunlight and heat.

- Cylinders should be stored in the vertical position standing on footrest.
- The protective cap should be properly fixed on the cylinder valve (whether in full or in empty conditions).

Equipment Set Up

- Normal LPG withdrawal rate should be within 0.5 kg./hr. For higher withdrawal rates (while cutting thicker sections) two or more cylinders should be banked.
- While connecting/disconnecting LPG cylinders the hose connection to the pressure regulator valve should not be disturbed too often.
- For disconnecting LPG cylinders, remove pressure regulator from the seat (instead of disconnecting the hose connection).
- Operator should be trained properly for opening, closing, fixing and disconnecting pressure regulator.
- In case of outdoor application, LPG cylinders should be brought back to safe storage after usage and should not be left in the open.

Safety in LPG Cutting Operation

- Carry out cutting operation in airy spaces, away from other source of fire, spark, oil, etc.
- Ensure the equipment set up is in order and free from leakage. The B-type cutting nozzle should fit to the nozzle holder of the torch with adequate tightness.

Start up Instructions

- Blow off any dust from seating surface. Check the rubber seal of the cylinder.
- Fit the click on type LPG regulator as prescribed.
- Open the cylinder valve and torch valve to purge the LPG line. Close both the valves.
- Follow procedure for fixing oxygen regulator.
- Set gas pressure at the regulators to correct settings. Follow nozzle manufacturers' guidelines in setting gas pressure.
- Open both cylinder valves.
- Crack open LPG torch valve and ignite the torch. Slowly increase the LPG flow.
- Open oxygen valve and set the flame to desired type.

Shut off Instructions

- Close LPG torch valve first and then close oxygen torch valve.
- Close cylinder valves – first LPG followed by oxygen.

- Open torch valves for LPG and oxygen to release residual gas inside the hose.
- Release frees the oxygen pressure regulator knob.
- Remove the click on type LPG regulator along with hose connection, ensuring that the hose connector is not damaged.

Oxygen Do nots

Oxygen is being used increasingly in industry. That's why 'The safe use of oxygen and oxygen equipment in the iron and steel industry' a manual prepared by BISF Accident Prevention Committee with the help of the British Oxygen Company Ltd., is being widely circulated, for those who have to handle oxygen equipment, the manual warns against eight examples of bad practice:

Do not inhale oxygen from cylinders or pipeline supplies and never give oxygen to others either seriously or in fun. Oxygen is 'the breath of life' but can harm or kill if administered carelessly or without proper control. Trained persons should carry out resuscitation only.

Do not release oxygen to sweeten air or to improve the working conditions; only a small increase of oxygen in the air greatly increases the hazard.

Do not smoke or carry smoldering materials about in areas where there is likely to be more oxygen than normal. The excess oxygen will make them burn more readily.

Do not leave a lance incorrectly fitted to its holder as the end of the tube may ignite. (The end of the tube should be free from internal burrs and held flush against the seating in the handle by the union nut.)

Do not disregard recommended lighting procedure. Flashbacks may occur when there is a mixture of gases in the equipment. Check all connections.

Do not use oxygen as a substitute for compressed air or use it to dust down clothing or cool down the body.

Do not leave cylinders where they are likely to become overheated.

Do not use them as work supports or improvised rollers.

PETROLEUM PRODUCT PIPELINE

Why Pipeline

The current highway system is approaching saturation with the ever-increasing traffic in both freight transportation and human movement. Many of the nation's roads are clogged and congestion continues to worsen. The conventional approach of building more roads has ceased to be effective in most areas of the country for both fiscal and environmental reasons. Research is being conducted to enhance capacities of the existing infrastructure. At the same time, it is important to study new transportation stations.

Pipeline: The term pipeline in broader sense means a facility used to transport commodities from point of receipt to the point of delivery. Many commodities are transported through pipelines. Crude oil and petroleum products are perhaps the most common commodities transported by pipelines.

Advantages of Pipeline Transportation

- Lower cost of transportation
- Lower transit losses
- Lower energy intensiveness
- Economics of scale
- Safety and reliability – minimum disruptions
- Environment friendliness
- Multiproduct handling.

Different Modes for Transportation of Petroleum – A Comparison

Head	Road	Rail	Pipeline
Energy cost	High	Very high	Low
Operating cost	Very high	High	Low
Pollution	High	Low	Nil
Movement congestion	High	Low	Nil
Handling loss	High	Low	Negligible
Safety hazards	High	Low	Negligible
Reliability	Low	Low	100%

PLAN A SAFE OFFICE

It is common knowledge that the right kind of furniture and fittings both for work and relaxation help the body to function at its best.

A firm, comfortable mattress on a solid base relaxes your body at night; so does a straight-backed chair to keep your back straight and your feet firmly on the floor, in concentrating fully in your work. You need a spacious enough table with elbow room on top and space underneath to stretch your legs sometimes, do not you feel choked in rooms that are crammed full of furniture? It's so difficult to work or relax in such a place.

Plan the placing of the office furniture in a way that leaves space enough for free and easy traffic. Jutting shelves and trailing electric wires are the twin menaces to life and limb. A high, narrow, overhead rack teetering on spindly legs might topple on you at the slightest provocation. Loose pieces of paper lying on a highly polished, shiny surface are virtual guarantees for slips and falls; so are spilt liquids-drops of water around filters and water coolers, for example; or tea or coffee cascading on the floor. Do not leave it to dry there, have it wiped up immediately; put the papers back into their proper places – shelves, files, drawers or waste baskets. Better have the floors covered with non-slip material.

Arrange the furniture in a way that leaves passages wide enough for people to move freely without constantly bumping into one another or blundering into obstructing shelves and cabinets. Clear visibility is also necessary for an accident free environment.

A business is started with growth and expansion in mind. When you buy and arrange furniture, plan in such a way that it leaves room enough for further acquisition and rearrangement without interfering with either free-passage-way or proper ventilation. A cluttered, badly ventilated room can induce claustrophobia and respiratory trouble that in turn might interfere with employee efficiency.

Proper storage is vital to good house keeping especially in offices where a large amount of paper, files, films and other highly combustible materials are routinely handled. It is important that every item is neatly and systematically stored in its own proper place.

Smoking should be strictly prohibited in and around the offices.

And be extremely careful of your electric appliances if you want to free from fire and injury. Be sure that the electrical outlets and connections are in sound condition and are regularly and frequently inspected. Replace and repair cracked, broken plugs, loose, faulty plug points, frayed wires immediately.

Electric faults, old defective wiring, wires running under carpets or between door ways can cause short circuits; wires under carpets, linoleum or between doorways are constantly stepped on and consequently get crushed and frayed and lie unnoticed for long – a very real fire hazard.

It's important to install properly functioning fire fighting equipment at strategic points. Have regular fire drills, and an emergency plan chalked out.

If you provide a healthy, safe, congenial work environment, the benefits would be readily reflected on the efficiency graph.

PREVENT ACCIDENTS IN THE OFFICE

An accident in the office can be just as painful and costly as an accident inside the manufacturing plant or a factory. One can fall while walking, climbing ladders and stairs. You can even trip over telephone and electrical wires, table drawers, equipment and packages left in aisles.

To protect yourself as well as others, be on the lookout for potential hazards in the office and follow the safety rules. Some of these are:

- Wipe up all spills immediately.
- Stack materials inside cabinets, not on top. Keep the piles neat and labeled.
- Use a stool or ladder, not a chair to reach top shelves in high cabinets.
- Keep all four legs of your chair on the floor. Tilting back in a chair can result in a fall.
- Dispose of waste or trash promptly. This includes flammable liquids, oily and paint-covered rags and waste paper.
- Disconnect electrical appliances when not in use.
- Get out-of-order defective switches repaired promptly including loose/broken switches.
- Use sufficient light to do the job safely and correctly.
- Beware of telephone and electrical wires lying across the floor.
- On stairways, use handrails and take one step at a time.
- Report worn treads and broken or loose stairs to management immediately.

SAFETY MEASURES FOR WORKING IN CONFINED SPACE

- Barricade/lock the confined spaces wherever possible to prevent unauthorized entry.
- Signpost the confined space to warn of dangers in these areas.
- The atmosphere must be tested for presence of toxic, flammable gas and oxygen deficiency.
- If the space is contaminated with toxic gas, then purge the atmosphere by blowing air or extracting toxic gases or both.
- Oxygen mask, air supplying respirators should be made available at site.
- People entering any confined space should use safety belts with a long lifeline held by persons standing outside for rescue in case of emergency.
- In case illumination is required inside the confined space 24 volts flame proof hand lamps should be used.
- Untrained, unequipped and unprepared people must not enter a confined space to rescue affected persons.
- Ensure strict supervision while people work inside confined space.
- While working in underground sewage at a particular manhole, the proceeding, the succeeding and that particular manhole must be kept opened at least one hour before starting of the job.

PROCEDURE TO WORK IN CONFINED SPACE

What is a Confined Space?

If we are building a tank or digging a hole in the ground, when the depth becomes greater than the diameter and the space is large enough for someone to enter, the space is considered confined. At such places we must take precautionary measures. If oil or chemical is stored in the tank it may drain out in the tank or on the ground and give off fumes or catch fire. If it contains acid, the atmosphere in the tank may contain toxic gas and people can be affected while cleaning.

Safety Precautions While Working in Confined Space

Always consider vessels more dangerous empty than full. Therefore, the following precautionary measures should be taken while working in confined spaces.

- If a part of the vessel can not be inspected and be seem to be safe, we should assume the vessel contains hazardous material. Gas tests alone are not conclusive. There may be some sludge present which gives off gas when heated or disturbed. Never take short cuts in entering a vessel.
- Stand by workers should not leave a vessel when others are inside it. Men working in confined spaces should be watched and "OUT OF SERVICE" tags must be displayed.
- In general, steam lines, heating coils, etc. should be de-pressured and isolated before entry is permitted to a confined space. The power supply should have been discontinued.
- Before allowing any one to enter a vessel or other confined space, ask how he will be rescued if he is overcome.
- Before entering the vessel always see that the power supply is isolated, i.e., fuses must be taken out and switches must be looked.
- If vessels are open, but entry is not yet authorized, the manhole should be covered by a barrier. Do not rely on contractors reading rules. Explain the rules to them.
- A man entering any confined space such as coal bunker, ash pit, or drain line should wear a life line and be watched by an attendant stationed on the outside.
- If a vessel or confined space contains a toxic gas, people can be overcome a meter or more from opening. In such areas two persons trained in rescue and resuscitation should be on duty outside the vessel.

FACTORIES ACT

Section 33 of the Factories Act says that in every factory every fixed vessel, sump, tank, pit, or opening in the ground or in the floor which, by reason of its depth, situation, construction or contents, is or may be a source of danger, shall be either securely covered or securely fenced.

Pressure Vessels, Boiler Safety

Pressure vessel means any vessel, which is used to store, handle any gas, vapor or liquid under pressure greater than atmospheric pressure.

- Ensure that the safety gadgets provided to the pressure vessels are in working condition.
- Any deviation in the working condition of the pressure vessels informs the supervisor immediately.
- Do not undertake repair without the instructions of the supervisors.
- Know the safe working pressure of the vessel.

BOILER SAFETY

Do's

- Ensure gauge cocks are working freely and there is no storage of water by testing or any other feed devices like pumps.
- While starting, vent the boiler and during use ease the safety valves periodically.
- Keep all the blow-down valves closed tight except the continuous blow-down valve.
- Ensure the feed mechanism is working properly and there is no air lock on suction side and water level indicated is actual.
- Ensure pressure gauge is working correctly and marking in red, visible from a distance highlights working pressure.
- Rise steams gradually and never pump large quantity of feed water at one go. Feed should be steady and gradual.
- Work at the permitted working pressure only.
- In the event of water level vanishing from the gauge glass, remove the fire, vent the boiler, and cool the same. Inspect for signs of overheat or distortion and re-fire only if there is no damage.
- Prior to blow down make use of low load suitable on the boiler.
- For openings, close through doors, spigot should be placed centrally to the hole and avoid round packing ropes.
- Drain the steam lines before opening. Stop valve opening should be gradual.
- Ensure no oil or grease enters the boiler and no scaling material is let in.

- To clean the boiler effectively, retain the water, vent the steam out through valve, and thus reduce the pressure, cool to room temperature, enter with cleaning tools as soon as the doors are opened.
- Ensure slightly alkaline pure feed enters the boiler and avoid priming, foaming.
- For efficient preservation, drain first and keep all the valves and other openings shut with some hygroscopic material like lime in side.
- Feel the boiler to its capacity with one percent caustic solution in water.

Do nots

- Never leave the boiler unattended or allow unauthorized persons to meddle.
- Never start forced draft fan before induced draft fan is started.
- Never bypass any automatic arrangement like interlocking of ID and FD, pressure and fuel cut-off system.
- Never start firing without reaching correct oil temperature and correct oil pressure.
- Never cut in the boiler unless the pressure is nearly same as the header pressure.
- Never soot blow without adjusting draft to higher value, a higher pressure in the boiler to make room for reduced condition in furnace, stick to sequence, refrain from non adherence to set pattern.
- Never ignore any abnormal condition like hissing sound, excessive white smoke in the chimney, investigate the cause like baffle crumbling, puncture etc.
- Never use oversize burner and cause loss in efficiency.
- Never allow formation of heavy clinker and failure due to overheating etc.
- Limit excess air supply in such a way that oxygen content in flue gas from chimney is limited to five percent only.
- Never work the boiler below its rated working pressure in preference to pressure reducing stations where steam at low pressure is sought.
- Never rely solely on automates, be alert than complacent.
- Never use the boiler without changing the fusible plug after annual inspection.
- Never hit the safety valve or other nuts of the boiler mountings with hammer while in use.

PRODUCER GAS

The producer gas is an essential gas for various processes and manufacturing activities. This gas is a mixture of carbon monoxide and other organic gases like methane etc. It is highly poisonous when inhaled by human beings over and above the permissible limits.

The mixture of producer gas and ordinary atmospheric air is highly inflammable and explosive. This is denser than the atmospheric air.

It is possible gas leakages may occur, when the human being comes in contact and breaths the producer gas, they are likely to have acute carbon monoxide poisoning. Depending on the concentration and duration of the exposure the symptoms of producer gas poisoning vary from:

- simple headache
- nausea
- vomiting to collapse, coma and death.

When a person is exposed to producer gas for longer period, certain observations can be made on the body of the person. The person will be struggling for breath with discolored nail beds and lips. The conjunctive will be red in color. Carbon monoxide poisoning could be established by estimating the levels of its presence in the blood, and this test is possible only at the laboratories attached to medical college hospitals or research institutions.

First Aid to Victims:

- Move the patient to fresh air.
- Do not crowd over the patient.
- If the patient is not able to breathe mouth to mouth artificial respiration has to be started.
- Simultaneously, external cardiac massage has to be started and continued till the victim reaches the hospital.
- In the mean time, action should be taken to plug the gas leakage.

Safety Measures:

- Do not keep the distribution points open when not required. Close them.
- Maintain the water levels in all the water seal drip pots.
- Ensure periodical checks of the pipe lines.
- The responsible agency needs to burn the excess gases in the pipe line, when required.

TIPS ON USE OF COMPRESSED AIR

Compressor air is a useful source of energy when utilized properly. Cleaning, painting, motive power for tools are some of the gainful uses of compressed air.

We often misuse compressed air from the tapings provided on the shop-floor for cleaning our dresses, body, floors and machines by blowing it and sometimes to horseplay on shop floor. Such misuses are dangerous and can result in serious accidents, injuries to persons causing permanent disability, even death.

Serious injuries occur because compressed air can:

- Injure the eardrums resulting in deafness.
- Damage the eyes by blowing particles of dust, oil etc. or even knock down the eyeballs.
- Damage the air circulation system of the body causing instant death by air bubbles entering the blood stream through a cut or abrasion.
- Can make a worker loose his balance while on the job when a jet of air is blown on his body as a horseplay or mischief.
- Because bursting of the vessel when compressed air is blown to clean it.

Remember:

A little blast of compressed air at as low as 35 psi can destroy an eye, ruptures an ear drum or may also be fatal:

- Do not use compressed air to cool off.
- Do not use compressed air to dust your clothes.
- Never play practical jokes with compressed air.

Never direct the compressed air jet at another person or to yourself

SAFETY, HEALTH AND ENVIRONMENT FOR GROWTH

Rememer:

"No job is so important and no service so urgent that it cannot take time to perform the work safely".

ABC of Safety

Always be careful. Do not endanger Fellow – workers. Get help if job knowledge is lacking. Maintain normal operational procedure. Quickly replace safety tackle. Use vigilance when expanding youthful zeal.

How Long

- It takes a minute to write a safety rule.
- It takes an hour to hold a safety meeting.
- It takes a week to plan a safety programme.
- It takes a month to put it into operation.
- It takes a year to win a safety award.
- It takes a lifetime to inculcate safety habits.
- It takes only one second to destroy it all with an accident.

SUPERVISORY RESPONSIBILITY FOR SAFETY

- Supervisor is the key person to carryout management's safety policy and to prevent injuries to workers.

An Effective Supervisor Knows

- His total responsibilities and integrate safety with them.
  - Area of operation, machineries and personnel.
  - Maintenance and repair.
  - Working conditions.
  - Provision of guard and protective devices.
- What disciplinary action is permitted, under what circumstances?
- Who is to instruct and train workers in safety, first-aid and fire-prevention.
- What is the safe work method for each job?
- What ppe's are to be used for each job?
- His commitments to rectify unsafe conditions.
- What to do in case of accident and what reports are required.

A Good Supervisor puts Safety to Work

- Take initiatives for safer layout, tools and process.
- Professional care taker of equipments to ensure safety.
- Know importance of guards and ensure it.
- Takes pride in using equipments safely.
- Takes charge of non-routine jobs with safety precautions.
- Arranges and ensures for good house keeping.
- Knows hazardous material and its handling procedure.
- Keeps eyes open for the employee under his control.
- Continues to "talk safety" and impress safety upon men.
- Establishes good relations with safety committee members.
- Sets the example in safety.
- Not only explains how to do a job, but shows how and ensures that it continues safely.
- Studies all accidents and takes corrective measures.

SAFETY INDICES

I.O.W.: injured on works. any injury sustained by a person inside the works. in all such cases accident report forms should be filled in by the supervisor and the injured person should be sent to the hospital with I.O.W. Forms.

I.O.D.: Injured on duty. any injury sustained by a person outside the works while on duty. No forms to be filled in, in such cases.

Lost time accident: When due to the injuries sustained by a person arising out of an accident he is unfit for work for 48 hours or more.

Minor accident: When a person is unfit for 2 days and up to 20 days due to injury sustained.

Serious accident: When a person is unfit for 21 days and overdue to injuries sustained.

Fatal accident: Death resulting from an accident.

Frequency rate: Total No. of accidents per one lakh man-hours worked.

$$\text{F.R.} = \frac{\text{No. of accident} \times 10^6}{\text{Man-hours worked}}$$

Severity rate: Total No. of man-hours lost due to accident per one lakh man-hours worked. For every fatal accident 48000 man-hours lost are taken in account.

$$\text{S.R.} = \frac{\text{Man-hours lost due to accident} \times 10^6}{\text{Man-hours worked}}$$

STATUTORY PERMISSIONS REQUIRED UNDER FACTORIES ACT

- Permission to construct, extend or take into use any building as a factory.
- Approval of site and building plans.
- Appraisal of site by state site appraisal committee (only for hazardous process units).
- Certificate of stability of factory building.
- Application for registration and notice of occupation of a factory.
- Application for license/renewal of license, of a factory.
- certificate of authorization for use of boiler from chief inspector of factories and boilers.

REPORTING OF ACCIDENTS UNDER FACTORIES ACT

As per Sec. 88 of the Act, if in any factory an accident occurs which causes death or any bodily injury, by reason of which the person injured is prevented from working for a period of 48 hours or more immediately following the accident or which is of such nature as prescribed in this behalf, the manager of the factory is required to send a notice thereof to the authorities and in the form prescribed by the state government.

Sec. 88-A of the act deals with notice of dangerous occurrences. if any "dangerous occurrence" of such nature as prescribed occurs in a factory, whether causing any bodily injury or not, the manager of the factory should send a notice thereof to the authorities and in the form prescribed by the state government.

SAFETY SIGNAGES TO BE PROVIDED UNDER FACTORIES ACT, 1948

Factories Act

- Marking of "Drinking Water" at the Drinking Water Centers [Section 18(2)].
- Label on Hoists, Lifts and Lifting machines etc. Marking of SWL identification number (Sections 28 and 29).
- Display notice of change of weekly holidays (Section 52).
- Display notice of periods of work for adult workers (Form 16).
- Display of the Scheme of regulation for granting of leave (Section 79).

Factories Rules

- Sign boards to be displayed on the latrine blocks – Rules framed under Section 19(3).
- Display of a Table showing SWL of every type of chain, rope or lifting tackle in use, in the store room – Rules framed under Section 29(2).
- Marking of safe working pressure and the date of last examination on every pressure vessel or pressure plant-Rules framed under Section 31(2).
- Exits shall be clearly marked – Rules framed under Section 38(1).
- Prohibitory notices: No Smoking, No naked lights or carrying of matches or any other source of sparks in high hazard chemical processes and under various processes declared dangerous (Rules framed under Section 41).
- – Safety Policy-Display copy of safety policy in conspicuous places – Rules framed under Section 7-A(3), 41-B(2) and 112.
  – Labeling or marking of all containers of hazardous substances – Rules framed under Section 7-A (3), 41-B(2) and 112.
  – Display of cautionary notices of work places where hazardous process or dangerous operation is carried on.
- Washing facilities – Notice/marking on washing facility for women workers – Rules framed under Section 42.

- **First-Aid Appliance:**
  - Marking of Red Cross on the F.A. Boxes.
  - Notice about names of F.A. trained persons, their availability, name and telephone number of the nearest hospital etc displayed in conspicuous places.
  - In the ambulance room or dispensary display notice about name, address and telephone number of the medical in charge and nearest hospital (Rules framed under Section 45).
- Prices of the foodstuff, etc. shall be conspicuously displayed in the Canteen-Rules framed under Section 46.
- Compensatory Holidays – display of the list of worker allowed compensatory holidays in the following month – Rules framed under Section 53(2).

20 CHAPTER

Work Permit System

PERMITTING PROCESS

A smooth work process is an important factor in safe maintenance. It enables factories to quickly execute a lot of work at a high level of security.

Operators, shift leaders, work preparation staff and production management have a clear overview of ongoing and planned activities. At the change of shifts it is clear which permits are still open, which need special attention and which work are planned.

Important work will get the attention it deserves, no valuable attention is lost! Better preparation and more effective communication ensure a more predictable production planning and reduce the number of disturbances, incidents and accidents.

GENERAL PRINCIPLES

The following aspects should be considered with respect to Permit to Work Systems:

- Human factors;
- Management of the work permits systems;
- Poorly skilled work force;

- Unconscious and conscious incompetence;
- Objectives of the work permit system;
- Types of work permits required; and
- Contents of the work permits.

The following issues may contribute towards a major accident or hazard:

- Failing of the site safety management system;
- Failure to recognize a hazard before and during maintenance;
- Failure to comply with the work permit system in hazardous environments; and
- Communication failures during the use of a work permit system.

Contributory Factors for An Assessor to Consider Concerning the Work Permits System

The Safety Report should address the following points:

- Whether staffs have been sufficiently informed, instructed, trained and supervised to minimize a potential human failing during operation of the work permit system;
- Whether the work permit system includes sufficient safety information, maintenance instructions, correct PPE and equipment for use;
- Whether the work permit contains sufficient information about the type of work required (Equipment removal excavation, hot/cold work, repairing seals, vessel entry, waste disposal, isolation);
- Whether there is sufficient provision available to fulfill the requirements of the work permit system;
- Whether the employees responsible for control of the maintenance work are identified within the work permit system and that the work is properly authorized by a responsible person;
- Whether the work permit system is managed, regularly inspected and reviewed;
- Whether all work permits are kept on file;
- Whether Human factors (stress, fatigue, shift work, attitude) are given importance.
- Whether sufficient precautions are taken prior to initiating a work permit (isolation, draining, flushing, environmental monitoring, risk assessments, communication, time allotted for the work);
- Whether staff are aware of the type of environment they are working in during the operation of a work permit (flammable, corrosive, explosive, zones 0, 1 and 2, electricity supplies);
- Whether the person responsible for operating the plant is aware of the type of maintenance involved and how long it is likely to take; and

- Whether the work permit system involves a formal procedure whereby the maintained plant or equipment is handed back to operation.

MAJOR HAZARDS

Major hazards could arise from the following:

- Wrong type of work permit used;
- Wrong information about work required on the work permit;
- Failure to recognize the hazards where work is carried out (e.g., flammable substances);
- Introduction of ignition source in controlled flameproof area (e.g., welding, non-spark-proof tools, non-intrinsically safe equipment used in intrinsically safe zones);
- Terms of work permit not adhered to (e.g., failure to isolate plant and/or drain lines of hazardous substances);
- Failure to hand-over plant in safe condition on completion of work/canceling of work permit;
- Unauthorized staff performing work permit functions;
- Poor management of the work permit system; and
- Insufficient monitoring of the work permit system.

A Work Permit system for controlling all work done in the plant is one of the most important safety systems existing in a chemical plant. With the permit, comes awareness of safety in general, safety rules, do's and don'ts etc.

All maintenance work, working at heights and excavation works is to be covered by a work permit system. The objectives are:

- To ensure proper authorization of non-routine work such as hot work in hazardous area like the chemical plant, storages, vessel entry excavation, working at heights etc.
- To make clear to persons carrying out the job the risk involved and precautions to be taken.
- To ensure that the person responsible for the area is aware of all work being done there.
- To provide a record showing that the method of working and the precautions needed have been checked by the appropriate persons and if necessary a second opinion is obtained to prevent errors of judgment or adopting short cuts which may increase the risk.
- The same work permit form could be used for company employees doing the work or for the engaged contractors. The contractor should inform his employees of the work permit procedure and ensure that they are followed.

- A work safety permit is intended primarily to safeguard people and property, but it also may be needed as evidence in case of claims against the company or their legal actions.
- A format of a safety work permit/excavation permit/confined space entry permit which could be modified if necessary to suit the requirements. It is suggested that the safety department involve the plant managers before finalizing the format so that any practical difficulties in implementation of the permit system could be sorted out prior to printing the same.

WHAT IS A HOT WORK PERMIT?

Hot work is defined as cutting and welding operations for construction/demolition activities that involve the use of portable gas or arc welding equipment. The use of these types of equipment for cutting and welding introduces significant fire hazards.

The hot work permit system is intended to educate the parties involved in construction of these hazards and to implement control measures to help mitigate them.

A hot work permit is the means by which the departments of Facilities Design and Construction and Risk Management and Safety can stay aware and keep track of construction activities that involve hot work. The hot work permit also provides a step-by-step check list for hot work fire safety and serves as a reminder to contractors of their fire prevention responsibilities before, during, and after any hot work is conducted.

HOW DOES THE HOT WORK PERMIT SYSTEM WORK?

Before a contractor can perform hot work for a construction project they need to get a hot work permit. To get a permit, the contractor must to go to the Department of Risk Management. After completing a sign-out form, the permit is issued to the contractor for a specified time period for the building where the work will be performed. The contractor may then perform the hot work, following the precautions outlined on the permit. After the hot work is completed, the contractor turns the permit over to their Construction Project Manager.

WHEN IS A HOT WORK PERMIT NECESSARY?

Hot work permits are needed for all cutting or welding activities that are conducted with portable gas or arc equipment on construction projects.

WHERE IS A HOT WORK PERMIT NECESSARY?

Hot work permits are needed for each building where hot work will be performed (utility tunnels are considered to be separate buildings). For example, if one contractor is performing work at several different buildings for one project, a permit is necessary for each building.

WHO NEEDS HOT WORK PERMITS?

Hot work permits are needed for each and every contractor or sub-contractor/trade performing hot work for a project. For example, if there are three different sub-contractors/trades performing hot work on one project, each sub-contractor/trade is responsible for obtaining a permit for their own work.

At the time the permit is obtained, a brief description of how the permit should be used will be provided to the contractor.

Once the permit is signed-out, Risk Management and Safety will notify the Construction Project Manager that a hot work permit has been issued for a particular project and the duration for which the permit has been issued.

HOW LONG IS A HOT WORK PERMIT VALID?

The duration of a hot work permit depends upon the type of project (new or existing construction) and the character of the hot work. The following are guidelines used to determine how long a permit is good for. These are guidelines. If there are conditions unique to the project or activities a contractor will be performing, exceptions can be made.

For **New Construction** permits are issued in 28-DAY intervals. New construction is defined as new buildings, additions to existing buildings, new tunnels (including vaults), and new exterior improvement work. The following are the types of work anticipated for new construction;

- Structural hot work-cutting/welding reinforcing steel and structural steel for all of the project's structural work (tunnels construction, building super-structure, site work).
- Mechanical hot work-tunnel services connections, building system installations, HVAC equipment installations.
- General activities hot work-all other cutting/welding for equipment/building component installations (handrails, guardrails, specialties, and ornamental metal).

For **Renovations and Remodels** permits are issued in 7-DAY intervals. Renovations and remodels are defined as new work that takes place in an existing building. The following are the types of hot work anticipated for renovations/remodels:

- Demolition hot work-dismantling built-in equipment, removal of discontinued/abandoned equipment.
- Mechanical hot work-removal of discontinued/abandoned services, new services tie-ins, building system installations/modifications.

- General activities hot work-all other cutting/welding for equipment/building component installations (handrails, guardrails, specialties, and ornamental metal).

WHERE SHOULD THE HOT WORK PERMIT BE POSTED?

Hot work permits should be posted at the job site in an accessible and conspicuous location. Job site trailers are an acceptable location.

WHO CHECKS TO SEE IF THE HOT WORK REQUIREMENTS ARE MET?

The contractor or sub-contractor/trade performing hot work is ultimately responsible for conducting their hot work activities in a sound, fire-safe manner and following the precautions outlined on the hot work permit. The responsible contractor or sub-contractor/trade supervisor or foreman shall review the work area and sign the card daily.

HOT WORK PERMIT FOR RENOVATIONS AND REMODELS

Date Issued ______________________________

Valid Until ______________________________

Building ______________________________

Building No. ______________________________

Project No. ______________________________

Location of Work ______________________________

Construction Project Manager/Phone No. ______________

Contractor/Phone No. ______________________________

The location where this work will take place will be examined before the start of cutting/welding operations and all the appropriate precautions (including any that exceed those outlined below) will be taken.

Signed (at issue of permit No.) ______________________

Date ______________________________

Print name ______________________________

FIRE SAFETY PRECAUTIONS BEFORE THE WORK

All of the following precautions must be taken:

- Cutting and/or welding equipment must be thoroughly inspected and found to be in good repair, free of damage or defects.

- A multi-purpose dry chemical, portable fire extinguisher must be located such that it is immediately available to the work and is fully charged and ready for use.
- At least one fire alarm pull station or means of contacting the fire department (i.e., site telephone) must be available and accessible to person(s) conducting the cutting/welding operation.
- Floor areas under and at least 35 feet around the cutting/welding operation must be swept clean of combustible and flammable materials.
- All construction equipment fueling activities and fuel storage must be relocated at least 35 feet away from the cutting/welding operation.

Where applicable, the following precautions will also be taken before the work begins:

- Fire resistant shields (fire retardant plywood, flameproof tarpaulin, metal, etc.), must cover combustible floors.
- Spark/slag catchers (fire retardant plywood, flameproof tarpaulins, metal, etc.) must be suspended below any elevated cutting/welding operation.
- All floor and wall openings must be covered to prevent sparks/slag from traveling to other, unprotected areas.
- Containers in or on which cutting/welding will take place must be purged of flammable vapors.

During/After the Work

The following precautions will be taken:

- Person(s) must be assigned to a fire watch during and for at least 30 minutes after all cutting/welding ceases.
- Fire watch person(s) are to be supplied with multi purpose dry chemical, portable fire extinguisher and trained in its use.
- A fire alarm pull station or means of contacting the fire department (i.e., site telephone) available and accessible to fire watch person(s).

APPLICATION OF WORK PERMIT SYSTEM

The work permit system is a document which sets out how the work to be done, the hazards involved and precautions to be taken. It predetermines a safety drill and is a clear record that all foreseeable hazards have been considered and that appropriate precautions are defined and put in correct sequence. The classification of systems and their requirements are as follows:

1. **Permit to Work in Hazardous Operation:**
   - Work in confined space.

- Breaking or operating equipment or pipelines containing hazardous chemicals.
- Hot work in areas or on equipment where flammables are stored or processed.
- Work on high voltage electric equipment.
- Loading and un-loading of hazardous substances.
- Excavation: underground cables, pipeline work, vessels etc.
- Operations involving disposal of hazardous substances.
- Operations for testing of systems, equipments, pipeline, pressure plants etc.

2. Permit to Work in Hazardous Location:

- Work on fragile roof or ceiling.
- Work at dangerous heights, on scaffoldings, walls and tall chimneys.
- Work on or below or in the vicinity of guarded or un-guarded electrically operated and or mechanically moving machinery or equipment.
- Work on equipment that requires complete isolation.
- Work involving propping and centering of RCC slabs.

3. Permit to Work in Hazardous Work Areas:

- Explosive building work.
- Acid area work
- Flammable area work.
- Noxious fumes area work.

4. Permit to Work for Special Hazard:

- Use of toxic materials, matches or lighter, flammables.
- Use of repaired, modified electrical and other tools, equipments and appliances.

5. Permit to Work in Equipment Operating:

- Operating vehicle, fork-lift etc.
- Closing of sprinkler valves etc.

CONFINED SPACE ENTRY: A SAMPLE PERMIT

(Also termed as Safe Entry Permit and Safe Entry & Hot Work Permit)

Class: ______________________________

Location of work: ______________________________

Description of work (Trades): ______________________________

Employee assigned: ______________________________

Entry date: ______________________________

Entry time: ______________

Outside contractors: ______________

Isolation checklist	**Needed**	**Not needed**	**Done**
Blanking and/or Disconnecting	–	–	–
Electrical	–	–	–
Mechanical	–	–	–
Other	–	–	–
Hazardous work:			
Burning	–	–	–
Welding	–	–	–
Brazing	–	–	–
Open flame	–	–	–
Other	–	–	–
Hazards Expected:			
Corrosive Materials	–	–	–
Hot Equipment	–	–	–
Flammable materials	–	–	–
Toxic materials	–	–	–
Drains open	–	–	–
Cleaning (e.g., Chemical or Water lance)	–	–	–
Spark producing operations	–	–	–
Spilled liquids	–	–	–
Pressure systems	–	–	–
Other	–	–	–
Personal safety:			
Ventilation requirements	–	–	–
Respirators	–	–	–
Clothing	–	–	–
Head, hand and foot protection	–	–	–
Shields	–	–	–
Lifelines & harness	–	–	–
Lighting	–	–	–
Communications	–	–	–

Employee qualified	_	_	_
Buddy system	_	_	_
Standby person	_	_	_
Emergency egress procedure	_	_	_

Vessel cleaned:

Deposits ____________________

Methods ____________________

Inspection ____________________

Neutralized with ____________________

Fire safety precautions: ____________________

____

____

Training sign off: (Supervisor or qualified person) ____________________

Remarks: ____________________

Atmospheric gas tests:

	Tests performed	Location	Reading
	________	________	________
	________	________	________
Example:	Oxygen	________	19.5%
Example:	Flammability	________	Less than 10% LFL
	________	________	________
	________	________	________

Remarks: ____________________

Test performed by: ____________________

Signature: ____________________

Time: ____________________

Authorizations:

Supervisor: ____________________

Production supervisor: ____________________

Line supervisor: ____________________

Safety supervisor: ____________________

Etc.: ____________________

Entry and emergency procedure understood:

Stand by person: ____________________

Rescue: ____

Telephones: ____

Permit expires: ____

Classification: ____

21 CHAPTER

Industrial Hazards

PHYSICAL HAZARDS

Physical hazards are the most common and present in most workplaces. They include unsafe conditions that can cause injury, illness and death. They are typically easiest to spot but, too often overlooked because of familiarity, lack of knowledge, resistance to spending time or money to make necessary improvements or simply delays in making changes to remove the hazards. None of these are acceptable reasons for workers to be exposed to physical hazards.

Examples of physical hazards include:

- Electrical hazards: frayed cords, missing ground pins, improper wiring
- Unguarded machinery and moving machinery parts: guards removed or moving parts that a worker can accidentally touch
- Constant loud noise
- High exposure to sunlight/ultraviolet rays, heat or cold
- Working from heights, including ladders, scaffolds, roofs, or any raised work area
- Working with mobile equipment such as fork lifts

- Spills on floors or tripping hazards, such as blocked aisle or cords running across the floor.

CHEMICAL HAZARDS

The use of chemicals has increased dramatically due to the economic development in various sectors including industry, agriculture and transport. As a consequence, workers are exposed to a large number of chemicals of both natural and man-made origin. Exposure occurs through the air they breathe, the water they drink or bathe in, the food they eat, and the soil they touch. They are exposed virtually wherever they are: at home, in the school, on the playground, and during transport.

Chemicals may have immediate, acute effects, as well as chronic effects, often resulting from long-term exposures. Many of these poisonings occur in, workers are unintentional and can be prevented if chemicals were appropriately stored and handled. Chronic, low-level exposure to various chemicals may result in a number of adverse outcomes, including damage to the nervous and immune systems, impairment of reproductive function and development, cancer, and organ-specific damage.

Sound management of chemicals, particularly heavy metals, pesticides and persistent organic pollutants, is a prerequisite for the protection of worker's health.

BIOLOGICAL HAZARDS

A biological hazard, also known as a biohazard, is an organism or a by-product from an organism that is harmful or potentially harmful to other living things, primarily human beings. Common types of biological hazards include viruses, medical waste, or toxins that were created by a particular organism or microorganism. The "biohazard symbol" is a familiar sight in hospitals, and any object that carries it should be treated with extreme caution.

There are four levels of biohazards. A level 1 biological hazard poses the least risk while a level 4 poses the greatest.

Sources of biological hazards include bacteria, viruses, insects, plants, birds, animals, and humans. These sources can cause a variety of health effects ranging from skin irritation and allergies to infections (e.g., tuberculosis, AIDS), cancer and so on.

Workers in the hairdressing, nail and beauty industry are at risk of exposure to biological hazards that cause infectious diseases, such as:

- Blood borne diseases, e.g., Hepatitis B, Hepatitis C and HIV
- Skin infections, e.g., staphylococcus aureus
- Skin infestations, e.g., head lice

- Hairdressing, nail and beauty therapy workers are exposed to blood and body substances through activities such as:
  - Shaving
  - Electrolysis
  - Tweezing
  - Ear and body piercing
  - Manicure and pedicure
  - Application of artificial nails
  - Tattooing
  - Waxing
  - Skin extractions

Exposure to blood and body substances may be from:

- Direct contact, e.g., applying first aid to a bleeding client
- Indirect contact, e.g., handling contaminated equipment.

Blood or body substances do not have to be visible on an instrument for an infection to be transmitted.

Infection with a blood borne disease can occur if infected blood or body substances enter a person's body. This could occur: by a skin penetrating injury, e.g., accidentally piercing skin with a used electrolysis needle through broken skin, e.g., a cut, wound or dermatitis.

Through mucous membranes, e.g., blood splashing into a person's eyes or mouth.

Clients may be exposed to blood and body substances from equipment that has not been correctly cleaned and disinfected or sterilized.

CONTROL MEASURES

Substitution

- Substitute reusable equipment with single-use, disposable equipment, e.g., needles, spatulas, emery boards, make-up brushes, razors, hand towels.

Redesign

- Provide dull-tip scissors for cutting hair to prevent scissor-induced trauma.
- Install surfaces, furniture and fittings that are made of non-absorbent materials and can be readily cleaned.
- Design the work area so that clean and contaminated instruments are kept separate from each other.

Isolation

- Make sure all used sharps are placed in a clearly labeled, rigid-walled, puncture resistant container immediately after use.
- Make sure all waste that is contaminated with blood or body substances is placed in a leak proof bag or container and sealed.

ADMINISTRATIVE CONTROLS

Develop and implement procedures for:

- Cleaning, disinfecting, sterilizing and storing reusable equipment, etc.
- Managing blood and body substance spills
- Managing accidental blood and body substance exposures and skin penetrating injuries
- Safe disposal of contaminated waste.
- Cleaning and storing laundry.
- Provide workers with supervision, information and training on infectious diseases and infection control practices and procedures.
- Provide Hepatitis B immunization for workers at risk of exposure to blood and body substances, particularly for workers performing skin penetrating procedures.
- Make sure workers do not reuse equipment marked by the manufacturer as 'single use'.
- Make sure workers do not reuse equipment that has been contaminated with blood or body substances unless it has been cleaned and disinfected or sterilized.
- Make sure workers dispose of dispensed creams, ointments and lotions and do not return them to the original container.
- Make sure workers do not reuse wax unless it has been decontaminated.
- Make sure workers treat all blood and body substances as potentially infectious and take standard precautions to prevent exposure, e.g., wear disposable gloves, good hygiene practices, safe handling of sharps.
- Provide adequate hand washing facilities at the workplace.
- Instruct workers to wash their hands using soap and water before and after client contact, and after contact with blood and body substances and contaminated equipment.
- Provide a number of sets of equipment to allow some equipment to be cleaned and disinfected or sterilized while others are in use.
- Instruct workers to follow the recommended dilutions and storage requirements for disinfectants and observe use-by dates.

PERSONAL PROTECTIVE EQUIPMENT

- Make sure workers wear disposable gloves for all contact with blood and body substances, and when performing skin penetration procedures, such as electrolysis, skin extractions, tattooing and ear and body piercing.
- Make sure workers wear gloves when cleaning contaminated equipment.
- Make sure all abrasions; cuts are covered by waterproof dressings.
- Make sure workers wear eye and/or face protection when performing a procedure, such as cleaning contaminated equipment, which may cause a splashing hazard.
- Provide devices, such as gloves and finger cots, to protect nail technicians from abrasive injuries from files.

ERGONOMIC HAZARD

Ergonomics is matching the job to the worker and product to the user. Ergonomics and human factors are often used interchangeably in workplaces. Both describe the interaction between the worker and the job demands. The difference between them is ergonomics focuses on how work affects workers, and human factors emphasize designs that reduce the potential for human error.

Ergonomic hazards refer to workplace conditions that pose the risk of injury to the musculoskeletal system of the worker. Examples of musculoskeletal injuries include tennis elbow (an inflammation of a tendon in the elbow) and carpal tunnel syndrome (a condition affecting the hand and wrist). Ergonomic hazards include repetitive and forceful movements, vibration, temperature extremes, and awkward postures that arise from improper work methods and improperly designed workstations, tools, and equipments.

NOISE HAZARDS IN THE WORKPLACE

Noise in the workplace may not seem like a big issue but excessive exposure to any noise for a long period of time can cause irreversible damage to the ears. Noise can come from equipment or people that are working around. If the people talk in normal tone, it indicates that the place is not prone to noise hazard. If they are yelling it is a good indication that wearing ear protection is safer. Another way to know if the work environment is too loud is if your ears are ringing after you have left work and if it takes a little while for you to hear clearly again.

NOISE HAZARDS EAR PROTECTION

The absolute best way to avoid damage to ears is to not work in loud places. Unfortunately some people can not avoid noise where they are working. If you must work in a loud area be sure to take all the proper precautions to protect your hearing. All areas where there is excessive noise should be clearly marked with signs that state hearing safety equipment is required. This is the best way to be sure everyone is aware of the risk and is taking the proper safety steps before entering the area. Protective equipment should be available to all employees and they should be trained on how to use them properly. In areas where the noise level is slightly elevated a pair of foam ear plugs should be fine. Many professions such as air traffic controllers use this type of ear protection. It is good for high noise areas.

Noise Hazard in the workplace cannot be avoided for some people. If you have to work in a loud place be sure to have your hearing checked annually. If you have your hearing checked on a regular basis the doctor will be able to see any damage before it becomes irreparable. Hearing loss is very common in factories and most people do not even realize it is work related. If the damage to the ears is too much it could result in permanent hearing loss.

CHEMICAL SAFETY

Chemical Safety is achieved by undertaking all activities involving chemicals in such a way as to ensure the safety of human health and the environment. It covers all chemicals, natural and manufactured, and the full range of exposure situations from the natural presence of chemicals in the environment to their extraction or synthesis, industrial production, transport use and disposal.

Chemical safety has many scientific and technical components. Among these are toxicology, eco toxicology and the process of chemical risk assessment which requires a detailed knowledge of exposure and of biological effects.

TOXICITY

Toxicity is the degree to which a substance is able to damage an exposed organism. Toxicity can refer to the effect on a whole organism, such as an animal, bacterium, or plant, as well as the effect on a substructure of the organism, such as a cell (cytotoxicity) or an organ (organotoxicity), such as the liver (hepatotoxicity). A central concept of toxicology is that effects are dose-dependent; even water can lead to water intoxication when taken in large enough doses, whereas for even a very toxic substance such as snake venom there is a dose below which there is no detectable toxic effect.

Types of Toxicity

There are generally three types of toxic entities; chemical, biological and physical:

Chemicals include inorganic substances such as lead, mercury, asbestos, hydrofluoric acid, and chlorine gas, organic compounds such as methyl alcohol, most medications, and poisons from living things.

Biological toxic entities include those bacteria and viruses that are able to induce disease in living organisms. Biological toxicity can be complicated to measure because the "threshold dose" may be a single organism. Theoretically one virus, bacterium or worm can reproduce to cause a serious infection. However, in a host with an intact immune system the inherent toxicity of the organism is balanced by the host's ability to fight back; the effective toxicity is then a combination of both parts of the relationship. A similar situation is also present with other types of toxic agents.

It is more difficult to assess the toxicity of chemical mixtures than of single, pure chemicals because each component displays its own toxicity and components may interact to produce enhanced or diminished effects. Common mixtures include gasoline, cigarette smoke, and industrial waste. Even more complex are situations with more than one type of toxic entity, such as the discharge from a malfunctioning sewage treatment plant, with both chemical and biological agents.

Global Classifications of Toxicity

For substances to be regulated and handled appropriately they must be properly classified and labeled. Classification is determined by approved testing measures or calculations and have determined cut off levels set by governments and scientists. Global Classification looks at three areas:

- Physical Hazards (explosions and pyrotechnics),
- Health Hazards, and
- Environmental Hazards.

Health Hazards

The types of toxicities where substances may cause lethality to the entire body, lethality to specific organs, major/minor damage, or cause cancer. These are globally accepted definitions of what toxicity is anything falling outside of the definition cannot be classified as that type of toxicant.

Acute Toxicity

Acute toxicity looks at lethal effects following oral, dermal or inhalation exposure. It is split into five categories of severity where Category 1 requires the least amount of exposure to be lethal and Category 5 requires the most exposure to be lethal.

The table below shows the upper limits for each category:

Method of administration	Category 1	Category 2	Category 3	Category 4	Category 5
Oral: LD50 measured in mg/kg of bodyweight	5	50	300	2,000	5,000
Dermal: LD50 measured in mg/kg of bodyweight	50	200	1,000	2,000	50,00

Gas Inhalation: LC50 measured in ppmV	100	500	2,500	20,000	Undefined
Vapor Inhalation: LC50 measured in mg/L	0.5	2.0	10	20	Undefined
Dust and Mite Inhalation: LC50 measured in mg/L	0.05	0.5	1.0	5.0	Undefined

Note: The undefined values are expected to be roughly equivalent to the category 5 values for oral and dermal administration.

Other Methods of Exposure and Severity

Skin corrosion and irritation are determined though a skin patch tests analysis. This examines the severity of the damage done; when it is incurred and how long it remains; whether it is reversible and how many test subjects were affected.

Skin corrosion from a substance must penetrate through the epidermis into the dermis within four hours of application and must not reverse the damage within 14 days. Skin irritation shows damage less severe than corrosion if: the damage occurs within 72 hours of application; or for three consecutive days after application within a 14 day period; or causes inflammation which lasts for 14 days in two test subjects. Mild skin irritation minor damage (less severe than irritation) within 72 hours of application or for three consecutive days after application.

Serious eye damage involves tissue damage or degradation of vision which does not fully reverse in 21 days. Eye irritation involves changes to the eye which do fully reverse within 21 days.

IDLH

IDLH is an initials for Immediately Dangerous to Life or Health, and is defined as "an atmosphere that poses an immediate threat to life, would cause irreversible adverse health effects, or would impair an individual's ability to escape from a dangerous atmosphere."

IDLH values are often used to guide the selection of breathing apparatus that are made available to workers or firefighters in specific situations.

CHEMICAL STORAGE AND TRANSPORTATION

Flammable and Combustible Liquid Storage

The storage of flammable and combustible liquids in a laboratory, shop, or building area must be kept to the minimum needed for research and operations. Flammable liquids have a flash point below 100°F. If more than 5 gallons of flammable liquids are stored outside safety cans per 100 square feet of area, a flammable-liquids storage cabinet is needed. Flammable-liquids storage cabinets are not intended for storage of anything other than flammable liquids.

The total quantity of flammable liquids permitted to be stored in a laboratory is 10 gallons per 100 square feet of laboratory space.

Flammable Liquids Storage in a Cabinet

- No more than 60 gallons of Class I flammable liquids (flash point below 100°F) or Class II combustible liquids (flash point between 100°F to 140°F) may be stored in a flammable-liquids storage cabinet.
- No more than 120 gallons of a Class III combustible liquid (flash point between 140°F and 200°F) may be stored in a flammable-liquids storage cabinet.
- Storage cabinets shall be designed and constructed to limit the internal temperature to not more than 325°F when subjected to a 10-minute fire test using the standard time temperature chart set forth in NFPA 251.
- All flammable-liquids cabinets shall be labeled in conspicuous letters **"Flammable."**
- Storage cabinets shall be constructed of at least No. 18 gauge sheet iron and shall be double walled with 1½ inch air space. Joints shall be riveted, welded, or made tight by some equally effective means. The door shall be provided with a three-point lock, and the door sill shall be raised at least 2 inches above the bottom of the cabinet.
- All flammable liquid storage cabinets must be grounded. A ground cable of 3/8" copper brain or a 12 gauge copper conductor can be used. The ground must be tested and resistance to ground cannot exceed one mega ohm. The grounding cable must be connected to a building structural member or an electrical building ground. Due to increased use of plastic piping, (which breaks the ground) water pipes must not be used for grounding.
- The NFPA Technical Committee on General Storage of Flammable Liquids considers that providing vents to storage cabinets reduces the limited fire protection provided by such cabinets because a single walled duct will transmit heat faster than a double-walled cabinet. Ventilation of storage cabinets is recommended only when highly odoriferous conditions exist. Ventilation requires a steel duct and an appropriate exhaust fan discharging to an appropriate location outside the building.
- All chemical storage in cabinets must be compatible.

Flammable Liquids Storage Outside of a Cabinet

Storage of flammable liquids outside of a storage cabinet should be avoided when possible. Flammable liquids that are not in use should be stored in an appropriate cabinet. The maximum quantity of flammable liquids allowed in a laboratory outside of a storage cabinet and not stored in a safety can is 5 gallons per 100 square feet of laboratory space.

Transportation of Hazardous Chemicals

The transportation of hazardous chemicals in laboratory buildings provides the greatest potential for chemical exposure to the building occupants. Spills occurring outside storerooms and laboratories may lead to hazardous concentrations of vapors and gases being distributed throughout the building.

The following guidelines should be observed when transporting chemicals outside the laboratory:

- **Elevators:** Freight elevators shall be used where available to transport hazardous materials. Under no circumstances are passenger elevators to be used for the transportation of hazardous materials if freight elevators are available.
- **Flammable Liquids**
  - Flammable liquids shall be transported in pressure-resistant safety cans.
  - Original containers of flammable liquids shall be placed in an outside container or acid-carrying bucket.
  - No more than 5 gallons of flammable liquids in glass containers shall be transported on the freight elevator unless the original shipping carton (box) is used and the materials are on an appropriate cart.
- **Corrosive or Oxidizing Materials**
  - Original glass shipping containers holding liquids acids and bases must be placed in an outside container or acid-carrying bucket.
  - Incompatible chemicals, for example, chromic acid (oxidizing acid) and ethyl acetate (flammable liquid), should not be transported on the same cart unless they are in original shipping cartons and physically separated.
- **Water Reactive Chemicals**
  - Wherever possible, use the original outside shipping containers (packaging) when transporting water reactive chemicals.
  - Once opened, water reactive chemicals must be placed in a rigid outside container or acid carrying bucket for transporting.
- **Pyrophoric (spontaneously igniting) Substances**
  - Whenever possible, the original outside shipping container (packaging) must be used to transport pyrophoric substances.
  - Once opened, pyrophoric substances must be placed in a rigid outside container or acid carrying bucket for transporting.

- **Acutely Toxic Compounds:** Whenever possible, the original outside shipping container (packaging) must be used to transport acutely toxic compounds.
- **General**
  - Chemical, substances and research materials must be clearly labeled with the correct chemical name when transported. Legible hand-printed labels are acceptable; chemical formulas and structural formulas alone are not acceptable.
  - Carts used for chemical transport must have sides, on each shelf, that are high enough to retain the containers. Cart wheels must be large enough to prevent the carts from being caught in floor cracks, and door and elevator thresholds.
  - Personnel transporting chemicals must (at a minimum) wear chemical resistant gloves and safety glasses.

General Considerations for Chemical Storage

- Carefully read the label before storing a hazardous chemical.
- The MSDS will also provide any special storage information and incompatibilities.
- Do NOT store un-segregated chemicals in alphabetical order or incompatible chemicals in close proximity to each other.

Chemicals should be separately stored by chemical class as follows:

Solids

- Oxidizing solids
- Flammable solids
- Water reactive solids
- All other solids

Liquids

- Acid liquids
- Caustic liquids
- Oxidizing liquids
- Perchloric acid solutions
- Flammable or combustible liquids

Gases

- Toxic gases
- Flammable gases
- Oxidizing and inert gases

(Once separated into hazard classes, chemicals may be stored alphabetically).

Use approved storage containers and safety cans for flammable liquids. Use spill trays under containers of strong corrosive reagents. **Do not store liquids above eye level.**

Ensure that all containers are properly labeled.

Compressed Gases

- Carefully read the label before using or storing compressed gas. The MSDS will provide any special hazard information. Always use the minimum size cylinder required to perform the work.
- Cylinders of compressed gases must be handled as high-energy sources. When storing or moving a cylinder, have the cap securely in place to protect the stem. Use suitable racks, straps, chains or stands to support cylinders. Compressed gas cylinders pose a crush hazard to hands and feet.
- Do not expose cylinders to temperature extremes.
- Always use the correct regulator. Do not use a regulator adapter. Oil or grease on the high pressure side of an oxygen cylinder can cause an explosion. Do not lubricate an oxygen regulator.
- Cylinders of toxic, flammable or reactive gases should be stored and used in a fume hood or with local ventilation.
- Never bleed a cylinder completely empty. Leave a slight pressure to keep contaminants out.
- Always wear safety glasses when handling compressed gases.

Designated Areas

All locations within the laboratory where acutely toxic, carcinogenic, or reproductive hazards are stored or handled should be demarcated with caution signs. Storage areas must be segregated from other chemical storage. This includes all fume hoods and bench tops where the acutely toxic, carcinogenic, or reproductive hazards are handled.

The use of a designated area for handling and storage of these three chemical classes will minimize the exposure to laboratory workers and prevent accidental contact by untrained faculty.

Flammable Gas Cylinders

The storage of flammable gas cylinders is limited to two (2) type 1 (10″ × 50″) cylinders per 500 square feet of non-sprinklered laboratory space.

Liquefied flammable gas containers should be limited to two (2) 9″ × 30″ cylinders per 500 square feet of non-sprinklered laboratory space or three (3) 9″ × 30″ cylinders per 500 square feet of sprinklered laboratory space.

General Guideline for Cleaning Up Chemical Spills

- Immediately alert others in the area and the supervisor, and evacuate the area, if necessary.
- If there is a fire or medical attention is needed, contact the appropriate Personnel.

- Attend to any persons who may be contaminated. Contaminated clothing must be removed immediately and the skin flushed with water for no less than fifteen minutes. Clothing must be laundered before reuse.
- If a volatile, flammable material is spilled, immediately warn others in the area, control sources of ignition, and ventilate the area.
- Wear personal protective equipment, as appropriate to the hazards.
- If the spill is a MAJOR one, if there has been a release to the environment, or if assistance is needed, contact the appropriate personnel.
- Consider the need for respiratory protection.
- Protect floor drains or other means for environmental release. Spill socks and absorbents may be placed around drains, as needed.
- Loose spill control materials should be distributed over the entire spill area, working from the outside, circling to the center. This reduces the chance of splash or spreading of the spilled chemical.

THE TRANSPORT EMERGENCY CARD (TREM CARD)

Providing drivers with training and written safety instruction is the first precautionary measure that needs to be taken to avoid accidents. It is also a mandatory requirement now. The cards contain the safety instructions and are called the TREM CARD or Transport Emergency Card. This card apart from being helpful to the driver is also of use to local police, fire brigade and hospitals. TREM Cards should have the following format:

Transport Emergency Card (Road)

- Cargo: Mention chemical identity of the dangerous and hazardous goods
- Nature of hazard
- Protection device
- Emergency action: Notify police and fire brigade immediately
- Spillage
- Fire
- First aid
- Additional information provided by manufacturer or sender
- Telephone numbers.

MECHANICAL HAZARDS

Mechanical hazards can mainly start from the following causes:

- Failure of components of a mechanical system due to faulty design, faulty assembly, faulty materials, lack of repair and maintenance.
- Complacency on the part of workers at the point of operation.
- Inadequate safeguards on the machine.
- Laxity in the use of personal protective equipment.

Few safety devices basically made for protecting the operators from the point of operation hazards are as follows:

- Adjustable or movable barriers or guards.
- Two hand control device.
- Pull-out or pull-away devices.
- Hold-out devices.
- Sweep guard.
- Optical sensor.
- Feeding tools.

Some mechanical hazardous tools are:

- Hand tools and power tools.
- Portable ladders.
- Ropes.
- Fly wheels
- Lifting tackles and lifting equipments.

Mechanical handling equipments

- Conveyors
- Rope ways
- Elevators/lifts
- Fork lift trucks
- Toeing vehicles.

Prevention of accidents due to mechanical hazards is:

- Proper training of workers.
- Adequate illumination in work areas.
- Safety devices including guards, railings etc.
- Proper lay-out and planning.
- Safe operational conditions or procedures.
- Regular repair and maintenance of mechanical equipments.
- Provisions of personal safety equipment.

22
CHAPTER

Hazard Evaluation Techniques

HAZARD DEFINITION

Hazard can be defined as physical or chemical characteristics that have the potential to cause harm to people, property and to the environment.

Hazard can be classified as:

- Acute hazard and
- Chronic hazard.

Acute hazard is defined as the potential for the injury or damage to occur due to instantaneous or short duration exposure.

Chronic hazard is defined as the potential for injury or damage to occur due to prolonged exposure to the undesirable events or conditions.

Hazard evaluation is the analysis of a hazardous situation or process safety concerns and help identification of the unexpected events in processes or in operations.

A number of methods are practiced to analyze both quantitatively and qualitatively about the plant safety, its operating and maintenance practices, and to match the design and construction standards.

Hazard evaluation can be approached by the following techniques:

- HAZOP study
- Job Safety Analysis (JSA)
- Fault Tree Analysis (FTA)
- Event Tree Analysis (ETA)
- Failure Mode and Effect Analysis (FMEA)
- Relative Ranking Technique (RRT)
- Safety Review and Safety Considerations (SR&SC)
- Checklist analysis and Ranking of Events
- Preliminary Hazard Analysis (PHA)
- Brain storming analysis: What – If Analysis
- Cause and Consequence Analysis (CCA)
- Human Reliability Analysis (HRA).

Requirement for Hazard Evaluation:

- Knowledge and experience of operating personnel.
- Materials used, intermediates and products, their physical, chemical and other pertinent data.
- Process chemistry and operations sequence.
- Materials inventories.
- Operating procedures.
- Code and standards.
- Flow chart procedures for start up.
- Normal drawings of equipments.
- Maintenance schedules.
- Emergency procedures.
- Personal injury reports.
- Hazards incident reports.
- Pressure vessel inspection reports.
- Inspection reports by internal staff and by external agencies.
- Previous safety study reports, if any.

Hazop Study

A hazard and operability study (HAZOP) is a structured and systematic examination of a planned or existing process or operation in order to identify and evaluate problems that may represent risks to personnel or equipment, or prevent efficient operation. The HAZOP technique was initially developed to analyze chemical process systems, but has later been extended to other types of systems and also to complex operations and to software systems. A HAZOP is a qualitative technique based on guide-words and is carried out by a multi-disciplinary team (HAZOP team) during a set of meetings.

Parameters and Guide Words

The key feature is to select appropriate parameters which apply to the design intention. These are general words such as Flow, Temperature, Pressure and Composition. Deviations from the design Intention. In order to identify Deviations, the Study Leader applies (systematically, in order) a set of Guide Words to each parameter for each section of the process. The current standard Guide Words are as follows:

Guide Word	Meaning
NO OR NOT	Complete negation of the design intent
MORE	Quantitative increase
LESS	Quantitative decrease
AS WELL AS	Qualitative modification/increase
PART OF	Qualitative modification/decrease
REVERSE	Logical opposite of the design intent
OTHER THAN	Complete substitution
EARLY	Relative to the clock time
LATE	Relative to the clock time
BEFORE	Relating to order or sequence
AFTER	Relating to order or sequence

The following table gives an overview of commonly used guide word-parameter pairs and common interpretations of them.

Parameter/ Guide Word	More	Less	None	Reverse	As well as	Part of	Other than
Flow	High flow	Low flow	No flow	Reverse flow	Deviating concentration	Contamination	Deviating material
Pressure	High pressure	Low pressure	Vacuum		Delta-p		Explosion

Temperature	High temperature	Low temperature					
Level	High level	Low level	No level		Different level		
Time	Too long/ too late	Too short/ too soon	Sequence step skipped	Back- wards	Missing actions	Extra actions	Wrong time
Agitation	Fast mixing	Slow mixing	No mixing				
Reaction	Fast reaction/ runaway	Slow reaction	No reaction				Unwanted reaction
Start-up/ Shut-down	Too fast	Too slow			Actions missed		Wrong recipe
Draining/ Venting	Too long	Too short	None		Deviating pressure	Wrong timing	
Inertising	High pressure	Low pressure	None			Contami- nation	Wrong material
Utility failure (instrument air, power)			Failure				
DCS failure			Failure				
Maintenance			None				
Vibrations	Too low	Too high	None				Wrong frequency

Once the causes and effects of any potential hazards have been established, the system being studied can then be modified to improve its safety. The modified design must then be subject to another Hazop, to ensure that no new problems have been added.

Job Safety Analysis

Job Safety Analysis is one of the safety management tools that can be used to define and control the hazards associated with a certain process, job or procedure. Job Safety Analysis is a term used interchangeably with Job Hazard Analysis and Risk Assessment. The purpose of a JSA is to ensure that the risk of each step of a task is reduced to ALARP (As Low As Reasonably Practicable).

The analysis starts with a summary of the whole job process. This is broken down into smaller steps and listed in table form. The hazards involved in each single step are identified and then the control measures to eliminate, reduce or mitigate each hazard are identified and described. By this means every aspect of the whole process is analyzed and safe methods of work determined.

When is a JSA Required?

Some type of risk analysis should be performed before every job. Some tasks are routine and the hazards and controls well understood. For routine tasks consider using a Standard Operating Procedure, a set of standing orders that control the known hazards. For tasks that are complex, unusual, difficult, require the interaction of many people or systems or involve new tools or methods, a JSA should be performed.

How is a JSA Created?

The JSA or JHA should be created by the work group performing the task. Sometimes it is expedient to review a JSA that has been prepared when the same task has been performed before but the work group must take special care to review all of the steps thoroughly to ensure that they are controlling all of the hazards for this job this time. The JSA is usually completed on a form. The most common form is a table with three columns. The headings of the three columns are: (1) Job Step (2) Hazard and (3) Controls. A Hazard is any factor that can cause damage to personnel, property or the environment. The work group firstly breaks down the entire job into its component steps. Then, for each step, hazards are identified. Finally, for each hazard identified, controls are recorded in the 3rd column. In the example below, the hazards are analyzed for the task of preparing and painting a handrail:

Step	Hazard	Control
1. Prepare Surface Using Electric Wire Brush	Hand Arm Vibration Syndrome	Wear thick gloves Use vibrating tool no more than 20 minutes at a time and for no more than 2 hours a shift.
	Paint dust possibly containing lead	Wear a organic vapor mask when disturbing old paint. Wear disposable coveralls. Wash hands thoroughly before eating or smoking. Thorough housekeeping.
	Slips trips and falls	Route all electrical cables sensibly to keep walkways and stairs free of hazards.
	Sunburn	Wear proper clothing as required.

2. Paint Handrails	Damage to adjacent surfaces from thinners and paint	Use drop sheets
	Exposure to fumes from thinners	If poorly ventilated, use P3 organic vapor mask
	Paint in eyes	Wear safety goggles when working above shoulder height, safety glasses at other times
	Fire	Keep containers of thinners and flammable solvents closed properly and stored in a cool place away from sources of sparks
3. Housekeeping	Slip and trip hazards	Remove waste to bin, tools to store, ensure barriers and signs are in place to denote wet paint.

Fault Tree Analysis

Fault tree analysis (FTA) is a failure analysis in which an undesired state of a system is analyzed. This analysis method is mainly used in the field of safety engineering to quantitatively determine the probability of a safety hazard.

Methodology

Since no system is perfect, dealing with a subsystem fault is a necessity and any working system eventually will have a fault in some place. However, the probability for a complete or partial success is greater than the probability of a complete failure or partial failure. Assembling a FTA is thus not as tedious as assembling a success tree which can turn out to be very time consuming.

Because assembling a FTA can be a costly and cumbersome experience, the perfect method is to consider subsystems. In this way, dealing with smaller systems can assure less error work probability, less system analysis. Afterward, the subsystems integrate to form the well analyzed big system.

An undesired effect is taken as the root ('top event') of a tree of logic. There should be only one Top Event and all concerns must tree down from it. Then, each situation that could cause that effect is added to the tree as a series of logic expressions.

When fault trees are labeled with actual numbers about failure probabilities (which are often in practice unavailable because of the expense of testing), computer programs can calculate failure probabilities from fault trees.

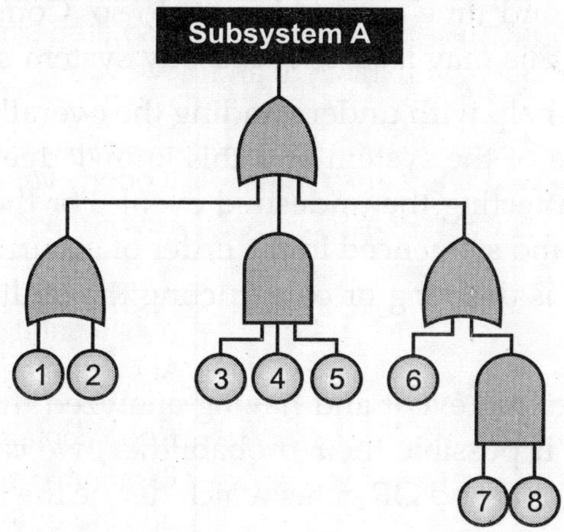

A Fault Tree Diagram

The Tree is usually written out using conventional logic gate symbols. The route through a tree between an event and an initiator in the tree is called a Cut Set. The shortest credible way through the tree from fault to initiating event is called a Minimal Cut Set. Some industries use both Fault Trees and Event Trees. An Event Tree starts from an undesired initiator (loss of critical supply, component failure etc.) and follows possible further system events through to a series of final consequences. As each new event is considered, a new node on the tree is added with a split of probabilities of taking either branch. The probabilities of a range of 'top events' arising from the initial event can then be seen.

Analysis

Many different approaches can be used to model a FTA, but the most common and popular way can be summarized in a few steps. Remember that a fault tree is used to analyze a single fault event and that one and only one event can be analyzed during a single fault tree.

FTA Analysis Involves Five Steps:

1. Define the undesired event to study.
2. Definition of the undesired event can be very hard to catch, although some of the events are very easy and obvious to observe. An engineer with a wide knowledge of the design of the system or a system analyst with an engineering background is the best person who can help define and number the undesired events. Undesired events are used then to make the FTA, one event for one FTA; no two events will be used to make one FTA.
3. Obtain an understanding of the system.
4. Once the undesired event is selected, all causes with probabilities of affecting the undesired event of 0 or more are studied and analyzed. Getting exact numbers for the probabilities leading to the event is usually impossible for the reason that it

may be very costly and time consuming to do so. Computer software is used to study probabilities; this may lead to less costly system analysis.

5. System analysts can help with understanding the overall system. System designers have full knowledge of the system and this knowledge is very important for not missing any cause affecting the undesired event. For the selected event all causes are then numbered and sequenced in the order of occurrence and then are used for the next step which is drawing or constructing the fault tree.

Construct the Fault Tree

After selecting the undesired event and having analyzed the system so that we know all the causing effects (and if possible their probabilities) we can now construct the fault tree. Fault tree is based on AND and OR gates which define the major characteristics of the fault tree.

Evaluate the Fault Tree

After the fault tree has been assembled for a specific undesired event, it is evaluated and analyzed for any possible improvement or in other words study the risk management and find ways for system improvement. This step is as an introduction for the final step which will be to control the hazards identified. In short, in this step we identify all possible hazards affecting in a direct or indirect way the system.

Control the Hazards Identified

This step is very specific and differs largely from one system to another, but the main point will always be that after identifying the hazards all possible methods are pursued to decrease the probability of occurrence.

Event Tree Analysis

An event tree is a graphical representation of the logic model that identifies and quantifies the possible outcomes following an initiating event. Event tree analysis provides an inductive approach to reliability assessment as they are constructed using forward logic. Fault trees use a deductive approach as they are constructed by defining TOP events and then use backward logic to define causes. Event tree analysis and fault tree analysis are, however, closely linked. Fault trees are often used to quantify system events that are part of event tree sequences. The logical processes employed to evaluate event tree sequences and quantify the consequences are the same as those used in fault tree analyses.

Failure Modes and Effects Analysis

A Failure Modes and Effects Analysis (FMEA) is a procedure in product development and operations management for analysis of potential failure modes within a system for classification by the severity and likelihood of the failures. A successful FMEA activity helps a team to identify potential failure modes based on past experience with similar products or processes, enabling the team to design those failures out of the system with the minimum of effort and resource expenditure, thereby reducing development time and costs. It is widely used in manufacturing industries in various phases of the product life cycle and is now increasingly finding use in the service industry. Failure modes are any errors or defects in a process, design, or item, especially those that affect the customer, and can be potential or actual. Effects analysis refers to studying the consequences of those failures.

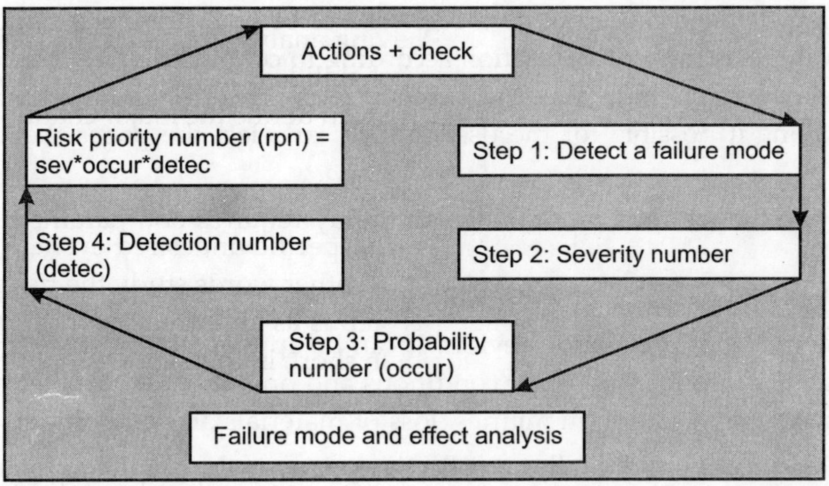

***Severity:** The consequences of a failure mode. Severity considers the worst potential consequence of a failure, determined by the degree of injury, property damage, or system damage that could ultimately occur.

FMEA Cycle

Failure mode: The manner by which a failure is observed; it generally describes the way the failure occurs.

Failure effect: Immediate consequences of a failure on operation, function or functionality, or status of some item.

Indenture levels: An identifier for item complexity. Complexity increases as levels are closer to one.

Local effect: The failure effect as it applies to the item under analysis.

Next higher level effect: The failure effect as it applies at the next higher indenture level.

End effect: The failure effect at the highest indenture level or total system.

Failure cause: Defects in design, process, quality, or part application, which are the underlying cause of the failure or which initiate a process which leads to failure.

Relative Ranking Technique

A ranking is a relationship between a set of items such that, for any two items, the first is either 'ranked higher than', 'ranked lower than' or 'ranked equal to' the second. In mathematics, this is known as a weak order or total preorder of objects. It is not necessarily a total order of objects because two different objects can have the same ranking. The rankings themselves are totally ordered. For example, materials are totally preordered by hardness, while degrees of hardness are totally ordered.

By reducing detailed measures to a sequence of ordinal numbers, rankings make it possible to evaluate complex information according to certain criteria. Thus, for example, an Internet search engine may rank the pages it finds according to an estimation of their relevance, making it possible for the user quickly to select the pages they are likely to want to see.

Analysis of data obtained by ranking commonly requires non-parametric statistics.

Safety Review and Safety Considerations

It is also known as loss prevention review. It can be applied at any stage of the process. The evaluation helps to identify plant conditions and operation details that might lead to unexpected accidents resulting in injuries, loss of materials and equipments etc.

The team members individually or collectively survey the plant and operations. They focus on risky situations, risky operations and failure prone equipments and accessories. House keeping, morale of the staff are also considered. Based on the facts, the team makes recommendations with justification. A follow up evaluation and a re-inspection planning is made to verify the corrective action whether carried or not. This method is a description of potential safety problems and corrective actions. The plant management is made responsible to carry out corrective actions.

Checklist Analysis and Ranking of Events

This method evaluates whether the standards and practices laid down by the designers are complied with, from safety view point. The checklists should be developed by well experienced and varied background people. A completed checklist contains answers yes or no. This is a versatile method of safety assurance.

Preliminary Hazard Analysis

This method is based on U.S Military Safety Standard system. Hazardous materials and processes are identified prior to the commencement of the operation. It concerns areas where energy release takes place in an un-controlled manner. Considerations are based on the following:

- Raw materials, intermediates and final products and their activities

- Plant equipment
- Lay out facility
- Operating environment
- Operating activities like testing, maintenance etc.
- Interfaces among system components.

This technique helps in ranking hazardous situations for reduction and elimination of hazards in subsequent phases of life cycle of the process.

Brain Storming Approach: What – if Analysis

This method is widely adopted by experts within the industry and experts from outside industries. Operational faults like operation of wrong valve, unexpected switching off of motors, electricity failure, personal failures and natural calamities are discussed by what if questioning method and experts advices were sought to avoid hazardous phenomenon. Only expert and experienced analysts to take part in what if question session, otherwise the desired results may not be achieved.

Causes and Consequence Analysis

This is a blend of Fault Tree and Event Tree Analysis. The cause and consequence diagram displays the relationship between accident outcomes and their basic causes. Due remedies are suggested based on the cause and consequence analysis. CCA techniques depend on the number, complexity and level of resolution of events included in the analysis.

Human Reliability Analysis

This is a systematic evaluation of operating personnel, technicians, and maintenance staff etc., involved in plant operations. The physical and environmental characteristics of the job requirements, skill, knowledge and capabilities of the individual are analyzed. The method analyses the error – likely situations of the human activity in the machine atmosphere, identify and pin points the human error leading to accidents. It is done along with other hazard evaluation techniques. Severities of consequences are analyzed. The result can be updated for design changes in the system, plant or training modification.

Job Hazard Analysis (Sample Report)

Basic job steps	Hazard present in each job step	Correct and safe procedure for completing the job
1. 2. 3. 4.		

Typical Uses for Hazard Evaluation Techniques

	Safety review	Check list	Relative ranking	PHA	What – If	HAZOP	FMEA	FTA	CCA	HRA
Research and development			X	X	X					
Conceptual design		X	X	X	X					
Pilot plant operation		X		X	X	X	X	X	X	X
Detailed engineering		X		X	X	X	X	X	X	X
Construction Start up	X		X	X						
Routine operation	X	X			X	X	X	X	X	X
Expansion/ modification	X	X	X	X	X	X	X	X	X	X
Incident investigation					X	X	X	X	X	X
Decommissioning		X			X					

X – Commonly used Blank – Rarely applied or inappropriate.

23 CHAPTER

Pep Talk/Tool Box Meeting at Work Place

WHY IT IS REQUIRED?

- There are more than some millions recorded workplace incidents involving employee injuries every year.
- More than some thousand workers die in work-related accidents annually.
- You can make a difference and help protect your employees by speaking up and speaking out about safety.
- The more your workers know about potential hazards and necessary protections, the safer they will be on the job.
- Even with a solid safety program in place, workers need a safety pep talk from time to time.

How do you know if it is time for a pep talk? Look for signs that employees are getting relaxed about safety. For example:

- An increase in accidents and near misses
- Dirty, disorganized, or dangerous work areas
- Workers not wearing required PPE

- Employees taking shortcuts, skipping steps, and not following safety rules
- Workers not using tools and equipment properly
- People apparently unaware of safety hazards or requirements—or simply not caring
- Workers rushing through their work, not looking out for co-workers, or fooling around
- Employees missing safety meetings or skipping safety training sessions
- Workers failing to report workplace hazards, accidents, or near misses.

Should you target individuals or talk to everybody? The answer depends on what you see when you take a good, hard look around the workplace. If it is just a few people taking risks or ignoring safety requirements, then certainly start by targeting those workers. Sit them down individually or as a group and give them a good pep talk. With hardcore safety shirkers you may have to do more than talk, of course. Those few who think the rules do not apply to them may need discipline to turn them around. But sometimes just reminding workers who have gotten careless about the possible consequences of their actions might be enough to change both their attitude and behavior. If a lot of employees are getting sloppy and careless, then talk to everybody. Talking up safety can never hurt. Even the safe workers need encouragement to keep focused on safety. A good pep talk might just prevent someone who is generally a safe worker from engaging in risk taking at some time in the future.

What can you say that could make your workplace safer? There is a lot you can say to boost employee safety awareness and encourage safe work behavior. For example, in addition to talking about safety issues specific to your workplace, you could emphasize fundamental safety dos and do nots like these in your pep talks:

Do:

- Treat safety as an important job responsibility.
- Think ahead all day, every day, no matter what you are doing.
- Plan each job before you start.
- Think about what could go wrong and how you will prevent problems and accidents.
- Use labels, MSDSs, and other safety information so that you can work safely.
- Inspect tools and equipment before you use them.
- Keep the safety rules in mind while you work.
- Pay attention to what you are doing and avoid distractions.
- Know what to do in an emergency.
- Take safety training seriously.
- Ask questions when you are unsure of what to do or how to do it.

Do not:

- Ignore any safety hazard—remove it, repair it, or report it.
- Turn a blind eye to co-workers' unsafe actions—talk to them about the risks and the precautions.
- Bypass safety procedures—or let others talk you into doing so.
- Neglect to use required PPE.
- Work on very hazardous jobs, such as tasks in confined spaces, without a buddy.
- Rush, take shortcuts, or skip steps.
- Fool around.
- Ignore good housekeeping requirements in your work area.

Toolbox Meeting Tips

When?: Ideally, you want to have a short toolbox safety meeting the first thing in the morning at the work sites.

Where?: You need room for every one to sit/stand comfortably and relax with as few distractions as possible, and where you can be easily seen and heard. If the topic is crane safety, try holding the meeting next to the sites crane if possible.

How Long?: Try to limit the safety meeting to five or ten minutes.

What to Say?: Do not grab a printed topic and read it. Pick a topic relevant to what the employees are doing or will be doing. Do some preparation so you can give the talk in your own words.

Get input from the crew about any concerns they may have or about topics that could be discussed. Discuss any unsafe acts or conditions observed during the past week and how they were corrected. Discuss new equipment on the job or upcoming activities.

Remember to prepare, start on time, end on time, talk do not read, and thank your audience for their time, for doing a good job, and maintaining a good safety record.

Some Important Topics for Pep talk:

General Safety Rules and Procedures

- Always follow all safety rules and regulations.
- Learn to recognize unsafe conditions and be sure to correct them.
- Make safety your responsibility. Do not depend on others.
- Handle hazardous materials properly. Check the MSDS for accurate information.
- Develop good housekeeping habits.
- Inspect electrical and hand tools before use.
- When it is heavy get some help. Do not be a hurt hero.

- Never smoke around flammables.
- Read and heed signs and other warnings.
- Do not take chances. Chance taker is accident maker.
- Watch out for pinch points and sharp edges.
- Keep your work area neat and clean.
- Avoid horseplay, someone always gets hurt.
- Report injuries to your supervisor promptly.
- Near misses are warnings, the next time could be much worse.
- Wear personal protective equipment properly and whenever required.
- When in doubt, lock it out.
- Select the right tool for the job.
- Wear your seat belt, the life you save may be yours.
- Check the label and read the manufacturer's instructions before use.
- Watch out for others on the job.
- Follow proper trenching safety guidelines, bench, shore, or sheet.
- Call for help when there is an emergency.
- Ask questions whenever you're in doubt.

Accident Prevention

You are part of a team of skilled workers and accident prevention is part of your job. It takes everyone's effort to keep a jobsite safe. The following rules may be observed to help prevent accidents.

- Come to work fully rested; wear proper clothing and sturdy footwear; jewelry, watches and rings must be left at home.
- Use the correct personal protective equipment when the task requires it, and keep this safety gear in good condition and replace it as necessary.
- Damaged or lost equipment should be reported to your supervisor.
- Keep your work area clean and neat. Do not let your housekeeping get out of hand.
- Follow the warnings written on labels.
- Observe signs, regulations and procedures; ask your supervisor about any you do not understand.
- Never bypass safety valves or devices.
- Follow lock out – tag out practices where required to do so.
- Remove protruding nails or bend them over.
- Wipe up spills of oil, water, or grease.

- Keep walkways, aisles, traffic lanes and fire exits clear of debris and other materials.
- When working in new areas of the jobsite take a few minutes to look around to locate obvious hazards.
- Do not leave any floor openings unprotected. Cover floor holes securely or guard with standard guardrails.
- Make sure you have the right type and size of ladder. Climb it facing the rungs and be sure your hands are free to hold onto the ladder.
- Check your electrical tools prior to use.
- Do not use tools with split, broken, or loose handles.
- Watch out for overhead power lines.
- Store flammable liquids in approved containers.
- Shut-off engines and let them cool down prior to refueling; and never smoke around flammables.
- Report any accidents to your supervisor.
- If you get injured get proper first aid and seek medical assistance if necessary.
- Keep your mind on your work.
- Drugs and alcohol do not have a place on the job.
- Horseplay and practical jokes cause accidents so keep them off the job.
- Practice accident prevention.

Try your best to follow these guidelines and all of us will have a safer place to work. Give your undivided attention to safety and prevent accident.

Confined Spaces

A 'confined or enclosed space' means any space having a limited means of access and egress, which is subject to the accumulation of toxic or flammable contaminants, has an oxygen deficient atmosphere, or could possibly cause suffocation due to entry of liquids, or harm from corrosives, acids, etc.

Confined or enclosed spaces include but are not limited to storage tanks, process vessels, bins, boilers, ventilation or exhaust ducts, sewers, underground utility vaults, tunnels, pipelines, and open top spaces more than 4 feet in depth such as pits, tubs, vaults and vessels.

The employer and supervisor, using standard tests, must determine if ventilation or atmospheric conditions within the space are hazardous, and whether any special safety equipment is required such as protective clothing, respiratory equipment, etc. Once this has been done make sure that everyone going into the confined space is familiar with exactly what work is to be done. Everyone involved must know what to do should an emergency take place. Remember, confined spaces are dangerous. Look out for yourself as well as your co-workers.

Do not Neglect Cuts

Infection is often called 'Blood Poisoning'. It might be of interest to know exactly what is meant by 'Blood Poisoning'. The term itself indicates that it is a poisoning directly related to blood.

There are two ways in which a poison can attack our bodies. It may be taken in through the mouth and enter the body by way of the digestive organs, or it may enter directly into the blood stream through an abrasion or cut in the skin. In any event, every poison eventually works through the blood and the poison of infections works into the blood stream directly.

The smallest cut, abrasion or scratch is large enough for germs to enter. If they are not wash off they will cause an infection which could lead to blood poisoning. If left untreated, a hand or arm could become so infected that it might possibly have to be amputated.

Dress for the Job

Our clothes and footwear are our first line of defense when it comes to protecting our bodies. Each day we wear our work clothes for eight, ten and sometimes even more hours, and there is nothing worse than working in uncomfortable clothing and/or poor fitting footwear. Although work clothes are very important to your safety and health, your comfort is also a consideration. You need to have clothes that are right for the job. They must be sturdy and durable, and capable of standing up to heavy wear and tear. You need clothes that will keep you warm in winter and cool in the summer, and that will keep you dry in wet weather. Proper footwear is another important part of work attire. Wear the right shoe or boot for the job. A good sturdy leather boot with steel toe cap will last a long time and also provide your feet with good support throughout the shift. Since you are on your feet most of the time, make sure the shoe or boot fits correctly. If you wear jewelry, watches or rings remember that they can be very dangerous around machinery and electricity. Use common sense and dress for the job you do, leave jewelry at home, wear appropriate clothing and sturdy footwear, and your workday will be a safer and more comfortable one. Set a good example for others and treat safety as one of the most important job responsibilities.

Electricity

There is a widespread but mistaken idea that 110 volts can not seriously injure or kill a person. Each of you should think about the dangers of low voltage electricity, especially if you use portable electric tools. The possibility of death from electric shock does not depend entirely on the voltage of the power supply. It also depends on the resistance of the human body, which varies greatly among individuals, and on the conditions under which a person is working. One cause of electric shock when using portable electric tools is the failure of the insulation between the current-carrying part and the frame of the tool. When insulation fails, fatal electric shock, severe burns, or even a fall from one level to another may result.

Electricity always tries to reach a ground potential and will always take the path of least resistance. If the outer metal shell of a defective tool becomes energized, the operator sets up a direct path through his own body between the energized tool and the ground itself. The ground can be the earth or it could be pipes or steel building structures that are in contact with the earth. Body resistance is lowered when you work in wet areas or sweat heavily; electricity can then flow easily through vital regions of the body.

When you work in a wet area, near a water pipe, grounded tank, or reinforcing rods that may be grounded, be extra careful to keep yourself as dry as possible. Stand on a wooden platform or use rubber boots. In places where tools may become wet, use only tools that are designed especially for that type of service.

Keep portable electric tools in good condition through the use of a regular inspection program. It is your responsibility to inspect your tools prior to use. Check both tools and cords and turn in any tool that needs repair as soon as you see any defect. There is no excuse for unsafe equipment. Remember, it only takes 1/10 of an amp to kill a person.

Eye Protection

Taste, smell, hearing, touch and sight are the five basic senses within us. Of the five, the sight is most depending upon. Everything we do involves the use of our eyes and God only gave us two. Eye protection begins with the ability to recognize those times that eye protection is needed, and then, to seriously commit to wear the protection whenever necessary. Any time you are working where there is the potential for flying particles eye protection is required. When using a saw, drill, pouring concrete, chipping, blasting or handling chemicals just to name a few. Dirt, dust, rust, rock, bits of concrete, etc. are all potential dangers in work site.

No one but a professional should attempt to remove a foreign body from the eye. Cover the eye lightly with a clean pad and either wait for medical help to arrive or take the employee to a doctor.

Do not forget that eye protection is also needed when using chemicals. Make sure you are using chemical goggles and a splash shield. You may need to flush the eyes should they come in contact with the chemical. Do not take chances with your vision, wear eye protection.

Falls – Causes and Cures

The only way to be safe from falls is to avoid them. Let us explore just a few of the factors contributing to falls and their serious results.

Scaffolds: Never erect a temporary scaffold. Even if the job will only last a very short time, the scaffold should be erected as if you were going to use it indefinitely. Make sure you install the entire cross braces both vertically and horizontally, be sure the scaffold is built on a level surface and fully checked, and proper access is provided.

Ladders: Select the right ladder for the job. Is it the right size, did you tie it off, did you inspect it prior to use? Always face the ladder when you climb and avoid carrying tools in your hands when climbing, one slip could send you down. Use a hand line or pouch for the tools. Never stand on the top two steps.

Floor Openings: Any floor opening measuring 12 inches across or larger must be covered or protection provided by a standard guard rail with toe board. A cover must be large enough and strong enough to prevent failure and be marked so that everyone on the job will be aware of its purpose. Guard rails must meet minimum strength requirements. Toe boards will prevent tools or materials from falling through the opening and injuring workers below.

Stairways: Slow down; do not run up or down. Avoid carrying objects that block your view of the steps. To help eliminate falls on stairways take your time, look where you step, and use the handrail. Keep stairways free of clutter to prevent tripping.

Housekeeping: A secure footing is a positive step in avoiding falls and good housekeeping is essential to secure footing. Debris, trash, oil and water left to accumulate on stairs, walkway etc. will lead to certain falls. A clean worksite is a safer worksite. Watch your step. Stay alert. Avoidance and prevention is your first line of defense.

First Aid

Knowing basic first aid is a must. The following is a list of helpful hints when first aid is needed.

- Act promptly but not hastily, look for breathing and airway obstructions, and check for bleeding and/or broken bones.
- Start mouth to mouth resuscitation if necessary.
- Stop the bleeding; a snug bandage or a pressure dressing will usually stop the bleeding. Use direct pressure, not a tourniquet. Avoid direct contact with blood, use gloves.
- Look for shock, skin cold and moist, weak pulse, face drained of colour and fainting.
- Caution, handle with care, a person with a suspected neck or back injury should not be moved until professional rescue personnel are on the scene. Assist them if requested.
- Splint broken bones, a splint can be made from any firm object that is long enough to reach beyond the broken bone. Immobilize the joints above and below the break.
- Never give liquids to an unconscious victim.
- Bandage wounds to help protect against infection. The wound should be covered with a sterile dressing before the bandage is applied.
- Remember to wear protective equipment.

First Day on the Job

Your safety on any job is important, so let us discuss the types of personal protective equipment you need to use.

- Hard hats are designed to protect your head, and statistics prove that they prevent most serious head injuries.
- Eye protection is required when there is any possibility of an eye injury. Safety glasses, and cutting goggles will protect eyes but they must be worn, not carried in the pocket.
- Other types of protective equipment include hearing protection, respirators, harnesses, lifelines, and proper work clothes. All of these are important to safety and should be used as required.
- Good housekeeping is a must. Keep aisles and walkways clear of obstructions.
- Always inspect electrical and hand tools prior to use. If you find anything wrong or damaged, let your supervisors know and tag the tool **'Needs Repair – Do Not Use'.**
- When it is required to use a ladder check it out, inspect it for any damage, make sure it is the right size for the job and never stand on the top two rungs or steps. If you are using a metal ladder keep a sharp eye out for overhead power lines coming in contact with them can be deadly.
- Have a right to know what hazardous materials are in use on the job. Copies of material safety data sheets are available and should be reviewed if you have any question about the handling or protective gear necessary when using any hazardous material. Always read the label on containers so you know what you are using.

Gas Cylinders

Oxygen, Acetylene, Argon, Air, LPG, Nitrogen and other gasses are found in metal cylinders. These portable containers, used for transporting and storing compressed gasses, can cause serious injuries. If used incorrectly, gas cylinders can cause an explosion, fire, or other hazardous situation. Handle them with care and follow appropriate safety rules. Let us review some of the safety do's and do nots for using compressed gas.

Do'S

- Always keep cylinders in a secure and upright position.
- Keep the protective valve cap in place when a cylinder is not in use.
- Keep oil and grease away from oxygen cylinders (oil and oxygen can ignite spontaneously).
- Open valves slowly, using the valve wheel or T-handle wrench provided by the supplier.
- Store oxygen and fuel gas cylinders at least 20 feet apart or separated by a 5 foot high noncombustible barrier.
- If the cylinder is too heavy to handle use a hand truck to move it, or ask a co-worker for help.

Do nots

- Do not permit sparks, flames, or molten metal to contact the cylinder.
- Never use grease or oil on valves.
- Do not lift cylinders without safety caps in place.
- Never use oxygen to blow or dust off your work clothes.
- Do not roll cylinders horizontally on the ground.
- Never drop cylinders on the ground or other work surfaces.
- Do not store oxygen cylinders with other fuel gas cylinders.
- Never use a leaking gas cylinder. Take it out of service immediately.
- Never mix or match acetylene gauges with oxygen gauges.

Hand Tools

- Keep all hand tools in good condition. Check to be sure that safety devices are in place and in proper working order. Lubricate tools on a regular schedule. Keep them sharp and they will help to perform the job safely.
- Typical hand tools include hammers, wrenches, screw drivers, hand saws, axes, hacksaws, shovels, rakes, picks, sledge hammers, wheelbarrows, levels, knives, punches, chisels, pliers, etc.
- Each hand tool has a particular job to do and it is your responsibility to use the tool as the manufacturer designed it. Short cuts, using the wrong tool will often cause an accident.
- When using hand tools remember to wear the proper personal protective equipment. If there is any potential for an eye injury, safety glasses are a must. Protect your hands by wearing gloves. Watch out for sharp pointed tools as well as sharp edges on saws, both will cause a nasty cut if handled improperly
- After you are done with a hand tool return it to the place it belongs. When you return it, place it properly so that the next person can pick it up without the possibility of injury.
- Should a tool get damaged take it out of service for repairs, and if it can not be repaired, dispose of it. Defective tools are dangerous and should not be used. Taking a chance with one last use of a defective tool may kill.

Hand tools make your job much easier. Care for them properly and use them wisely.

Horse Play

Horse play does not have a place on the work site. All of us like to have fun, but when horse play gets started on the job it usually ends up with someone getting injured, and none of us really wants that to happen.

Sometimes horse play goes even further. A worker decides to play a trick on another worker by taking off or changing the position of a safety device on a power tool. Something like this is not only stupid but extremely dangerous and could cause an accident with serious injuries.

Practical jokes should be banned from all work sites. If you see any kind of horse play taking place stop it at once. Let the other person know that you do not like it, and if it continues you will notify your supervisor to put a stop to it.

Be a safe worker. Check your work area for hazards, inspect your tools before use, set a good example.

Housekeeping

Good housekeeping is the first law of accident prevention and should be a primary concern of all supervisors, foremen and the entire workforce. Poor housekeeping often results in unsafe conditions and also implies that the work is poorly managed. Many accidents and injuries charged to other causes are actually caused by unsafe conditions due to poor housekeeping.

A safe worker knows he can do his best work easier and more quickly if good housekeeping is maintained. Learning the habit of good housekeeping takes practice. The familiar expression 'a place for everything and everything in its place', will assist you in your efforts.

Materials left on the job should be stored in a central location and if at all possible stacked out of the way. When cleaning up be sure that all combustible materials are disposed off proper so as to curtail the possibility of fires. Tripping accident's can be reduced significantly by frequent clean-ups. Make it a habit to remove or bend over all nails protruding from scrap lumber to protect against puncture wounds. Sharp-edged and pointed tools should be stored in such a way as to prevent injuries.

Each member of the crew has a responsibility to insure good housekeeping in all phases of their work. It is a lot easier to pick up as you work instead of waiting for the end of the shift. The importance of the relationship between an orderly job and a safe job cannot be overstressed.

We can have clean, well appearing, accident free jobs only if we really want them and insist at everyone cooperates. Good housekeeping requires constant effort and vigilance to make certain the job and equipment are kept in good condition. Remember, good housekeeping promotes safety in the workplace, improves performance, protects you and the public, and just makes good sense.

'A clean job is a safe job'. Housekeeping starts at the beginning of the shift and needs to continue throughout the entire workday. Do not let scrap materials build up; dispose off them daily. Another common housekeeping problem arises with the use of welding leads, air compressor hoses, and extension cords. If placed improperly they become tripping hazards. Keep walkways free for passage. Scrap cardboard and packing materials left lying around provide excellent fuel for fires. Housekeeping is a never ending process. Do your part by keeping your work area and adjacent walkways and stairs clean and orderly.

No doubt about it – if everyone does their share, good housekeeping will make Your Job a Safer Job.

Illumination

Good illumination is important to maximize production and maintain quality control. Poor lighting on the job-site will lead to personal injury accidents; tripping, falling and injuries from tools and equipment.

All areas, including stairs, ramps, corridors, storage areas, shops, offices, etc. be lighted by natural or artificial illumination. Generally speaking, if you are able to read drawings and follow layout marks without difficulty and use cutting tools effectively and with ease, there is sufficient lighting on the site. Plant and shop areas, first aid stations and offices require higher intensities of illumination.

All temporary wiring and lighting on the site must comply with the same codes as permanent wiring. Undersized wiring or overloaded circuits lead to work stoppages, electrical shocks and even fires. Be sure wiring is protected from damage in high traffic areas.

Flexible cords used for temporary or portable lights must be designed for hard or extra-hard usage, all lamps for general illumination must be protected from accidental contact or breakage; metal case sockets must be grounded, and temporary lights must not be suspended by their cords unless specifically designed for this means of suspension.

120 volt, portable lighting may be used in wet or other conductive locations such as vessels, drums and tanks but only if protected by a ground fault circuit interrupter, otherwise the maximum permitted is 12 volts or less. Temporary wiring must be removed immediately upon completion of work.

New Employee and New Job

Supervisor should take time necessary to explain the safety requirements to the new employees. Here are several safety topics to think about.

- **First Aid and Emergency:** Where is the first aid station located? Where are the first aid supplies? Who is certified to provide first aid? Where are emergency phone numbers posted?
- **Housekeeping and Sanitation:** Where is the waste disposal area? Are there any materials which must be disposed off in a special manner? What are the procedures for daily cleanup? Where is drinking water located?
- **Personal Protective Equipment:** Are hard hats required at this work site? Are soft soled shoes prohibited? Check eye and ear protection requirements. What other kinds of Personal Protective Equipment are needed?

- **Hand and Power Tools:** Are you qualified to use the tools you will be using on this job? Are all the required guards in place? Are your tools properly grounded?
- **Ladders:** Is the ladder the right one for the job? Is it in good condition? Be sure the ladder is properly set up and secured. Always check a ladder prior to using it.
- **Hazard Communication:** Are you going to have to work with chemicals? Do you understand all of the precautions which must be taken? Find out where Material Safety Data Sheets are kept, as well as where the main chemical inventory list is located.

Shortcuts are Killers

The following is a list of things we often do, even though we know we should not.

- We fool with safety devices; we remove safety guards for our convenient.
- We should not take a chance when operating heavy equipment; we do not use the seat belt that is provided.
- We know that flames or sparks are not permitted around flammable liquids; but some of us smoke around them.
- A protruding nail in a guard rail can cause an injury; but we do not bother to remove it or bend it over.
- Horseplay causes a lot of injuries on the job; but we continue to play practical jokes.
- A circular saw can amputate a finger; but we insist on using the saw without a guard.
- We know the safe way to climb a ladder; but we climb it with one hand full of tools.
- We should wear goggles while grinding; but we leave our goggles strapped up on helmet.
- We know better that chemicals should be used after reading the MSDS; but we use the chemical any way.
- We know wearing a life jacket is essential when working over water; but we go out over the water without one.
- A head injury may be fatal; but we continue to work without our hard hats.
- It is dangerous to block fire fighting equipment; but we stack boxes of material in front of fire extinguishers.
- We know not to work within 10 feet of a power line; but there is just one more load of steel to be unloaded and it will not happen to me.

We all, at one time take shortcuts. Usually it is because we are attempting to save some time. Our life is too important to risk by taking chances. Think safety first always. Do not take shortcuts. The minute you saved may cost you days, weeks, or months of recovery time.

A Single Second

- It takes a minute to write a safety rule.
- It takes an hour to hold a safety meeting.
- It takes a week to plan a good safety program.
- It takes a month to put that program into operation.
- It takes a year to win a safety award.
- It takes a lifetime to make a safe worker.
- But it takes only a second to destroy it all – with one accident.

Take the time now to work safe and help your fellow employees to be safe.

After Thoughts and Regrets

Here are some afterthoughts which, unfortunately, too many of us have experienced:

- "That's how we have always done it before."
- "I never thought that a little bolt dropped from that distance would cause so much bleeding."
- "If I had taken that first-aid/CPR course, I probably could have helped him."
- "I should have taken care of that board with the projecting rusty nails earlier."
- "Wow, I never realized that a fire could get out of control so fast."
- "I know they were always preaching that we should lift with the leg muscles instead of the back muscles."
- "For few more money, I could have bought safety shoes."
- "My safety glasses were in the tool box, but I was just going to grind off this one little piece...."
- "We were only going to use the scaffold for one day. I never thought a hammer would fall off the plank and strike someone."

"They always insisted that the tool rest should be no more than one-eighth inch from the grinding wheel. What difference does another quarter inch make?"

Learn from others' mistakes and have no regrets.

Attitude and Behavior

Humans instinctively seek to avoid pain and death. And yet, we may behave in a manner that is a threat to our well-being. There are a couple of reasons why this occurs.

- The first is lack of knowledge. What you do not know, can hurt.
- The second reason we may act in a risky manner is attitude. What is our attitude toward safety? Our attitude affects almost all that we do and how we do it.
- People who are successful in life, or are just happy, tend to have a positive attitude and so it is with safety. Safety rules and procedures are written to protect us from

harm. They are not written to make our work life more uncomfortable or inconvenient.

- If we cooperate in safety matters, not only is there a lesser likelihood of our getting hurt we will not be doing battle with the boss who is just trying to do his duty by enforcing the safety rules.
- Even the best of us can forget or make errors in judgment. To maximize our safety efforts, we must look out for one another.
- If you see someone doing something unsafe, speak up, but do so diplomatically. Treat others just as you would like to be treated in the same situation.
- Remember, attitude affects behavior. If you have a positive attitude, you will exhibit safe behavior. A negative attitude toward safety will only cause conflict, stress and, ultimately, an accident.

Mentally Prepared for Emergencies

You should be able to answer the following:

- How and who do you notify in an emergency?
- Are you prepared to react responsibly?
- Should you stay with the injured person or run for help?
- If you are not First Aid certified, do you know who in your crew is?
- Does the emergency scene need to be secured?
- Do you know the chain of command? Who is in charge during an emergency?

When an emergency does occur, it is your responsibility to be mentally ready.

Know the Fire Extinguishers

The vast majority of portable, hand held fire extinguishers are loaded with a dry chemical powder that will extinguish the majority of fires you might encounter in your daily environment. This powder is not toxic but will make you sneeze and cough if you inhale it. (It tastes like sodium bicarbonate which is its base powder.) This powder will extinguish Class "A", "B", and "C" fires.

Class "A" fires involve material such as paper, plastic, wood and other common combustibles.

Class "B" fires involve grease, oil or gasoline. Dry chemical extinguishers will work, but these fires can be harder to extinguish and should be approached with extreme caution.

Class "C" fires involve burning electrical motors or transformer. This type of fire changes from "C" to Class "A" or "B" as soon as the power is cut off (or shorts out). Dry chemical can be used here also because it will not conduct electricity and will put out "A" or "B" type fires.

Know where the general use fire extinguishers in your work area. Do not hang your coat over them, or stack material in front of them. Extinguishers are never needed until they are needed NOW. Keeping them easily visible and easily accessible at all times helps ensure that when a fire emergency occurs, a fire extinguisher can be easily and quickly reached.

And remember-extinguishers are made for relatively small fires. If the fire is too big or moving too fast to control, hold others away and wait for the Fire Department.

Carelessness

The fact is that approximately 20% of injuries are due to unsafe conditions and 80% are caused by unsafe acts. If most unsafe conditions are brought about by human failure, then virtually all accidents are brought about by unsafe acts. If you knew the proper, safe way to do the job, then you cannot claim ignorance. What is left, whether you like it or not, is carelessness. So what causes temporarily disregard to own safety?

External Pressure: Disregarding safe practices is not going to save enough time to make a significant difference. However, any accident or injury is guaranteed to have an effect. As a matter of fact, when the pressure is applied, it is worthwhile to pay more attention to safety because such situations frequently lead to more accidents.

Bad Habits: You fail to follow the established procedure and you do not get hurt. Psychologically, this is a reward and so you do it again and again and finally meet with an accident.

Internal Pressure: There is just so much to do and not enough time. Haste makes waste.

Attitude: This safety stuff does not apply to me. There is nothing like status that will protect from injury except following the safe procedure.

Safety is no more than doing the job the right way, every day.

Common Sense and Accident Prevention

The experts say at least 80% of industrial accidents are caused by unsafe acts on the part of employees and 18% due to unsafe conditions. By avoiding unsafe acts and practicing common sense, work will go smoother, with less chance for accidents.

Statistically, most accidents are caused by unsafe acts, including:

- Being in a hurry
- Taking chances
- Being preoccupied
- Having a negative attitude
- Failing to look for hidden hazards

Maintaining a positive attitude pays in safety.

Employee Responsibility

Employees are responsible to:

- Listen and learn from safety training.

- Be an active participant in learning a job skill or safety issue.
- Ask for assistance if the training or instruction is not clear.
- Report unsafe acts and near misses immediately.
- Address problems to the supervisor. But always try to give solutions to every problem.
- Re-address issues with the supervisor.
- Be an active member in the safety of the workplace.
- Participate in Safety Committee Meetings, Safety Meetings, and when trained on a safety issue.

24 CHAPTER

Safe Handling, Operation and Use

MANUAL MATERIALS HANDLING GUIDE

Lifting/Lowering:

- Use mechanized lifts whenever possible.
- Minimize the distance loads need to be lifted/lowered.
- Avoid storing materials directly on the floor. (Use table or shelving so loads can be placed no lower than knuckle height.)
- Tag/label unstable/heavy loads.
- Reduce the weight of the load by limiting capacity (i.e., smaller containers).
- Clear spaces/paths to improve access to materials being handled.
- Stretch before and after lifting heavy loads.
- Keep loads as close to the body as possible.
- Lift with the legs, not the back.
- Keep the back straight, by sticking out the butt and keep your head up looking forward.
- Balance lifts on both sides of the body.

- Get a secure grip.
- Avoid twisting, pivot with the feet instead.
- Use both hands if possible.
- Use a ladder for overhead loads.

Carrying:

- Slide, drag, push or pull loads instead of carrying whenever possible.
- Clear the path.
- Tag/label heavy/unstable loads.
- Reduce capacity of container.
- Keep loads close to the body.
- Keep loads between knuckle and chest height.
- Minimize carrying distance by using wheeled dollies or carts.
- When carrying load with one hand, alternate hands throughout the carry.
- Use both hands when possible.
- Increase size of handles when possible.

Pushing/Pulling:

- When possible, push instead of pull.
- Clear the path.
- Reduce capacity of container to reduce weight of load.
- Use wheeled carts/containers whenever possible.
- Stagger the legs to generate pushing/pulling force, avoid using the back.
- Use entire body to push/pull loads, avoid using the shoulders and arms.
- Push and pull with both hands whenever possible.
- Use equipment with four swivel wheels or castors to improve control.
- Proper maintenance of wheeled carts (lubricate, clean, replace wheels frequently).

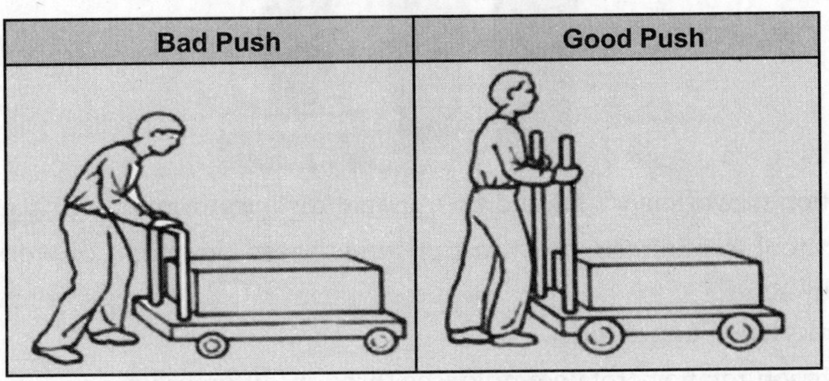

Work Station Design:

- Height of table should encourage the elbow to relax at 90 degrees.
- Workbench height should be adjustable to accommodate the variance in individual height.
- Workbench height should be adjusted for the type of work:
  - **Light-work:** At-elbow-height
  - **Hard-work:** Below-elbow-height
  - **Precision work:** Above elbow height.

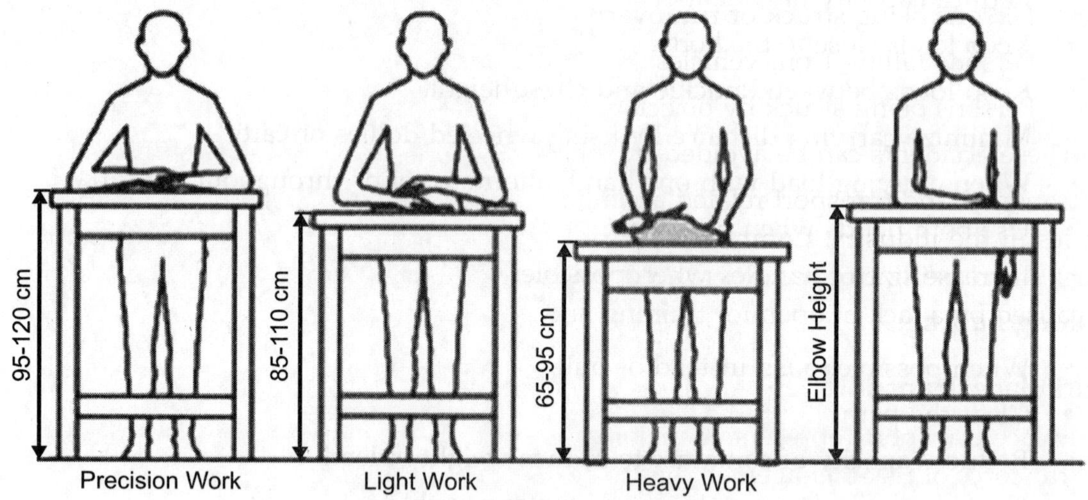

- Location of workbench should be minimal distance from other necessary tools.
- Select tool to minimize awkward postures based on height of work and surface orientation.

General Workplace Suggestions:

- Utilize job rotation (rotate employees through different jobs).

- Utilize job enlargement (increase variety by involving more tasks or employees in the process).
- Ensure adequate rest periods.
- Modify work practices/environment to maintain neutral postures.

SAFE OPERATION OF VEHICLES

Introduction

Transport accidents usually involve:

- Persons being struck or run over by moving vehicles (e.g., during reversing);
- Persons falling from vehicles;
- Persons being struck by objects falling from vehicles; or vehicles overturning.

These accidents can be avoided by effective management and prevention measures.

Transport and transport related accidents are among the most common causes of fatal injuries in the industry. Common scenarios involve being struck or run over by moving vehicles and being trapped or crushed when vehicles overturn. Many of these accidents are caused by a lack of operator training and poor visibility.

Workplace Transport

Workplace transport represents a major cause of fatal accidents and serious injuries, and thus the force of risk management has to be exercised to minimize the potential harm. The dangers of workplace transport are identified and the risks are assessed, making it important for employers to take responsibility, to consider what could happen and the ways in which to prevent accidents occurring.

Vehicle Oriented Preventive Measures

The first step in preventing workplace transport accidents is to carry out a risk assessment to identify who is at risk and where and when it occurs. This risk assessment should be used to decide what action must be taken to remove or reduce this risk. Consulting the workforce is a requirement. Using their knowledge helps to ensure hazards are correctly spotted and workable solutions implemented.

Prevention measures can be divided up into:

- Workplace prevention measures
- Vehicle orientated prevention measures
- Worker orientated prevention measures
- Safe systems of work.

Better design of the workplace. Check that the layout of routes is appropriate for vehicle and pedestrian activities. The priority should always be to segregate pedestrians and vehicles. If this is not possible, adequate warnings must be in place. Ensure there are suitable pedestrian crossing points on vehicle routes. Consider introducing a one-way traffic system to reduce the risk of collisions. Check that vehicle traffic routes are suitable for the types and quantity of vehicles that use them. Ensure they are wide enough and that floor and road surfaces are kept in good condition. Remove obstructions where possible, otherwise, make sure they are clearly visible. Avoid including sharp bends in road layouts. Provide suitable fixed mirrors at blind corners, to enable good visibility around the corner.

Check that suitable safety features are provided. Direction, speed limit and priority signs may be needed. Determine whether physical speed restrictions such as speed bumps are necessary. Edges of loading bays, pits etc. must be clearly marked and fitted with a barrier if possible.

Check that lighting and visibility provide safe passage through the work site (both inside and outside). Potential hazards, e.g., road junctions, pedestrians and instructions must be clearly visible. High visibility clothing may be needed for drivers and/or pedestrians if they cannot be segregated adequately.

Ensure that vehicles are maintained appropriately. Preventive maintenance programs are required. Drivers should carry out basic safety checks before using vehicles, e.g., pre-shift check of brakes and lights.

Ensure that a safe and suitable vehicle is being used. Vehicles should be purchased with appropriate safety features and comply with required standards. There must be safe means of access to and exit from the vehicle. The driver may need protection against overturning or being hit by falling objects. (Falling object and roll over protection.) Consider using audible warning devices, e.g., on reversing lorries and flashing beacons on vehicles to increase their visibility.

Worker Orientated Prevention Measures

Check that selection and training procedures ensure that drivers are capable of working safely. Drivers should be competent to operate their vehicles and carry out daily maintenance. Drivers should be medically fit, with good mobility, hearing and vision. Only people who have been selected, trained and authorized to do so should be allowed to drive vehicles.

Training

Driver training is essential and a legal requirement. An untrained driver is a danger to him/herself and others. Employees have duties to co-operate actively with employers' preventive measures.

SAFE USE OF COMPRESSED GAS CYLINDERS

Do	Do nots
1. Issue/Receipt of Gas Cylinders:	
– Check conformity of the gas cylinder as per the standard or color code.	– Never issue/receive any gas cylinder before the identification of its contents. – Do not issue/receive any gas cylinder without its valve cap.
2. Loading/Unloading:	
– Unload cylinders directly on a raised platform by rolling over a coir mattress, wherever possible. – Make sure that cylinder lowered on the mattress is rolled away before the next one is slide down. – Use only properly maintained fiber rope sling to lift cylinder one at a time. – Use a properly designed cradle with suspension if more than one cylinder has to be handled by a crane. – Use suitable hand cart equipped with a chain or belt to transport cylinder in plant area.	– Do not drop or allow dropping cylinders from height. – Do not use a lifting magnet for loading and unloading any cylinder. – Do not use a chain sling to lift a cylinder. – Do not roll a cylinder on ground over a long distance. – Never drag the cylinder.
3. Storage:	
– Store cylinders in a well ventilated place away from rain, snow, strong sunlight and any other storage of corrosive or combustible substances. – Store empty cylinders away from full cylinders. – Display 'full' or 'empty' notices on each relevant stack of cylinders. – Secure cylinders by suitable brackets. – Use proper chokes or blocks at each end of stack to prevent rolling of horizontally stacked cylinders. – Place large size cylinders at the bottom when stacked horizontally.	– Do not place cylinders against unsecured wall or bench. – Do not keep the cylinders in a battery charging room or in room where oils, acids or corrosive liquids are stored. – Do not use tarpaulin or any other cover in direct contact with cylinder as a protection against the sun. – Do not place cylinders directly on wet soil. Use proper dunn-age. – Do not keep unidentified cylinders in store. – Do not keep cylinders near door ways or passage ways.

– Store cylinders away from sources of heat such as furnaces, boilers, heating appliances etc. – Store cylinders of combustible gases separately from other gases in a well ventilated area above ground level.	– Do not store or use liquid gas cylinder in horizontal condition. – Do not keep cylinders in emergency escape route or difficult to reach place.
4. Transportation: – Transport cylinders with cap on. – Secure cylinder against falling from the vehicle.	– Do not let cylinder be subjected to jolting and damage during vehicle movements.
5. Handling: – Ensure that grit or dust of any sort or oil does not enter regulator assemblies. – Use safety shoes while handling cylinders. – Avoid mechanical damage to the cylinder (dents, cuts etc.). – Do not keep more than necessary number of gas cylinders in working areas or occupied building. – Before allowing any person to handle gas cylinders of poisonous or irritating gases, e.g., ammonia, chlorine etc. ensure that he has received proper training and information and required personal protective equipments are given to him.	– Do not use cylinder as a roller, work support or back support. – Do not allow cylinder to come in contact with electrical apparatus or live wires. – Do not lubricate cylinder valves, or handle cylinder or valve assembly with greasy hands or oily rags. – Do not increase the leverage of keys or spanners. – Do not make any attempt to get gas from cylinder with broken valve spindles. – Do not bang jolt or drop cylinders violently. – Do not hoist the cylinder in an inverted position. – Never tamper with safety devices.
6. Operation/Use: – Use standard valve only. – Use standard key only for opening the valves and make sure that these are free of any oil or grease. – Be familiar with basic knowledge of gas before its handling. – Read labels of instruction carefully before use. – Connect only to equipments meant for the particular service.	– Do not use adopter for valve. – Do not operate valves hastily. – Do not use leaking cylinders or equipments. – Do not use damaged tools to operate valve, or excessive force while making connections. – Do not use oxygen instead of compressed air or some other gas. – Do not allow smoking where flammable gases are stored or used.

– Keep the connections clean and in good order. Check the tubing, valve and regulators etc. for leakage at regular intervals. – Protect cylinders against contamination from pressurized equipments, since back flow from other gases or liquid may lead to serious accidents. Use proper non-return valves, clock-and-bend arrangement or the like. – Use flame arresters in flammable gas lines where they are used with compressed air or oxygen. – Have fire extinguishers and heat protecting gloves available when gas cylinders are used along with welding equipment.	– Do not remove valve key when the cylinder is in use. – Do not leave the valve in open condition when the cylinder is not in use. – Do not leave cylinders or connected equipment in confined spaces when not in use even for short breaks. – Do not use acetylene without properly reducing pressure.
7. In Case of Fire: – Stop the supply of flammable gas in area of fire. – Check the valve by using protecting gloves and remove the cylinder from the fire. – Put cylinder into a river, canal, or the like to cool down or cool it with water sprays, if it becomes hotter.	– Do not panic and run away when an emergency arise.

SAFE USE OF EQUIPMENT AND MACHINERY

Circular Saw

Handling Kickback

Kickback is a common problem while using a circular saw. It is caused by the timber that is being cut, bending in some way, so that it jams on the back of the blade, making the saw buck or stall.

In the sketch above when all is going well the action of the teeth cutting into the timber at "A" helps to keep the saw bed and the timber in close contact. If the timber starts pinching the blade at "B" the opposite happens, the saw wants to climb out of the timber, sometimes with a jerk. The easy answer is clamping the work as firm as possible.

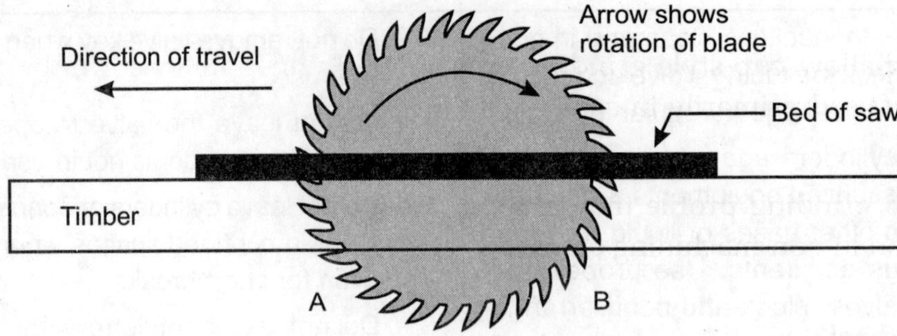

Circular saw – Saw blade action.

ABRASIVE WHEELS

A **grinding wheel** is an abrasive compound used for various grinding (abrasive cutting) and abrasive machining operations. They are used in grinding machines.

The wheels are generally made from a matrix of coarse particles pressed and bonded together to form a solid, circular shape, various profiles and cross sections are available depending on the usage. There are five characteristics of a cutting wheel: material, grain size, wheel grade, grain spacing and bond type. They will be indicated by codes on the wheel's label.

Straight Wheel

These are by far the most common style of wheel and can be found on bench or pedestal grinders. They are used on the periphery only and therefore produce a slightly concave surface (hollow ground) on the part. This can be used to advantage on many tools such as chisels.

Cylinder or Wheel Ring

Cylinder wheels provide a long, wide surface with no center mounting support (hollow). They can be very large, up to 12" in width. They are used only in vertical or horizontal spindle grinders. Cylinder or wheel ring is used for producing flat surfaces, the grinding being done with the end face of the wheel.

Tapered Wheel

A straight wheel that tapers outward towards the center of the wheel. This arrangement is stronger than straight wheels and can accept higher lateral loads. Tapered face straight wheel is primarily used for grinding thread, gear teeth etc.

Straight Cup

Straight cup wheels are an alternative to cup wheels in tool and cutter grinders, where having an additional radial grinding surface is beneficial.

Dish Cup

A very shallow cup-style grinding wheel. The thinness allows grinding in slots and crevices. It is used primarily in cutter grinding and jig grinding.

Saucer Wheel

A special grinding profile that is used to grind milling cutters and twist drills. It is most common in non-machining areas, as saw filers use saucer wheels in the maintenance of saw blades.

Diamond Wheel

Diamond wheels are grinding wheels with industrial diamonds bonded to the periphery.

They are used for grinding extremely hard materials such as carbide cutting tips, gemstones or concrete.

Diamond Mandrels

Diamond mandrels are very similar to their counterpart, a diamond wheel. They are tiny diamond rasps for use in a jig grinder doing profiling work in hard material.

Cut Off Wheels

Cut off wheels, also known as parting wheels are self-sharpening wheels that are thin in width and often have radial fibers reinforcing them. They are often used in the construction industry for cutting reinforcement bars (rebar), protruding bolts or anything that needs quick removal or trimming.

Use

To use the grinding wheel it must first be clamped to the grinding machine. The wheel type (e.g., cup or plain wheel below) fit freely on their supporting arbors, the necessary clamping force to transfer the rotary motion being applied to the wheels side by identically sized flanges (metal discs).

Grinding Dresser

Grinding wheels are self sharpening to a small degree, for optimal use they may be dressed and trued by the use of wheel or grinding dressers. Dressing the wheel refers to removing the current layer of abrasive, so that a fresh and sharp surface is exposed to the work surface. Truing the wheel makes the grinding surface parallel to the grinding table or other reference plane, so the entire grinding wheel is even and produces an accurate surface.

Safety

- Before mounting and balancing a grinding wheel, the wheel must be sounded. Care must be taken not to damage the wheel when sounding. A wheel that is safe to use will ring clearly and solidly, like a bell or tuning fork. A damaged wheel will not make any resonating sound; it will sound more like a dull thud.

- The clamping force of the grinding wheel flanges is an important safety parameter of a grinding operation. It must be high enough to drive the wheel without slippage under the most severe operating conditions of the machine. It must not apply to the wheel an excessive compression stress which could weaken the wheel. It must not distort the flanges.
- When flanges are clamped by screws it is essential to know the torque to use when tightening these screws to make sure that the needed clamping force is obtained and that each screw is loaded enough to avoid loosening. The design of the flanges and their tightening parameters are the manufacturer's responsibility.

SAFE USE OF INDUSTRIAL LUBRICANTS

Understanding basic safety precautions when working with lubricants is important for any employee working in an industrial plant and especially gear-manufacturing operations. The potential hazards are associated with handling, storing and using petroleum-products.

High-pressure Injection Hazards

High-pressure injection injuries, also known as grease gun injuries, are caused by the accidental injection of a foreign material such as grease, oil or solvent under pressure through the skin and into the underlying tissue. Accidents involving injection injuries can occur when using any type of pressurized equipment.

The most common sites of injury are the fingers or hand. However, any part of the body can be involved. With grease guns, especially, accidents usually occur when the injured person wipes the tip of the nozzle with his finger or the nozzle slips off the grease fitting while being held in place. Grease may also be injected into the body from a leak in the grease line. In hydraulic system accidents, a leak in a hydraulic line can emit a high-velocity stream of oil and cause injury if it strikes a person. Workers are commonly injured when they try to stop the leak by covering it with their hand or finger.

Chemical irritation is not a major problem with most petroleum products because hydraulic oils and greases are generally non-irritating and present low toxicity to the skin. However, the resulting bacterial infection can be a problem because of the damaged tissue and circulation in the wound, even though it has been surgically opened and the foreign material removed. One of the dangers from this type of injury is that it is not recognized quickly by the injured person as being serious. Often the initial wound may be very small and essentially painless. The injured person may even continue working. However, in every case in which a person receives this type of injury, he should stop work and get immediate medical treatment.

In case of a grease gun accident, seek immediate medical treatment. Identify the grease or oil involved in the accident. Contact the supplier or the manufacturer to obtain the product's. Material Safety Data Sheet (MSDS) about possible toxicity if a physician or hospital needs more information.

Mechanical Hazards

Handling drums: If a drum is dropped, it may bounce out of control or burst at a seam, creating a spill and/or fire hazard. Two people should overturn or up bend a drum to prevent muscle strains and other injuries. When rolling a drum, always check its motion; never allow it to free roll. When hoisting a drum, use a drum sling that hooks over the ends of the drum. Do not use air pressure to empty a drum as it may burst open.

Oil and grease spills: Oil or grease spilled on floors, catwalks, and ladders can present fall and fire hazards. Wipe up lubricant spills immediately or use absorbent drying pads. Repair or report sources of lubricant leaks.

Application to machines: Do not apply lubricants to machines in operation unless the machine is equipped with central lubrication systems or the fittings and oil caps are piped out to a safe place. For machinery that specifically requires shut down for lubrication, ensure that the machinery is properly locked and tagged out of service.

Machine guards: Guards on belt or chain drives, open gears, couplings, etc., should be removed only after the machine is shut down and properly locked and tagged out of service. Replace guards promptly after lubrication work is done and report damaged guards.

Ladders and work lifts: A ladder should be of suitable material; for example, a metal ladder or lift should not be used where there is possible contact with electrical wiring or equipment. Use ladders of the proper length; do not overextend extension ladders. The ladder or lift should be inspected to be sure that the safety feet, rungs, and slide rails are in good condition and free of oil and grease. Use both hands when climbing; carry equipment in a sling, bag, or pockets, or hoist it up to the point of use.

Safe clothing: Follow plant rules for the proper kind of safety shoes, hats, goggles, glasses, gloves, or special clothing. Do not wear loose or torn clothing that can be caught in moving parts of a machine. Wear long sleeves in the vicinity of hot surfaces.

Hand tools: Take special care when using hand tools. Use the right tool for the job; do not improvise or change its configuration for a purpose for which it was not intended. High pressure grease guns can pierce the skin.

Hazards to the skin: The skin may be sensitive to prolonged exposure to petroleum products such as cutting fluids, solvents and rust preventatives. Irritation, itching, or skin rashes (dermatitis) may develop. To prevent trouble or escalation, wear rubber gloves whenever possible. Wash hands and affected skin areas frequently with mild soap and warm water.

Fire-hazards: Most petroleum products will burn. Lube oils and greases have relatively high flash points, but solvents, kerosene, diesel fuel, and gasoline have much lower flash points and will burn readily. Do not use gasoline for cleaning and do not smoke around any petroleum product.

In case of fire: In the event of a fire, sound the alarm and dial plant's emergency line. Do not let the fire cut off your escape route. Stay upwind and do not breathe any more smoke than is necessary, since smoke from certain petroleum fires can be dangerous. Firefighting should only be performed by designated and trained individuals. For extinguishing agent, dry chemical, foam, and carbon dioxide (CO_2) are recommended. Water can also be used, but be cautious of using a solid stream of water as it can disperse across the affected area and will conduct electricity if sprayed directly on a live electrical panel. Use of water sprays should be left to trained firefighting personnel.

Oily rags: Keep oily rags in a labeled, closed, oily waste can. Rags soaked with paint or linseed oil should not be kept in a closed container, but instead should be hung up to dry and then disposed off according to plant practices and governmental regulations.

Handling solvents: Many solvents emit enough vapors to form flammable mixtures with air. Any spark, even from static electricity, can cause a fire. Before opening or dispensing solvents or fuels, make sure the containers are grounded, either with ground wires, metal to metal contact between containers or direct contact with the ground. Handle solvents in well-ventilated areas and keep containers closed when not in use.

Hazards to lungs: Dangerous vapors, mists, or dusts can form in plant working areas and prolonged exposure can be hazardous. If overexposed, get out of the area and get first aid. Do not enter any large confined spaces such as empty tanks, vats, kettles, etc., alone and without checking for oxygen deficiency with approved measuring devices. Regardless of toxicity levels, approved respiratory devices are recommended for use in these areas. Always use the "two-man rule" when working in these spaces and talk to each other frequently. If entering into a confined space wear approved ropes/harnesses, especially in dark areas. Consult your local and state officials for published Lower Explosive Limits (LEL) and Permissible Exposure Limits (PEL).

25 CHAPTER

'On-Site' and 'Off-Site' Emergency Plans

WHY EMERGENCY PLANNING IS REQUIRED?

After the incident of Bhopal Gas Disaster, the Factories Act has been amended and a new chapter (Provision relating to hazardous processes) has been added to the Factories Act. All hazardous process industries are covered under the provision of Section 41A, 41B, 41C, 41D, 41E, 41G and 41H as per the provision of the Section 41B (4), every occupier of hazardous process shall draw up an "On-site Emergency Plan" with the approval of Chief inspector of factories. He has to prepare detailed disaster control measures for his factory and make known to the workers employed therein and as well as to the general public living in the vicinity of the factory. The safety measures to be taken in the event of an accident taking place. This is the statutory provision laid down in the Act for preparation of on-site emergency plan to control disaster in the factories. Major accidents may cause emergency and it may lead to disaster. This may cause heavy damage to plant property, harm to person and environment and creates adverse affects on production. Many disasters like Bhopal gas tragedy, Chernobyl nuclear disaster etc. have occurred at many places in the world causing heavy loss of life, environment and property. Emergency situation arises all on a sudden and creates havoc, damage to person, property, production and environment. Therefore such situations and risks should be thought in advance and it should be planned before hand to tackle them immediately and control them within the shortest possible time.

WHAT IS AN EMERGENCY?

A major emergency can be defined as an accident/incident that have potential to cause serious injuries or loss of life. It may cause extensive damage of property, serious disruption of both in production and working of factory and may adversely affect the environment. The following factors may cause major emergency:

- Plant failure
- Human failure
- Vehicle crash
- Sabotage
- Earthquake
- Natural calamities.

On-site Emergency: If an accident/incident takes place in a factory and its affects are confined to the factory premises, involving the persons working in the factory and the property inside the factory it is called an "On-site Emergency."

Off-site Emergency: If the accident is such that it affects inside the factory are uncontrollable and it may spread outside the factory premises, it is called as "Off-site Emergency."

Objectives: The main objectives of an emergency plan are:

(i) To control and contain the incident/accident and eliminate it if possible.

(ii) To minimize the effects of the incident on person, property and environment.

Statutory Provisions: After the Bhopal gas tragedy (1984) and Supreme Court direction in case of M/s Sriram Foods and Fertilizers, the Government of India has made some important amendments to the Factories Act 1948 in the year 1987 with incorporation of special provisions relating to hazardous process. Under Section 41 (B) (4) every occupier is to prepare an On-site Emergency Plan and detailed disaster control measures for his factory. Again under provision of Rule 13 of the Manufacture, Storage and Import of Hazardous chemicals Rules 1989, the occupier shall prepare and keep up to date On-site Emergency Plan containing details how major accidents can be dealt with on the site where the industrial activity is carried on and that plan shall include the name of the person who is responsible for safety on the site and names of those who are authorized to take action in accordance with the plan in case of an emergency.

Each major hazard factory should prepare an emergency plan incorporating details of action to be taken in case of any major accident/disaster occurring inside the factory. The plan should cover all types of major accident/occurrences and identify the risk involved in the plant. Mock drills on the plan should be carried out periodically to make the plan foolproof and persons are made fully prepared to fight against any incident in the plant. The plan will vary according to the type of industry and emergency.

Main Elements of On-site Emergency Plan:

- Leadership and administration.
- Role and responsibilities of key personnel.
- Emergency action.
- Light and power.
- Source of energy control.
- Protective and rescue equipment.
- Communication.
- Medical care.
- Mutual aid.
- Public relation.
- Protection of vital records.
- Training.
- Periodical revision of plan.

Emergency Action Plan:

The action plan should consist of:

- Designated Emergency Control Centre/Room
- Key Personnel

Emergency Control Centre: This is the main centre from where the operations to handle the emergency are directed and coordinated.

The major facilities to be made available in the Emergency Control Centre are:

- Internal and external communications.
- Computer and other essential records.
- Daily attendance of workmen employed in the factory.
- Storage of hazardous material records and manufacturing records.
- Pollution records.
- Walky-talky.
- Plan of the plant showing:
  - Storage area of hazardous materials.
  - Storage of safety equipments.
  - Fire-fighting system and additional source of water.

  - Site clearance, roadway and emergency exit.
  - Assembly points.
  - Truck parking area.
  - Surrounding location.
- Note book, pad and pencil.
- List of key personnel with addresses, telephone number etc.

Assembly Points: A safe place far away from the plant should be predetermined as assembly point where in case of emergency personnel evacuated from the affected areas are to be assembled. The plant workers, contract workers and visitors should assemble in assembly point in case of emergency and should be taken their attendance so as to assess the missing person during emergency.

The Key Personnel for On-site Emergency:

- Works Main Controller (WMC).
- Works Incident Controller (WIC).
- Communication Officer.
- Security and Fire Officer.
- Telephone Operators.
- Medical Officer.
- Personnel/Administrative Officer.
- Essential Work Team Leaders.

Works Main Controller: The General Manager of the plant should act as Works Main Controller. His duties are to:

- Assess the magnitude of the situation and decide whether the evacuation of staff from the plant is needed.
- Exercise and direct operational control over areas other than those affected.
- Maintain a continuous review of possible development and assess in consultation with Work Incident Controller and other Key Personnel.
- Liaison with Police, Fire Service, Medical Services, Factory Inspectorate and other Government Agencies.
- Direct and control rehabilitation of affected area after emergency.
- Intimate Off-site Emergency Controller if the emergency spreads beyond the factory premises and likely to affect the surrounding area.
- Ensure that evidence is preserved for enquiries to be conducted by Statutory Authorities.

The Works Main Controller will declare the emergency and he will instruct main gate office to operate the emergency siren after assessing the gravity of the situation.

Works Incident Controller: He is the next responsible officer after the Works Main Controller. Generally the Plant Manager is designated as Works Incident Controller. His duties are:

- In case of emergency he will rush to the place of occurrence and take overall charge and report to the Works Main Controller by personnel communication system like cell phones or walky-talky and inform about the magnitude of emergency.
- He will assess the situation and considering the magnitude of emergency he will take decision and inform Communication Officer to communicate the news of emergency to different agencies.
- He will give direction to stop all operations within the affected area.
- He will take charge of main controller till the main controller arrives.
- He will order for shut-down and evacuation of workers and staffs from affected area.
- He will inform all Key Personnel and all outside agency for help.
- He will inform Security and Fire Officers and State Fire Services.
- He will ensure that all non-essential workers/staff are evacuated to assembly point and areas searched for casualties.
- He will report all significant development to Communication Officer.
- Moreover he will advise to preserve evidence of emergency into the cause of emergency.

Other Key Personnel and their duties:

Communication Officer:

- On hearing the emergency siren/alarm he will proceed to the Control Centre and communicate to Works Incident Controller.
- He will collect information from the emergency affected area and send correct message to Works Main Controller for declaration of emergency.
- He will maintain a log book of incident.
- He will contact all essential departments.
- He will take stock of the meteorological condition from local meteorological department.
- He will communicate all information as directed by Works Main Controller.

Security and Fire Officer: The Security and Fire Officer will be responsible for the fire fighting. His duties are:

- On hearing the emergency alarm/siren, he will reach the incident area with fire and security staff.

- Immediately after arrival to the emergency area, he will inform through telephone or walky-talky to Communication Officer.
- He will inform to the Works Incident Controller about the situation and requirement of outside help like State Fire Service and other Mutual Aid Members.

At the site, the entire fire squad member will respond to the advice and information given by the Works Incident Controller. The security will control the visitors and the vehicle entry.

Telephone Operator:

- In case fire is discovered but no emergency siren is operated, he shall ensure the information about the location of fire/emergency incident from the person discovered/notices the above and communicate to different Key Personnel immediately with clear message.

Medical Officer:

- Medical Officer with his team will report to the Works Incident Controller on hearing the fire/emergency siren immediately.
- The ambulance will be parked nearest to the site of incident.
- Name of injured and other casualties carried to the hospital will be recorded and handed over to works incident controller.
- The ambulance will carry the injured to the nearest hospital for treatment.

Personnel/Administrative Officer:

He should work as a Liaison Officer, liaison with Works Main Controller and other essential departments such as Police, Press and Statutory Authorities. His responsibilities shall include:

- To ensure that casualties receive adequate attention to arrange additional help if required and inform relatives.
- To control traffic movement into the factory and ensure that alternative transport is available when needed.
- When emergency is prolonged, arrange for the relief of personnel and organize refreshment and catering facilities.
- Arrange for finance for the expenditure to handle the emergency.

Essential Works and Team Leaders:

During emergency the plants immediately affected or likely to be affected, as determined by the works Main Controller, need to be shut down for safety. In the area immediately affected, it may be possible to isolate equipment from which flammable or toxic material is leaking. Plant supervisors and essential operators must immediately carry out this work.

Workers/staffs need to be nominated to carry out the following essential works at the time of emergency:

- Extra first aid personnel to deal with casualties.
- Emergency engineering works, provision of extra or replacement of light, isolation of equipment, temporary bypass electrical lines etc.
- Moving tankers or other vehicles from area of risk.
- To carry out tests on ambient air quality.
- To act as runner in case of communication system fails.

The Works Main Controller will require a task force of suitable trained people for the following work:

- Manning of assembly points to record the arrival of evacuated people.
- Assistance of casualty arrival areas to record the details of casualties.
- Manning the factory entrance in liaison with security to direct emergency vehicle at the gate, e.g., ambulance, fire tenders etc.

For these essential jobs designated teams should be made available. The responsibilities of the team and the leader should be given.

The essential work teams are:

- Task force and repair team.
- Fire-fighting team.
- Communication team.
- Security team.
- Transport team.
- First aid and Medical team.
- Safety team.

Alarm System: Alarm system varies and will depend upon the size of the works area. Simple fire bell, hand operated siren, break open type fire alarm etc. Automatic alarm may be needed for highly hazardous nature of plant.

Communication System: Communication is a key component to control an emergency. The following communication system may be provided in the plant:

- Walky-talky
- Telephone (internal and external)
- Cell phone.
- Intercom/paging
- Runners (verbal or written messages).

Siren for emergency: Siren for emergency should be different from the normal siren. The emergency siren should be audible to a distance of 5 km radiuses. The emergency siren should be used only in case of emergency.

Escape Route: The escape route from each and every plant should be clearly marked. The escape route is the shortest route to reach out of the plant area to open area, which leads to assembly point. This route should be indicated on the layout plan attached to the On-site Emergency Plan.

Evacuation: All non-essential staff should be evacuated from the emergency site. As soon as the emergency siren rings the workers have to shut down the plant and move to the assembly point. The plant shut down procedure in case of emergency should be prepared and kept ready and responsible person should be nominated for the purpose.

Counting of Personnel: All personnel working in the plant should be counted. Time office person should collect the details of personnel arriving at the assembly point. These should be checked with the attendances of regular workers, contract workers present in the site on the day of emergency. The accident control should be informed and arrangement should be made for searching missing person in the emergency affected area. The employees address, contact number of next to kin should be maintained in time office so that during emergency relatives of those affected due to emergency may be informed accordingly. Information in respect of emergency should be given to the media and other agency.

All Clear Signal: After control of emergency the Works Incident Controller will communicate to the Works Main Controller about the cessation of emergency. The Main Controller can declare all clear by instructing the time office to sound "All Clear Sirens'.

Mutual Aid System: Mutual aid scheme should be introduced among industries so that in case of emergency necessary help from mutual aid partner may be extended. Essential elements of this scheme are:

- Mutual aid must be a written document signed by the Chief executive of the industries concerned.
- Specify key personnel who are authorized to give requisition of materials from other industries.
- Specify the available quantity of material/equipment that can be spared.
- Mode of requisition during emergency.
- Mode of payment/replacement of material given during an emergency.
- May be updated from time to time based on experience gained.

Mock Drills: Mock drills on emergency planning should be conducted once in 6 months and sequence of events should be recorded for improvement of the exercise. Exercise on On-site Emergency Planning should be monitored by Factory Inspectorate and the high officials of the organization and the plan should be reviewed every year.

Emergency Facilities: The following facilities should be provided in any factory to tackle any emergency at any time.

- Fire protection and fire fighting facilities.
- Emergency lighting and standby power.
- Emergency equipment and rescue-equipment.
  - Breathing apparatus with compressed air cylinder.
  - Fire proximity suit.
  - Resuscitator.
  - Water gel blanket.
  - Low temperature suit.
  - First aid kit.
  - Stretchers.
  - Torches.
  - Ladders.
- Safety equipment
  - Respirators.
  - Gumboots.
  - Safety helmets.
  - Asbestos rubber hand gloves.
  - Goggles and face shield.
  - Toxic gas measuring instruments.
  - Explosive meter.
  - Oxygen measuring instruments.
  - Wind direction indicator.

On-site Emergency Plan should contain:

- Site plan and topographic plan.
- Plan showing the fire fighting facilities.
- Plan showing hazardous material storage area.
- Material safety data sheets for hazardous chemicals.
- Facilities available in main control centre.
- List of emergency equipment.
- List of safety equipment.
- List of important telephone numbers and addresses.
  - Nearest hospitals and ambulance service centre.
  - Nearest fire station.

- Government officials.
- Transport providers.

- Names and address and contact telephone number of key personnel.

The On-site emergency plan so prepared shall be documented in a printed form in sufficient copies to give all concerned for knowledge, study and easy follow up. The emergency plan shall be rehearsed and practiced at regular intervals to test efficiency of personnel, equipments, coordinated efforts, to increase confidence and experience to operate such plan.

OFF-SITE EMERGENCY PLAN

The main objectives of the plan are:

- To save lives and injuries.
- To prevent or reduce property losses.
- To provide for quick resumption of normal situation or operation.

Risk Assessment:

Risk assessment is most essential before preparing any off site emergency plan. Hazardous factories and their hazard identification, other hazard prone areas, specific risks, transportation risks, storage risks, pollution risks by air and water pollution, catastrophic risks such as disasters, natural calamities, acts of God, earthquake, landslide, storm, high wind, cyclone, flood, scarcity, heavy rain, lightning, massive infection, heavy fire, heavy explosion, volcano, heavy spill, toxic exposure, environmental deterioration etc., risks from social disturbances, risks from the past accidents, must be considered while carrying out risk assessment of a particular area (district) for which the off-site emergency plan is to be prepared.

Central Control Committee

As the off-site plan is to be prepared by the Government, a Central Control Committee shall be formed under the Chairmanship of the District Collector. Other Officers from Police, Fire Service, Factory Inspectorate, and Medical Department shall be incorporated as members of the Central Control Committee. Under the Central Control Committee the following committees shall be constituted under the Control of the District Collector.

- Incident and Environment Control Committee.
- Fire Control Committee.
- Traffic Control, Law and Order, Evacuation and Rehabilitation Committee.
- Medical Help, Ambulance and Hospital Committee.
- Welfare, Restoration and Resumption Committee.
- Utility and Engineering Services Committee.
- Press, Publicity and Public Relations Committee.

The District Collector in consultation with the factory management and government agencies shall prepare the Off-site Emergency Plan. The plan contains up-to-date details of out side emergency services and resources such as Fire Services, Hospitals and Police etc. with telephone number. The district authorities are to be included in the plan are:

- Police Department.
- Revenue Department.
- Fire Brigade.
- Medical Department.
- Municipality.
- Gram Panchayat.
- Railway Department.
- Telephone Department.
- Factory Department.
- Electricity Department.
- Pollution Control Department.
- Explosive Department.
- Press and Media.

Mock exercises on Off-site plan should be carried out at least once in a year to train the employees, up to date the plan, observe and rectify the deficiencies.

Hazop Study: Before making the On-site and Off-site plans Hazop study has to be carried out to identify the potential hazardous situations and to find out possible control measures. Hazop study is to be carried out by a team of experts. The team should consist of:

- Mechanical engineer.
- Chemical engineer.
- R & D Chemist.
- Works Manager.
- Project Manager.
- Outside Experts.
- Safety Officer/Manager.

Conclusion: To carry out mock exercises and rehearsal of the Off-site plan, to ensure its efficiency, test and response, interaction and co-ordination of operators various service organizations evaluate the effectiveness and adequacy of the equipments and to gain experience and confidence to implement the plan. The finalized Disaster/Off-site plan shall be given to all concerned for implementation and rehearsal for preparedness.

26 CHAPTER

Basic Elements of Safety Programmes

- **Environmental Health and Safety Policy**
  - Ensure employees are aware of the policy and its requirements.
  - Ensure that all are working safely as per Occupational Health and Safety Regulations.
- **Management Meetings:** Include safety as an agenda item on management meetings and document in the minutes.
- **Joint Health and Safety Committees**
  - Ensure a joint health and safety committee is in place and meets monthly.
  - Ensure that meetings are well attended and documented.
- **Orientation, Training and Supervision of Employees**
  - Ensure employees and trainees receive proper training.
  - Ensure that they are getting proper instruction and supervision.
- **Hazard Assessment and Worksite Inspections**
  - Work areas must be inspected regularly.
  - Inspections must be documented.

- Unsafe conditions should be corrected immediately.
- Prior to initiating new projects, conduct a hazard assessment and take appropriate steps to control/eliminate the hazards identified.
- Document hazard assessments.

- **Incident Investigations**
  - All incidents should be reported and documented.
  - Lost time incidents should be investigated and documented.
- **Written Safe Work Instructions:** Written instructions should be available for each job as reference.
- **Records and Statistics:** Document all training, meetings, disciplinary actions, inspections, incident reports and investigations, employee or trainee safety concerns.
- **First Aid and Emergency Services**
  - Ensure employees and trainees are familiar with location of first aid services, fire stations, fire exits and assembly areas and telephone number to report emergencies and request assistance.
  - Ensure the department has a fire safety plan and emergency response plan.
- **Program Review**
  - Regularly review the program components and update as necessary.
  - Document all these process.

MONITORING OF SAFETY PERFORMANCE STATISTICS OF ACCIDENTS

Industrial Injuries

Under the Factories Act, 1948, statistics of injuries resulting from industrial accidents by reasons due to which the persons injured are prevented from attending to work for a period of forty-eight hours or more immediately following the accidents are collected. The coverage remains limited and varies from year to year because many factories fail to submit the returns. The numbers of injuries are based on the notices of accidents.

The important statistical measures for injuries are:

- Frequency Rate,
- Severity Rate, and
- Incidence Rate.

The Frequency Rate is calculated by dividing the total number of injuries by corresponding number of man days worked in lakhs.

The Severity Rate, which takes into account the duration of disability as well, is calculated by dividing the number of man days lost due to injuries by the number of man days in lakhs. This rate is calculated only in respect of those non-fatal injuries in which workers returned to work during the same year.

The incidence rate is calculated by dividing the injuries by average daily employment per thousand. The statistics are based on injuries reported in the annual returns.

FREQUENCY RATE AND SEVERITY RATE

- **Frequency rate** is the number of disabling injuries (lost time injuries) per one million man hours worked.

$$\textbf{Frequency rate} = \frac{\text{No. of disabling (or lost time injuries)}}{\text{Man hours worked}} \times 10{,}00{,}000$$

- **Severity rate** is the total number of man days lost or charged to accidents per one million man hours worked.

$$\textbf{Severity rate} = \frac{\text{Man days lost in a year due the accidents}}{\text{Man hours worked}} \times 10{,}00{,}000$$

- **Number of man days charged** per injury equals and man days lost and man days charged for fatal accidents per accident. That is

$$\textbf{No. of man days charged per injury} = \frac{\text{Man days lost + man days charged (as per disabling injuries)}}{\text{Man hours worked}}$$

Examples of Computation of Frequency Rate and Severity Rate

An engineering company has the following data on its safety records:

Number of workers	= 250
Number of disabling injuries	= 10
Average number of hours worked per worker per year	= 2000

(A) Calculate frequency rate

(B) Calculate severity rate if the number of man days lost due to accident were 60 and assuming that

(a) None of the accidents caused any permanent disability or death.

(b) One of the accident caused loss of one finger.

(Man days lost according to schedule of charges for loss of one finger is 1200)

Solution:

$$\text{(A) Frequency rate} = \frac{\text{Number of disabling (or lost time) injuries}}{\text{Number of man hours worked}} \times 10{,}00{,}000$$

$$= \frac{10 \times 10{,}00{,}000}{250 \times 2{,}000} \doteq 20$$

(B) (i) Severity rate $= \dfrac{\text{Days lost in a year due to accidents}}{\text{Number of man hours worked}} \times 10{,}00{,}000$

$$= \frac{\text{Man days lost + man days charged for permanent disability or death}}{\text{Number of man hours worked}} \times 10{,}00{,}000$$

$$= \frac{60 + 0}{250 \times 2{,}000} \times 10{,}00{,}000 = 120$$

(ii) Severity rate (Loss of one finger) $= \dfrac{60 + 120}{250 \times 2{,}000} \times 10{,}00{,}000 = 2520$

SAFE-T-SCORE

$$\text{Safe-T-Score} = \frac{\text{(Frequency-rate-now)} - \text{(Frequency-rate-past)}}{\text{[((Frequency-rate-past)/million-worker-hours-now)(1/2)]}}$$

A positive Safe-T-Score indicates a worsening record; a negative Safe-T-Score indicates an improved record over the past.

- If the Safe-T-Score is between = 2.00 and – 2.00, the change is not significantly different and the variation is due to random fluctuation
- If the Safe-T-Score is greater than + 2.00, the record is significantly worse and something has gone wrong.
- If the Safe-T-Score is less than – 2.00, the record is significantly better than before and something has changed for the better.

SAFETY INSPECTIONS

I. Safety Audit

A good safety audit program does not come easily. The effort requires careful planning and diligent preparation. A good starting point is deciding why you want to do a safety audit. Or, more specifically, asking what is it you want to achieve? Answering this question gives your audit a focus and purpose. It also provides the foundation on which the audit program will be built.

Consider the following questions when planning for a safety audit program:

- What departments or operations are to be covered in the inspection tour?
- What items or activities are to be checked?
- How often are the inspections to be carried out?

- Who will conduct the tours?
- How will the inspections be conducted?
- What follow-up activity will ensure that corrections are, in fact, made?

Does management understand that hazards or unsafe work practices need to be corrected and that this requires human resources, management and engineering expertise?

II. Safety Surveys

The safety survey is a key element of successful safety program. Supervisors should make detailed surveys of their areas to detect unsafe conditions, such as those arising from mishandling of materials, scrap accumulation or wear and tear of machinery.

Supervisors should also observe employees' unsafe work practices. Identifying unsafe acts is also as important as finding unsafe conditions.

Safety survey should identify things that are right, as well as things that are wrong and target improvements that can reduce accident exposures. Cover your entire operation and all areas of safety whether it takes one survey or series of surveys to obtain complete picture.

Safety surveys conducted by safety officers or representatives from safety committees can reveal hazards overlooked by supervisors.

Safety surveys should be conducted at regular intervals and the deficiencies found must be corrected in time. Use checklist to evaluate your safety survey to ensure you have not missed anything.

Individuals conducting safety surveys must wear the necessary personal protective equipments and observe safety practices in the areas they visit. They should not talk to workers without their supervisor's approval. Avoid criticism, stick strictly to facts.

Safety surveys include complete written reports recommending corrective actions for any hazards or unsafe practices. Include target dates and names of those responsible for completion of hazard correction.

III. Plant Safety Inspection Checklists

Safety Checklists were made with the idea of making inspection work much safer. These checklists prove very useful when wanting to verify whether a production site is fit to do work according to safety regulations.

The essential things that are to be included in a Safety Checklist are:

- *Site Inspections:* Walk around the site and check.
- *Employee site orientation:* Prior to starting the work, the workers must be made aware of the unique risks and hazards present in the work.
- *Worksite fenced off:* Placing a fence around the site would keep away outsiders from getting in and exposing themselves to the potential dangers in the work.

- *Protective equipment:* Must be used.
- *First aid:* Make sure that there is sufficient first aid equipment and facilities are made available and easily accessible. First aid must be quick in response and done in a proper manner.
- *Caution signs:* Placement of caution signs around the parameters of the site to keep the general public a good distance from the site would do well to ensure their safety.
- *Tools and equipment:* Testing tools and equipment to verify that they are working properly is another measure that needs to be taken just before work starts. This must also be applied to all electrical leads or outlets. The list above is merely something to start off with and build up on. Safety Checklists could include many more things. This may very well prove to be a good starter.

IV. Plant Hazard Identification Checklist

Sl. No.	Elements/Items of Checklist	Yes/No	Further Information
1.	**Lay out of the plant**		
1.1	Is area properly demarcated?		
1.2	Is aisles provided?		
1.3	Are there areas for emergency vehicles?		
1.4	Do demarcated storages for raw materials and products exist?		
1.5	Are there safe clearances from overhead electrical lines?		
1.6	Are the interdistances between units and between equipment adequate?		
1.7	Is there adequate platforms and railings wherever required for safe working?		
2.	**Safe operating procedures**		
2.1	Are written procedures available for all critical operations?		
2.2	Are employee and contractors' workers made aware of these procedures?		
2.3	Are procedures available for handling hazardous chemicals?		

2.4	Are MSDS available for all hazardous chemicals?		
2.5	Are hazardous chemicals stored as required?		
3.	**House keeping**		
3.1	Are the floors, staircases and aisles clean and free from obstructions?		
3.2	Is there any oil/chemical spillage in the work areas?		
3.3	Are all tools and accessories kept in their designated place?		
3.4	Is there any accumulation of dry grasses in and around work space?		
4.	**Personal protective equipment (PPE)**		
4.1	Are there adequate PPE's available to various activities, available?		
4.2	Are employees and contractor' workers adequately trained to use PPE's?		
4.3	Is there proper storage of PPE's?		
4.4	Are the PPE's maintained?		
4.5	Are there adequate replacements available?		

Index

B

C

D

E

F

G

H

R

S

NOTES

NOTES